PROPERTY OF:

Beverly Carrillo

May 2019

ALSO BY AMERICA'S TEST KITCHEN

The New Essentials Cookbook

Dinner Illustrated

Cooking at Home with Bridget and Julia

The Complete Slow Cooker

The Complete Make-Ahead Cookbook

The Complete Mediterranean Cookbook

The Complete Vegetarian Cookbook

The Complete Cooking for Two Cookbook

How to Roast Everything

Nutritious Delicious

What Good Cooks Know

Cook's Science

The Science of Good Cooking

The Perfect Cookie

The Perfect Cake

Bread Illustrated

Master of the Grill

Kitchen Smarts

Kitchen Hacks

100 Recipes: The Absolute Best Ways to Make the
True Essentials

The New Family Cookbook

The America's Test Kitchen Cooking School Cookbook

The Cook's Illustrated Meat Book

The Cook's Illustrated Baking Book

The Cook's Illustrated Cookbook

The America's Test Kitchen Family Baking Book

The Complete America's Test Kitchen TV Show
Cookbook 2001–2019

Sous Vide for Everybody

Multicooker Perfection

Food Processor Perfection

Pressure Cooker Perfection

Vegan for Everybody

Naturally Sweet

Foolproof Preserving

Paleo Perfected

The How Can It Be Gluten-Free Cookbook: Volume 2

The How Can It Be Gluten-Free Cookbook

The Best Mexican Recipes

Slow Cooker Revolution Volume 2: The Easy-Prep Edition

Slow Cooker Revolution

The Six-Ingredient Solution

The America's Test Kitchen D.I.Y. Cookbook

THE COOK'S ILLUSTRATED ALL-TIME BEST SERIES

All-Time Best Brunch

All-Time Best Dinners for Two

All-Time Best Sunday Suppers

All-Time Best Holiday Entertaining

All-Time Best Appetizers

All-Time Best Soups

COOK'S COUNTRY TITLES

One-Pan Wonders

Cook It in Cast Iron

Cook's Country Eats Local

The Complete Cook's Country TV Show Cookbook

FOR A FULL LISTING OF ALL OUR BOOKS

CooksIllustrated.com

AmericasTestKitchen.com

PRAISE FOR AMERICA'S TEST KITCHEN TITLES

"Buy this gem for the foodie in your family, and spend the extra money to get yourself a copy, too."
THE MISSOURIAN ON *THE BEST OF AMERICA'S TEST KITCHEN 2015*

"The book offers an impressive education for curious cake makers, new and experienced alike. A summation of 25 years of cake making at ATK, there are cakes for every taste."
THE WALL STREET JOURNAL ON *THE PERFECT CAKE*

"*The Perfect Cookie* . . . is, in a word, perfect. This is an important and substantial cookbook. . . . If you love cookies, but have been a tad shy to bake on your own, all your fears will be dissipated. This is one book you can use for years with magnificently happy results."
THE HUFFINGTON POST ON *THE PERFECT COOKIE*

Selected as one of the 10 Best New Cookbooks of 2017
THE LA TIMES ON *THE PERFECT COOKIE*

"If there's room in the budget for one multicooker/Instant Pot cookbook, make it this one."
BOOKLIST ON *MULTICOOKER PERFECTION*

"It's all about technique and timing, and the ATK crew delivers their usual clear instructions to ensure success. . . . The thoughtful balance of practicality and imagination will inspire readers of all tastes and skill levels."
PUBLISHER'S WEEKLY (STARRED REVIEW) ON *HOW TO ROAST EVERYTHING*

Selected as the Cookbook Award Winner of 2017 in the Baking Category
INTERNATIONAL ASSOCIATION OF CULINARY PROFESSIONALS (IACP) ON *BREAD ILLUSTRATED*

"Use this charming, focused title to set a showstopping table for special occasions."
LIBRARY JOURNAL ON *ALL-TIME BEST HOLIDAY ENTERTAINING*

"A one-volume kitchen seminar, addressing in one smart chapter after another the sometimes surprising whys behind a cook's best practices. . . . You get the myth, the theory, the science and the proof, all rigorously interrogated as only America's Test Kitchen can do."
NPR ON *THE SCIENCE OF GOOD COOKING*

"This book upgrades slow cooking for discriminating, 21st-century palates—that is indeed revolutionary."
THE DALLAS MORNING NEWS ON *SLOW COOKER REVOLUTION*

"The 21st-century *Fannie Farmer Cookbook* or *The Joy of Cooking*. If you had to have one cookbook and that's all you could have, this one would do it."
CBS SAN FRANCISCO ON *THE NEW FAMILY COOKBOOK*

"The sum total of exhaustive experimentation . . . anyone interested in gluten-free cookery simply shouldn't be without it."
NIGELLA LAWSON ON *THE HOW CAN IT BE GLUTEN-FREE COOKBOOK*

"This book is a comprehensive, no-nonsense guide . . . a well-thought-out, clearly explained primer for every aspect of home baking."
THE WALL STREET JOURNAL ON *THE COOK'S ILLUSTRATED BAKING BOOK*

THE BEST OF

AMERICA'S TEST KITCHEN

BEST RECIPES, EQUIPMENT REVIEWS, AND TASTINGS

2019

AMERICA'S TEST KITCHEN

AMERICA'S TEST KITCHEN
21 Drydock Avenue, Boston, MA 02210

THE BEST OF AMERICA'S TEST KITCHEN 2019
Best Recipes, Equipment Reviews, and Tastings

ISBN: 978-1-945256-53-0
ISSN: 1940-3925

Manufactured in the United States of America

10 9 8 7 6 5 4 3 2 1

Distributed by Penguin Random House Publisher Services
Tel: 800-733-3000

EDITORIAL DIRECTOR, BOOKS: Elizabeth Carduff
SENIOR MANAGING EDITOR: Debra Hudak
PROJECT EDITOR: Elizabeth Wray Emery
ASSISTANT EDITOR: Samantha Ronan
ART DIRECTOR: Lindsey Chandler
PRODUCTION DESIGNER: Reinaldo Cruz
PHOTOGRAPHY DIRECTOR: Julie Bozzo Cote
PHOTOGRAPHY PRODUCER: Meredith Mulcahy
FRONT COVER PHOTOGRAPH: Keller + Keller
SENIOR STAFF PHOTOGRAPHER: Daniel J. van Ackere
STAFF PHOTOGRAPHER: Steve Klise
ADDITIONAL PHOTOGRAPHY: Carl Tremblay
FOOD STYLING: Catrine Kelty and Marie Piraino
PHOTOSHOOT KITCHEN TEAM:
    MANAGER: Timothy McQuinn
    LEAD TEST COOK: Daniel Cellucci
    TEST COOK: Jessica Rudolph
    ASSISTANT TEST COOK: Mady Nichas
ILLUSTRATIONS: John Burgoyne
PRODUCTION MANAGER: Christine Spanger
IMAGING MANAGER: Lauren Robbins
PRODUCTION AND IMAGING SPECIALISTS: Heather Dube, Dennis Noble, and Jessica Voas
COPYEDITOR: Cheryl Redmond
PROOFREADER: Jane Tunks Demel
INDEXER: Elizabeth Parson

CHIEF CREATIVE OFFICER: Jack Bishop
EXECUTIVE EDITORIAL DIRECTORS: Julia Collin Davison and Bridget Lancaster

PICTURED ON FRONT COVER: Pomegranate–Walnut Cake (page 238)

CONTENTS

WELCOME TO AMERICA'S TEST KITCHEN

This book has been tested, written, and edited by the folks at America's Test Kitchen. Located in Boston's Seaport District in the historic Innovation and Design Building, it features 15,000 square feet of kitchen space including multiple photography and video studios. It is the home of *Cook's Illustrated* magazine and *Cook's Country* magazine and is the workday destination for more than 60 test cooks, editors, and cookware specialists. Our mission is to test recipes over and over again until we understand how and why they work and until we arrive at the best version.

We start the process of testing a recipe with a complete lack of preconceptions, which means that we accept no claim, no technique, and no recipe at face value. We simply assemble as many variations as possible, test a half-dozen of the most promising, and taste the results blind. We then construct our own recipe and continue to test it, varying ingredients, techniques, and cooking times until we reach a consensus. As we like to say in the test kitchen, "We make the mistakes so you don't have to." The result, we hope, is the best version of a particular recipe, but we realize that only you can be the final judge of our success (or failure). We use the same rigorous approach when we test equipment and taste ingredients.

All of this would not be possible without a belief that good cooking, much like good music, is based on a foundation of objective technique. Some people like spicy foods and others don't, but there is a right way to sauté, there is a best way to cook a pot roast, and there are measurable scientific principles involved in producing perfectly beaten, stable egg whites. Our ultimate goal is to investigate the fundamental principles of cooking to give you the techniques, tools, and ingredients you need to become a better cook. It is as simple as that.

To see what goes on behind the scenes at America's Test Kitchen, check out our social media channels for kitchen snapshots, exclusive content, video tips, and much more. You can watch us work (in our actual test kitchen) by tuning in to *America's Test Kitchen* or *Cook's Country from America's Test Kitchen* on public television or on our websites. Listen in to test kitchen experts on public radio (SplendidTable.org) to hear insights that illuminate the truth about real home cooking. Want to hone your cooking skills or finally learn how to bake—with an America's Test Kitchen test cook? Enroll in one of our online cooking classes. However you choose to visit us, we welcome you into our kitchen, where you can stand by our side as we test our way to the best recipes in America.

facebook.com/AmericasTestKitchen
twitter.com/TestKitchen
youtube.com/AmericasTestKitchen
instagram.com/TestKitchen
pinterest.com/TestKitchen
google.com/+AmericasTestKitchen

AmericasTestKitchen.com
CooksIllustrated.com
CooksCountry.com
OnlineCookingSchool.com

STARTERS AND SALADS

CARAMELIZED ONION DIP

✓ **WHY THIS RECIPE WORKS:** We set out to create a simple dip that showcased the savory-sweet flavor of caramelized onions. We started by cooking the onions in a covered nonstick skillet over high heat with ¾ cup water; the water and steam helped the onions soften quickly. After removing the lid, we lowered the heat and pressed the softened onions into the bottom and sides of the skillet to allow for maximum contact with the hot pan. Instead of finishing with sugar or honey as many recipes call for, we added baking soda, which speeds up the reaction that converts flavorless inulin (a polysaccharide present in onions) to fructose. After chopping the caramelized onions, we combined them with the remaining dip ingredients: Sour cream and yogurt provided tang and a subtle richness that balanced the sweetness of the onions, while chives offered a welcome burst of freshness.

With nothing more than heat and time, onions can undergo an extraordinary transformation. Sweet and complex caramelized onions can improve everything from soups, dips, and sandwiches to pizzas, casseroles, pastas, and salads. The traditional approach is long, careful cooking over a low flame for upwards of 1¼ hours. There are shortcut recipes that rely on cranking up the heat, but the results are never as richly flavored as the real deal. I've also found that when I cut one of these quick-caramelized strands in half, I reveal a pale, watery interior lurking beneath the brown exterior. I set myself the challenge of finding a way to shave off time and still produce exemplary caramelized onions, which I could then incorporate into a dip that would be simple to prepare but complex in flavor.

First, I reviewed the science behind the traditional approach: Cooking causes the onions to break down and soften, releasing water, sugars, and proteins. The water evaporates, concentrating flavor. Given heat and time, the sugars and proteins undergo two reactions. One is caramelization, in which sugar molecules recombine into hundreds of new flavor, color, and aroma compounds. The other is Maillard browning, where sugars react with amino acids to produce a different array of flavors and colors.

In the test kitchen, we often turn to baking soda to speed up browning. This is because it creates a high-pH (basic) environment, which allows browning reactions to occur more readily. It's also handy for softening vegetables because altering the pH helps weaken their structure. I wanted to speed up both processes, so why not add baking soda here?

I sliced three pounds onions and added them to a nonstick skillet (its surface would ensure that the fond stuck to the onions, not to the pan) with 2 tablespoons of oil and ⅛ teaspoon of baking soda. After just 45 minutes over moderate heat, they were impressively browned, sweet, and complex-tasting. In fact, they were much sweeter than any I'd had before. Our science editor explained that the baking soda sped up the conversion of flavorless compounds called inulin into the simple sugar fructose. So while many recipes for caramelized onions call for adding sugar or honey to boost sweetness, there was no need for that in my recipe.

But there was a drawback to the baking soda. It caused the onions to break down too much; by the time they were browned, I had a skillet full of onion jam instead of the tender, distinct strands I wanted. To keep the flavor benefits of baking soda without ending up with mush, I added it at the last minute. Doing so, even at the last minute, deepened the color and flavor. But I still had to cook the onions for well over an hour. I'd have to look for other ways to speed things up.

Here's the thought that came to mind: Moisture is usually regarded as the enemy of browning, since food needs to rise above 212 degrees in order to brown, and that can't happen until most of the moisture burns off. But I knew that adding water and covering the skillet could help speed up the cooking without working against me. After all, the first part of the cooking process isn't about browning but rather softening the onions and breaking down their structure. Surrounding the onions with steam (and submerging some of them in the added water) would heat them more quickly and thoroughly than just relying on the heat generated by the cooking surface of the skillet alone. When cooked with ¾ cup of water, the onions wilted about 10 minutes faster. I then uncovered the skillet and turned the heat to medium-high. Since browning occurs only where the onions are in direct contact with the hot pan, I gently pressed the softened onions into the bottom and sides of the skillet to allow for maximum contact. I let them sit for about 30 seconds and then stirred them; I repeated the pressing and stirring process for the rest of the cooking time. Repeating this

CARAMELIZED ONION DIP

technique thoroughly softened and deeply browned the onions in just 15 minutes; start to finish, the entire cooking time took less than half an hour.

There are countless ways to use these tender, sweet, richly flavored onions, but an upscale take on the classic onion dip was at the top of my list. With the onions cooked, my dip came together effortlessly: I simply chopped a portion of the sweet, sticky onions and combined them with sour cream, yogurt, chives, and a little vinegar (for a dash of acidity).

LAN LAM, *Cook's Illustrated*

Caramelized Onion Dip

MAKES 2 CUPS

You will only need a portion of the caramelized onions for this dip; reserve the rest for another use. The dip can be refrigerated for up to 24 hours before serving.

    1 cup sour cream
    ⅔ cup caramelized onions, chopped fine (recipe follows)
    ⅓ cup yogurt
    2 tablespoons minced fresh chives
    ¾ teaspoon distilled white vinegar
       Salt and pepper

Stir together sour cream, onions, yogurt, chives, vinegar, ½ teaspoon salt, and ⅛ teaspoon pepper. Refrigerate dip for at least 1 hour. Season with salt and pepper to taste. Serve.

Caramelized Onions

MAKES ABOUT 2 CUPS

We prefer yellow or Spanish onions in this recipe for their complex flavor. Slicing the onions through their root end prevents them from breaking down too much during cooking. Caramelized onions are a great addition to countless meals. Try them in an omelet, in a frittata, or with scrambled eggs. They taste fantastic on grilled cheese sandwiches, BLTs, and burgers or thrown into pasta dishes and green salads. Try sprinkling them over bruschetta, focaccia, or pizza. They also can be used to spiff up baked and mashed potatoes, rice, risotto, and polenta.

    3 pounds onions, halved and sliced
       through root end ¼ inch thick
    ¾ cup plus 1 tablespoon water
    2 tablespoons vegetable oil
    ¾ teaspoon salt
    ⅛ teaspoon baking soda

1. Bring onions, ¾ cup water, oil, and salt to boil in 12-inch nonstick skillet over high heat. Cover and cook until water has evaporated and onions start to sizzle, about 10 minutes.

2. Uncover, reduce heat to medium-high, and use rubber spatula to gently press onions into sides and bottom of skillet. Cook, without stirring onions, for 30 seconds. Stir onions, scraping fond from skillet, then gently press onions into sides and bottom of skillet again. Repeat pressing, cooking, and stirring until onions are softened, well browned, and slightly sticky, 15 to 20 minutes.

3. Combine baking soda and remaining 1 tablespoon water in bowl. Stir baking soda solution into onions and cook, stirring constantly, until solution has evaporated, about 1 minute. Transfer onions to bowl. (Onions can be refrigerated for up to 3 days or frozen for up to 1 month.)

ASPARAGUS FRIES

✔ **WHY THIS RECIPE WORKS:** Golden-brown, crunchy fried asparagus spears are a favorite at some restaurants; we wanted to be able to make these snappy spears at home, too. For the crispiest coating, we relied on the tried-and-true bound breading technique but found that the coating wasn't adhering as steadfastly as we wanted. The solution was to rinse the spears under cold running water before dipping them in the flour. The residual moisture was just enough to help the flour (and the coating) stick. We used fresh white bread for a sweeter crumb. A bright yet creamy sauce made with sour cream, lemon juice, and mustard was the perfect accompaniment.

When asparagus season hits, it hits hard. I never tire of this ubiquitous-in-spring vegetable, but I am always looking for new ways to prepare it. When I tried an order of breaded and fried asparagus—crunchy on the outside, tender inside—at a restaurant recently, I knew I wanted to create my own recipe.

ASPARAGUS FRIES

My first step was to sort through the breading options. After several tests, I landed on a classic three-step process: dipping the spears in flour, then beaten eggs, and finally bread crumbs. I tested store-bought crumbs (both regular and crunchier panko) alongside fresh crumbs made by grinding bread in a food processor; the fresh crumbs won for their clean flavor and softer texture when fried. Adding a little flour to the crumbs while processing them made the coating more uniform. But the crumbs weren't sticking perfectly and were a little patchy in places. Rinsing the raw asparagus under the tap and then dropping the still-wet spears into the flour produced an even breading that stayed put throughout frying—and eating. Another bonus: The breading sopped up the moisture, so there was no splattering during frying.

Since I was using thinner (about ½-inch-thick) spears, they needed only a minute or two in the hot oil to cook through and for the coating to crisp. I found that it was easiest to bread a full pound of spears and let them rest on a baking sheet before frying one-third of them at a time. A simple mixture of sour cream, lemon juice, and Dijon mustard made a perfectly bright, sharp sauce for dipping.

ALLI BERKEY, *Cook's Country*

Asparagus Fries

SERVES 4 TO 6

Do not use asparagus that is thinner than ½ inch in this recipe. The bottom 1½ inches or so of asparagus is woody and needs to be trimmed. To know where to cut the spears, grip one spear about halfway down; with your other hand, hold the stem between your thumb and index finger about 1 inch from the bottom and bend the spear until it snaps. Using this spear as a guide, cut the remaining spears with your knife.

- ½ **cup sour cream**
- 1 **tablespoon lemon juice**
- 1 **tablespoon Dijon mustard**
  Salt and pepper
- ¼ **cup plus 3 tablespoons all-purpose flour**
- 3 **large eggs**
- 4 **slices hearty white sandwich bread, torn into 1-inch pieces**
- 1 **pound (½-inch-thick) asparagus, trimmed**
- 4 **cups peanut or vegetable oil**

1. Combine sour cream, lemon juice, mustard, ½ teaspoon salt, and ¼ teaspoon pepper in bowl; set aside sauce.

2. Place ¼ cup flour in shallow dish. Beat eggs in second shallow dish. Process bread, 1 teaspoon salt, ½ teaspoon pepper, and remaining 3 tablespoons flour in food processor until finely ground, about 1 minute. Transfer crumbs to 13 by 9-inch baking dish.

3. Place asparagus in colander and rinse under cold running water. Shake colander to lightly drain asparagus (asparagus should still be wet). Transfer one-third of asparagus to flour and toss to lightly coat; dip in egg, allowing excess to drip off; then transfer to breadcrumb mixture and press lightly to adhere. Transfer breaded asparagus to baking sheet. Repeat with remaining asparagus in 2 batches.

NOTES FROM THE TEST KITCHEN

MAKING PERFECT FRIED ASPARAGUS

1. Determine trimming point of 1 spear, then use that spear as guide to trim remaining spears.

2. Moisten spears under cold running water.

3. Toss moistened spears in flour, dip them in beaten egg, and coat them in bread crumbs before frying.

4. Line large plate with paper towels. Heat oil in large Dutch oven over medium-high heat to 350 degrees. Carefully add one-third of asparagus to hot oil and cook until golden brown, 1 to 2 minutes. Transfer to prepared plate. Repeat with remaining asparagus. Serve with sauce.

MULTICOOKER BUFFALO CHICKEN WINGS

✅ **WHY THIS RECIPE WORKS:** Great wings should boast juicy, tender meat and a crisp coating. The multicooker turned out to be the perfect all-in-one vessel for this crowd-pleasing bar snack. Both pressure and slow cooking the wings did a great job rendering excess fat and producing perfectly tender meat, while using hot sauce as our cooking liquid infused the wings with great flavor from the outset. Since the multicooker has a temperature regulator built right in, we found that we could maintain a consistent temperature at the highest sauté or browning function to fry our wings. As a bonus, the high sides of the pot prevented the oil from splattering and making a mess. Finally, we tossed our crisp, golden-brown wings with a classic Buffalo sauce made with a combination of Frank's RedHot sauce and Tabasco for extra kick, along with a little brown sugar and cider vinegar for deeper flavor.

The multicooker makes dinner easier, whether you plan to use the pressure-cook setting to significantly speed up cooking time or the slow-cook setting to have a warm meal ready when you get home. But during testing for our new multicooker cookbook, *Multicooker Perfection*, we discovered that these appliances can do a lot more than just make simple dinners—they can be used to make everything from oatmeal to cheesecake. Clearly, we were just scratching the surface as to their versatility, so I set my sights on making one of my favorite appetizers: Buffalo wings. They're undeniably a crowd-pleasing snack, but I don't often make them at home—frying on the stovetop is messy and leaves me stuck standing over a hot pot of oil, fussing with a burner dial to maintain a constant temperature. Could the multicooker be my new secret weapon for wings?

If I was going to haul out my multicooker to make wings, I wanted them to be perfect: fall-off-the-bone tender inside, with crispy skin that maintained its crunch even under a layer of spicy sauce. I already knew the moist heat of the pressure- or slow-cook setting would produce tender meat; the real challenge would be achieving that hallmark crispy skin.

To give home cooks maximum flexibility, all the recipes in our book offer the option to use either the pressure-cook setting or the slow-cook setting, and this one was no exception. I started with pressure cooking, and found that just 5 minutes under pressure produced meltingly tender meat and rendered the excess fat nicely so that my wings weren't greasy. As for slow cooking, just an hour or two did the trick and produced the same great result. Since I needed to add some liquid to the pot (both to help the pot pressurize and to keep the wings moist while they slow cooked), I tested adding small amounts of water, chicken broth, and hot sauce. My tasters liked hot sauce best since it infused the wings with Buffalo flavor from the start. These were easily some of the most tender wings I'd ever tasted, but the skin was, of course, unpalatably limp.

In the past, the test kitchen has turned to the broiler to crisp up wings that have been parcooked in a traditional slow cooker, but I wondered whether I could find a way to maximize my use of the multicooker here. On closer inspection, I realized the answer was right in front of me—the sauté function. Let me explain: Most multicooker models have a sauté setting, which we usually use to perform tasks such as browning aromatics before pressure or slow cooking, or reducing sauces after. Since a multicooker is an electric appliance, this function sets the heating element (which is in the bottom of the pot) to a specific, preset temperature—and keeps it there. I hoped that I could use this built-in regulator to keep frying oil at a consistent temperature.

During our testing of multicookers (see page 298), we had learned that the highest sauté function (which might be called "high sauté," "brown," or "sear," depending on the model) worked best for the usual tasks like cooking an onion or adjusting the consistency of a dish at the end of cooking—the lower settings never got hot enough to do these things. I knew that

MULTICOOKER BUFFALO CHICKEN WINGS

if the lower settings weren't hot enough in those cases, they wouldn't be hot enough to fry, either, so I opted for the highest setting and heated several cups of oil in the pot. A temperature test after a few minutes of heating revealed that the temperature was ideal: between 325 and 350 degrees.

I quickly discovered that trying to fry all of the wings at once was a nonstarter: The temperature of the oil dropped too low, producing soggy wings. Cooking in three batches worked much better, allowing the multicooker to better maintain the heat. I was also happy to find that the multicooker's high sides prevented the oil from splattering across the counter as it would in a Dutch oven. For due diligence, I ran three more tests to see just how crispy I could get the wings: I tried simply patting them dry before putting them in the oil, and I also ran tests in which I tossed them with cornstarch or baking soda before frying. The cornstarch and the baking soda, I hoped, would help to further dry out the skin and promote and enhance browning. Ultimately, I found the extra steps didn't provide enough benefit to make them worthwhile. Simplest was best: I dried the wings with paper towels and into the oil they went, unadorned.

The skin on my wings was now deeply and evenly bronzed—as golden brown as any I'd ever enjoyed in a restaurant. I kept the first batch warm in the oven while I fried the second and third batches, and then tossed them in the test kitchen's go-to Buffalo sauce (a mixture of melted butter and classic Frank's RedHot along with some dark brown sugar, cider vinegar, and Tabasco for balance and zing). My tasters were thrilled, and so was I. My wings now tasted great inside and out, and I didn't have to constantly fiddle with a stovetop burner to maintain the heat of the frying oil, nor spend time cleaning my stovetop and counters afterward. Perfect, foolproof, and fuss-free Buffalo wings? I was a convert. With a simple and creamy blue cheese dressing served alongside, I'll be making these wings every chance I get.

—ANNE WOLF, *America's Test Kitchen Books*

Multicooker Buffalo Chicken Wings

SERVES 6

PRESSURE COOK TOTAL TIME: 1 HOUR
SLOW COOK TOTAL TIME: 2 HOURS 45 MINUTES

Serve these wings with carrots and celery sticks.

CREAMY BLUE CHEESE DRESSING

2½ ounces blue cheese, crumbled (½ cup)
 3 tablespoons buttermilk
 3 tablespoons sour cream
 2 tablespoons mayonnaise
 2 teaspoons white wine vinegar
   Salt and pepper

WINGS

 3 pounds chicken wings, cut at joints, wingtips discarded
 1 cup hot sauce, preferably Frank's RedHot Original Cayenne Pepper Sauce
 4 cups peanut or vegetable oil
 4 tablespoons unsalted butter, melted
 2 tablespoons Tabasco sauce or other hot sauce
 1 tablespoon packed dark brown sugar
 2 teaspoons cider vinegar

1. FOR THE CREAMY BLUE CHEESE DRESSING: Mash blue cheese and buttermilk in small bowl with fork until mixture resembles cottage cheese with small curds. Stir in sour cream, mayonnaise, and vinegar and season with salt and pepper to taste. Cover and refrigerate until ready to serve. (Dressing can be refrigerated for up to 4 days.)

2. FOR THE WINGS: Combine chicken wings and ½ cup hot sauce in multicooker.

3A. TO PRESSURE COOK: Lock lid in place and close pressure release valve. Select high pressure cook function and cook for 5 minutes. Turn off multicooker and quick-release pressure. Carefully remove lid, allowing steam to escape away from you.

3B. TO SLOW COOK: Lock lid in place and open pressure release valve. Select low slow cook function and cook until wings are tender, 1 to 2 hours. (If using

Instant Pot, select high slow cook function.) Turn off multicooker and carefully remove lid, allowing steam to escape away from you.

4. Adjust oven rack to middle position and heat oven to 200 degrees. Set wire rack in rimmed baking sheet. Using slotted spoon, transfer wings to paper towel–lined plate and pat dry with paper towels. Discard cooking liquid and wipe multicooker clean with additional paper towels.

5. Using highest sauté or browning function, heat oil in now-empty multicooker until it registers between 325 and 350 degrees. Carefully place one-third of wings in oil and cook until golden and crisp, 8 to 10 minutes, turning halfway through cooking. (If using Instant Pot, increase cooking time to about 15 minutes.) Using slotted spoon, place wings on prepared sheet and keep warm in oven. Return oil to 325 to 350 degrees and repeat with remaining wings in 2 batches.

6. Whisk melted butter, Tabasco, sugar, vinegar, and remaining ½ cup hot sauce together in large bowl. Add wings and toss to coat. Serve immediately.

CHINESE PORK DUMPLINGS

✓ **WHY THIS RECIPE WORKS:** If you have the right recipe, Chinese dumplings can be as much fun to make as they are to eat. We started by making a boiling water and flour dough that was easy to roll out. For our filling, we added vegetable oil and sesame oil to ground pork to mimic the richness of the fatty pork shoulder that is traditionally used. Soy sauce, ginger, Chinese rice wine, hoisin sauce, and white pepper added flavor, and cabbage and scallions contributed subtle crunch. Mixing the filling in the food processor encouraged the development of myosin, a protein that helps the filling hold together when cooked. We swapped the traditional multipleat crescent for a simpler two-pleat shape. Our recipe makes 40 dumplings, so you can cook some right away and freeze some for later.

Chinese dumplings are like carefully wrapped gifts: juicy, deeply seasoned pork encased in soft, slightly stretchy dough. Boiled, they are delicately chewy; pan-fried, they are crisp on one side. But whether found in a restaurant or in a supermarket, they're rarely bad.

Unfortunately, they're rarely great. I've always wanted to make my own so I could stock my freezer with high-quality dumplings.

As I cooked and ate my way through several versions, I realized that though there are few truly bad dumplings, there are bad dumpling recipes. Some made too much filling for the amount of dough or vice versa. Some doughs too dry, so the dumplings wouldn't seal, while others were wet and stuck to my fingers. I wanted a supple-but-not-sticky dough; a juicy, cohesive filling; and a simple shaping technique.

Premade dumpling wrappers are thin and lack the stretch and chew of the homemade kind. Happily, you need only two ingredients to make your own: all-purpose flour and boiling water. Boiling water hydrates the starch in flour faster than cold water does, making a dough that is moist but not sticky, and it makes the gluten (the network of proteins that gives the dough structure) looser and less prone to snapping back. I buzzed 1 cup of boiling water and 12½ ounces of all-purpose flour in a food processor, and the dough came together in less than a minute. Then I kneaded it briefly until it was smooth, wrapped it in plastic wrap, and set it aside to rest.

For the filling, I started with 12 ounces of ground pork, saving myself the traditional step of finely chopping a fatty cut such as pork shoulder. I seasoned it with soy sauce, ginger, sesame oil, hoisin sauce, white pepper, and sherry, plus a little oil to compensate for the ground pork's relative leanness. For the vegetable component, I chopped cabbage in the food processor. I then salted it to draw off excess moisture and squeezed it dry before gently mixing it with the seasoned meat. Next I wrapped and pan-fried a batch to check the flavor and texture of the filling. The dumplings tasted good, but instead of being cohesive, the filling was crumbly.

I had mixed the filling gently to avoid releasing excess myosin, the sticky meat protein responsible for sausage's springy texture. But I noticed that some dumpling recipes call for vigorously mixing the filling, so I wondered if a little myosin development might actually help. This time I pulsed the pork and seasonings in the food processor until the mixture was slightly sticky, added the cabbage along with some scallions, buzzed it a bit more, and cooked another batch. Now the filling was on point: juicy and well seasoned, with the perfect balance of tenderness and cohesion.

CHINESE PORK DUMPLINGS

I knew I'd have to carefully portion the dough and the filling, but trying to eyeball either was maddening. I divided the dough into quarters and divided each quarter into tenths. I then did the same with the filling. I flattened one dough piece into a round, placed about 1 tablespoon of filling in its center, and contemplated how best to close it. The classic approach is to pleat the wrapper so that the dumpling curves and is stable enough to stand up and brown on its flat side. To do it, you gather one side of the wrapper into a series of pleats and seal them to the other side, which remains flat. The motion becomes muscle memory if you do it often enough, but otherwise it's tricky to execute. I came up with a simpler two-pleat method that achieved the appearance and functionality of a crescent.

I brushed vegetable oil over the surface of a cold nonstick skillet (in a hot pan, oil would pool and dumplings with no oil under them wouldn't crisp) and snugly arranged 20 dumplings before turning on the heat. When the bottoms started to brown, I added water and a lid, lowered the heat, and let the dumplings steam. Minutes later, I removed the lid and cranked the heat so that the remaining water would evaporate and the bottoms would crisp.

The results were ideal—a flavorful, juicy, cohesive filling tucked inside a soft, slightly chewy wrapper—and the method was user-friendly and fun. No more takeout for me; from now on, I'll be making dumplings and stockpiling them in my freezer.

ANDREA GEARY, *Cook's Illustrated*

Chinese Pork Dumplings

MAKES 40 DUMPLINGS

For dough that has the right moisture level, we strongly recommend weighing the flour. For an accurate measurement of boiling water, bring a full kettle of water to a boil and then measure out the desired amount. To ensure that the dumplings seal completely, use minimal flour when kneading, rolling, and shaping so that the dough remains slightly tacky. Keep all the dough covered with a damp towel except when rolling and shaping. There is no need to cover the shaped dumplings. A shorter, smaller-diameter rolling pin works well here, but a conventional pin will also work.

DOUGH

2½ cups (12½ ounces) all-purpose flour
1 cup boiling water

FILLING

5 cups 1-inch napa cabbage pieces
   Salt
12 ounces ground pork
1½ tablespoons soy sauce, plus extra for dipping
1½ tablespoons toasted sesame oil
1 tablespoon vegetable oil, plus 2 tablespoons for pan frying (optional)
1 tablespoon Chinese rice wine or dry sherry
1 tablespoon hoisin sauce
1 tablespoon grated fresh ginger
¼ teaspoon ground white pepper
4 scallions, chopped fine
   Black or rice vinegar
   Chili oil

1. FOR THE DOUGH: Place flour in food processor. With processor running, add boiling water. Continue to process until dough forms ball and clears sides of bowl, 30 to 45 seconds longer. Transfer dough to counter and knead until smooth, 2 to 3 minutes. Wrap dough in plastic wrap and let rest for 30 minutes.

2. FOR THE FILLING: While dough rests, scrape any excess dough from now-empty processor bowl and blade. Pulse cabbage in processor until finely chopped, 8 to 10 pulses. Transfer cabbage to medium bowl and stir in ½ teaspoon salt; let sit for 10 minutes. Using your hands, squeeze excess moisture from cabbage. Transfer cabbage to small bowl and set aside.

3. Pulse pork, soy sauce, sesame oil, 1 tablespoon vegetable oil, rice wine, hoisin, ginger, pepper, and ½ teaspoon salt in now-empty food processor until blended

and slightly sticky, about 10 pulses. Scatter cabbage over pork mixture. Add scallions and pulse until vegetables are evenly distributed, about 8 pulses. Transfer pork mixture to small bowl and, using rubber spatula, smooth surface. Cover with plastic and refrigerate.

4. Line 2 rimmed baking sheets with parchment paper. Dust lightly with flour and set aside. Unwrap dough and transfer to counter. Roll dough into 12-inch cylinder and cut cylinder into 4 equal pieces. Set 3 pieces aside and cover with plastic. Roll remaining piece into 8-inch cylinder. Cut cylinder in half and cut each half into 5 equal pieces. Place dough pieces on 1 cut side on lightly floured counter and lightly dust with flour. Using palm of your hand, press each dough piece into 2-inch disk. Cover disks with damp towel.

5. Roll 1 disk into 3½-inch round (wrappers needn't be perfectly round) and re-cover disk with damp towel. Repeat with remaining disks. (Do not overlap disks.)

6. Using rubber spatula, mark filling with cross to divide into 4 equal portions. Transfer 1 portion to small bowl and refrigerate remaining filling. Working with 1 wrapper at a time (keep remaining wrappers covered), place scant 1 tablespoon filling in center of wrapper. Brush away any flour clinging to surface of wrapper. Lift side of wrapper closest to you and side farthest away and pinch together to form 1½-inch-wide seam in center of dumpling. (When viewed from above, dumpling will have rectangular shape with rounded open ends.) Lift left corner farthest away from you and bring to center of seam. Pinch to seal. Pinch together remaining dough on left side to seal. Repeat pinching on right side. Gently press dumpling into crescent shape and transfer to prepared sheet. Repeat with remaining wrappers and filling in bowl. Repeat dumpling-making process with remaining 3 pieces dough and remaining 3 portions filling.

7A. TO PAN-FRY: Brush 12-inch nonstick skillet with 1 tablespoon vegetable oil. Evenly space 16 dumplings, flat sides down, around edge of skillet and place 4 in center. Cook over medium heat until bottoms begin to turn spotty brown, 3 to 4 minutes. Off heat, carefully add ½ cup water (water will sputter). Return skillet to heat and bring water to boil. Cover and reduce heat to medium-low. Cook for 6 minutes. Uncover, increase heat to medium-high, and cook until water has evaporated and bottoms of dumplings are crispy and browned, 1 to 3 minutes. Transfer dumplings to platter,

crispy sides up. (To cook second batch of dumplings, let skillet cool for 10 minutes. Rinse skillet under cool water and wipe dry with paper towels. Repeat cooking process with 1 tablespoon vegetable oil and remaining dumplings.)

NOTES FROM THE TEST KITCHEN

SHAPING DUMPLINGS

1. Place scant 1 tablespoon filling in center of wrapper.

2. Seal top and bottom edges to form 1½-inch-wide seam.

3. Bring far left corner to center of seam and pinch together.

4. Pinch rest of left side to seal. Repeat process on right side.

5. Gently press dumpling into crescent shape.

7B. TO BOIL: Bring 4 quarts water to boil in large Dutch oven over high heat. Add 20 dumplings, a few at a time, stirring gently to prevent them from sticking. Return to simmer, adjusting heat as necessary to maintain simmer. Cook dumplings for 7 minutes. Drain well.

8. Serve dumplings hot, passing vinegar, chili oil, and extra soy sauce separately for dipping.

TO MAKE AHEAD: Freeze uncooked dumplings on rimmed baking sheet until solid. Transfer to zipper-lock bag and freeze for up to 1 month. To pan-fry, increase water to ⅔ cup and covered cooking time to 8 minutes. To boil, increase cooking time to 8 minutes.

CHINESE SMASHED CUCUMBERS

✔ **WHY THIS RECIPE WORKS:** Smashed cucumbers, or *pai huang gua,* is a Sichuan dish that is typically served with rich, spicy food. We started with English cucumbers, which are nearly seedless and have thin, crisp skins. Placing them in a zipper-lock bag and smashing them into large, irregular pieces sped up a salting step that helped expel excess water. These craggy pieces also did a better job of holding on to the dressing. Using Chinese black vinegar, an aged rice-based vinegar, added a mellow complexity to the soy and sesame dressing while a little sugar added subtle sweetness. Toasted sesame seeds contributed crunch and a touch of richness to the otherwise lean dish.

My longtime definition of cucumber salad—cool, crisp slices tossed with a tangy vinaigrette or a sour cream dressing—was recently upended when, at a Sichuan restaurant, I was presented with a plate of large, craggy, skin-on cucumber pieces sparingly coated with dressing. The cukes had a crunchy, almost pickle-like texture and hinted at garlic and sesame, with mild acidity and touches of sweetness and salinity. The simple preparation proved to be an ideal accompaniment to the rich, spicy food.

The dish, called *pai huang gua,* is drop-dead easy to make. Smash the cukes with a skillet or rolling pin (or, as is traditional, with the flat side of a Chinese cleaver). Once they're smashed, tear them into rough pieces and

briefly salt them to expel excess water. Finally, dress the chunks with a quick vinaigrette of soy sauce, vinegar, minced garlic, and sesame oil.

Why smash the cukes? I found a couple of reasons. The first was speed. When I treated equal amounts of smashed versus chopped cucumbers with salt and measured the amount of liquid each batch exuded, the smashed cucumbers were crisp and had lost about 5 percent of their water weight after only 15 minutes. It took the chopped cucumbers four times as long to shed the same amount of water.

The second benefit was textural. Smashing breaks up the vegetable in a haphazard way that exposes more surface area than chopping or slicing, so more vinaigrette can adhere.

As for the best type of cuke, I dismissed American cucumbers, finding their thick, wax-coated skins too tough. That left nearly seedless English cucumbers, pickling cucumbers, or small Persian cucumbers. All had thin, crisp skins, but the pickling type can have a lot of seeds and the Persian type lacked a thick layer of flesh and was therefore missing the refreshing crispness of the English variety, my ultimate choice.

Regarding the dressing, soy sauce, garlic, and toasted sesame oil provided a complex base that I accented with sugar, but what really made it special was Chinese black vinegar, which is made by fermenting rice.

Finally, I whipped up a spicy chili oil for drizzling when serving the cucumbers with a mild entrée. And there I had it: an all-new (and more interesting) take on cucumber salad.

KEITH DRESSER, *Cook's Illustrated*

NOTES FROM THE TEST KITCHEN

SMASHING CUCUMBERS

Cut cucumbers into thirds and place in zipper-lock bag before gently pounding with small skillet or rolling pin.

Smashed Cucumbers (Pai Huang Gua)

SERVES 4

We recommend using Chinese Chinkiang (or Zhenjiang) black vinegar in this dish for its complex flavor. If you can't find it, you can substitute 2 teaspoons of rice vinegar and 1 teaspoon of balsamic vinegar. A rasp-style grater makes quick work of turning the garlic into a paste. We like to drizzle the cucumbers with Sichuan Chili Oil (recipe follows) when serving them with milder dishes such as grilled fish or chicken.

  2 **(14-ounce) English cucumbers**
1½ **teaspoons kosher salt**
  4 **teaspoons Chinese black vinegar**
  1 **teaspoon garlic, minced to paste**
  1 **tablespoon soy sauce**
  2 **teaspoons toasted sesame oil**
  1 **teaspoon sugar**
  1 **teaspoon sesame seeds, toasted**

1. Trim and discard ends from cucumbers. Cut each cucumber crosswise into three equal lengths. Place pieces in large zipper-lock bag and seal bag. Using small skillet or rolling pin, firmly but gently smash cucumbers until flattened and split lengthwise into 3 to 4 spears each. Tear spears into rough 1- to 1½-inch pieces and transfer to colander set in large bowl. Toss cucumbers with salt and let stand for at least 15 minutes or up to 30 minutes.

2. While cucumbers sit, whisk vinegar and garlic together in small bowl; let stand for at least 5 minutes or up to 15 minutes.

3. Whisk soy sauce, oil, and sugar into vinegar mixture until sugar has dissolved. Transfer cucumbers to medium bowl and discard any extracted liquid. Add dressing and sesame seeds to cucumbers and toss to combine. Serve immediately.

Sichuan Chili Oil

MAKES ABOUT 1½ CUPS

Asian chili powder is similar to red pepper flakes but is milder and more finely ground. A Sichuan chili powder is preferred, but Korean red pepper flakes, called *gochugaru*, are a good alternative.

½ **cup Asian chili powder**
2 **tablespoons sesame seeds**
2 **tablespoons Sichuan peppercorns, crushed**
½ **teaspoon salt**
1 **cup vegetable oil**
1 **(1-inch) piece ginger, unpeeled, sliced into ¼-inch rounds and smashed**
2 **bay leaves**
3 **star anise pods**
5 **green cardamom pods, crushed**

Place chili powder, sesame seeds, half of peppercorns, and salt in heatproof bowl. Heat oil, ginger, bay leaves, star anise, cardamom pods, and remaining peppercorns in small saucepan over low heat. Cook, stirring occasionally, until spices have darkened and mixture is very fragrant, 25 to 30 minutes. Strain oil mixture through fine-mesh strainer into bowl with chili powder mixture (mixture may bubble slightly); discard solids in strainer. Stir well to combine. Once cool, transfer mixture to airtight container and let stand for at least 12 hours before using. (Oil can be stored at room temperature for up to 1 week or refrigerated for up to 3 months.)

RADICCHIO SALAD

✔ WHY THIS RECIPE WORKS: Radicchio has a pleasing bitter flavor and satisfying texture that make it a welcome presence in a variety of dishes. For an intriguing addition to our fall salad rotation, we paired bitter, ruby-red radicchio with peppery arugula, sweet sliced apple, and nutty shaved Parmesan cheese. Honey and a little Dijon mustard contributed sweetness and a spicy kick to a bright vinaigrette that was the perfect foil to the bitter radicchio. A sprinkling of chopped toasted almonds finished the dish with richness and crunch. To soften the fibrous texture of the radicchio, we let it sit in the dressing for 15 minutes before tossing it with the rest of the ingredients.

Radicchio is often reserved for braises or pasta dishes, but that's a shame: The sharp, pleasantly bitter flavor of this vibrant purple and white, softball-size sphere can be a welcome addition to many dishes. For this recipe,

I wanted to highlight radicchio in its crisp, raw form by simply tossing it with a handful of ingredients to make a refreshing, flavorful, and brightly colored salad.

I began by making a handful of the recipes that I found for radicchio salads. Some salads were surprisingly delicate, combining the radicchio with assorted fruit and nuts and finishing with sweet vinaigrettes. Others were more aggressive, featuring strong cheeses and spicy dressings. I set out to find a sweet spot somewhere in the middle; I also wanted to find a way to tone down the hearty chew of this vegetable's somewhat fibrous leaves.

My tasters loved how sweet vinaigrettes played off the radicchio's bitterness in the delicate versions we tried, so I whisked together honey, white wine vinegar, olive oil, and potent Dijon mustard. For added interest and a pop of green, I tossed in a few handfuls of peppery baby arugula. Parmesan cheese—thinly shaved with a vegetable peeler, a fancy-looking touch that couldn't be easier to produce—added salty depth. Finally,

a generous handful of toasted and chopped almonds and some crisp sliced apple added even more crunch.

As for the radicchio, one recipe dealt with the chewiness issue by calling for finely shredding the leaves, but that seemed like a lot of work for a simple salad. Instead, I found that simply coring the radicchio, chopping it into 1-inch pieces, and letting it sit in the vinaigrette for about 15 minutes before adding the other ingredients softened its texture and made for more pleasant eating.

This salad was so good that I decided to create another version with the flavor pumped up a bit. I substituted rich balsamic vinegar for the white wine vinegar and used pear instead of apple. Whole parsley leaves replaced the baby arugula, and I swapped in crumbled blue cheese for the Parmesan shavings and toasted and chopped pistachios for the almonds.

ASHLEY MOORE, *Cook's Country*

Radicchio Salad with Apple, Arugula, and Parmesan

SERVES 4

Letting the radicchio sit in the dressing for 15 minutes softens its fibrous texture. The easiest way to make thin Parmesan shavings is with a sharp vegetable peeler.

- 5 tablespoons extra-virgin olive oil
- 3 tablespoons honey
- 2 tablespoons white wine vinegar
- 1 teaspoon Dijon mustard
  Salt and pepper
- 1 head radicchio (10 ounces), halved, cored, and cut into 1-inch pieces
- 1 apple, cored, halved, and sliced thin
- 2 ounces (2 cups) baby arugula
- 2 ounces Parmesan cheese, shaved with vegetable peeler
- ¼ cup whole almonds, toasted and chopped

1. Whisk oil, honey, vinegar, mustard, 1 teaspoon salt, and ½ teaspoon pepper together in large bowl. Fold in radicchio and let sit until slightly softened, about 15 minutes.

2. Add apple, arugula, and Parmesan to radicchio mixture and toss to combine. Season with salt and pepper to taste. Transfer to platter, sprinkle with almonds, and serve.

NOTES FROM THE TEST KITCHEN

PREPPING RADICCHIO

1. Use chef's knife to halve radicchio through core.

2. Use tip of knife to cut out tough, woody core.

3. Place each half cut side down; cut it into strips and then into 1-inch pieces.

RADICCHIO SALAD WITH PEAR, PARSLEY, AND BLUE CHEESE

VARIATION

Radicchio Salad with Pear, Parsley, and Blue Cheese

Substitute balsamic vinegar for white wine vinegar, 1 ripe pear for apple, 1 cup fresh parsley leaves for arugula, ½ cup crumbled blue cheese for Parmesan, and pistachios for almonds.

TOMATO AND CORN SALAD

✔ **WHY THIS RECIPE WORKS:** It's hard to beat the ripe juiciness of in-season tomatoes and the sweet flavor of late summer corn. We wanted to combine these two favorites in a fresh, flavorful summertime salad. Heirloom tomatoes are ideal, but we found that any ripe tomato worked well as long as we shopped carefully and selected fragrant specimens that felt heavy for their size (an indication they are ripe with juice). Peak-season corn is so sweet and tender that we found we could simply add it to the salad raw, eliminating the step of cooking it. To give our salad a little Southwestern flair, we added some jalapeño and fresh cilantro leaves, along with crumbled *queso fresco* for a touch of richness.

If you asked me to choose a favorite summertime vegetable, I'd have a hard time choosing between tomatoes and corn. At peak ripeness, each is perfect on its own. But together? Even better—that is, if you don't mess with them too much. I wanted a simple salad with a subtle Southwestern profile, just right for a relaxed summer supper, preferably outdoors.

I started my recipe development process not in the kitchen but at the market. Heirloom tomatoes are great when you can get your hands on them. Juicy and delicate, they usually can't withstand shipping so they're more likely to be grown locally. But if your market's fresh out at the moment, look for a tomato that has a strong tomatoey aroma and feels heavy with juice. I picked up 1½ pounds of the ripest tomatoes I could find and cut them into bite-size wedges.

To add corn into the mix, I tried blanched, sautéed, and raw kernels sliced fresh from a perfect cob. The blanched version required two extra dishes and the kernels lost some of their signature crunch. The charred flavor in the sautéed corn distracted from the fresh, vibrant flavor of the tomatoes. Surprisingly, the taste-test favorite was also the easiest: raw kernels. They are easy to slice off an ear, and they added little bursts of sweetness, a welcome complement to the deeply flavorful, juicy tomatoes.

I tossed the tomatoes and corn with a range of vinaigrettes using different ratios, starting with 3 parts extra-virgin olive oil to 1 part acid (in this case, lime juice) and working my way down. Eventually, I arrived at a ratio of 6 parts oil to 1 part lime juice, which gave me the bright—but not sour—flavor I wanted without getting in the way of the star ingredients.

Since I was taking this salad in a Southwestern direction, I added a bit of minced jalapeño for heat and a sprinkling of mild *queso fresco* cheese for just a bit of richness. A few leaves of cilantro tied it all together. Enjoying this salad at a patio table while the sun goes down, perhaps with a margarita nearby . . . that's the sort of moment that makes summer the very best time of year.

MORGAN BOLLING, *Cook's Country*

Southwestern Tomato and Corn Salad

SERVES 4

If *queso fresco* is unavailable, you can substitute farmer's cheese or a mild feta.

- 1½ **pounds ripe, mixed tomatoes, cored**
- **Salt and pepper**
- 1 **ear corn, kernels cut from cob**
- ¼ **cup extra-virgin olive oil**
- 1 **tablespoon minced shallot**
- 1 **tablespoon minced jalapeño chile**
- 2 **teaspoons lime juice**
- 2 **ounces queso fresco, crumbled (½ cup)**
- 2 **tablespoons fresh cilantro leaves**

1. Cut tomatoes into ½-inch-thick wedges, then cut wedges in half crosswise. Arrange tomatoes on large, shallow platter, alternating colors. Season with salt and pepper to taste. Sprinkle corn over top.

2. Whisk oil, shallot, jalapeño, lime juice, ½ teaspoon salt, and ¼ teaspoon pepper together in bowl. Spoon dressing evenly over tomatoes. Sprinkle with queso fresco and cilantro. Serve.

SOUTHWESTERN TOMATO AND CORN SALAD

CHOPPED CARROT SALAD WITH CELERY AND RAISINS

CHOPPED CARROT SALAD

✓ **WHY THIS RECIPE WORKS:** In search of a carrot salad with superior texture and flavor, we started by ditching two typically essential steps: grating and peeling. Finely chopping carrots in the food processor, instead of grating them by hand, produced a delicately crunchy, light-textured base for our salad. The food processor broke down the carrots in seconds, and we saved even more time by not peeling the carrots; scrubbing them was sufficient, and the skins contributed a subtle but pleasant bitterness. We added bulk and contrasting flavor to the carrots with fresh mint, tart pomegranate seeds, and toasted pistachios. A bright, lemony dressing bound it all together.

I'd spent days scraping pounds of carrots—and my knuckles—against a box grater, but I still wasn't any closer to improving upon the classic shredded carrot salad, which is usually damp and clumpy. Using the shredding disk on my food processor wasn't any help; it produced long, overly thick shreds. In fact, it wasn't until I stumbled upon an unusual recipe from cookbook author Joan Nathan that I realized I'd been approaching my revamp of this dish all wrong. It wasn't so much the flavors or the ratio of dressing to carrots or even my shredding technique that needed to change. It was the method itself: The grater had to go.

Nathan's recipe, based on an Israeli technique, calls for finely chopping the carrots in a food processor. The resulting texture is entirely different from the wet, heavy consistency of a shredded carrot salad. The fine bits deliver the vegetable's juicy, earthy sweetness but offer a texture that's more like grains with a pleasant crunch. To lighten things up, Nathan mixes the chopped carrots with lots of fresh herbs, garlic, and nuts and binds the salad together with a bright lemony dressing. The result is a surprising and refreshing take on a too-familiar vegetable and a frustrating technique. Best of all, it takes mere seconds to make, since the food processor does the lion's share of the work.

I was sold on this template but had a few ideas for tweaking the technique, starting with exactly how thoroughly to process the carrots and herbs to produce even pieces. Another change on my list was to dial down the garlic flavor and mix in other components to add complexity and further lighten the consistency of the salad.

I wanted the bits of carrots and herbs to be fine, not ground. But as anyone who's blitzed vegetables or herbs in the food processor knows, if you process until every last piece is finely chopped, some of the mixture inevitably breaks down into mush. However, if you are too conservative and don't process the pieces enough, you're likely to leave large carrot chunks or whole herb leaves in the processor bowl. Cutting the whole peeled carrots into 1-inch chunks before adding them to the processor helped produce the fine, even bits that I wanted.

The herbs—I started with ½ cup of cilantro leaves—were more challenging. No matter when I added the leaves to the processor bowl (before, with, or after the carrots), some inevitably turned to mush, muddying the salad's fresh flavor and sabotaging the delicately crunchy texture I was after. Mincing the cilantro by hand was a bit more work, but it gave me much better control over the final product.

The only part of the vegetable prep that was a bit of a drag was peeling all those carrots, and it made me wonder if I could skip peeling altogether and just give the roots a trim and a good scrub instead. I gave it a shot and was pleased to discover that it was actually advantageous: Not only was the skin's slightly tougher texture imperceptible in those tiny pieces but the skin also lent the salad a subtle earthy bitterness that matched well with the vegetable's sweeter core and all those grassy-tasting fresh herbs.

Circling back to the garlic, I tried mincing it by hand to make sure it was fine enough, along with incrementally reducing the amount. But in both cases, its harsh taste overwhelmed the more subtle flavors of the other components. It was better to leave it out altogether.

Now for some salads with flavors of my own. The first was a nod to Nathan's original: I kept the lemon-based dressing and the pistachios but added a touch of honey, swapped out the cilantro for mint, seasoned the mixture with smoked paprika and a touch of cayenne, and mixed in pomegranate seeds for bursts of tangy sweetness and vibrant color. I liked the addition of fruit with the carrots, so I mixed up a couple more variations in the same vein: One was a riff on classic American carrot salad, with raisins, celery, and parsley, and the other featured chopped fennel, toasted hazelnuts, orange juice and zest, and chives. The last salad, a kimchi-inspired version, paired a rice vinegar–based dressing with cilantro, plus coarsely chopped radishes and toasted sesame seeds for extra crunch.

ANDREW JANJIGIAN, *Cook's Illustrated*

Chopped Carrot Salad with Mint, Pistachios, and Pomegranate Seeds

SERVES 4 TO 6

We prefer the convenience and the hint of bitterness that leaving the carrots unpeeled lends to this salad; just be sure to scrub the carrots well before using them.

- ¾ cup shelled pistachios, toasted
- ¼ cup extra-virgin olive oil
- 3 tablespoons lemon juice
- 1 tablespoon honey
  Salt and pepper
- ½ teaspoon smoked paprika
- ⅛ teaspoon cayenne pepper
- 1 pound carrots, trimmed and cut into 1-inch pieces
- 1 cup pomegranate seeds
- ½ cup minced fresh mint

Pulse pistachios in food processor until coarsely chopped, 10 to 12 pulses; transfer to small bowl. Whisk oil, lemon juice, honey, 1 teaspoon salt, ½ teaspoon pepper, paprika, and cayenne in large bowl until combined. Process carrots in now-empty processor until finely chopped, 10 to 20 seconds, scraping down sides of bowl as needed. Transfer carrots to bowl with dressing; add ½ cup pomegranate seeds, mint, and half of pistachios and toss to combine. Season with salt to taste. Transfer to serving platter, sprinkle with remaining pomegranate seeds and pistachios, and serve.

VARIATIONS

Chopped Carrot Salad with Celery and Raisins

Omit pistachios, paprika, cayenne, and pomegranate seeds. Substitute parsley for mint. Add 3 celery ribs, sliced thin, and ¾ cup raisins to dressing with carrots.

Chopped Carrot Salad with Fennel, Orange, and Hazelnuts

Substitute toasted and skinned hazelnuts for pistachios. Omit paprika, cayenne, and pomegranate seeds. Substitute ¼ teaspoon grated orange zest plus ⅓ cup juice and 2 tablespoons white wine vinegar for lemon juice. Substitute chives for mint, saving ¼ cup to use as garnish. Before processing carrots, pulse 1 fennel bulb, stalks discarded, bulb halved, cored, and cut into 1-inch pieces, in food processor until coarsely chopped, 10 to 12 pulses, then add to dressing.

Chopped Carrot Salad with Radishes and Sesame Seeds

Omit pistachios. Substitute 3 tablespoons vegetable oil and 2 teaspoons toasted sesame oil for olive oil. Substitute rice vinegar for lemon juice and 1½ teaspoons Korean red pepper flakes for paprika, cayenne, and pepper. Increase honey to 2 tablespoons and salt to 1¼ teaspoons. Before processing carrots, pulse 8 ounces radishes, trimmed and halved, in food processor until coarsely but evenly chopped, 10 to 12 pulses; add to dressing. Substitute ¼ cup toasted sesame seeds for pomegranate seeds and cilantro for mint.

NOTES FROM THE TEST KITCHEN

WHEN BETTER IS ALSO FASTER

Carrots that are finely chopped in the food processor make a salad that's much lighter and more open-textured than the shredded kind. Best of all, processing the carrots takes mere seconds and keeps your knuckles out of harm's way.

GRATED
Clumpy and damp

PROCESSED
Fine and fluffy

GRILLED SWEET POTATO SALAD

☑ **WHY THIS RECIPE WORKS:** To bring together two summer traditions—potato salad and grilling—we used the grill to both steam and char sweet potatoes, so all the cooking was done outside. We first tossed the potatoes with a spiced vinaigrette in a disposable aluminum pan; the vinaigrette generated steam and helped cook the potatoes through while also seasoning them. Once the sweet potatoes were steamed, we transferred them from the pan to the hot cooking grate to give them some flavorful char. Threading toothpicks through the onion rounds kept them intact and prevented them from falling through the grate during cooking.

Summer is the season of potato salads and grilling. I decided to combine these two traditions, with a little twist—I'd use sweet potatoes.

The first step was cutting the tubers down to size; they're dense and would take a long time to cook through if left whole. After experimenting with chunks and rounds, I found that rounds took on more charred flavor. Still, it wasn't easy to get them to grill evenly. By the time the centers cooked through, the exteriors looked like coal.

The answer was to drop the rounds into a disposable aluminum pan, cover the pan tightly with aluminum foil, set it over the fire, and let the water in the potatoes steam them through. I then transferred the steamed potatoes from the pan to the cooking grate to char. At this point, they were good, but not great. For a flavor boost, I tossed the rounds with a sweet-smoky vinaigrette of lime juice, honey, cumin, and chipotle chile before grilling.

I also grilled a red onion, sliced into rounds that I skewered with toothpicks to help them hold together on the grill. To assemble the salad, I tossed the charred spuds and onions with a bit more vinaigrette and topped it all with salty feta, sliced scallions, and fresh cilantro.

ALLI BERKEY, *Cook's Country*

Grilled Sweet Potato Salad

SERVES 4 TO 6

Buy medium sweet potatoes, 2 to 3 inches in diameter, because they'll fit neatly in the disposable aluminum pan.

1 small red onion, sliced into ½-inch-thick rounds
3 tablespoons lime juice (2 limes), plus lime wedges for serving
2 tablespoons honey
1 teaspoon minced canned chipotle chile in adobo sauce
½ teaspoon ground cumin
Salt and pepper
⅓ cup vegetable oil
2½ pounds sweet potatoes, peeled and cut into ½-inch-thick rounds
1 (13 by 9-inch) disposable aluminum pan
2 ounces feta cheese, crumbled (½ cup)
3 scallions, sliced thin on bias
¼ cup coarsely chopped fresh cilantro

1. Thread 1 toothpick horizontally through each onion round. Whisk lime juice, honey, chipotle, cumin, ½ teaspoon salt, and ¼ teaspoon pepper together in bowl. Slowly whisk in oil.

2. Toss potatoes, onion rounds, ¼ cup vinaigrette, ½ teaspoon salt, and ½ teaspoon pepper together in separate bowl. Place onion rounds in bottom of disposable pan, layer potatoes over top, then pour in any remaining liquid from bowl. Cover disposable pan tightly with aluminum foil.

3A. FOR A CHARCOAL GRILL: Open bottom vent completely. Light large chimney starter filled with charcoal briquettes (6 quarts). When top coals are partially covered with ash, pour evenly over grill. Set cooking grate in place, cover, and open lid vent completely. Heat grill until hot, about 5 minutes.

3B. FOR A GAS GRILL: Turn all burners to high, cover, and heat grill until hot, about 15 minutes. Turn all burners to medium. Adjust burners as needed to maintain grill temperature around 400 degrees.

4. Clean and oil cooking grate. Place disposable pan on grill. Cover grill and cook until vegetables are tender, 20 to 25 minutes, shaking disposable pan halfway through cooking to redistribute potatoes. Remove disposable pan from grill.

5. Place vegetables on cooking grate. Cook (covered if using gas) until lightly charred and tender, 2 to 4 minutes per side. Transfer vegetables to platter. Remove toothpicks from onion rounds and separate rings. Pour remaining vinaigrette over vegetables and toss to coat. Sprinkle feta, scallions, and cilantro over top. Serve with lime wedges.

SOUPS AND STEWS

POSTHOLIDAY TURKEY SOUP

✓ **WHY THIS RECIPE WORKS:** Our simple approach to stock making delivers pure turkey flavor with very little effort. Using the roasted carcass as is, without further browning the bones in the oven, saved time and allowed the turkey flavor to come to the fore. Gently simmering the bones in water for just 2 hours extracted enough gelatin to give this stock rich homemade flavor and body. Omitting *mirepoix* (carrot, celery, and onion) from the recipe allowed the essence of the poultry to shine through. With our simple stock complete, we then used it as the base for a few soups featuring leftover turkey meat, a starchy ingredient (such as barley, orzo, or rice), and simple vegetables (such as carrots, celery, mushroom, and hearty greens). Limiting seasonings to herbs, a squeeze of lemon juice, and salt and pepper allowed the pure turkey stock to shine through.

I've been the primary cook for my family's Thanksgiving feast for about 20 years now. I gladly inherited this honor from my mom, but there's one task I never took off her plate: making a batch of stock from the leftover turkey carcass. I've always felt guilty about saddling her with the job, so this year I vowed to take it on myself. Anticipating a bit of postholiday fatigue, I intended to keep this recipe as simple as possible.

As it happened, a colleague was roasting lots of whole turkeys, producing a ready supply of carcasses that I could use for testing purposes. I gathered two that had the leg quarter and breast meat removed but still included meaty bits, the wings, and a fair amount of skin. I prepared two bone-and-water stocks, the first using a carcass straight from the roasted turkey and a second one for which I roasted the carcass for 45 minutes, thinking that this might produce a richer-tasting stock.

The first stock simmered into a lovely pale gold hue, whereas the roasted-carcass stock turned a deep mahogany brown. I assumed that the darker sample would be more popular, so I was pleasantly surprised when tasters gravitated toward the easier-to-make golden stock. It tasted clearly and deeply of turkey, whereas the stock made with twice-cooked bones tasted more generically of roasted meat.

I experimented with aromatics next. To one stockpot containing 4 quarts of water and a whole carcass, I added raw mirepoix (chopped carrots, onion, and celery); to a second, the same mix of vegetables that I had first caramelized to a deep golden brown in the oven. Finally, I made a third stock with only water and a carcass. To my delight, we preferred the near-effortless bone-only stock to those made with vegetables. The raw mirepoix stock was too vegetal and the roasted one too sweet, but the bone-only stock boasted nothing but pristine, though slightly weak, poultry flavor.

Happy with the way things were progressing, I made one more bone-only stock, but rather than use the carcass whole, I broke it into smaller pieces—a step easily accomplished with a heavy knife or kitchen shears—so I would need only 2½ quarts of water (enough for a batch of soup) instead of 4 quarts to cover the bones. The upshot was a more concentrated stock. I also found that I could squeeze a broken carcass into a Dutch oven, a boon for cooks who don't own a stockpot.

Next up: consistency. To attain the viscosity I wanted, the stock needed plenty of gelatin, which develops from collagen, a protein found in connective tissue, skin, and bones. It lends subtle body you won't find in commercial products and is the hallmark of a good homemade stock. Many recipes call for simmering bones all day to ensure adequate gelatin extraction. Was that truly necessary?

To find out, I filled four pots with equal weights of bones and water and cooked them for 1, 2, 3, and 4 hours, respectively. After an overnight chill in the refrigerator, the 1-hour stock was slightly thickened, indicating the presence of a small amount of gelatin. However, the 2-, 3-, and 4-hour stocks were all lightly set and wiggled like Jell-O when I shook its container. Although the 3- and 4-hour stocks were slightly firmer when cold, when we tasted them hot, they were nearly impossible to distinguish from the 2-hour stock—each was richly flavored and infused with an ample amount of gelatinous body.

Scoring yet another victory for simplicity, I went with a 2-hour simmer. I occasionally skimmed the surface of the bubbling liquid to remove any foam or impurities. Then, once the time was up, I strained out the bones, let the stock cool for 20 minutes, and spooned off the surface fat. Energized by the fact that my stock required nothing more than water, bones, and time, I decided to use the reserved turkey fat to sauté aromatics for a quick batch of soup.

My first try at an easy postholiday soup—with

TURKEY ORZO SOUP WITH KALE AND CHICKPEAS

fennel, rosemary, and kale—was a little too complex; the bold ingredients overwhelmed the poultry flavor I had been at pains to create in my stock. I altered the ingredient list, ultimately ending up with three variations; each one combined 2 cups of shredded leftover turkey meat with a starchy component—barley, orzo, or rice—along with carefully selected aromatics, complementary vegetables, mild-mannered seasonings, and a last-minute addition of fresh lemon juice to brighten things up.

Now I was guaranteed to eat well on the Friday after Thanksgiving while still having plenty of time to kick back on the couch.

STEVE DUNN, *Cook's Illustrated*

Simple Turkey Stock

MAKES 8 CUPS

Pick off most of the meat clinging to the carcass and reserve it. However, don't pick the carcass clean: The stock will have a fuller flavor if there is some meat and skin still attached. If you have the bones from the drumsticks and thighs, add them to the pot.

1   carcass from 12- to 14-pound roasted turkey
10   cups water

1. Using chef's knife, remove wings from carcass and separate each wing at joints into 3 pieces. Cut through ribs to separate breastbone from backbone, then cut backbone into 3 or 4 pieces. Using kitchen shears or heavy knife, remove ribs from both sides of breastbone. (You should have roughly 4 pounds of bones broken into 10 to 12 pieces.)

2. Arrange bones in stockpot or large Dutch oven in compact layer. Add water and bring to boil over medium-high heat. Reduce heat to low, cover, and cook for 2 hours, using shallow spoon to skim foam and impurities from surface as needed.

3. Strain stock through fine-mesh strainer into large container; discard solids. Let stock cool slightly, about 20 minutes. Skim any fat from surface (reserve fat for making soup). Let stock cool for 1½ hours before refrigerating. (Stock can be refrigerated for up to 2 days or frozen for up to 4 months.)

Turkey Barley Soup

SERVES 6

If you don't have turkey fat, you can substitute unsalted butter.

2   tablespoons turkey fat
1   onion, chopped fine
½   teaspoon dried thyme
    Pinch red pepper flakes
2   garlic cloves, minced
1   recipe Simple Turkey Stock
¾   cup pearled barley
1   bay leaf
2   celery ribs, cut into ¼-inch pieces
2   carrots, peeled and cut into ¼-inch pieces
2   cups shredded turkey
1   tablespoon lemon juice
    Salt and pepper

1. Heat fat in Dutch oven over medium heat until shimmering. Add onion, thyme, and pepper flakes and cook, stirring occasionally, until onion is softened and translucent, about 5 minutes. Add garlic and cook until fragrant, about 1 minute. Add stock, barley, and bay leaf; increase heat to high and bring to simmer. Reduce heat to medium-low and simmer, partially covered, for 15 minutes.

2. Add celery and carrots and simmer, partially covered, until vegetables start to soften, about 15 minutes.

3. Add turkey and cook until barley and vegetables are tender, about 10 minutes. Off heat, stir in lemon juice and season with salt and pepper to taste. Serve.

Turkey Orzo Soup with Kale and Chickpeas

SERVES 6

If you don't have turkey fat, you can substitute extra-virgin olive oil. Our favorite canned chickpeas are Pastene Chick Peas.

2   tablespoons turkey fat
1   onion, chopped fine
    Pinch red pepper flakes
3   garlic cloves, minced
¼   teaspoon ground cumin
¼   teaspoon ground coriander

1 recipe Simple Turkey Stock

3 ounces curly kale, stemmed and cut
into ½-inch pieces (6 cups)

1 (15-ounce) can chickpeas, rinsed

½ cup orzo

2 cups shredded turkey

2 tablespoons lemon juice

Salt and pepper

1. Heat fat in Dutch oven over medium heat until shimmering. Add onion and pepper flakes and cook, stirring occasionally, until onion is softened and translucent, about 5 minutes. Add garlic, cumin, and coriander and cook until fragrant, about 1 minute. Add stock; increase heat to high and bring to simmer. Stir in kale, chickpeas, and orzo; reduce heat to medium-low and simmer, partially covered, for 10 minutes.

2. Add turkey and cook until orzo and kale are tender, about 2 minutes. Off heat, stir in lemon juice and season with salt and pepper to taste. Serve.

Turkey Rice Soup with Mushrooms and Swiss Chard

SERVES 6

If you don't have turkey fat, you can substitute extra-virgin olive oil.

2 tablespoons turkey fat

1 onion, chopped fine

½ teaspoon dried sage

Pinch red pepper flakes

3 garlic cloves, minced

1 recipe Simple Turkey Stock

¾ cup long-grain white rice

4 ounces cremini mushrooms, trimmed and sliced thin

3 ounces Swiss chard, stems chopped fine, leaves sliced into ½-inch-wide strips (5 cups)

2 cups shredded turkey

2 tablespoons lemon juice

Salt and pepper

1. Heat fat in Dutch oven over medium heat until shimmering. Add onion, sage, and pepper flakes and cook, stirring occasionally, until onion is softened and translucent, about 5 minutes. Add garlic and cook until fragrant, about 1 minute. Add stock; increase heat to high and bring to simmer. Stir in rice, reduce heat to medium-low, and simmer, partially covered, for 10 minutes.

2. Add mushrooms and chard stems and simmer, partially covered, until vegetables start to soften, about 5 minutes.

3. Add chard leaves and turkey and cook until rice is cooked and chard leaves are wilted, about 2 minutes. Off heat, stir in lemon juice and season with salt and pepper to taste. Serve.

CHICKEN NOODLE SOUP

✓ WHY THIS RECIPE WORKS: We were after a comforting, deeply flavored chicken noodle soup that would be easy enough to make when you're feeling under the weather. Browning bone-in chicken pieces (our recipe lets you customize the soup with dark meat, white meat, or both) before simmering them in store-bought chicken broth created an intensely chicken-y soup base. A standard mix of onion, celery, and carrot simmered alongside the chicken enhanced rather than distracted from the chicken broth's richness. And though egg noodles are common in homemade versions, tasters preferred spaghetti broken into bite-size pieces, which gave a nostalgic nod to canned versions but had loads more flavor.

When you're wrapped in blankets on the couch feeling lousy, nothing beats a comforting bowl of steaming, deeply flavored chicken noodle soup to make you feel cared for. Unfortunately, most of the salty, mystery-meat canned versions (I'll admit to having popped a few tops myself in moments of sickness) fall short of the mark.

We all deserve a little TLC when we're not feeling well, so I decided I needed to do better. I set out to create a recipe for a rich, satisfying homemade soup that screamed "comfort food" but was also fast and easy enough to make in about an hour.

To get my bearings, I gathered a handful of different chicken noodle soup recipes from our cookbook library. Those that called for making homemade chicken stock tasted great but required hours of simmering and piles of ingredients, while those that skipped this step came out watery, dull, and totally unsatisfying.

OLD-FASHIONED CHICKEN NOODLE SOUP

I found a better starting point in a previous test kitchen recipe for a rich chicken stew that developed a deep base of flavor by browning skin-on, bone-in chicken parts and then simmering them in store-bought broth with aromatics until the pieces were cooked through.

This effectively created a hybrid stock of prefab broth bolstered by real chicken parts, aromatic onion, cut-up carrot, and some faintly astringent celery. The result was a full-flavored stock that, after just 15 minutes of simmering, tasted like it had been carefully nurtured on the back burner for several hours. What's more, because this stock simmered for just a short time, the vegetables weren't totally spent.

To determine the best chicken parts to use, I put together a side-by-side test of stock made with just chicken breasts versus stock made with just legs and thighs. The result was a draw: Some tasters preferred the tender shreds of clean white meat in their soup, while others sought the deeper, more savory flavor that chicken thighs gave the broth. I decided to call for a combination of the two to get the best of both worlds.

Once the stock had simmered, I removed the chicken pieces and let them cool down just enough so that I could easily remove the bones and skin. I then shredded the meat with two forks and returned it to the pot.

After perfecting this two-part broth technique, I returned to my lineup of vegetables to see if there were any improvements to make. I tried everything from leeks to peas to parsnips, but in the end I found that my initial lineup, a standard mix of celery, onion, and carrot, enhanced rather than distracted from the chicken's richness and kept the soup in the familiar comfort zone.

A single bay leaf and a couple of sprigs of fresh thyme added a complex herby background. My soup was now ready for noodles. While egg noodles are a common ingredient in many homemade versions of this soup, I decided to hold a tasting pitting egg noodles against orzo, spaghetti, and several other pasta shapes. To my surprise (and delight), my tasters preferred spaghetti, broken up into bite-size pieces. Some colleagues noted that this choice gave a nostalgic nod to those old canned versions, bringing up memories of sick days past.

Many recipes call for cooking the noodles separately before adding them to the soup, but this seemed silly to me and required another pot. Instead, I cooked the

KEYS TO EASY HOMEMADE CHICKEN NOODLE SOUP

1. Sear chicken to create flavorful browned bits on bottom of pot.

2. Boost flavor of store-bought broth by adding aromatics.

3. Use 2 forks to shred chicken into bite-size pieces.

4. Add pasta toward end of cooking to ensure it doesn't overcook.

spaghetti right in the soup, which was easier and allowed the noodles to soak up plenty of rich, savory chicken flavor. Some minced fresh parsley tossed over the top of the soup added a final pop of freshness.

With chicken-infused noodles, hearty vegetables, and shreds of tender meat all simmering in a golden, comforting broth, this soup will help you weather any cold. But I'm not waiting until the next time I'm really sick to make a batch, slip on my fuzzy socks, and stake out a spot on the couch, where I'll settle in with a bowl of this supremely comforting soup.

MORGAN BOLLING, *Cook's Country*

Old-Fashioned Chicken Noodle Soup

SERVES 4 TO 6

The easiest way to break the noodles is to wrap them in a clean dish towel and snap them on the edge of your counter. If you prefer, 4 ounces (2 cups) of egg noodles can be substituted for the spaghetti. Fresh dill can be substituted for the parsley.

1½ pounds bone-in chicken breasts and/or
      thighs, trimmed
      Salt and pepper
  1 tablespoon vegetable oil
  8 cups chicken broth
  1 onion, chopped
  1 carrot, peeled and cut into ½-inch pieces
  1 celery rib, cut into ½-inch pieces
  2 sprigs fresh thyme
  1 bay leaf
  5 ounces spaghetti, broken into 1-inch
      pieces (1½ cups)
  1 tablespoon minced fresh parsley

1. Pat chicken dry with paper towels and sprinkle with ¼ teaspoon salt and ¼ teaspoon pepper. Heat oil in Dutch oven over medium-high heat until shimmering. Cook chicken until well browned all over, 8 to 10 minutes.

2. Add broth, onion, carrot, celery, thyme sprigs, bay leaf, and ¼ teaspoon salt, scraping up any browned bits. Bring to boil, cover, and reduce heat to low. Simmer until breasts register 160 degrees and/or thighs register at least 175 degrees, 14 to 17 minutes.

3. Remove pot from heat; discard thyme sprigs and bay leaf. Transfer chicken to plate and let cool slightly. Using 2 forks, shred chicken into bite-size pieces; discard skin and bones.

4. Return soup to boil over medium-high heat and add pasta. Cook, uncovered, until pasta is tender, 9 to 11 minutes, stirring often. Add chicken and parsley and cook until chicken is warmed through, about 2 minutes. Season with salt and pepper to taste. Serve. (Soup can be made through step 3, covered, and refrigerated for up to 2 days.)

GARLIC-CHICKEN SOUP

✔ WHY THIS RECIPE WORKS: Both chicken soup and garlic soup have been lauded as remedies for what ails you. Our goal was to combine the two for a supercharged dose of comfort. We started our testing with a generous 2 tablespoons of garlic, but it wasn't until we reached a whopping ½ cup that tasters praised its bright yet balanced presence. Blooming the garlic before adding liquid gave it a toasty sweetness. Wild rice is nutrient-dense and was a hearty addition, and cooking it directly in the soup infused it with garlicky flavor. To ensure tender, juicy chicken, we simmered it during the last few minutes of cooking. Several handfuls of baby spinach and plenty of chopped parsley gave our soup a vegetal boost that complemented the deep garlic notes.

No matter what ails me, chicken soup has always been my go-to remedy; the rich aroma and warm broth take the edge off of even the most punishing cold. But when I lived in Spain, I was introduced to their version of the cure-all: garlic soup. Called *sopa de ajo*, this pungent, brothy soup hails from the mountainous region of Castile and exists in many forms throughout Spain. My mother-in-law's Catalan version, *sopa d'all i farigola*, is exquisitely perfumed with thyme. Both of these healthy, nourishing soups have been in my repertoire for years, but I wondered if combining the two might deliver the ultimate supercharged cold-weather meal.

Here in the test kitchen, we've cranked out our fair share of chicken soups, but garlic soup was untrodden territory. A little research introduced me to the broad range of garlic soups simmered all across Europe, from potato-packed Czech *česnečka* to creamy Austrian *knoblauchcremesuppe* to egg-thickened Provençal *aïgo boulido*. These options were all tempting, but I wanted a simple soup, so I decided to make an easy brothy version. And while noodles or white rice add texture and help thicken the base of my favorite chicken soups, I wanted my garlic-infused version to be wholly nutritious, so I opted for nutrient-dense wild rice.

My first challenge lay in determining the best way to harness the garlic's flavor. Roasting is a hands-off way to bring out its nutty sweetness, but I was hoping for a speedier flavor boost. I opted to mince the garlic, and began with a generous 2 tablespoons. Gently blooming the garlic in oil unlocked its complex flavor,

GARLIC-CHICKEN SOUP WITH WILD RICE

but after combining it with aromatics and the broth, the garlic presence was barely discernible. I prepared a few more batches, incrementally upping the amount of garlic, but my tasters were not satisfied until I'd incorporated a whopping ½ cup of minced cloves.

The wild rice needed to simmer for just under an hour to turn perfectly chewy, which was enough time for the garlic to infuse the broth and rice with plenty of flavor; bay leaves, minced thyme, and umami-rich tomato paste deepened the supersavory profile of my soup. I still wanted tender bites of chicken so I added pieces of breast meat, which contributed plenty of lean protein for a more substantial soup. A few handfuls of iron-rich baby spinach added a final nutrition boost.

As I finished my final batch of soup with a handful of chopped parsley, I didn't need to call for tasters—the enticing garlic aroma had drawn a small, hungry crowd. We tucked into our bowls of soup and all agreed: A soup this good shouldn't have to wait for a sick day.

NICOLE KONSTANTINAKOS,
America's Test Kitchen Books

Garlic-Chicken Soup with Wild Rice

SERVES 6

You will need at least two heads of garlic. We prefer to use homemade broth (recipe follows) in this recipe.

- 3 tablespoons extra-virgin olive oil
- ½ cup minced garlic (about 25 cloves)
- 2 carrots, peeled and sliced ¼ inch thick
- 1 onion, chopped fine
- 1 celery rib, minced
  Salt and pepper
- 2 teaspoons minced fresh thyme or ½ teaspoon dried
- 1 teaspoon tomato paste
- 6 cups chicken broth
- 2 bay leaves
- ⅔ cup wild rice, picked over and rinsed
- 8 ounces boneless, skinless chicken breasts, trimmed and cut into ¾-inch pieces
- 3 ounces (3 cups) baby spinach
- ¼ cup chopped fresh parsley

1. Heat oil and garlic in Dutch oven over medium-low heat, stirring occasionally, until garlic is light golden, 3 to 5 minutes. Add carrots, onion, celery, and ¼ teaspoon salt, increase heat to medium, and cook, stirring occasionally, until vegetables are just beginning to brown, 10 to 12 minutes.

2. Stir in thyme and tomato paste and cook until fragrant, about 30 seconds. Stir in broth and bay leaves, scraping up any browned bits, and bring to simmer. Stir in rice, return to simmer, cover, and cook over medium-low heat until rice is tender, 40 to 50 minutes.

3. Discard bay leaves. Stir in chicken and spinach and cook over low heat, stirring occasionally, until chicken is cooked through and spinach is wilted, 3 to 5 minutes. Off heat, stir in parsley and season with salt and pepper to taste. Serve.

Chicken Broth

MAKES ABOUT 8 CUPS

This rich and well-rounded chicken broth is perfect as a base for soups, stews, and sauces; as a cooking medium; and even on its own. Many recipes for chicken broth call for simmering a whole chicken, but we found that cutting the chicken into pieces yielded more flavor by providing more surface area for browning. If using a slow cooker, you will need one that holds 5½ to 7 quarts.

- 1 tablespoon extra-virgin olive oil
- 3 pounds whole chicken legs, backs, and/or wings, hacked into 2-inch pieces
- 1 onion, chopped
- 8 cups water
- 3 bay leaves
  Kosher salt

1. Heat oil in Dutch oven over medium-high heat until just smoking. Pat chicken dry with paper towels. Brown half of chicken, about 5 minutes; transfer to large bowl. Repeat with remaining chicken; transfer to bowl.

NOTES FROM THE TEST KITCHEN

WHAT IS COLD-PRESSED OIL?

Expeller- or cold-pressed oils are healthier than chemically extracted oils. But they involve trade-offs. Both are minimally refined oils, processed without chemicals. Cold pressing involves lower temperatures and is used for heat-sensitive oils such as olive oil. These oils retain more of their antioxidants but spoil more quickly and may need to be refrigerated. They may also have lower smoke points.

2. Add onion to fat left in pot and cook over medium heat until softened, about 5 minutes. Stir in 2 cups water, bay leaves, and 1 teaspoon salt, scraping up any browned bits.

3A. FOR THE STOVETOP: Stir remaining 6 cups water into pot, then return browned chicken and any accumulated juices to pot and bring to simmer. Reduce heat to low, cover, and simmer gently until broth is rich and flavorful, about 4 hours.

3B. FOR THE SLOW COOKER: Transfer browned chicken and any accumulated juices and onion mixture to slow cooker. Stir in remaining 6 cups water. Cover and cook until broth is rich and flavorful, about 4 hours on low.

4. Remove large bones from pot, then strain broth through fine-mesh strainer into large container; discard solids. Let broth settle for 5 to 10 minutes, then defat using wide, shallow spoon or fat separator. (Cooled broth can be refrigerated for up to 4 days or frozen for up to 1 month.)

MULTICOOKER CHIPOTLE PORK AND HOMINY STEW

✔ WHY THIS RECIPE WORKS: Also known as posole, this fragrant New Mexican stew combines toothsome hominy and tender chunks of pork in a mildly spicy, verdant base. We wanted to use the multicooker to make a streamlined version that would maintain the stew's complex flavor. Plenty of onion plus jalapeños and garlic offered a bold base, while a bit of chipotle chile brought smoky depth and spice. In the insulated heat of the multicooker, the pork cooked up ultratender. Adding the hominy before pressure or slow cooking allowed it to soak up lots of flavor from the porky broth; the fluffy, chewy kernels also released some starch, which nicely thickened the stew.

If you've been on the Internet lately, you've probably heard about multicookers (such as the Instant Pot). Legions of devoted fans sing the praises of these electric pressure-cooking/slow-cooking/rice-cooking/yogurt-making devices, and, it seems, for good reason: They promise to make getting dinner on the table faster and easier than ever. Multicookers are touted as being especially well suited for recipes such as soups and stews, since the enclosed environment of the cooker can concentrate flavors without requiring much hands-on time. Intrigued, I decided to develop a weeknight-friendly recipe for one of my favorite stews, pork posole, for our new book of multicooker recipes.

Posole is the Mexican name for both hominy (dried field-corn kernels treated with lime and boiled until tender but still chewy) and the full-flavored stew made with hominy and meat. Traditional versions of this stew can require multiple cuts of meat and hours of stovetop simmering, making them impractical for anything but a weekend project. The balance of porky broth, spicy chiles, and earthy hominy is key to a great posole, and I hoped the multicooker could help me achieve that—without my having to hover over the stove.

In addition to choosing the best ingredients and techniques for my recipe, I would also need to overcome an additional hurdle: For our book, we had decided to develop every recipe so that it would work on both the pressure-cook setting and the slow-cook setting of the multicooker. We loved the idea of giving home cooks the option to choose the setting (and therefore, the timing) that works best for them. After all, the appeal of the multicooker is in making life easier, so we aimed to truly deliver on that promise.

With this ambitious, multifaceted goal in mind—a deeply flavorful and satisfying stew that would require a minimum of hands-on work and that could be made on either the pressure- or slow-cook setting of the multicooker—I got to work.

While traditional recipes for posole start out with multiple, sometimes obscure cuts of pork (like head, neck, and shank), the test kitchen has had great success using pork butt. Pork butt's hearty marbling gives it great flavor, and it's easy to find and work with. I opted for a boneless butt, which would speed up the cooking time. Cutting the pork into small pieces before cooking shaved off even more time, and allowed me to trim the pork of excess fat, avoiding a greasy stew.

For my stew base, I used the multicooker's sauté function. The sauté function is one of my favorite aspects of these appliances, since this built-in setting makes most multicooker dishes one-pot affairs. I sautéed onions and garlic along with some jalapeño chiles (for grassy, bright flavor) and a spoonful of minced canned chipotle chile in adobo sauce, which was an easy way to add smoky depth. A bit of flour gave the stew nice body. Finally, I whisked in some wine (for balancing acidity) and chicken broth (for savory backbone).

MULTICOOKER CHIPOTLE PORK AND HOMINY STEW (POSOLE)

While we typically brown meat for stews, I wondered if it was really necessary here. I would have to brown the pork in batches, which was time-consuming, and I suspected that the stew's potent ingredients would overwhelm any flavor benefit from browning anyway. A quick side-by-side test of my working recipe revealed that browning was in fact unnecessary.

After a few more tests, I discovered that 25 minutes under pressure or 4 to 5 hours on the slow-cook setting tenderized the pork beautifully and gave the stew complexity. Tasters' one complaint was that the broth was on the thin side (since I was using boneless pork, this wasn't surprising, as I wasn't getting any body-building gelatin from bones). I didn't want to add more flour, but I did have another idea. Up until now, I had been adding the hominy at the end of cooking, afraid that it would turn mushy in the intense heat of the pressure cooker or with extended slow cooking. But the starchy hominy might be just the thickener my stew needed. When I tested adding the hominy before pressure or slow cooking, it worked like a charm, offering just enough starch to give the broth a little more body. As a bonus, the hominy soaked up some of the savory broth during cooking, saturating the kernels with flavor. I also added carrots for a bit of sweetness and heft.

With a handful of fresh cilantro added just before serving, my recipe was nearly done. I had just the balanced, hearty stew I was after, and in the multicooker I was using, it worked perfectly every time. But in an initial testing of different models, we had discovered that they don't all work the same way. While the pressure-cook settings and the sauté settings usually produce similar results, the slow-cook settings can vary wildly. We found this was especially true of one of the most popular models of multicooker, the Instant Pot Duo.

While the low slow-cook setting on many multicookers reaches about 200 degrees, the Instant Pot's low slow-cook setting only gets up to about 187 degrees. When we tried to cook food on the low slow-cook setting in the Instant Pot, it took hours longer than in other models. Cooking recipes on the high slow-cook setting in the Instant Pot, which runs at about 206 degrees, helped, but even then, we sometimes needed to extend cooking time ranges. Why was this, even though the temperature was technically higher than our winner on low? It has to do with more than just temperature. Dr. Robert A. Heard, professor of materials science and engineering at Carnegie Mellon University, helped us calculate the potential amount of energy, in the form of heat, that ends up in each machine's insert to cook the food, based on the dimensions of each machine's base and insert and its wattage (power). He explained that since the Instant Pot's potential energy is lower than many multicookers, it cooks much slower. Basically, the heat was taking longer to get to the food.

Lucky for us, once we were armed with this info, adjusting recipes was easy: We simply defaulted to the high slow-cook setting in the Instant Pot, instead of low as in the other models, then tested each of our working recipes to see how long they needed to cook.

Finally, my recipe was not only delicious and doable on a weeknight, but it was absolutely foolproof—no matter which setting or model you choose.

LEAH COLINS, *America's Test Kitchen Books*

Multicooker Chipotle Pork and Hominy Stew (Posole)

SERVES 6 TO 8

PRESSURE COOK TOTAL TIME: 1 HOUR 10 MINUTES
SLOW COOK TOTAL TIME: 5 HOURS 40 MINUTES

Pork butt roast is often labeled Boston butt in the supermarket. If using the pressure cook function, be sure to cover the valve with a dish towel when releasing the pressure to protect from hot steam or splatters. Serve with diced tomato, diced avocado, and thinly sliced radishes.

- 1 tablespoon vegetable oil
- 2 onions, chopped fine
- 2 jalapeño chiles, stemmed, seeded, and minced
- ⅓ cup all-purpose flour
- 4 garlic cloves, minced
- 1 tablespoon minced canned chipotle chile in adobo sauce
- 2 teaspoons minced fresh oregano or ½ teaspoon dried
- 1 cup dry white wine
- 2 cups chicken broth, plus extra as needed
- 2 (15-ounce) cans white or yellow hominy, rinsed
- 8 ounces carrots, peeled and sliced 1 inch thick
- 2 bay leaves
- 3 pounds boneless pork butt roast, pulled apart at seams, trimmed, and cut into 1-inch pieces
  Salt and pepper
- ¼ cup minced fresh cilantro
  Lime wedges

1. Using highest sauté or browning function, heat oil in multicooker until shimmering. Add onions and jalapeños and cook until vegetables are softened and lightly browned, 5 to 7 minutes. Stir in flour, garlic, chipotle, and oregano and cook until fragrant, about 1 minute. Slowly whisk in wine, scraping up any browned bits and smoothing out any lumps. Stir in broth, hominy, carrots, and bay leaves. Season pork with salt and pepper and st ir into multicooker.

2A. TO PRESSURE COOK: Lock lid in place and close pressure release valve. Select high pressure cook function and cook for 25 minutes. Turn off multicooker and quick-release pressure. Carefully remove lid, allowing steam to escape away from you.

2B. TO SLOW COOK: Lock lid in place and open pressure release valve. Select low slow cook function and cook until pork is tender, 4 to 5 hours. (If using Instant Pot, select high slow cook function and increase cooking range to 6 to 7 hours.) Turn off multicooker and carefully remove lid, allowing steam to escape away from you.

3. Discard bay leaves. Using large spoon, skim excess fat from surface of stew. Adjust consistency with extra hot broth as needed. Stir in cilantro and season with salt and pepper to taste. Serve with lime wedges.

NOTES FROM THE TEST KITCHEN

CHOOSING THE RIGHT SETTING ON YOUR MULTICOOKER

Because each multicooker model runs differently—and the temperatures given in the manuals are not always accurate—getting slow-cooked recipes just right may require some trial and error. If you like, you can run a simple test that will tell you the approximate temperature of your multicooker on the slow settings, sidestepping some of the guesswork. You want to aim to slow-cook at a temperature between 195 and 210 degrees, so choose high or low based on which setting falls in that range.

To perform the test, fill your multicooker with 4 quarts of room-temperature water (70 degrees). Turn on the low slow setting and let the multicooker run for 1 hour. Using an instant-read thermometer, take the temperature of the water. Repeat with the high slow setting if necessary.

MOROCCAN LENTIL AND CHICKPEA SOUP

WHY THIS RECIPE WORKS: Our recipe for the classic Moroccan chickpea and lentil soup known as *harira* carefully streamlines the ingredient list and technique of this dish to deliver all the bold flavors you'd expect in just a fraction of the time. Using canned chickpeas rather than dried saved about 2 hours of cooking time. And while spices play more than just a supporting role in this hearty North African soup, we were able to pare down the number we used to a key five, for a dish most people can prepare without a special trip to the market. Using large amounts of just two herbs—cilantro and parsley—made for quicker prep and a more efficient use of fresh ingredients. Finishing the dish with fresh lemon juice helped focus all the flavors.

If you only know lentil soup as a plain and rather homogeneous dish, prepare to be wowed by the Moroccan version known as *harira*. Not only is this soup—which is native to the Maghreb region of North Africa—full of warm spices and fresh herbs, but it's usually bulked up with chickpeas or fava beans, pasta or rice, tomatoes, hearty greens, and sometimes even lamb, beef, or chicken. The hearty base is usually brightened with a good bit of lemon juice and maybe a spoonful of the spicy North African chili paste, harissa. No wonder it's often the first dish Muslims eat when they break their daily fast during Ramadan.

Like countless other regional dishes, harira's exact ingredients vary from region to region and even from family to family. I wanted my version to be doable on a weeknight and ideally call mainly for staples I already had on hand. I also decided to omit any meat—with all the other robust flavors and textures in the mix, I wasn't sure what more it could offer.

Happily, dried lentils take only about 20 minutes to cook. Since fava beans in any form are hard to find, I opted for chickpeas—and canned were a must. Harira recipes can call for a dozen or more spices, but I pared down the list to five that would contribute different flavor notes: cumin and cinnamon for warmth; smoked paprika for depth; coriander for nutty, floral notes;

MOROCCAN LENTIL AND CHICKPEA SOUP (HARIRA)

and a tiny bit of red pepper flakes for a hint of heat. Instead of the dried ginger I saw in some recipes, I opted for the brighter zing of fresh ginger. I decided to limit the fresh herbs to cilantro and parsley, and to use an abundance of them, for a total of more than 1 cup. I began by sautéing onion, celery, garlic, and ginger in oil and then added tomato paste, my dried spices, and the fresh herbs. Dried lentils, canned chickpeas, and water went in next, followed by crushed tomatoes and a handful of orzo, a common choice. When the orzo was halfway cooked, I added some chopped Swiss chard before finishing the soup with lemon juice. The result? My soup tasted more like Italian minestrone than North African harira.

In my next batch, I eliminated the tomato paste and increased the smoked paprika and coriander, two of the most distinctive spices in the mix. For more depth, I also replaced half the water with chicken broth (any more and the soup tasted too chicken-y).

My soup was just about there, but it lacked the freshness of some versions I'd tried. The solution: I reserved ¼ cup each of the parsley and cilantro to add off the heat before serving.

My tasters all certainly agreed: This wonderfully complex-tasting, spice-filled soup, made almost entirely from pantry ingredients, brings humble lentils to a whole new level.

STEVE DUNN, *Cook's Illustrated*

Moroccan Lentil and Chickpea Soup (Harira)
SERVES 6 TO 8

For a vegetarian version, substitute vegetable broth for the chicken broth and water. We like to garnish this soup with a little harissa, a fiery North African chili paste, which is available at some supermarkets.

⅓ cup extra-virgin olive oil
1 large onion, chopped fine
2 celery ribs, chopped fine
5 garlic cloves, minced
1 tablespoon grated fresh ginger
2 teaspoons ground coriander
2 teaspoons smoked paprika
1 teaspoon ground cumin
½ teaspoon ground cinnamon
⅛ teaspoon red pepper flakes
¾ cup minced fresh cilantro
½ cup minced fresh parsley
4 cups chicken broth
4 cups water
1 (15-ounce) can chickpeas, rinsed
1 cup brown lentils, picked over and rinsed
1 (28-ounce) can crushed tomatoes
½ cup orzo
4 ounces Swiss chard, stemmed and cut into ½-inch pieces
2 tablespoons lemon juice, plus lemon wedges for serving
Salt and pepper

1. Heat oil in large Dutch oven over medium-high heat until shimmering. Add onion and celery and cook, stirring frequently, until translucent and starting to brown, 7 to 8 minutes. Reduce heat to medium, add garlic and ginger, and cook until fragrant, 1 minute. Stir in coriander, paprika, cumin, cinnamon, and pepper flakes and cook for 1 minute. Stir in ½ cup cilantro and ¼ cup parsley and cook for 1 minute.

2. Stir in broth, water, chickpeas, and lentils; increase heat to high and bring to simmer. Reduce heat to medium-low, partially cover, and gently simmer until lentils are just tender, about 20 minutes.

3. Stir in tomatoes and pasta and simmer, partially covered, for 7 minutes, stirring occasionally. Stir in chard and continue to cook, partially covered, until pasta is tender, about 5 minutes longer. Off heat, stir in lemon juice, remaining ¼ cup cilantro, and remaining ¼ cup parsley. Season with salt and pepper to taste. Serve, passing lemon wedges separately.

NOTES FROM THE TEST KITCHEN

DETERMINING THE FRESHNESS OF SPICES
Our soup calls for more than 5 teaspoons of dried spices—so make sure yours are fresh. How to tell? Give them a sniff. If they've lost their pungent aroma, it's time to replace them. In general, ground spices retain their flavor and aroma for about a year when stored in a cool, dark place.

TUSCAN WHITE BEAN AND ESCAROLE SOUP

✓ **WHY THIS RECIPE WORKS:** Our version of *acquacotta*, one of Italy's traditional vegetable soups, features creamy cannellini beans, tender fennel, and faintly bitter escarole. Though acquacotta translates to "cooked water," we used chicken broth and amped up the flavor with a *soffritto*, a mixture of sautéed onion, celery, and garlic. A food processor made quick work of finely chopping these ingredients as well as the canned tomatoes that flavor the broth. Aromatic parsley, oregano, and fennel fronds gave our soup its distinctive taste. Finally, we thickened the broth with a mixture of the bean canning liquid and egg yolks and ladled our finished soup over toasted bread, turning a humble vegetable soup into a hearty one-bowl meal.

Don't let the name *acquacotta*, meaning "cooked water" in Italian, deceive you. In this Tuscan soup, a cousin of the better-known minestrone and *ribollita*, water, vegetables, beans, and herbs are transformed into a rustic meal when whole eggs or yolks are whisked into the broth before it's ladled over stale bread, which is often first topped with a poached egg.

Though its name references water, many modern recipes for this soup call for broth. No matter which liquid is used, the soup is usually bolstered with *soffritto*: sautéed minced onion, celery, and garlic. From there, recipes vary wildly. To choose between chicken broth and water, I made two batches of soffritto and added broth to one and water to the other. I also added fennel, for its anise notes, and bitter escarole. Canned tomatoes contributed acidity, cannellini beans brought heartiness, and a Pecorino rind lent salty savoriness. Tasters preferred the broth-based soup, though it still tasted somewhat lean.

That's because I had yet to add the egg. Most recipes call for stirring raw eggs or yolks directly into the soup, but curdling is always a risk. Would diluting the egg proteins with liquid make it harder for them to link up and form firm clumps when heated? I whisked two yolks into the canning liquid from the beans, which was already pretty viscous; this mixture thickened the broth beautifully.

I sprinkled in lots of parsley and oregano for freshness and, taking a cue from thrifty Italian cooks, added the sweet fronds from the fennel bulb. Finally, with no stale bread on hand, I toasted a few slices under the broiler. Placing a poached egg on the toast before ladling the soup into the bowl made a more substantial meal. With a sprinkling of Pecorino and a spritz of lemon juice, this was a remarkably satisfying soup, all the more enjoyable for its frugal provenance.

LAN LAM, *Cook's Illustrated*

Tuscan White Bean and Escarole Soup (Acquacotta)

SERVES 8 TO 10

If escarole is unavailable, you can substitute 8 ounces of kale. Parmesan can be substituted for the Pecorino Romano, if desired. If your cheese has a rind, slice it off the wedge and add it with the broth (remove it before serving). We like to serve this soup the traditional way, with a poached or soft-cooked egg spooned on top of the toast before the broth is ladled into the bowl.

SOUP

- 1 large onion, chopped coarse
- 2 celery ribs, chopped coarse
- 4 garlic cloves, peeled
- 1 (28-ounce) can whole peeled tomatoes
- ½ cup extra-virgin olive oil
- Salt and pepper
- ⅛ teaspoon red pepper flakes
- 8 cups chicken broth
- 1 fennel bulb, 2 tablespoons fronds minced, stalks discarded, bulb halved, cored, and cut into ½-inch pieces
- 2 (15-ounce) cans cannellini beans, drained with liquid reserved, rinsed
- 1 small head escarole (10 ounces), trimmed and cut into ½-inch pieces (8 cups)
- 2 large egg yolks
- ½ cup chopped fresh parsley
- 1 tablespoon minced fresh oregano
- Grated Pecorino Romano cheese
- Lemon wedges

TOAST

- 10 (½-inch-thick) slices thick-crusted country bread
- ¼ cup extra-virgin olive oil
- Salt and pepper

TUSCAN WHITE BEAN AND ESCAROLE SOUP (ACQUACOTTA)

1. FOR THE SOUP: Pulse onion, celery, and garlic in food processor until very finely chopped, 15 to 20 pulses, scraping down sides of bowl as needed. Transfer onion mixture to Dutch oven. Add tomatoes and their juice to now-empty processor and pulse until tomatoes are finely chopped, 10 to 12 pulses; set aside.

2. Stir oil, ¾ teaspoon salt, and pepper flakes into onion mixture. Cook over medium-high heat, stirring occasionally, until light brown fond begins to form on bottom of pot, 12 to 15 minutes. Stir in tomatoes, increase heat to high, and cook, stirring frequently, until mixture is very thick and rubber spatula leaves distinct trail when dragged across bottom of pot, 9 to 12 minutes.

3. Add broth and fennel bulb to pot and bring to simmer. Reduce heat to medium-low and simmer until fennel begins to soften, 5 to 7 minutes. Stir in beans and escarole and cook until fennel is fully tender, about 10 minutes.

4. Whisk egg yolks and reserved bean liquid together in bowl, then stir into soup. Stir in parsley, oregano, and fennel fronds. Season with salt and pepper to taste.

5. FOR THE TOAST: Adjust oven rack about 5 inches from broiler element and heat broiler. Place bread on aluminum foil–lined rimmed baking sheet, drizzle with oil, and season with salt and pepper. Broil until bread is deep golden brown.

6. Place 1 slice bread in bottom of each individual bowl. Ladle soup over toasted bread. Serve, passing Pecorino and lemon wedges separately.

NOTES FROM THE TEST KITCHEN

ALL ABOUT ESCAROLE
A member of the chicory family, escarole can add crispness and personality to plain green salads. Its broad, white-spined, curly-topped leaves start out light at the bottom and darken to a rich green at the top, and its head yields very little waste.

Escarole is also a key player in many Italian soups, including our Tuscan White Bean and Escarole Soup. Though escarole is less assertive than its cousins Belgian endive and frisée, its bitterness brings complexity to the soup. Also, its resilient leaves turn supple when cooked but don't fall apart, and the base and spine of each leaf add a little texture. Look for heads bristling with sturdy, unblemished leaves.

MONTEREY BAY CIOPPINO

✓ WHY THIS RECIPE WORKS: To create a home recipe inspired by the cioppino served up at Phil's Fish Market & Eatery in Moss Landing, California, we started by making a marinara base that relied on pantry staples and came together quickly. Instead of breaking out the food processor to make a traditional pesto to flavor our stew as Phil does, we simply added the classic pesto ingredients (olive oil, basil, and garlic) to the mix. Phil's version is brimming with a wide range of seafood, but we wanted to keep our version streamlined, so we bypassed clams and calamari, opting instead for easy-to-find shrimp, scallops, sea bass, and mussels. Adding our seafood to the pot in stages and finishing the cooking off the heat ensured that each component was perfectly cooked.

Cioppino is an Italian American fish stew from San Francisco featuring an abundance of seafood in a garlicky broth of tomatoes, stock, and wine. It's a treasured dish, a staple in Bay Area restaurants. But on a recent trip, our executive food editor, Bryan Roof, visited Phil's Fish Market in nearby Moss Landing and fell for a slightly sweeter, more herby version that locals and visitors alike line up for. After hearing him rave about this dish, I knew I had to try it.

Phil DiGirolamo's cioppino is built on a tomato-based broth, which is traditional. But then DiGirolamo sets his cioppino apart from others: He makes a basil pesto and sautés mussels and clams in that pesto, along with a few other surprising ingredients—Worcestershire sauce, saffron, cinnamon, brown sugar for sweetness, and a healthy dose of Sauternes, a white dessert wine. These additions make DiGirolamo's cioppino sweeter and more complex and aromatic than the standard version. He then brings the dish together by incrementally adding the rest of the seafood—sea bass, calamari, shrimp, scallops, and Dungeness crab—along with the tomatoey broth and a long pour of clam juice.

To create a home recipe inspired by this variation, I needed to make some strategic adjustments. The marinara base stayed straightforward, relying on pantry staples and coming together quickly. And while DiGirolamo makes a separate pesto for cooking the seafood, I decided to skip the food processor and simply add pesto's key ingredients (olive oil, basil, and garlic) to the mix. My tasters approved.

It's easy enough for a seaside restaurant to have access to such a wide range of seafood, but for a home version, I wanted to tighten the roster. I ditched the clams and calamari, leaving me with easy-to-find shrimp, scallops, sea bass, and mussels. (Rest assured, this stew is delicious even if you decide to leave out one or more of these ingredients; see "Seafood Substitutions" below.) DiGirolamo also adds Sauternes, an expensive choice to use as a cooking wine. When I tried a few cheaper substitutes, dry sherry stood out as a clear favorite, adding a comparable complex sweetness.

When I brought out my simplified version of DiGirolamo's cioppino, it drew raves. But I had my eyes on only one taster, the one who had tried the real thing. Bryan didn't rave; he was too busy spooning cioppino into his mouth.

MATTHEW FAIRMAN, *Cook's Country*

Monterey Bay Cioppino

SERVES 6 TO 8

We recommend buying "dry" scallops, which don't have chemical additives and taste better than "wet" scallops. Dry scallops will look ivory or pinkish; wet scallops are bright white. If you can't find fresh dry scallops, you can substitute thawed frozen scallops. If you can't find sea bass, you can substitute cod, haddock, or halibut fillets.

MARINARA

- 3 tablespoons extra-virgin olive oil
- 1 large onion, halved and sliced thin
- 3 garlic cloves, sliced thin
- ¾ teaspoon salt
- 1 (15-ounce) can tomato sauce
- 1 cup canned tomato puree
- ½ cup chopped fresh basil
- 1 tablespoon packed light brown sugar
- 1½ teaspoons Worcestershire sauce
- ¼ teaspoon ground cinnamon

CIOPPINO

- 1½ pounds skinless sea bass fillets, 1 to 1½ inches thick, cut into 1½-inch pieces
- 12 ounces extra-large shrimp (21 to 25 per pound), peeled, deveined, and tails removed
- 12 ounces large sea scallops, tendons removed, cut in half horizontally
    Salt and pepper

- 3 tablespoons extra-virgin olive oil
- 1 pound mussels, scrubbed and debearded
- ½ cup chopped fresh basil
- ¼ cup dry sherry
- 3 garlic cloves, minced
- 1 teaspoon Worcestershire sauce
- ½ teaspoon saffron threads, crumbled
- 2 (8-ounce) bottles clam juice
- 1 (12-inch) baguette, sliced and toasted
    Lemon wedges

1. FOR THE MARINARA: Heat oil in large saucepan over medium heat until shimmering. Add onion, garlic, and salt and cook until onion is softened and just beginning to brown, about 8 minutes. Add tomato sauce, tomato puree, basil, sugar, Worcestershire, and cinnamon and bring to boil. Reduce heat to medium-low and simmer until marinara is slightly thickened, 10 to 12 minutes. Remove from heat, cover, and set aside.

2. FOR THE CIOPPINO: Season sea bass, shrimp, and scallops with salt and pepper; set aside. Heat oil in Dutch oven over medium-high heat until shimmering. Add mussels, basil, sherry, garlic, Worcestershire, saffron, and ½ teaspoon salt. Cover and cook until mussels start to open, about 2 minutes.

3. Stir in clam juice and marinara until combined. Nestle sea bass and scallops into pot and bring to boil. Reduce heat to medium, cover, and simmer until seafood is just turning opaque, about 2 minutes. Nestle shrimp into pot and return to simmer. Cover and cook until all seafood is opaque, about 3 minutes. Remove from heat and let sit, covered, for 5 minutes. Serve with baguette slices and lemon wedges.

NOTES FROM THE TEST KITCHEN

SEAFOOD SUBSTITUTIONS

Our version of Phil's cioppino uses a carefully considered collection of seafood, but that doesn't mean you can't make it if you can't find everything on the ingredient list. Below are a few suggestions.

- Substitute cod, haddock, or halibut fillets of a similar size for the sea bass.
- Double the amount of shrimp or scallops if you can't find one or the other.
- Use small clams in place of the mussels, or use half clams and half mussels.
- Garnish the stew with cooked crabmeat—or, for the full Phil's effect, cooked crab legs—before serving.

MONTEREY BAY CIOPPINO

VEGETABLES AND SIDES

BUTTER-BRAISED VEGETABLES

✔ **WHY THIS RECIPE WORKS:** To prevent our medley of spring vegetables from becoming waterlogged, we cooked them in a steamer basket, staggering their additions so that each ended up perfectly crisp-tender. Spreading the vegetables on a platter immediately after cooking allowed excess heat to dissipate, so the vegetables didn't overcook while we made the sauce. Instead of plain melted butter, which has a tendency to slip off the vegetables and pool on the platter below, we made a version of the creamy, tangy French butter sauce *beurre blanc* by emulsifying chilled butter into a mixture of sautéed shallot, vinegar, salt, sugar, and water. The emulsified sauce clung to and coated each vegetable. A sprinkle of chives made this simple platter of vegetables worthy of a special occasion.

Recipes for butter-braised spring vegetables abound, but don't let them lead you astray. Braising simply doesn't work for tender spring produce.

Winter vegetables are another story: If you slowly braise sturdy carrots, parsnips, and potatoes in butter over low heat in a covered pot, they stew in their own juices, turning perfectly tender with an earthy sweetness. But do the same with delicate asparagus and peas and you get sodden, drab mush.

That's why most so-called butter-braised spring vegetables aren't technically braised. Instead, they're cooked rapidly in a covered skillet with a small amount of butter and water or broth. But I reject those recipes, too. Because the vegetables cook directly in the buttery liquid, they become dull and waterlogged and the buttery richness is lost. For spring vegetables that retained their vibrant colors and crisp textures and butter that clung to their surfaces, I'd have to find another way.

But first, which vegetables to cook? Asparagus, emblematic of spring, was a must. Sugar snap peas would provide the sweetness of their shelled cousins but with extra, well, snap. And I confess I chose radishes mostly for their dazzling color. Turnips' hint of bitterness rounded out my medley.

To prevent the vegetables from becoming soggy, I decided to cook them in a steamer basket over a small amount of water. I halved the radishes and cut the asparagus and turnips to match the size of the whole sugar snap peas, hoping similar dimensions would help the vegetables cook at the same rate.

It didn't quite work out, though. The asparagus and turnips were perfectly crisp-tender after 5 minutes, but by that time the peas had long lost their snap. Much of the radishes' color had leached into the water below, and their crisp pepperiness had given way to a vaguely cabbage-like flavor.

For my next batch, I gave the asparagus and turnips a 2-minute head start before adding the peas. And I added the radishes, cut into slim half-moons, for the last minute to warm through. I lifted the steamer basket out of the saucepan, discarded the water, and tumbled the vegetables back into the saucepan. I stirred in some butter and a bit of salt and transferred everything to a platter.

The colors were beautiful and the vegetables nearly perfectly cooked. However, the butter had slipped right off the food and pooled on the platter.

For my next batch, I spread the vegetables on the platter right after steaming to let excess heat escape and prevent them from overcooking while I made a quick version of the French butter sauce called *beurre blanc*. An emulsion of flavorful liquid and butter, a beurre blanc coats food much better than butter alone. That's because water droplets in butter contain remnants of the cream from which it was made—proteins. These proteins act as emulsifiers, coating and separating tiny fat droplets as they disperse into the liquid when the butter melts. Because these fat droplets become separated by water, the resulting sauce is more viscous than either melted butter or water alone. It also clings to moist vegetables because the fat droplets are surrounded by water (water is attracted to water but resists fat).

I poured off most of the water from the saucepan and added minced shallot, white wine vinegar, salt, and a bit of sugar. Once the shallot softened, I whisked in chilled butter, tablespoon by tablespoon, until the sauce had the viscosity of heavy cream. I added the vegetables to the sauce, gave them a stir, and returned everything to the platter, finishing with a light sprinkle of minced chives.

The result was a platter of buttery, vibrant, perfectly cooked vegetables worthy of a spring celebration—and certainly worth celebrating.

ANDREA GEARY, *Cook's Illustrated*

Buttery Spring Vegetables

SERVES 6

To ensure that the turnips are tender, peel them thoroughly to remove not only the tough outer skin but also the fibrous layer of flesh just beneath. This recipe works best with thick asparagus spears that are between ½ and ¾ inch in diameter.

    1 pound turnips, peeled and cut into ½-inch
       by ½-inch by 2-inch batons
    1 pound asparagus, trimmed and cut on bias
       into 2-inch lengths
    8 ounces sugar snap peas, strings removed, trimmed
    4 large radishes, halved and sliced thin
    1 tablespoon minced shallot
  1½ teaspoons white wine vinegar
   ¾ teaspoon salt
   ¼ teaspoon sugar
    6 tablespoons butter, cut into 6 pieces and chilled
    1 tablespoon minced fresh chives

1. Bring 1 cup water to boil in large saucepan over high heat. Place steamer basket over boiling water. Add turnips and asparagus to basket, cover saucepan, and reduce heat to medium. Cook until vegetables are slightly softened, about 2 minutes. Add snap peas, cover, and cook until snap peas are crisp-tender, about 2 minutes. Add radishes, cover, and cook for 1 minute. Lift basket out of saucepan and transfer vegetables to platter. Spread into even layer to allow steam to dissipate. Discard all but 3 tablespoons liquid from saucepan.

2. Return saucepan to medium heat. Add shallot, vinegar, salt, and sugar and cook until mixture is reduced to 1½ tablespoons (it will barely cover bottom of saucepan), about 2 minutes. Reduce heat to low. Add butter, 1 piece at a time, whisking vigorously after each addition, until butter is incorporated and sauce has consistency of heavy cream, 4 to 5 minutes. Remove saucepan from heat. Add vegetables and stir to coat. Dry platter and return vegetables to platter. Sprinkle with chives and serve.

NOTES FROM THE TEST KITCHEN

STAGGER YOUR STEAMING
Perfect timing when steaming results in perfectly crisp-tender vegetables.

START WITH TURNIPS AND ASPARAGUS
Steam for 2 minutes

ADD SUGAR SNAP PEAS
Steam for 2 minutes

ADD RADISHES
Steam for 1 minute more

SKILLET-ROASTED BRUSSELS SPROUTS

✔ **WHY THIS RECIPE WORKS:** To create stovetop Brussels sprouts that were deeply browned on the cut sides while still bright green on the uncut sides and crisp-tender within, we started the sprouts in a cold skillet with plenty of oil and cooked them covered. This gently heated the sprouts and created a steamy environment that cooked them through without adding any extra moisture. We then removed the lid and continued to cook the sprouts cut sides down so they had time to develop a substantial, caramelized crust. Using enough oil to completely coat the skillet ensured that all the sprouts made full contact with the fat to brown evenly from edge to edge.

It was a memorable kitchen moment: I had been experimenting with cooking Brussels sprouts on the stovetop when I produced a batch unlike any I'd ever had. Over intense, direct heat, the tiny cabbages developed a deeply caramelized crust that was unusually thick and dark, contributing a rich, nutty sweetness. With their attractively browned cut sides juxtaposed against bright green, tender-but-crisp rounded sides, these sprouts were impossible to resist.

SKILLET-ROASTED BRUSSELS SPROUTS WITH MUSTARD AND BROWN SUGAR

Getting there hadn't been easy: Producing even browning from edge to edge and from sprout to sprout was a challenge, as was getting their dense interiors tender before the exteriors burned. I'd started by halving 1 pound of sprouts to create flat surfaces for browning. I heated a bit of oil in a skillet until smoking and then frantically arranged the sprouts cut sides down, later tossing them about. I had to remove the sprouts from the skillet when they started to burn in spots, but unfortunately, they were still crunchy. Adding a little water to a subsequent batch and covering the pan only made them too soft.

Since a hot skillet wasn't working, what about starting with a cold one? I set an oiled pan full of sprouts, cut sides down, over medium-high heat, covered, for 5 minutes. I then removed the lid and continued to cook the sprouts, without stirring, until they were just tender, which took only a few minutes more.

This was real progress. The cold start allowed the sprouts to heat slowly and release their moisture, so they steamed without additional liquid. Plus, I'd eliminated the hectic arrangement in a hot, oil-slicked skillet. That said, the sprouts' bottoms were somewhat dry, and a few burnt patches remained, especially in their very centers.

I'd been using just a small amount of oil. Would more oil help? Sure enough, a full 5 tablespoons worked wonders. As the sprouts heated, their tightly packed leaves separated and expelled moisture (a requirement for them to get hot enough to brown). This created space for oil to be trapped in the nooks and crannies and to spread from edge to edge for even contact with the skillet. Some oil was also absorbed by pores in the browned leaves rather than just sitting on the surface. The upshot? Gorgeous, evenly browned sprouts that weren't greasy. Rather, they took on a satisfying richness that sprouts typically lack.

Another advantage of this approach was that it was easier and less messy to arrange the sprouts in a dry skillet; I just drizzled the oil on top and it seeped underneath. And if any of the sprouts near the edges of the pan didn't brown as quickly as those in the center, I simply used tongs to reconfigure them.

Here was that unforgettable moment: These sprouts boasted brilliant green rounded sides and crisp-tender interiors contrasted by nutty-sweet, crusty façades. To balance the sweetness, I stirred in lemon juice and sprinkled Pecorino Romano on top.

ANNIE PETITO, *Cook's Illustrated*

Skillet-Roasted Brussels Sprouts with Lemon and Pecorino Romano

SERVES 4

Look for Brussels sprouts that are similar in size, with small, tight heads that are no more than 1½ inches in diameter, as they're likely to be sweeter and more tender than larger sprouts. Parmesan cheese can be substituted for the Pecorino, if desired.

- 1 **pound small (1 to 1½ inches in diameter) Brussels sprouts, trimmed and halved**
- 5 **tablespoons extra-virgin olive oil**
- 1 **tablespoon lemon juice**
  Salt and pepper
- ¼ **cup shredded Pecorino Romano cheese**

1. Arrange Brussels sprouts in single layer, cut sides down, in 12-inch nonstick skillet. Drizzle oil evenly over sprouts. Cover skillet, place over medium-high heat, and cook until sprouts are bright green and cut sides have started to brown, about 5 minutes.

2. Uncover and continue to cook until cut sides of sprouts are deeply and evenly browned and paring knife slides in with little to no resistance, 2 to 3 minutes longer, adjusting heat and moving sprouts as necessary to prevent them from overbrowning. While sprouts cook, combine lemon juice and ¼ teaspoon salt in small bowl.

NOTES FROM THE TEST KITCHEN

AVOIDING THE BULL'S-EYE
When there isn't enough oil in the skillet for even contact, the sprout browns (or even burns) only in the center instead of browning evenly across the cut side. Adding more oil solves the problem.

3. Off heat, add lemon juice mixture to skillet and stir to evenly coat sprouts. Season with salt and pepper to taste. Transfer sprouts to large plate, sprinkle with Pecorino, and serve.

VARIATIONS

Skillet-Roasted Brussels Sprouts with Cider Vinegar and Honey

Substitute 2 teaspoons cider vinegar, 2 teaspoons honey, and ¼ teaspoon red pepper flakes for lemon juice and omit pepper and Pecorino.

Skillet-Roasted Brussels Sprouts with Maple Syrup and Smoked Almonds

Omit pepper. Substitute 1 tablespoon maple syrup and 1 tablespoon sherry vinegar for lemon juice and ¼ cup smoked almonds, chopped fine, for Pecorino.

Skillet-Roasted Brussels Sprouts with Pomegranate and Pistachios

Substitute 1 tablespoon pomegranate molasses and ½ teaspoon ground cumin for lemon juice. Omit pepper. Substitute ¼ cup shelled pistachios, toasted and chopped fine, and 2 tablespoons pomegranate seeds for Pecorino.

Skillet-Roasted Brussels Sprouts with Chile, Peanuts, and Mint

Substitute 1 Fresno chile, stemmed, seeded, and minced; 2 teaspoons lime juice; and 1 teaspoon fish sauce for lemon juice. Omit pepper. Substitute 2 tablespoons finely chopped dry-roasted peanuts and 2 tablespoons chopped fresh mint for Pecorino.

Skillet-Roasted Brussels Sprouts with Gochujang and Sesame Seeds

Omit pepper. Substitute 1 tablespoon gochujang and 1 tablespoon rice vinegar for lemon juice and 2 teaspoons toasted sesame seeds for Pecorino.

Skillet-Roasted Brussels Sprouts with Mustard and Brown Sugar

Substitute 1 tablespoon Dijon mustard, 1 tablespoon packed brown sugar, 2 teaspoons white wine vinegar, and ⅛ teaspoon cayenne pepper for lemon juice. Omit pepper and Pecorino.

SPICE-ROASTED BUTTERNUT SQUASH

✔ **WHY THIS RECIPE WORKS:** To end a rut of plain roasted butternut squash, we turned to the spice cabinet; the delicate sweetness of cinnamon and the savoriness of cumin complemented these same subtle qualities in the squash. After tossing 1-inch chunks of squash (which were easy to prep and eat) in the spice mixture along with extra-virgin olive oil, salt, pepper, and a pinch of cayenne for warmth, we spread them on a rimmed baking sheet lined with parchment paper to prevent sticking and roasted them at 425 degrees until they were browned on the bottom and tender. We served the spiced squash drizzled with an easy microwave butter sauce flavored with honey, lemon juice, and thyme for richness and brightness that paired nicely with this earthy vegetable.

Butternut squash is a versatile yet underappreciated vegetable; its earthy sweetness is great when it's cut into cubes and roasted on its own, but it is also adept at taking on a variety of other flavors. I wanted to get out of my personal rut of roasting the squash with just salt, pepper, and oil and see how I could accent its flavor in a new way. The spice cabinet was a natural starting point.

I tried a handful of recipes for spice-roasted butternut squash and found a range of approaches, from composed salads featuring delicately spiced cubes to chile-coated wedges to simple preparations that looked a lot like home fries. While all were sprinkled with spices and roasted, some were dressed with vinaigrettes, others were sprinkled with chopped herbs, and a few had no further flourishes.

The first order of business was to establish a method for preparing and roasting the squash, one that would result in a tender texture and nice browning. After testing slices, cubes, chunks, and planks at a variety of temperatures, I settled on 1-inch pieces (easy to both prep and eat) and a 425-degree oven. To prevent the squash from getting messy and sticking, I lined my chosen vessel, a rimmed baking sheet, with parchment paper.

I had taken a shine to a few recipes that used warm spices, so I proceeded down that same road. Cinnamon, which has a delicate sweetness of its own, complemented that same quality in the squash. To draw out

SPICE-ROASTED BUTTERNUT SQUASH WITH HONEY-LEMON BUTTER

the savory qualities of the vegetable, I added some ground cumin to the mix; the combination of these spices gave the dish a North African flair that my tasters loved. After tossing the squash with the spices and roasting it, I drizzled it with a flavored butter (with honey, lemon, and thyme) that I quickly made in the microwave just before serving. Truly amazing squash? Yes indeed.

My tasters were so happy with this recipe that I decided to make two flavor variations. The first one was based on a combination of allspice and cumin, with the lemon juice swapped out for lime juice. For the second variation, I went with coriander instead of the cinnamon, orange juice in lieu of lemon, and fresh oregano in place of thyme. Knockouts, all three, with perfectly cooked, deeply seasoned squash and a drizzle of easy butter sauce.

ASHLEY MOORE, *Cook's Country*

Spice-Roasted Butternut Squash with Honey-Lemon Butter

SERVES 4

When peeling the squash, be sure to also remove the fibrous yellow flesh just beneath the skin.

- 3 tablespoons extra-virgin olive oil
  Salt and pepper
- 1 teaspoon ground cumin
- 1 teaspoon ground cinnamon
  Pinch cayenne pepper
- 3 pounds butternut squash, peeled, seeded, and cut into 1-inch pieces (7¾ cups)
- 2 tablespoons unsalted butter
- 1 tablespoon honey
- 1 teaspoon coarsely chopped fresh thyme
- 1 teaspoon lemon juice

1. Adjust oven rack to middle position and heat oven to 425 degrees. Line rimmed baking sheet with parchment paper.

2. Whisk oil, 1 teaspoon salt, 1 teaspoon pepper, cumin, cinnamon, and cayenne together in large bowl. Add squash and toss until evenly coated. Arrange squash in even layer on prepared sheet. Roast until squash is tender and browned on bottom, 30 to 35 minutes.

3. Microwave butter, honey, and ¼ teaspoon salt in small bowl until butter is melted, about 30 seconds. Stir in thyme and lemon juice. Using spatula, transfer squash to serving platter. Drizzle with butter mixture and serve.

VARIATIONS

Spice-Roasted Butternut Squash with Honey-Lime Butter

Substitute ground allspice for cinnamon, 1 tablespoon minced fresh chives for thyme, and lime juice for lemon juice.

Spice-Roasted Butternut Squash with Honey-Orange Butter

Substitute ground coriander for cinnamon, oregano for thyme, and orange juice for lemon juice.

NOTES FROM THE TEST KITCHEN

HOW TO PREP BUTTERNUT SQUASH

1. Lop ends off squash and use chef's knife to cut it into 2 pieces where bulb meets neck.

2. Use vegetable peeler to peel away skin and fibrous yellow flesh down to bright orange flesh.

3. Halve bulb end, then scoop out and discard seeds and pulp. Chop as directed.

GRILLED CAULIFLOWER

✓ **WHY THIS RECIPE WORKS:** To make grilled cauliflower with a tender interior and a flavorful, nicely browned exterior, we first microwaved it until it was cooked through and then briefly grilled it to pick up color and flavor. Dunking the cauliflower in a salt and sugar solution before microwaving seasoned it all over, even in the nooks and crannies. To ensure that the cauliflower held up on the grill without falling through the grate and to provide sufficient surface area for browning, we cut the head into large wedges, which were easy to handle and provided three sides to pick up flavorful browning. Just 10 minutes on the grill was enough time to allow the cauliflower to lightly char and caramelize, bringing new dimension to this versatile vegetable.

In the vegetable world, cauliflower is like Superman. Well, maybe it's more like his alter ego, Clark Kent. Initially, you might think it mild-mannered or bland. But when thrown into a hot oven, the vegetable is transformed, gaining a crisp, browned exterior; a tender interior; and sweet, nutty flavor. In the summer, though, I spend most of my time outside by the grill. Could I get the same results there?

Since small florets would be likely to fall through the cooking grate, I tried prepping the cauliflower other ways. The simplest treatment was to leave the head whole, but it took more than an hour to cook through. And without exposure to direct heat, the interior tasted sulfurous and steamed. Cutting the cauliflower head crosswise gave me uniform slabs with ample surface for charring, but I could get only a couple of slabs from one head, since the end pieces just crumbled into florets. In the end, I opted to cut the cauliflower through the core into six large wedges. The wedges yielded a good amount of surface area for browning, and the intact core provided a handle I could use to flip the wedges.

But once the wedges were on the grill, the exteriors browned and dried out before the interiors became tender. That's because cauliflower is so dense that it takes a while to cook through. Precooking was in order, so I turned to the microwave.

I arranged the wedges in a single layer on a plate so they would cook evenly and simply inverted a large bowl over the plate to trap steam. After 15 minutes of microwaving, the wedges had softened nicely. Now all I'd have to do was put the wedges on the grill just long enough to pick up color and smoky flavor. I patted them dry and transferred them to a medium-hot grill until they developed some crisp char all over—just a few minutes per side.

My cauliflower wedges were tender and nicely browned, but one issue lingered: seasoning. With all the nooks and crannies, it was difficult to evenly season the wedges with salt. The answer was simple: I stirred together a solution of 2 cups of water, ¼ cup of salt, and 2 tablespoons of sugar (added to encourage browning). I then dunked the wedges in the solution before microwaving them.

To garnish the wedges, I developed two spice-nut blends and a bright relish. But even with just a drizzle of olive oil, a sprinkle of chives, and a squeeze of lemon, the cauliflower was a true hero on the plate.

ANNIE PETITO, *Cook's Illustrated*

Grilled Cauliflower

SERVES 4 TO 6

Look for a head of cauliflower with densely packed florets that feels heavy for its size. Using tongs or a thin metal spatula to gently flip the wedges helps keep them intact. This dish stands well on its own, but to dress it up, serve it sprinkled with Pistachio Dukkah; Almond, Raisin, and Caper Relish; or Za'atar (recipes follow).

- 1 head cauliflower (2 pounds)
- ¼ cup salt
- 2 tablespoons sugar
- 2 tablespoons extra-virgin olive oil
- 1 tablespoon minced fresh chives
  Lemon wedges

1. Trim outer leaves of cauliflower and cut stem flush with bottom. Cut head through core into 6 equal wedges so that core and florets remain intact.

2. Whisk 2 cups water, salt, and sugar in medium bowl until salt and sugar dissolve. Holding wedges by core, gently dunk in salt-sugar mixture until evenly moistened (do not dry—residual water will help cauliflower steam). Transfer wedges, rounded side down, to large plate and cover with inverted large bowl. Microwave until cauliflower is translucent and tender and paring knife inserted in thickest stem of florets (not into core) meets no resistance, 14 to 16 minutes.

3. Carefully (bowl and cauliflower will be very hot) transfer cauliflower to paper towel–lined plate and pat dry. (Microwaved cauliflower can be held at room temperature for up to 2 hours.)

4A. FOR A CHARCOAL GRILL: Open bottom vent completely. Light large chimney starter three-quarters filled with charcoal briquettes (4½ quarts). When top coals are partially covered with ash, pour evenly over grill. Set cooking grate in place, cover, and open lid vent completely. Heat grill until hot, about 5 minutes.

4B. FOR A GAS GRILL: Turn all burners to high, cover, and heat grill until hot, about 15 minutes. Turn all burners to medium-high.

5. Clean and oil cooking grate. Brush cut sides of wedges with 1 tablespoon oil. Place cauliflower, cut side down, on grill and cook, covered, until well browned with spots of charring, 3 to 4 minutes. Using tongs or thin metal spatula, flip cauliflower and cook second cut side until well browned with spots of charring, 3 to 4 minutes. Flip again so cauliflower is sitting on rounded edge and cook until browned, 1 to 2 minutes.

6. Transfer cauliflower to large platter. Drizzle with remaining 1 tablespoon oil, sprinkle with chives, and serve with lemon wedges.

Pistachio Dukkah
MAKES ABOUT ⅓ CUP

This Middle Eastern spice blend can be sprinkled on a plate of extra-virgin olive oil and served as a dip for bread or sprinkled over soups, grain dishes, or bean salads as a garnish. If you do not own a spice grinder, you can process the spices in a mini food processor.

- 1½ tablespoons sesame seeds, toasted
- 1½ teaspoons coriander seeds, toasted
- ¾ teaspoon cumin seeds, toasted
- ½ teaspoon fennel seeds, toasted
- 2 tablespoons shelled pistachios, toasted and chopped fine
- ½ teaspoon salt
- ½ teaspoon pepper

Process sesame seeds in spice grinder or mortar and pestle until coarsely ground; transfer to bowl. Process coriander seeds, cumin seeds, and fennel seeds in now-empty grinder until finely ground. Transfer to bowl with sesame seeds. Stir pistachios, salt, and pepper into sesame mixture until combined. (Dukkah can be refrigerated for up to 1 month.)

Almond, Raisin, and Caper Relish
MAKES ABOUT ½ CUP

Champagne vinegar can be used in place of white wine vinegar and regular raisins in place of golden raisins, if desired.

- 2 tablespoons golden raisins
- 2 tablespoons hot water
- 1 teaspoon white wine vinegar
- ¼ cup almonds, toasted and chopped fine
- 1 tablespoon capers, rinsed and chopped fine
- 1 teaspoon minced fresh parsley
-   Pinch red pepper flakes
- 3–4 tablespoons extra-virgin olive oil
-   Salt and pepper

Combine raisins and hot water in small bowl and let stand for 5 minutes. Drain raisins and chop fine. Toss raisins and vinegar in bowl, then stir in almonds, capers, parsley, and pepper flakes. Stir in 3 tablespoons oil; mixture should be well moistened. If still dry, add remaining 1 tablespoon oil. Season with salt and pepper to taste.

NOTES FROM THE TEST KITCHEN

FLIPPING THE MICROWAVING SETUP
We often rely on the microwave to parcook vegetables before using them in a recipe, as we do in our recipe for Grilled Cauliflower. It's a common practice to place cut-up vegetables in a bowl and cover the bowl with a plate so that the pieces steam while they cook. But in the case of our cauliflower recipe, we flip the script by evenly arranging the wedges of cauliflower on a plate and covering them with a bowl. Arranging the cauliflower in a single layer allows for more even cooking and prevents us from having to stop the microwave to rearrange the hot wedges.

GRILLED CAULIFLOWER

CORN FRITTERS

MAKES ABOUT ⅓ CUP

Try sprinkling some of this Middle Eastern spice mix over olive oil as a dip for bread. You can also use it in grain dishes or as a flavorful topping for hummus or other dips.

- 2 tablespoons dried thyme
- 1 tablespoon dried oregano
- 1½ tablespoons sumac
- 1 tablespoon sesame seeds, toasted
- ¼ teaspoon salt

Process thyme and oregano in spice grinder or mortar and pestle until finely ground and powdery. Transfer to bowl and stir in sumac, sesame seeds, and salt. (Za'atar can be stored at room temperature in airtight container for up to 1 year.)

SOUTHERN CORN FRITTERS

WHY THIS RECIPE WORKS: For the lightest corn fritters, we minimized the number of fillers we added. We processed some of the kernels to use as a thickener rather than more flour or cornmeal. This step also helped the fresh corn flavor shine through. Browning the corn puree in a skillet drove off excess moisture and deepened the flavor even more, and heating the oil until it was shimmering before cooking the fritters ensured that they turned out crispy but not greasy. Adding cayenne, nutty Parmesan cheese, and oniony chives balanced the natural sweetness of the corn, and a touch of cornstarch crisped the exteriors and helped provide a wonderful textural contrast with the light and creamy interiors.

Ask a Northerner about corn fritters and you're sure to get, well, an earful: They'll describe crispy-on-the-outside, tender-on-the-inside dumplings dotted with fresh corn and deep-fried in a pot of oil, drizzled with honey or maple syrup, and served as a sweet treat. Southerners, on the other hand, will talk about fritters formed into patties and skillet-fried in a modest amount of oil. These contain cheese, herbs, and/or chiles and, accompanied by a dollop of creamy sauce, are served as a side dish or appetizer. As a Yankee, I have an affinity for the drenched-in-maple-syrup variety, but for this recipe I decided to focus my energies on the Southern type.

To start, I dove into the world of Southern corn fritters, researching dozens of recipes before settling on a handful to try in the test kitchen. The results ranged from fragile, barely-there patties made with only whipped egg whites and fresh corn kernels to thick, stodgy disks in which corn seemed to be an afterthought. Versions with too many extra ingredients lost their corn soul, whereas those with too few were boring and bland. I wanted just enough batter to hold a patty shape and form a crispy exterior and a tender interior popping with sweet and savory corn flavor.

The first order of business was to order a bushel of corn and get to work on creating a batter that would give me a structurally sound fritter. I began by whisking together an ultrasimple mixture of just 2 tablespoons of flour, a beaten egg, baking powder, the kernels from two ears of corn, and some salt and pepper. The first thing I noticed was that the liquid-y batter just barely coated the corn kernels. I forged ahead, gently frying 2-tablespoon portions in ½ cup of vegetable oil—just enough to cover the bottom of a 12-inch skillet—until all the nooks and crannies of the fritters were evenly golden brown.

The result? Bland, cakey disks featuring one smooth side and a flip side pebbled with overcooked kernels. The thin batter spread too much in the skillet, settling into a uniform crust on the bottom of the fritter and leaving all the kernels exposed to the heat when I flipped it. Without any insulating batter, the bare kernels overbrowned and turned tough and chewy.

For the next go-round, I ditched the leavener since it was contributing to the unwelcome cakey texture. I also bumped up the amount of flour to ⅓ cup, hoping that more would thicken the batter enough to support the kernels and keep them suspended. It worked, but the extra gluten made the fritters slightly tough. To the next batch I added cornmeal; alas, it only made the fritters cornbread-esque.

Then I got a better idea: How about creating a fresh corn puree that might thicken the batter without making the fritters cakey or heavy? I stripped the kernels from two cobs and blitzed them in the food processor into a chunky, starchy puree. I then stirred the puree together with just ¼ cup of flour, an egg, salt, and pepper. Finally, I folded in the kernels from two more ears of corn. Sure enough, this lightly thickened batter fully enrobed the corn, keeping the kernels suspended in the finished fritter. What's more, pureeing some of the kernels liberated their flavor, boosting the patties' overall corniness. The downside was that processing the kernels had freed so much of their milky liquid that the fritters were somewhat wet and custardy. To correct that problem, I tried cutting back on the amount of corn puree I was adding, but that resulted in less fresh corn flavor.

For my next attempt, I cooked the pulp in a skillet to rid it of moisture and lightly brown it, which helped develop complexity. With this concentrated puree, the fritters had soft and tender—not gooey and wet—interiors.

Lightly browning the corn puree had worked so well that I wondered if I should briefly sauté the whole kernels I was adding as well. It would be easy to do right before cooking the puree. Sure enough, this simple step gave the kernels a less sweet, more roasty profile.

I wondered if I could do even more to balance the corn's sweetness, so I evaluated potential seasonings. I didn't want to add much, as simple corn goodness was my goal. I found that a couple of tablespoons of grated Parmesan brought just the right salty-umami counterpoint. I also settled on a pinch of cayenne for depth and some minced chives for color and earthy grassiness.

The only aspect of my fritters that I still wasn't crazy about was their exteriors, which tended toward limp rather than crispy. I knew that adding more flour would only toughen the fritters. Coating them with panko bread crumbs crisped up their exteriors—so much that the coating distracted from the tender kernels. Frying the fritters over higher heat or for a longer period only burned them in spots. I even played with taking the "fry" out of the fritters (the word "fritter" is derived from *friture*, the French word for frying) by cutting way back on the oil, but that rendered them dry and unevenly cooked.

Finally, a colleague wondered if cornstarch might help. After a series of tests, I settled on stirring 1 tablespoon into the batter. This delivered fritters with a delicate crunch at their lacy edges.

My testing came to a close after I'd created a few complementary sauces for my fritters, one of which included a little maple syrup in a nod to their Northern cousins. While these tasty corn patties may not be my first fritter love, they've certainly earned a prominent place in my heart.

STEVE DUNN, *Cook's Illustrated*

Corn Fritters

MAKES 12 FRITTERS

Serve these fritters as a side dish with steaks, chops, or poultry or as an appetizer with a dollop of sour cream or with one of our flavored sauces (recipes follow).

  4 **ears corn, kernels cut from cobs (3 cups)**
  1 **teaspoon plus ½ cup vegetable oil**
     Salt and pepper
  ¼ **cup all-purpose flour**
  ¼ **cup minced chives**
  2 **tablespoons grated Parmesan cheese**
  1 **tablespoon cornstarch**
     Pinch cayenne pepper
  1 **large egg, lightly beaten**

1. Process 1½ cups corn kernels in food processor to uniformly coarse puree, 15 to 20 seconds, scraping down sides of bowl halfway through processing. Set aside.

2. Heat 1 teaspoon oil in 12-inch nonstick skillet over medium-high heat until shimmering. Add remaining 1½ cups corn kernels and ⅛ teaspoon salt and cook, stirring frequently, until light golden, 3 to 4 minutes. Transfer to medium bowl.

3. Return skillet to medium heat, add corn puree, and cook, stirring frequently with heatproof spatula, until puree is consistency of thick oatmeal (puree clings to spatula rather than dripping off), about 5 minutes. Transfer puree to bowl with kernels and stir to combine. Rinse skillet and dry with paper towels.

4. Stir flour, 3 tablespoons chives, Parmesan, cornstarch, cayenne, ¼ teaspoon salt, and ⅛ teaspoon pepper into corn mixture until well combined. Gently stir in egg until incorporated.

5. Line rimmed baking sheet with paper towels. Heat remaining ½ cup oil in now-empty skillet over medium heat until shimmering. Drop six 2-tablespoon portions batter into skillet. Press with spatula to flatten into 2½- to 3-inch disks. Fry until deep golden brown on both sides, 2 to 3 minutes per side. Transfer fritters to prepared sheet. Repeat with remaining batter.

6. Transfer fritters to large plate or platter, sprinkle with remaining 1 tablespoon chives, and serve immediately.

Maple-Chipotle Mayonnaise

MAKES ⅔ CUP

For the fullest maple flavor, use maple syrup labeled "Grade A, Dark Amber."

- ½ cup mayonnaise
- 1 tablespoon maple syrup
- 1 tablespoon minced canned chipotle chile in adobo sauce
- ½ teaspoon Dijon mustard

Combine all ingredients in small bowl.

Red Pepper Mayonnaise

MAKES 1¼ CUPS

Letting the minced garlic sit in the lemon juice mellows the garlic's flavor.

- 1½ teaspoons lemon juice
- 1 garlic clove, minced
- ¾ cup jarred roasted red peppers, rinsed and patted dry
- ½ cup mayonnaise
- 2 teaspoons tomato paste
- Salt

Combine lemon juice and garlic in small bowl and let stand for 15 minutes. Process red peppers, mayonnaise, tomato paste, and lemon juice mixture in food processor until smooth, about 15 seconds, scraping down sides of bowl as needed. Season with salt to taste. Refrigerate until thickened, about 2 hours.

Basil Mayonnaise

MAKES ¾ CUP

Blue Plate Real Mayonnaise is our favorite mayonnaise. It's one of the top-selling mayonnaises in the country, but you'll have to mail-order it unless you live in the South or Southeast. Hellmann's Real Mayonnaise, which is available nationwide (it's sold as Best Foods west of the Rockies), is our runner-up.

- ½ cup mayonnaise
- ½ cup fresh basil leaves
- 1 tablespoon water
- 1 teaspoon lemon juice
- Salt and pepper

Process all ingredients in blender until smooth, about 10 seconds, scraping down sides of blender jar as needed; transfer to bowl and season with salt and pepper to taste.

Sriracha-Lime Yogurt Sauce

MAKES ⅔ CUP

Our favorite Greek yogurt is Fage Total Classic Greek Yogurt.

- ½ cup plain Greek yogurt
- ½ teaspoon grated lime zest plus 1 teaspoon juice
- ½ teaspoon Sriracha sauce
- 1 tablespoon minced fresh cilantro
- Salt

Combine all ingredients in small bowl and season with salt to taste.

NOTES FROM THE TEST KITCHEN

PRESS FOR BETTER TEXTURE

Pressing each portion of batter into a thin disk as soon as you drop it into the hot oil ensures that the fritters are evenly cooked and not gummy inside.

OVEN FRIES

✓ WHY THIS RECIPE WORKS: When traditional French fries are fried, water is rapidly driven out of the starch cells at the surface of the potato, leaving behind tiny cavities. It's these cavities that create a delicate, crispy crust. Since oven fries don't heat fast enough for air pockets to form, we coated our potatoes in a cornstarch slurry that crisped up like a deep-fried fry would. We arranged the coated planks on a rimmed baked sheet that we coated with both vegetable oil spray and vegetable oil; the former contains a surfactant called lecithin, which prevents the oil from pooling and, in turn, prevents the potatoes from sticking. Using the oil spray also allowed us to use only 3 tablespoons of oil, just enough to evenly coat the fries. Covering the baking sheet with aluminum foil for the first half of cooking ensured that the potatoes were fully tender by the time they were browned.

Peel, cut, fry, let cool, fry again, drain. Repeat with remaining batches. Let oil cool and, finally, discard oil. I think I speak for French fry lovers everywhere when I say that the tawny, crispy crusts and velvety interiors you get from a proper fry job are worth all the grease—elbow and otherwise. But given what the process entails, I make real fries about as often as I make croissants or pasta from scratch, which is to say almost never.

Most people's alternative to deep-fried fries is oven fries, which are usually less fussy to make, often less greasy, and always a disappointment. OK, that might be a bit harsh, but I think you'll agree that oven fries frequently fall short. The most basic methods call for simply tossing cut potatoes with a few tablespoons of oil, spreading them in a single layer on a rimmed baking sheet, and roasting them in a hot oven for about 30 minutes, turning them a few times so that all sides make contact with the hot surface and brown. More-involved recipes take the time to parcook (usually by boiling or microwaving) the cut potatoes before the oven phase, which helps the insides turn tender by the time the outsides are brown.

The perks are obvious: No lengthy potato prep work, no grease-splattered stovetop to clean, no vat of hot oil to deal with afterward. But in my experience, oven-fried potatoes rarely cook up with a French fry's evenly golden exterior, instead emerging pale or flabby in spots or shriveled and tough at the edges. Worse still, they lack that unmistakably lush, nutty, subtly savory "fry" flavor of French fries. What do they taste like? Compromise and wasted potential.

But what if you could have it both ways: the flavor and crispiness of deep-fried fries produced with no more work than roasting potatoes? For the sake of French fry lovers everywhere, I had to try.

To understand what goes wrong when you "fry" in the oven, I took a closer look at the aforementioned basic method. I cut 2 pounds of peeled russet potatoes into ½-inch-thick planks; tossed them with 4 tablespoons of vegetable oil, a common amount used in other oven fry recipes; spread them on a heavy-duty rimmed baking sheet that wouldn't warp in the hot oven; and cooked them at 425 degrees for about 30 minutes. (If the oven were any hotter, the oil would smoke and give the fries an acrid flavor.) I flipped the planks a few times during cooking so that they could brown all over.

There were two problems. First, the potatoes weren't tender by the time their exteriors were brown, which explained why some oven fry recipes called for parcooking the potatoes. Second, while each side of the potatoes was at least somewhat brown, only the sides originally in contact with the hot baking sheet were actually crispy; the other surfaces were tough and leathery.

Those flaws made sense when I considered how fried fries are typically made. Most recipes call for frying the potatoes twice. The first fry, often called blanching, cooks the potatoes through and causes the surface starch to gel. You then remove the potatoes and let them cool briefly before frying them again, which rapidly drives the water out of the starch gel at the surface, leaving behind tiny cavities. It's these cavities that lighten the crust during the second fry so that it shatters when you bite through it.

The problem with my oven fries was that the water in the potatoes wasn't heating rapidly. It was heating slowly, because air doesn't conduct heat as quickly as oil does. Consequently, no air pockets are formed and the starch molecules nestle together, leading to a tough crust.

THICK-CUT OVEN FRIES

To ensure tender fries, parcooking the potatoes was definitely in order. I could blanch them in water, but it would be more efficient to cover the baking sheet tightly with foil for the first part of cooking so that they could steam. After a few trial rounds, I determined that about 12 minutes under cover parcooked the potatoes enough that they would be fully tender by the end of the uncovered phase.

As for creating a crispy exterior, what if I could put a different starchy coating on the outside instead of relying on hot, bubbling oil to crisp the potato starch? Cornstarch is what I had in mind: Like those of potato starch, its particles are quite small, which is why we've had good luck in the past using it as a fry coating on everything from chicken wings to sweet potato wedges. Plus, its starch granules—much finer than those of potatoes—don't hold on to much water and don't hold on to it tightly, so it can easily form a crispy crust. Also, it's an ingredient that most cooks keep on hand. But instead of simply dusting cornstarch directly on the food, which we've found can leave a chalky film in your mouth, we prefer to mix the cornstarch with water to make a slurry. Doing so hydrates the starch, essentially creating a batter that coats the food.

I spent the next several tests mixing cornstarch and water in different ratios, but no matter what I tried, I couldn't produce a batter that coated the potatoes evenly. Thinner slurries slid right off the potatoes and pooled on the sheet, while thicker batches formed goopy clumps. What I wanted was that loose, pudding-like consistency you get when cooking cornstarch in a warm liquid, as you would when thickening a sauce. So for the next test I microwaved the slurry (3 tablespoons of cornstarch mixed with ¾ cup of water) for a minute or so, giving it a stir periodically. That helped; the cornstarch absorbed the water and thickened into a smooth pudding that coated the potatoes beautifully. I had, in effect, re-created the starch gel found on the surface of traditional oil-blanched fries.

I arranged the slurry-covered spuds on the oiled baking sheet, covered the sheet tightly with greased aluminum foil (to prevent it from sticking), and cooked the potatoes for 12 minutes before pulling off the cover and letting the potatoes brown for about 10 more minutes. I then flipped the fries and let them brown for another 10 minutes. The results were better than any I'd had to date: On most pieces, the coating was crispy and delicate and gave way to a fluffy, evenly tender interior. The problem was that the oil was pooling on the baking sheet, leaving some of the fries saturated and a tad greasy and others almost dry, meaning that they stuck to the pan and didn't crisp. And they still didn't deliver that rich "fry" flavor.

One quick change I made was to swap the russet potatoes for Yukon Gold potatoes, since the latter have a naturally buttery flavor that hinted at the richness of real fries. Their skins are also thinner than those of russets, so they didn't require peeling.

NOTES FROM THE TEST KITCHEN

PUTTING THE "FRY" IN OVEN FRIES
We discovered a couple key steps for achieving perfectly crisp, golden-brown oven fries.

USE A CORNSTARCH SLURRY: Microwaving a mixture of cornstarch and water evenly hydrates the starch molecules, creating a smooth mixture. This batter coats the potatoes evenly, forming a delicate crust as it fries.

ADD JUST ENOUGH OIL: A moderate 3 tablespoons of oil gives our fries truly fried flavor. More oil was unnecessary, and too little yielded off-flavors since it heated faster and broke down into unpleasant flavor compounds.

DON'T SKIP THE SPRAY
Vegetable oil spray contains a surfactant (an ingredient that reduces tension between a surface and a liquid) called lecithin that helps the oil flow to coat the metal evenly, so it forms a thin, complete layer between the baking sheet and the food. As a result, the potatoes in our recipe don't stick and we can use less oil.

Oil pooling on the cooking surface is a problem we've run into before. Our solution has been to spray the baking sheet with vegetable oil spray before coating it with oil. Odd as that sounds—grease held in place with grease—the cooking spray contains a key ingredient that oil doesn't: lecithin, a surfactant (an ingredient that reduces tension between a surface and a liquid) that helps the oil flow to coat the metal evenly and form a thin, complete layer between the baking sheet and the food.

I made another batch of fries, this time spraying the sheet before adding the 4 tablespoons of oil, and the results were much better. No more sticking, and the fries were evenly golden on the two flat sides. But now that the sticking wasn't a problem, did I even need 4 tablespoons of oil? After all, relative leanness is another supposed selling point of oven fries. Maybe I could get away with less, and that would help the greasiness, too.

I made several more batches, coating the potatoes with varying amounts of fat, including an ambitious batch where I used only the spray. I was able to take the oil down to 3 tablespoons and the fries still cooked up crispy; even better, the greasiness was gone and they delivered that rich, savory, from-the-fryolator flavor.

These spuds cooked in the oven truly deserved the title of "fries." They were delicately crispy on the outside, fluffy within, and full of fry flavor. In other words, they tasted like victory.

LAN LAM, *Cook's Illustrated*

Thick-Cut Oven Fries

SERVES 4

Choose potatoes that are 4 to 6 inches in length to ensure well-proportioned fries. Trimming thin slices from the ends of the potatoes in step 2 ensures that each fry has two flat surfaces for even browning. This recipe's success is dependent on a heavy-duty rimmed baking sheet that will not warp in the heat of the oven. Spraying the sheet with vegetable oil spray will help the oil spread evenly and prevent sticking. The rate at which the potatoes brown is dependent on your baking sheet and oven. After removing the foil from the baking sheet in step 5, monitor the color of the potatoes carefully to prevent scorching.

> 3 **tablespoons vegetable oil**
> 2 **pounds Yukon Gold potatoes, unpeeled**
> 3 **tablespoons cornstarch**
> **Salt**

1. Adjust oven rack to lowest position and heat oven to 425 degrees. Generously spray rimmed baking sheet with vegetable oil spray. Pour oil into prepared sheet and tilt sheet until surface is evenly coated with oil.

2. Halve potatoes lengthwise and turn halves cut sides down on cutting board. Trim thin slice from both long sides of each potato half; discard trimmings. Slice potatoes lengthwise into 1/3- to 1/2-inch-thick planks.

3. Combine 3/4 cup water and cornstarch in large bowl, making sure no lumps of cornstarch remain on bottom of bowl. Microwave, stirring every 20 seconds, until mixture begins to thicken, 1 to 3 minutes. Remove from microwave and continue to stir until mixture thickens to pudding-like consistency. (If necessary, add up to 2 tablespoons water to achieve correct consistency.)

4. Transfer potatoes to bowl with cornstarch mixture and toss until each plank is evenly coated. Arrange planks on prepared sheet, leaving small gaps between planks. (Some cornstarch mixture will remain in bowl.) Cover sheet tightly with lightly greased aluminum foil and bake for 12 minutes.

5. Remove foil from sheet and bake until bottom of each fry is golden brown, 10 to 18 minutes. Remove sheet from oven and, using thin metal spatula, carefully flip each fry. Return sheet to oven and continue to bake until second sides are golden brown, 10 to 18 minutes longer. Sprinkle fries with 1/2 teaspoon salt. Using spatula, carefully toss fries to distribute salt. Transfer fries to paper towel–lined plate and season with salt to taste. Serve.

BAKED SWEET POTATOES

✔ **WHY THIS RECIPE WORKS:** Producing baked sweet potatoes with creamy, deeply flavorful interiors isn't just about cooking the spuds to a particular temperature (200 degrees or so). We discovered that we needed to hold them at that temperature for about an hour, which allowed time for the cell walls to break down, starches to gelatinize, and moisture to evaporate so that flavor concentrated. Because the whole process could have taken about 3 hours of baking time, we jump-started the potatoes by zapping them in the microwave until they hit 200 degrees. Then we transferred them to a 425-degree oven for just an hour to finish cooking. Baking them on a wire rack set in a rimmed baking sheet allowed air to circulate around the potatoes; the sheet also caught any sugary syrup that inevitably oozed from the potatoes as they cooked.

Though they share a name, white potatoes and sweet potatoes couldn't be more different. The most familiar sweet potato varieties in American supermarkets, which have rusty orange or red-purple skin and deep orange flesh, come from a different botanical family than white potatoes such as russets and contain far less starch and more sugar. As a result, they cook very differently—a fact that is never more apparent than when preparing a simple baked potato.

Not long ago, we discovered that baking a russet potato in a 450-degree oven for about 45 minutes produced an ideally fluffy interior. But when I followed the same approach using a sweet potato, the interior was dense and watery. Meanwhile, I tried a handful of baked sweet potato recipes and came upon one from chef Michael Solomonov of Philadelphia's Zahav restaurant that revealed how truly extraordinary a baked sweet potato can be. After the spuds had spent about 3 hours in a 275-degree oven, their interiors were not just tender but downright plush, and their flavor was concentrated to the point of tasting caramelized, with hints of molasses. These were unlike any sweet potatoes I'd ever eaten.

But tying up my oven for 3 hours when I wanted to bake sweet potatoes wasn't an option. My aim was to expedite the process (about an hour seemed reasonable) without compromising the exceptional flavor and texture the potatoes got from the longer method.

The difference in starch content between russet potatoes and orange-fleshed sweet potatoes (the kind that I'll refer to throughout this story) is actually twofold: First, russets contain roughly 21 percent starch versus 15 percent in sweet potatoes. That 6-percent gap is significant because starch absorbs free moisture in the potato as it cooks, so a russet ends up with a drier texture after baking. Second, the starch granules in russets are almost twice as big as those in sweet potatoes; when they swell with water, they eventually force the cells to separate into distinct clumps that result in a texture we perceive as dry. Sweet potatoes have fewer and finer starch granules, so they absorb less water and thus bake up soft and creamy instead of dry.

My question was, when does a baked sweet potato reach the stage when it turns soft and creamy throughout? Per the Zahav approach, I baked three 8-ounce sweet potatoes in a 275-degree oven (I set them on a wire rack in an aluminum foil–lined rimmed baking sheet, knowing that they tend to ooze sugar during baking) and pulled one out every hour to check its temperature and consistency. As expected, the longer a potato cooked, the higher its temperature rose and the more uniformly soft it became. The potato pulled at 1 hour reached about 180 degrees, the 2-hour potato reached about 190 degrees, and the 3-hour potato reached about 200 degrees. Only the potato that cooked for the full 3 hours boasted the creamy, soft consistency and caramelized sweetness I wanted.

Could this mean that all I had to do was figure out the fastest way to get the potatoes to 200 degrees? No, because baking them in a 450-degree oven until they hit 200 degrees, which took about 45 minutes, would bring me back to my original problem: a barely tender, watery core.

Clearly, there was a benefit to baking the potatoes longer, so I put another set of potatoes in a 275-degree oven to take a closer look. This time I weighed the potatoes before and after baking to track moisture loss, which I assumed would correspond to flavor concentration, and inserted probes into each potato so that I could monitor its progress. As I recorded temperatures every 10 minutes, I noticed that the potatoes reached 200 degrees shortly after the 2-hour mark, meaning they spent almost the entire last hour at that temperature. They also lost an average of about 30 percent of their starting weight—about twice as much as the

BEST BAKED SWEET POTATOES

potatoes baked quickly in the 450-degree oven, I later discovered—and boasted a creamy consistency with complex flavor. But why?

Our science editor explained that when a sweet potato approaches 200 degrees, the pectin that gives its cell walls structure begins to break down so that the flesh softens and allows free moisture to escape. At the same time, starch granules within the cell walls take up free water and gelatinize, which makes the potato appear smooth and creamy. But it turns out that at 200 degrees and up to about 212 degrees, the pectin breakdown becomes more rapid, leading to greater softening. It also leads to moisture loss, which causes the spud's sugars to both concentrate and caramelize, leading to more complex flavor. And the longer the potatoes hover in that 200-plus zone, the creamier and more flavorful they become.

Now that I understood why the potatoes needed that extra hour at 200-plus degrees, I wondered if I could short-cut the front end of cooking by getting the potatoes to 200 degrees as quickly as possible and then let them linger in the oven. I baked the next batches in ovens set to 400, 425, and 450 degrees, weighing the potatoes before and after and probing them as I had before. Baked at 450, the potatoes reached 200 degrees in about 35 minutes. But after another hour in the oven, they had nearly burned on the outside. When baked any lower, they still took almost 2 hours to turn creamy and deeply flavorful—too long for a simple side.

There was one approach I hadn't yet tried: microwaving the potatoes until they hit 200 degrees and then finishing them in the oven. I was skeptical, since when we developed the baked russet recipe, we found that microwaving the spuds turned the flesh gummy. That's because their large and abundant starch granules are relatively fragile, and heating them rapidly in the microwave made them burst and release starch, which created a texture that we perceive as gluey.

But since sweet potatoes contain fewer and finer starch granules, I gave it a shot. I microwaved them until they had reached approximately 200 degrees at their cores, which took less than 10 minutes. Then I transferred them to a 425-degree oven—the hottest temperature I could use without burning them—to bake for a full hour. This hybrid cooking method did the trick: Their texture was creamy, almost fudgy; their flavor, complex and sweet; and their skin nicely tanned but not burnt. Best of all, barely more than an hour had passed, and they tasted just as good as the 3-hour version.

In fact, my sweet potatoes were so moist and creamy that they didn't need any butter or toppings, though I couldn't resist putting together a couple of simple ones to dress them up (yes, they're company-worthy). The first is an Indian-spiced yogurt; the second, a garlicky sour cream laced with chives.

ANNIE PETITO, *Cook's Illustrated*

NOTES FROM THE TEST KITCHEN

SWEET POTATOES AND WHITE POTATOES ARE NOT THE SAME

Sweet potatoes look, taste, and cook differently from white potatoes because they're from different botanical families. Sweet potatoes are members of the Convolvulaceae family, which includes plants with fleshy storage roots, such as morning glories, while white-fleshed potatoes belong to the Solanaceae (or nightshade) family. Their nutrient makeups—including their starch and sugar contents—also differ.

RUSSET POTATO

WATER: 74% to 78%
STARCH: 20% to 24%
SUGAR: < 1%

SWEET POTATO

WATER: 75% to 78%
STARCH: 15% to 18%
SUGAR: 4% to 7%

Best Baked Sweet Potatoes

SERVES 4

Any variety of orange- or red-skinned, orange-fleshed sweet potato can be used in this recipe, but we highly recommend using Garnet (also sold as Diane). Avoid varieties with tan or purple skin, which are starchier and less sweet than varieties with orange and red skins. When shopping, look for sweet potatoes that are uniform in size and weigh between 8 and 12 ounces (we prefer smaller potatoes). Top potatoes as desired or with one of our two sauces, Garam Masala Yogurt or Garlic and Chive Sour Cream (recipes follow).

4 small sweet potatoes (8 ounces each), unpeeled, each lightly pricked with fork in 3 places

Salt and pepper

1. Adjust oven rack to middle position and heat oven to 425 degrees. Place potatoes on large plate and microwave until potatoes yield to gentle pressure and centers register 200 degrees, 6 to 9 minutes, flipping potatoes every 3 minutes.

2. Set wire rack in aluminum foil–lined rimmed baking sheet and spray rack with vegetable oil spray. Using tongs, transfer potatoes to prepared rack and bake for 1 hour (exteriors of potatoes will be lightly browned and potatoes will feel very soft when squeezed).

3. Slit each potato lengthwise; using clean dish towel, hold ends and squeeze slightly to push flesh up and out. Transfer potatoes to serving platter. Season with salt and pepper to taste. Serve.

Garam Masala Yogurt
MAKES ABOUT ½ CUP

The warm flavors of garam masala, an Indian spice blend, complement the potatoes' sweetness.

½ cup plain yogurt

2 teaspoons lemon juice

½ teaspoon garam masala

⅛ teaspoon salt

Combine all ingredients in bowl.

Garlic and Chive Sour Cream
MAKES ABOUT ½ CUP

This garlicky sauce adds tang to balance the potatoes' caramel-y sweetness.

½ cup sour cream

1 tablespoon minced fresh chives

1 garlic clove, minced

⅛ teaspoon salt

Combine all ingredients in bowl.

BUBBLE AND SQUEAK

WHY THIS RECIPE WORKS: The name's a little quirky, but this dish—a deliciously crispy mess of fried mashed potato and cabbage—is pure comfort. The classic dish is traditionally made with leftovers, but for our version, we added softened savoy cabbage to easy mashed potatoes to make a quick hash and then browned the mixture on all sides to enhance the savory combo's flavors. Adding butter during cooking boosted flavor and helped the potatoes brown quickly without burning. Cooking the potatoes and cabbage separately to start ensured that they wouldn't burn in the hot skillet before they cooked through.

Leftovers from a holiday meal are never a bad thing, but bubble and squeak, a quick (and thrifty) hash of mashed potato and cabbage with an English accent, makes having—and eating—leftovers a joy. The dish, which picks up loads of tasty browning in the pan, gets its funny name from the sound the mixture makes when it pops in the hot skillet.

Bubble and squeak always contains potato and cabbage, but in Great Britain (where it's often eaten for breakfast, in addition to as a dinner side dish), it serves as a catchall for whatever other vegetables and meats are kicking around the refrigerator. While I found recipes that call for additions of cooked beets, carrots, peas, parsnips, and even roast beef, I decided to create a more basic version using just mashed potatoes, cabbage, and plenty of butter.

I didn't want my recipe to be limited to those occasions when you have leftover mashed potatoes, so I knew I'd have to start by cooking the spuds. I boiled 1½ pounds of russet potatoes until tender, drained them, and mashed them up with a good knob of butter. Easy.

For the cabbage, my tasters preferred the lighter texture of sautéed savoy cabbage (the traditional choice) to the denser regular green variety. I stirred the cabbage into the potatoes and got busy figuring out the best way to fry it all up. Some recipes call for frying the vegetable-studded mash in one big mass until brown on the bottom and then flipping the whole thing; this was too tricky and too much work for a simple hash. Other recipes call for forming the mixture

BUBBLE AND SQUEAK

into individual cakes and frying them on each side, but that seemed more like delicate restaurant fare than hearty home cooking.

Instead, I channeled my inner diner cook and "hashed" the whole thing right in a hot buttered non-stick skillet. I spread the green-flecked mash into an even layer and let it cook, undisturbed, until the bottom was nicely browned. Then I dug in, one spatula width at a time, and flipped it piece by piece. I continued the flipping until I'd created loads of delicious, crispy browning throughout the pan. Did the mixture bubble? Yes. Was there squeaking? Yes—by me, after sampling this crispy, buttery delight.

ALLI BERKEY, *Cook's Country*

Bubble and Squeak

SERVES 4 TO 6

A well-seasoned cast-iron skillet can be used here. Preheat it over low heat for 5 minutes before starting step 3. This side dish pairs just as well with roast chicken or beef as it does with eggs.

1½	**pounds russet potatoes, peeled and sliced ¼ inch thick**
	Salt and pepper
8	**tablespoons unsalted butter, cut into 8 pieces**
1	**small onion, chopped**
½	**small head savoy cabbage, cored and cut into 1-inch pieces (5 cups)**

1. Place potatoes and 1 tablespoon salt in medium saucepan and cover with water by 1 inch. Bring to boil over high heat. Reduce heat to medium and simmer until tip of paring knife inserted into potatoes meets no resistance, 8 to 10 minutes.

2. Drain potatoes and return them to saucepan. Add 3 tablespoons butter and ¼ teaspoon pepper. Using potato masher, mash until smooth. Set aside.

3. Melt 1 tablespoon butter in 12-inch nonstick skillet over medium heat. Add onion and cook until softened, about 4 minutes. Stir in cabbage, 2 tablespoons water, and ½ teaspoon salt. Cover and cook until cabbage is wilted and lightly browned, 8 to 10 minutes, stirring

occasionally. Transfer cabbage mixture to saucepan with potato mixture and stir to combine. Wipe skillet clean with paper towels.

4. Melt 2 tablespoons butter in now-empty skillet over medium-high heat. Add potato-cabbage mixture to skillet and, using rubber spatula, press into even layer. Cook, undisturbed, until bottom is well browned, about 7 minutes.

5. Flip spatula-size portions of potato mixture and lightly repack in skillet. Break remaining 2 tablespoons butter into small pieces and distribute around edge of skillet. Repeat flipping process every few minutes until potato-cabbage mixture is evenly browned, 8 to 10 minutes longer. Serve.

NOTES FROM THE TEST KITCHEN

PREPPING CABBAGE

1. Cut cabbage into quarters, then trim and discard hard core.

2. Separate cabbage into small stacks of leaves that flatten when pressed. Chop or slice as directed.

ALL ABOUT SAVOY CABBAGE

The traditional choice for this savory mash, savoy cabbage is mellow in flavor and has a light texture, with a loose, full head of wrinkly leaves. When shopping, look for leaves that are crisp with no sign of browning and be sure to choose a head that feels heavy for its size. Stored loosely in plastic wrap in the refrigerator, the cabbage should keep for about four days.

CHAPTER 4

PASTA, PIZZA, SANDWICHES, AND MORE

SLOW-COOKER GROWN-UP MACARONI AND CHEESE

✓ **WHY THIS RECIPE WORKS:** Mac and cheese is a guaranteed crowd-pleaser, and preparing it in a slow cooker makes a simple recipe even easier. With the process almost entirely hands-off, it's an ideal choice for company. Our goal was to boost its flavor and further broaden its appeal; in other words, we wanted a mac and cheese for the grown-ups. Inspired by the flavors of Swiss-style fondue, we started with an aged Gruyère, but the resulting sauce was grainy. Swapping the Gruyère for Comté—a younger, moister cheese with a similar flavor profile—greatly improved the texture, as did the addition of some easy-melting Monterey Jack. Just ¼ cup of white wine provided a welcome crisp acidity, while a handful of dried porcini contributed meaty flavor and a subtle earthiness.

The appeal of a slow cooker is undeniable: It can turn a multipot affair into a one-dish meal, and it allows for maximum flexibility in terms of timing. These advantages undoubtedly make for a fuss-free meal, but unfortunately many slow-cooker recipes prioritize ease over flavor. Take macaroni and cheese, for example. Slow-cooker recipes for this family favorite eliminate the pot of boiling water, making it entirely hands-off, but the resulting flavor is often disappointingly similar to the box version. That's a shame, because another advantage of a slow cooker is the long cooking time, which provides ample opportunity for deep, complex flavor to develop. I wanted a slow-cooker recipe that would give me mac and cheese with rich, cheesy flavor and an ultracreamy texture. And while I was at it, I wanted to give this classic comfort food a serious upgrade by introducing decidedly grown-up flavors to the mix.

The test kitchen has been perfecting slow-cooker pastas for years, so I already had some helpful tricks up my sleeve as I began my testing. First, to prevent the macaroni from overcooking and becoming flabby, I started by toasting the uncooked elbows with some oil in the microwave. This simple step set the pasta's protein, preventing it from becoming bloated as it cooked through. Pouring boiling water over the toasted pasta jump-started the cooking process and shortened the overall cooking time, while lining the slow-cooker insert with a collar of aluminum foil prevented any hot spots from burning the food. With my pasta's integrity secured, I turned my attention to the cheese sauce.

For my grown-up casserole, I wanted to bring in a cheese that was distinctly heady but still struck a comforting chord. My musings brought me back to the fragrant, indulgent pots of Swiss fondue I crave after a day on the ski slopes. Recipes for fondue typically include nutty, pleasantly funky aged Gruyère, so I decided to start there. But I wrestled with what to use as my cheese sauce's base. Many stovetop versions of mac and cheese incorporate flour in the form of a béchamel sauce to prevent the cheese from separating, but I wanted to keep my recipe all in one pot so I nixed that option. A few ultramodern recipes rely on a bit of kitchen chemistry, using sodium citrate or sodium phosphate (compounds that keep cheese's dairy fat and water emulsified) to create a reliably smooth texture. I was intrigued, but realized that incorporating a mail-order ingredient flew in the face of my simple approach. Further research pointed me to a more accessible alternative: a combination of condensed cream of cheddar soup and evaporated milk, two pantry items rich in the stabilizing and emulsifying agents I needed. I decided to give the pair a shot.

I emptied two cans of soup and two cans of evaporated milk into the slow cooker along with my shredded Gruyère, but after an hour's cooking time it was clear I still had work to do. While the soup and milk had successfully warded off a total grease slick, the Gruyère had melted unevenly, creating an unpleasantly grainy texture. Not ready to abandon that authentic Alpine flavor quite yet, I swapped out half of the Gruyère for mild Monterey Jack, a cheese that melts exceptionally well. This was a step in the right direction, but some of that unwanted graininess still remained. Seeking a younger alternative to the aged Gruyère, I swapped in a few moist, creamy cheeses that were still plenty pungent, and I found my answer in a close cousin to Gruyère: buttery, rich Comté. Although slightly milder than Gruyère, this French mountain cheese still had plenty of Alpine funk but produced a velvety texture and melted far more evenly.

With my selection of cheeses settled, I looked for ways to add complexity to the sauce. In a further nod to fondue, I decided that white wine was a must; it contributed a crisp, bright tang that perfectly complemented the cheese. I found that ¼ cup wine was as high as I could go; any more and the sauce curdled. Dried porcini mushrooms offered a meaty umami boost and a layer of earthiness, without watering down the sauce the way fresh mushrooms would. A touch of dry mustard heightened the savory flavors. These tweaks had upped the sauce's complexity, but I wondered if I could swap the cheddar soup for another creamy soup that would be more in line with my sauce's flavor profile. Cream of celery soup was a nonstarter—its boiled celery flavor was out of place here—but cream of onion soup delivered a balance of sweet and savory flavors that perfectly complemented the Comté.

Finished with a sprinkling of crunchy bread crumbs, this was finally it: a creamy, richly flavored slow-cooker macaroni and cheese that was still plenty easy to prepare. And with layers of nutty, earthy flavor, this is one mac and cheese that's pure sophistication—comfort food fit for a dinner party.

JOSEPH GITTER, *America's Test Kitchen Books*

Slow-Cooker Grown-Up Macaroni and Cheese with Comté and Porcini

SERVES 6 TO 8

COOKING TIME: 1 TO 2 HOURS ON HIGH
SLOW COOKER SIZE: 4 TO 7 QUARTS

Look for a Comté aged for about one year (avoid Comté aged for longer; it won't melt well). You can substitute an equal amount of fontina cheese for the Comté. You will need an oval slow cooker for this recipe. For an accurate measurement of boiling water, bring a full kettle of water to a boil and then measure out the desired amount.

1 pound elbow macaroni or small shells

1 tablespoon extra-virgin olive oil

3 cups boiling water, plus extra as needed

2 (12-ounce) cans evaporated milk

2 (11-ounce) cans condensed onion soup

8 ounces Comté cheese, shredded (2 cups)

8 ounces Monterey Jack cheese, shredded (2 cups)

¼ cup dry white wine

¼ ounce dried porcini mushrooms, rinsed and minced

1 teaspoon dry mustard

Salt and pepper

1 recipe Bread-Crumb Topping (optional)

1. Line slow cooker with aluminum foil collar and lightly coat with vegetable oil spray. Microwave macaroni and oil in bowl at 50 percent power, stirring occasionally, until macaroni begin to look toasted and blistered, 5 to 8 minutes.

2. Transfer hot macaroni to prepared slow cooker and immediately stir in 2¾ cups boiling water. Stir in evaporated milk, condensed soup, Comté, Monterey Jack, wine, mushrooms, mustard, 1 teaspoon pepper, and ½ teaspoon salt. Cover and cook until macaroni are tender, 1 to 2 hours on high.

3. Discard foil collar. Gently stir remaining ¼ cup boiling water into macaroni until combined. Season with salt and pepper to taste. Adjust consistency with extra boiling water as needed. Sprinkle individual portions with bread-crumb topping, if using. Serve. (Macaroni can be held on warm or low setting for up to 30 minutes.)

Bread-Crumb Topping

MAKES ABOUT 1 CUP

1 cup panko bread crumbs

2 tablespoons extra-virgin olive oil

Salt and pepper

1 ounce Parmesan cheese, grated (½ cup)

2 tablespoons minced fresh chives

Toss panko with oil in bowl and season with salt and pepper. Microwave panko, stirring occasionally, until deep golden brown, 2 to 4 minutes; let cool completely. Stir in Parmesan and chives. (Topping can be refrigerated for up to 2 days; bring to room temperature before using.)

NOTES FROM THE TEST KITCHEN

MAKING A FOIL COLLAR

Fold sheets of aluminum foil to make 6-layered foil rectangle that measures roughly 16 inches long by 4 inches wide. Press collar into back side of slow cooker; food will help hold collar in place.

BEEF SHORT RIB RAGU

SIMPLE BEEF RAGU

✔ **WHY THIS RECIPE WORKS:** A typical Sunday gravy is an all-day affair and calls for multiple meats. We wanted a rich sauce using one cut of beef that could be made in about 2 hours. For this ragu, we chose a flavorful, beefy cut of meat—boneless short ribs—and paired it with umami-rich ingredients to produce a deeply flavored sauce that required far less time and work. Boneless beef short ribs contributed a velvety texture and robust flavor while porcini mushrooms, tomato paste, and anchovies added savory notes to make this relatively quick sauce taste as though it had taken all day to make. Braising it in the oven made it a largely hands-off proposition, and removing the lid partway through cooking browned the meat, deepening its flavor and eliminating the messy step of browning it before braising.

I have fond memories of my Italian nonna's hearty meat ragu, or Sunday gravy. Made with sausages, meatballs, and braciole and served over a heaping pile of pasta, it was the backbone of a feast that fed a crowd—and it took her all day to prepare. With fall's cool, crisp arrival, I usually look forward to making a big batch, but this year I wondered if there wasn't an easier alternative. There are numerous versions of ragu from all over Italy, and some research turned up a particularly interesting version relying on just one type of meat: beef short ribs. Certainly they're a great cut, well marbled and flavorful, but I wondered if they alone could make a sauce as satisfyingly meaty as a traditional Sunday gravy.

Many of the recipes called for browning the short ribs and then braising them for 3 to 5 hours (relatively quick, compared with the all-day approach). The most involved recipe was indeed delicious, but it took even more work than my nonna's, so I left it behind. Simpler versions were mostly thin in body and flavor. However, a subset of this category, *ragù di manzo e funghi porcini* (beef ragu with porcini mushrooms), caught my attention and eventually became my point of departure. The version I tried was a bit lackluster and tasted more of woodsy porcini than of short ribs, but I felt that with a little work I could transform it into a luscious, rich, and deeply beefy sauce in just a couple of hours.

Although some recipes called for bone-in short ribs, I quickly settled on boneless short ribs, which are less expensive and have more meat. (Confusingly, they are not actually bone-in ribs without the bone, but are cut from the chuck, or shoulder, of the cow.) I browned the meat and set it aside, sautéed an array of aromatics, and then returned the short ribs to the pot along with a can of whole tomatoes I had chopped (canned diced tomatoes were too firm and didn't break down during cooking), a sprig of fresh rosemary, and some dried porcini mushrooms I'd rehydrated in beef broth. I set the pot to braise over a low flame and checked the meat periodically for doneness. The good news: The beef became silky and tender enough for me to shred and stir back into the sauce in just 2 hours. However, the ragu wasn't without problems. Despite my having turned down the flame here and there, the sauce at thebottom of the pot scorched over the direct heat. But, I thought, switching to oven braising would easily fix that.

The other problem presented more of a challenge: The sauce seemed to struggle to highlight the beef's savory quality. This lack of depth was probably at least partly due to the relatively short cooking time. Having too many competing flavors in the pot surely wasn't helping either, so I eliminated ingredients: Carrots, celery, and rosemary all got the ax. After browning the beef, I simply sautéed onion and garlic and then added the mushrooms, their rehydrating liquid, and the tomatoes, along with some dry red wine for acidity. Sure enough, as the sauce became focused on a few key ingredients, more beefiness came to the fore.

But the dish tasted a little too earthy from the porcini. I was hesitant to cut back on the mushrooms since I wanted their presence to be noticeable; I just needed the beef flavor to be equally prominent. To balance things out, I turned to two powerhouses: tomato paste and minced anchovies. Just 1 tablespoon of the former and three fillets of the latter did the trick, bringing deep meaty flavor to the ragu. That's because both ingredients are rich in umami-boosting glutamates. For the skeptics in the group, we did a side-by-side taste test of ragus prepared with and without anchovies and found that the minced fillets made a marked difference in the dish's savoriness—they added roundness and depth of flavor with nary a trace of fishiness.

As planned, I also switched to braising the ragu in the oven, covered, rather than on the stovetop, which eliminated the scorching issue. The sauce wasn't getting as thick as I wanted, though, so I removed the lid halfway through braising to allow it to thicken via evaporation. This move also prompted the meat sitting above the surface of the liquid to brown, enhancing its beefy taste. In fact, it worked so well that I eliminated the step of browning the meat prior to braising. I saved about 20 minutes of cooking time and my stovetop was splatter-free—a win-win scenario.

Finally, many of the ragù di manzo recipes I found called for a touch of warm spices, a nod to the importance of the spice route that passed through Italy from the 15th to the 17th century and introduced Europe to Asian flavors. I wanted to maintain this tradition in my dish, so as a final tweak I played with sprinkling in various amounts of cinnamon, cloves, and nutmeg. The spices worked beautifully, adding subtle background notes that underscored the taste of the beef and mushrooms. It occurred to me that I could trade in the separate spices for a single blend: five-spice powder. Just ½ teaspoon of this mix of cinnamon, cloves, fennel, white pepper, and star anise contributed sweet and warm flavors without being identifiably Asian. My colleagues applauded the deeply beefy flavor and velvety texture of my ragu. And I think that my nonna would also approve.

STEVE DUNN, *Cook's Illustrated*

NOTES FROM THE TEST KITCHEN

SHREDDING SHORT RIBS

Using 2 forks, pull beef into bite-size pieces, discarding any large pieces of fat or connective tissue.

Beef Short Rib Ragu

MAKES 5 CUPS; ENOUGH FOR 1 POUND PASTA

If you can't find boneless short ribs, don't substitute bone-in short ribs. Instead, use a 2½-pound chuck-eye roast, trimmed and cut into 1-inch chunks. This recipe yields enough to sauce 1 pound of pasta or a batch of Creamy Parmesan Polenta (recipe follows)—our favorite way to serve it. This recipe can be doubled, and the sauce can be frozen. Better Than Bouillon Roasted Beef Base is our taste test winner.

- 1½ cups beef broth
- ½ ounce dried porcini mushrooms, rinsed
- 1 tablespoon extra-virgin olive oil
- 1 onion, chopped fine
- 2 garlic cloves, minced
- 1 tablespoon tomato paste
- 3 anchovy fillets, rinsed, patted dry, and minced
- ½ teaspoon five-spice powder
- ½ cup dry red wine
- 1 (14.5-ounce) can whole peeled tomatoes, drained with juice reserved, chopped fine
- 2 pounds boneless beef short ribs, trimmed
  Salt and pepper

1. Adjust oven rack to middle position and heat oven to 350 degrees. Microwave ½ cup broth and mushrooms in covered bowl until steaming, about 1 minute. Let sit until softened, about 5 minutes. Drain mushrooms in fine-mesh strainer lined with coffee filter, pressing to extract all liquid; reserve liquid and chop mushrooms fine.

2. Heat oil in Dutch oven over medium heat until shimmering. Add onion and cook, stirring occasionally, until softened, about 5 minutes. Add garlic and cook until fragrant, about 1 minute. Add tomato paste, anchovies, and five-spice powder and cook, stirring frequently, until mixture has darkened and fond forms on pot bottom, 3 to 4 minutes. Add wine, increase heat to medium-high, and bring to simmer, scraping up any browned bits. Continue to cook, stirring frequently, until wine is reduced and pot is almost dry, 2 to 4 minutes. Add tomatoes and reserved juice, remaining 1 cup broth, reserved mushroom soaking liquid, and mushrooms and bring to simmer.

3. Toss beef with ¾ teaspoon salt and season with pepper. Add beef to pot, cover, and transfer to oven. Cook for 1 hour.

4. Uncover and continue to cook until beef is tender, 1 to 1¼ hours longer.

5. Remove pot from oven; using slotted spoon, transfer beef to cutting board and let cool for 5 minutes. Using 2 forks, shred beef into bite-size pieces, discarding any large pieces of fat or connective tissue. Using large spoon, skim off any excess fat that has risen to surface of sauce. Return beef to sauce and season with salt and pepper to taste. Serve. (Sauce can be refrigerated for up to 3 days or frozen for up to 2 months.)

Creamy Parmesan Polenta

SERVES 6 TO 8

Coarse-ground degerminated cornmeal such as yellow grits (with grains the size of couscous) works best in this recipe. Avoid instant and quick-cooking products, as well as whole-grain, stone-ground, and regular cornmeal. Do not omit the baking soda—it reduces the cooking time and makes for a creamier polenta. The polenta should do little more than release wisps of steam. If it bubbles or sputters even slightly after the first 10 minutes, the heat is too high and you may need a flame tamer, available at most kitchen supply stores.

7½ **cups water**

    Salt and pepper

    Pinch baking soda

1½ **cups coarse-ground cornmeal**

4 **ounces Parmesan cheese, grated (2 cups), plus extra for serving**

2 **tablespoons unsalted butter**

1. Bring water to boil in heavy-bottomed large saucepan over medium-high heat. Stir in 1½ teaspoons salt and baking soda. Slowly pour cornmeal into water in steady stream while stirring back and forth with wooden spoon or rubber spatula. Bring mixture to boil, stirring constantly, about 1 minute. Reduce heat to lowest possible setting and cover saucepan.

2. After 5 minutes, whisk polenta to smooth out any lumps that may have formed, about 15 seconds. (Make sure to scrape down sides and bottom of saucepan.) Cover and continue to cook, without stirring, until grains of polenta are tender but slightly al dente, about 25 minutes longer. (Polenta should be loose and barely hold its shape but will continue to thicken as it cools.)

3. Off heat, stir in Parmesan and butter and season with pepper to taste. Let polenta stand, covered, for 5 minutes. Serve, passing extra Parmesan separately.

NOTES FROM THE TEST KITCHEN

WHEN A RIB IS NOT A RIB

Flavorful, easy-to-prep boneless short ribs aren't actually cut from the rib section of the cow, as their name implies. They are cut from the chuck, or shoulder, of the animal. For that reason chuck roast is the best substitute when boneless short ribs are unavailable.

Why not just buy a less expensive chuck roast and cut it into chunks? When we purchased near-equal weights of boneless short ribs and chuck roast and then trimmed both, the former took half as much time to trim and the difference in cost of edible trimmed meat per pound didn't even add up to $0.50. We'll spend the extra pocket change and save time.

And what about bone-in short ribs? We don't recommend them as a substitute for boneless short ribs. They are cut from a different part of the cow—the plate, or front belly—and they cost significantly more per edible pound.

BONELESS SHORT RIBS
Cut from the chuck, or shoulder, these "ribs" are basically butchered and trimmed chuck roast.

NEXT BEST CHOICE
Chuck roast provides the same flavor and texture but requires more prep.

ENTIRELY DIFFERENT
Bone-in short ribs come from the plate, or front belly, and are much fattier.

BAKED ZITI WITH SAUSAGE AND BROCCOLI RABE

✔ **WHY THIS RECIPE WORKS:** We wanted to incorporate the classic Italian pairing of sausage and broccoli rabe into an easy yet elegant make-ahead casserole. Boiling the pasta until it just started to soften kept it from becoming bloated and mushy in the oven, and blanching the broccoli rabe helped it maintain its bright green color. Garlic, lemon zest, and pepper flakes provided a solid flavor base for our sauce, and a couple of minced anchovies contributed savory flavor without any detectable fishiness. A modest amount of white wine brightened our sauce, while fontina and Parmesan cheeses contributed creamy texture and a subtle nutty flavor. We found that we could refrigerate the assembled casserole for up to a day before baking; covering it with foil at the outset of baking prevented the casserole from drying out and ensured that it heated evenly, while baking it uncovered for the remainder of the time allowed for the sauce to thicken and the cheese to develop an irresistible golden-brown crust.

Baked pasta dishes are comforting, satisfying, and great for serving a crowd. There's just one problem: They're usually pretty labor-intensive, so making one during the week is pretty much out of the question. And if I'm having company for dinner—even on a weekend—the prospect of making a baked pasta as well as the appetizers, drinks, sides, and dessert necessary for a dinner party is overwhelming, and I inevitably opt for something simpler.

So when I started working on the test kitchen's new book devoted solely to make-ahead recipes, I knew just what I wanted to create: a hearty yet elegant baked pasta dish that could be prepared in advance without sacrificing any of the flavor or texture that makes these dishes so appealing.

First, I would need to nail down exactly what I wanted by developing the recipe as I normally would—that is, I would make the recipe straight through, without preparing anything in advance. Then, I could test my way into the make-ahead instructions, thereby ensuring that both versions were identical.

I chose a few flavor profiles for my tasters to try—one with tomato sauce and cheese, one with chicken and broccoli, and a third with sausage and broccoli rabe. While all were good, the consensus was clear: The classic Italian pairing of sausage and broccoli rabe was deemed the most elegant and company-worthy. But the dish itself wasn't perfect. The pasta was overcooked and mushy, and the broccoli rabe had turned an unappealing army green in the oven. Plus, the overall flavor of the casserole was a bit flat.

The texture of the pasta was an easy fix: I simply boiled it for less time—until it was just starting to soften—before adding it to the sauce. It then finished cooking to a perfect al dente in the oven. As for the broccoli rabe, a quick blanch in boiling water and then a dunk into ice water helped preserve its bright green color even after baking.

On to flavor: While the richness of the Italian sausage contrasted beautifully with the bitterness of the broccoli rabe, tasters wanted some additional depth. I realized that, since I was already cooking the sausage, I could use some of its flavorful rendered fat to build the base of my sauce. Garlic was a given, and tasters liked the mellow flavor and distinct presence of sliced garlic. For a subtle floral note, I added a little lemon zest. Finally, I rounded out my flavor base with a slightly unusual addition: anchovies. We often use these little fish in the test kitchen to add savory flavor (without any fishiness) to dishes, and it worked here, too: Just a couple of minced fillets were all I needed.

Up to this point, I had been making a simple roux-based cream sauce by adding flour to the aromatics and then whisking in equal parts broth and cream. But my tasters found the sauce a bit dull, so I replaced some of the cream with white wine; the wine's acidity livened up the sauce nicely. A squeeze of lemon juice added off the heat further accented the brightness.

While Pecorino is the traditional cheese of choice for pasta with sausage and broccoli rabe, it proved overpowering here. Instead, I opted for a combination of mild fontina and nutty Parmesan. I stirred half of the cheese into the sauce for a cohesive final dish, and sprinkled the rest on top to give the casserole a crisp, browned lid.

With my just-made casserole perfected—al dente pasta, perfectly balanced flavor, and a creamy yet bright sauce—I turned my attention to making it ahead. I had a few questions: Should I refrigerate it before or after baking? Would the pasta turn mushy if left to sit in the sauce? How long would it take to heat up on the second day? I knew freezing was off the table, since we've found in the past that cream-based sauces tend to break when frozen, creating a gritty texture in the

MAKE-AHEAD BAKED ZITI WITH SAUSAGE AND BROCCOLI RABE

baked casserole—not exactly the elegant solution I was after. So I focused my efforts on the fridge.

A few tests revealed that I could store the unbaked casserole, assembled and covered, in the fridge for up to a full day. This was great news, as all I would have to do the next day was bake it. But after 30 minutes in the oven—the time called for in my regular recipe—the pasta was still cold in the center, while the top and edges were dried out. That wouldn't do; this baked ziti was worlds away from my freshly made version.

I was hesitant to increase the amount of liquid in the sauce, since it would make the casserole too soupy if I did want to bake it the same day. And I couldn't leave the refrigerated dish out on the counter to come to room temperature before baking—such a dense casserole would take so long to warm up that I'd be pushing the limits of food safety. Could I use the moisture that was already in the sauce to my advantage? This time, after taking the dish out of the fridge, I covered it with foil before putting it in the oven. It was a step in the right direction: The pasta heated through evenly and remained moist. But new problems emerged. The foil prevented the cheese on top from browning, and the lack of evaporation meant the sauce hadn't thickened to the proper consistency. Luckily, both were easy to fix: I simply removed the foil once the pasta was hot throughout and let the casserole continue to bake uncovered for the rest of its time in the oven.

Finally, I had a baked pasta dish that was just as good made ahead as freshly made. In fact, in a side-by-side test, tasters couldn't tell the difference between the two. And with that, I knew what I was making next time I had company for dinner.

KATHRYN CALLAHAN, *America's Test Kitchen Books*

Make-Ahead Baked Ziti with Sausage and Broccoli Rabe

SERVES 8

Broccoli cut into 1½-inch pieces can be substituted for the broccoli rabe.

> 1 pound broccoli rabe, trimmed and cut into 1½-inch pieces
> Salt and pepper
> 1 pound ziti
> 2 tablespoons extra-virgin olive oil
> 1 pound sweet or hot Italian sausage, casings removed
> 1 onion, chopped fine
> 8 garlic cloves, sliced thin
> 2 anchovy fillets, rinsed and minced
> 2 teaspoons lemon zest plus 2 tablespoons juice
> 1 teaspoon red pepper flakes
> ⅓ cup all-purpose flour
> 2 cups chicken broth
> 1½ cups heavy cream
> ½ cup dry white wine
> 8 ounces fontina cheese, shredded (2 cups)
> 2 ounces Parmesan cheese, grated (1 cup)

1. Bring 4 quarts water to boil in large pot. Fill large bowl halfway with ice and water. Add broccoli rabe and 1 tablespoon salt to boiling water and cook until crisp-tender, about 1 minute. Using slotted spoon, transfer broccoli rabe to ice water and let cool, about 2 minutes; drain and pat dry.

2. Return pot of water to boil, add pasta, and cook, stirring often, until just starting to soften, about 5 minutes. Drain pasta in colander and toss with 1 tablespoon oil; leave in colander and set aside.

3. Adjust oven rack to middle position and heat oven to 400 degrees. Dry now-empty pot and heat remaining 1 tablespoon oil over medium heat until shimmering. Add sausage and cook, breaking up meat with wooden spoon, until no longer pink, about 3 minutes. Using slotted spoon, transfer sausage to paper towel-lined plate.

4. Pour off all but 1 tablespoon fat from pot, add onion and ½ teaspoon salt, and cook until softened and lightly browned, 5 to 7 minutes. Stir in garlic, anchovies, lemon zest, and pepper flakes and cook until fragrant, about 30 seconds. Add flour and cook, stirring constantly, until golden, about 1 minute. Slowly whisk in broth, cream, and wine, scraping up any browned bits and smoothing out any lumps. Bring to simmer and cook until thickened slightly, about 2 minutes.

5. Off heat, gradually whisk 1 cup fontina and ½ cup Parmesan into sauce until cheese is melted and sauce is smooth. Stir in lemon juice, broccoli rabe, pasta, and sausage, breaking up any clumps. Season with salt and pepper to taste. Transfer pasta mixture to 13 by 9-inch baking dish and sprinkle with remaining 1 cup fontina and remaining ½ cup Parmesan.

6. Place baking dish on aluminum foil–lined rimmed baking sheet and bake until golden and bubbling around edges, 25 to 35 minutes. Let casserole cool for 20 minutes before serving.

TO MAKE AHEAD: Casserole, prepared through step 5, can be refrigerated for up to 24 hours. To bake, cover with greased aluminum foil and bake on foil-lined sheet in 400-degree oven until hot throughout, about 35 minutes; remove foil and continue to bake until cheese is golden, 25 to 35 minutes.

LINGUINE WITH SEAFOOD

✔ **WHY THIS RECIPE WORKS:** To create a seafood pasta with savory seafood flavor in every bite, we made a sauce with clam juice and four minced anchovies, which fortified the juices shed by the shellfish. Cooking the shellfish in a careful sequence—adding hardier clams and mussels first and then adding the shrimp and squid during the final few minutes of cooking—ensured that every piece was plump and tender. We parboiled the linguine and then finished cooking it directly in the sauce; the noodles soaked up flavor while shedding starches that thickened the sauce. Fresh cherry tomatoes, lots of garlic, fresh herbs, and lemon made for a bright, clean, complex-tasting sauce.

Italian seafood pastas such as *frutti di mare* and *pescatore* promise noodles teeming with shellfish and saturated with clean, briny-sweet flavor. And while many versions are chock-full of shrimp, clams, mussels, lobster, scallops, squid, or any combination thereof, I've yet to eat one in which the pasta actually tastes much like the sea. The shellfish flavor tends to be locked up in the pieces of seafood themselves rather than awash throughout the dish. Together with the typical tomato-based sauce, these dishes resemble nothing more than pasta drenched in marinara and punctuated by the occasional bite of seafood.

Most recently I came across this problem in a bowl of *linguine allo scoglio*, another mixed shellfish-and-pasta classic that's named for the rocky Italian seashores where seafood is abundant (*scoglio* means "rock"). Tangled in the noodles were shell-on mussels and clams, shrimp, and squid, as well as cherry tomatoes, garlic, and fresh herbs. The sauce was white wine–based, which gave me hope that the seafood flavor might come through more clearly than it does in tomato-based preparations. But instead the pasta barely tasted like seafood and was relatively dry, as the thin sauce had slipped right off the linguine and puddled in the bowl. Worse, the mussels, shrimp, and squid were dense and rubbery, obviously having toughened while waiting for the longer-cooking clams to pop open.

Overcooked seafood would be easy enough to fix with a strategic cooking method. But I also had my sights set on a light-bodied sauce that clung nicely to the noodles and infused them with the flavor of the sea.

I ignored recipes that suggested sautéing or simmering the shrimp, clams, mussels, and squid together in a pot until every piece was cooked through, since that would surely lead to the rubbery results I'd had before. But I didn't want to tediously cook one type of shellfish at a time. I had to figure out how long it would take each type of seafood to cook, add the longest-cooking item first, and stagger the additions of the others.

First I sautéed minced garlic and red pepper flakes over moderately high heat, which would get the sauce base going. In went the clams, which popped open after about 8 minutes, followed midway through cooking by the mussels. With no hard, protective shells, shrimp and squid cook very quickly, so I lowered the flame and added them to the pot. They plumped nicely in about 4 minutes and 2 minutes, respectively, but would have toughened if I hadn't kept a close watch on them. Down the road, I'd see if there was an even gentler way to cook them, but for now, I had at least established a sequence.

Left behind in the pot were the aromatics and the liquor shed by the cooked shellfish, which would fortify my sauce. It wasn't much, though, so I borrowed a technique we've used in other shrimp preparations and made a quick stock with the shells by browning them

LINGUINE WITH SEAFOOD (LINGUINE ALLO SCOGLIO)

in a skillet and simmering them with wine. In this case, I finished building the sauce by adding lots of chopped parsley, a dash of fresh thyme, and about ¾ pound of whole cherry tomatoes; as the sauce simmered, the tomatoes collapsed into a pulp that added body to the sauce. Meanwhile, I boiled the linguine in a separate pot. I then tossed the cooked seafood into the sauce and poured it over the drained pasta.

The seafood was well cooked, but the sauce was still thin in both body and seafood flavor. This time I skipped the shrimp broth and instead added a bottle of clam juice and four minced anchovies. If that sounds like it would be unpleasantly fishy, trust me that it's not; we often use anchovies to add rich, savory flavor in both seafood and nonseafood preparations, and mincing them to a fine paste ensures that they meld seamlessly.

Adding a little tomato paste along with the anchovies and simmering the liquid until it had reduced by about one-third yielded much richer, rounder flavor—but only marginally better body. When I poured the sauce over the linguine, it still slipped to the bottom of the bowl.

That's when I realized I hadn't implemented one of the oldest Italian pasta-cooking tricks in the book: parboiling the pasta until it's just shy of al dente, draining it, and simmering it directly in the sauce to finish cooking. Doing so not only allows the pasta to soak up the flavor of the sauce but the starches it sheds during cooking also thicken the liquid. At last, the sauce was viscous enough to cling to the strands.

I was about to declare my recipe finished when I got a forkful of squid that was a tad rubbery. So were the shrimp, I realized with another bite. Both had overcooked as they'd sat in the warm bowl, so I decided to add them to the sauce along with the pasta rather than precook them with the clams and mussels. After I'd let the pasta simmer in the sauce for about 2 minutes, I lowered the heat and added the shrimp and a lid. About 4 minutes later, I followed with the squid.

Now plump and tender, the shrimp and squid were perfect. To freshen up the flavors before serving, I added lemon zest, halved cherry tomatoes, and more parsley along with the squid, plus a drizzle of olive oil and a squeeze of lemon juice. Every bite was bright, fresh, perfectly cooked, and—most important—packed with seafood flavor from top to bottom.

STEVE DUNN, *Cook's Illustrated*

Linguine with Seafood (Linguine allo Scoglio)
SERVES 6

For a simpler version of this dish, you can omit the clams and squid and increase the amounts of mussels and shrimp to 1½ pounds each; you'll also need to increase the amount of salt in step 2 to ¾ teaspoon. If you can't find fresh squid, it's available frozen (thaw it before cutting and cooking) at many supermarkets and typically has the benefit of being precleaned. Bar Harbor makes our favorite clam juice.

- 6 tablespoons extra-virgin olive oil
- 12 garlic cloves, minced
- ¼ teaspoon red pepper flakes
- 1 pound littleneck clams, scrubbed
- 1 pound mussels, scrubbed and debearded
- 1¼ pounds cherry tomatoes, half of tomatoes halved, remaining tomatoes left whole
- 1 (8-ounce) bottle clam juice
- 1 cup dry white wine
- 1 cup minced fresh parsley
- 1 tablespoon tomato paste
- 4 anchovy fillets, rinsed, patted dry, and minced
- 1 teaspoon minced fresh thyme
  Salt and pepper
- 1 pound linguine
- 1 pound extra-large shrimp (21 to 25 per pound), peeled and deveined
- 8 ounces squid, sliced crosswise into ½-inch-thick rings
- 2 teaspoons grated lemon zest, plus lemon wedges for serving

1. Heat ¼ cup oil in large Dutch oven over medium-high heat until shimmering. Add garlic and pepper flakes and cook until fragrant, about 1 minute. Add clams, cover, and cook, shaking pan occasionally, for 4 minutes. Add mussels, cover, and continue to cook, shaking pan occasionally, until clams and mussels have opened, 3 to 4 minutes longer. Transfer clams and mussels to bowl, discarding any that haven't opened, and cover to keep warm; leave any broth in pot.

2. Add whole tomatoes, clam juice, wine, ½ cup parsley, tomato paste, anchovies, thyme, and ½ teaspoon salt to pot and bring to simmer over medium-high heat. Reduce heat to medium and cook, stirring occasionally, until tomatoes have started to break down and sauce is reduced by one-third, about 10 minutes.

3. Meanwhile, bring 4 quarts water to boil in large pot. Add pasta and 1 tablespoon salt and cook, stirring often, for 7 minutes. Reserve ½ cup cooking water, then drain pasta.

4. Add pasta to sauce in Dutch oven and cook over medium heat, stirring gently, for 2 minutes. Reduce heat to medium-low, stir in shrimp, cover, and cook for 4 minutes. Stir in squid, lemon zest, halved tomatoes, and remaining ½ cup parsley; cover and continue to cook until shrimp and squid are just cooked through, about 2 minutes longer. Gently stir in clams and mussels. Remove pot from heat, cover, and let stand until clams and mussels are warmed through, about 2 minutes. Season with salt and pepper to taste and adjust consistency with reserved cooking water as needed. Transfer to large serving dish, drizzle with remaining 2 tablespoons oil, and serve, passing lemon wedges separately.

RED WINE RISOTTO WITH BEANS

✓ **WHY THIS RECIPE WORKS:** Making this deeply flavored, hearty winter specialty is typically a lengthy process of combining a minestrone-like soup with risotto. We eliminated the need to make two separate dishes and simplified its preparation to make one hearty risotto. Sautéed pancetta and *mirepoix* made a strong flavor base to which we added tomato paste and garlic for more savory depth. In place of the hard-to-find traditional Italian *salam d'la duja*, we used mild Italian-style salami, sautéing it with the Arborio rice before adding red wine and broth. Using our streamlined risotto method, we incorporated most of the liquid in one addition, making the cooking mostly hands-off. Near the end of cooking, we added chopped cabbage and creamy canned pinto beans. We finished the dish with butter for even more richness and red wine vinegar to brighten the meaty flavors.

I was skeptical when I first heard of *paniscia*, a specialty from the city of Novara in Piedmont, northern Italy. It is essentially a merger of two dishes: risotto—flavored with cured meats and red wine—and a minestrone-like bean and vegetable soup. Bean, meat, and red wine risotto? Figuring that paniscia must be experienced to be understood, I headed into the kitchen.

I first made a minestrone, simmering dried soaked cranberry beans in chicken broth along with *mirepoix* (chopped carrot, celery, and onion), cabbage, and pancetta. Meanwhile, I started a risotto, first browning Genoa salami (my sub for the traditional but hard-to-find lard-cured salami called *salam d'la duja*) and then toasting Arborio rice in the fat before pouring in red wine. Adhering to the established risotto method, I stirred liquid (here, the soup) into the rice in multiple additions. I finished the dish with a little butter.

I ate every grain. This was pure, soul-satisfying nourishment with deep, layered flavor.

With all hesitations about paniscia cast aside, I started thinking on a practical level. Was it truly necessary to prepare two dishes to make one? Specifically, could I use our Almost Hands-Free Risotto method to combine the minestrone ingredients with the rice?

The trick in that recipe is to add most of the liquid to the rice up front rather than in stages, which helps the grains cook evenly so that you need to stir only a couple of times. We also cover the pot, which helps evenly distribute the heat so that every grain is tender.

I sautéed pancetta and then added the mirepoix. Next, I added the rice, salami, and wine, stirring until the wine was absorbed. I then incorporated hot chicken broth all at once. Cabbage went in next, followed by canned pinto beans (our favorite substitute for dried cranberry beans). A cup of hot water thinned the texture, and after a few minutes the rice was beautifully creamy. But the dish didn't taste very meaty. Also, I wondered if I could skip preheating the broth.

For more savoriness, I added tomato paste and minced garlic and tripled the amount of salami. As for the broth question, the recipe worked seamlessly with room-temperature broth, saving me a pan to wash.

My streamlined recipe boasted tangy salami, just-wilted cabbage, and creamy beans, combined in a luscious risotto. Fresh parsley and red wine vinegar offset its rich flavors. And, though it's not traditional, I couldn't pass up a bit of grated Parmesan as well.

ANNIE PETITO, *Cook's Illustrated*

Red Wine Risotto with Beans (Paniscia)
SERVES 6 TO 8

We prefer to use a smaller, individually packaged, dry Italian-style salami such as Genoa or *soppressata*, but unsliced deli salami can be used.

RED WINE RISOTTO WITH BEANS (PANISCIA)

2 tablespoons extra-virgin olive oil

2 ounces pancetta, chopped fine

1 onion, chopped fine

1 carrot, peeled and chopped fine

1 celery rib, chopped fine

   Salt and pepper

6 garlic cloves, minced

1½ cups Arborio rice

6 ounces salami, cut into ¼-inch dice

2 tablespoons tomato paste

1 cup dry red wine

4 cups chicken broth

1 small head green cabbage, halved, cored,
   and cut into ½-inch pieces (4 cups)

1 (15-ounce) can pinto beans, rinsed

1 cup hot water, plus extra as needed

1 ounce Parmesan cheese, grated (½ cup),
   plus extra for serving

2 tablespoons unsalted butter

2 teaspoons red wine vinegar

2 tablespoons chopped fresh parsley

1. Heat oil in Dutch oven over medium heat until shimmering. Add pancetta and cook, stirring occasionally, until beginning to brown, 3 to 5 minutes. Add onion, carrot, celery, ½ teaspoon salt, and ¼ teaspoon pepper and cook, stirring occasionally, until vegetables are softened, 5 to 7 minutes. Add garlic and cook until fragrant, 30 seconds. Add rice and salami and cook, stirring frequently, until rice grains are translucent around edges, about 3 minutes.

2. Stir in tomato paste and cook until fragrant, about 1 minute. Add wine and cook, stirring constantly, until fully absorbed, 2 to 3 minutes. Stir in broth, reduce heat to medium-low, cover, and simmer for 10 minutes, stirring halfway through simmering.

3. Stir in cabbage and continue to cook, covered, until almost all liquid has been absorbed and rice is just al dente, 6 to 9 minutes longer.

4. Add beans and hot water and stir gently and constantly until risotto is creamy, about 3 minutes. Remove from heat, cover, and let stand for 5 minutes. Stir in Parmesan and butter. If desired, add up to 1 cup extra hot water to create fluid, pourable consistency. Stir in vinegar and season with salt and pepper to taste. Sprinkle with parsley and serve immediately, passing extra Parmesan separately.

ONE-HOUR PIZZA

✔ **WHY THIS RECIPE WORKS:** For our One-Hour Pizza recipe, we employed a handful of tricks to get a crust that was crisp, tender, and light without the need for a prolonged proofing period. First, we used a high percentage of yeast and warm water in the dough to make sure it proofed in 30 minutes. We also used a combination of semolina and bread flours. Finally, to create a light and tender crust, we rolled the dough between two sheets of lightly oiled parchment paper immediately after mixing so that it could relax while it proofed. For a supercrisp crust, we preheated the baking stone at 500 degrees; then, for a blast of heat before baking, we turned on the broiler for 10 minutes.

If there is anything in life I can claim to have mastered, it's making pizza: It was the first food I learned to cook, at age 15. Since then, I've developed nine pizza recipes. I've built two outdoor pizza ovens. Heck, I even teach pizza-making classes in my free time. But mastery can turn to complacency, so I was intrigued when editor in chief Dan Souza tasked me with the following challenge: Make really good pizza from scratch in just 1 hour, start to finish.

It would be the ultimate test, as it went against the gospel I've been preaching for years, which says that for superlative pizza—a mildly yeasty, slightly tangy crust that's crisp on the outside and pleasantly chewy within—you must let the dough proof in the refrigerator for at least one day or up to three days.

Time is so important because it significantly affects both flavor and texture. During a slow, cold rise, yeast creates fermented and acidic flavor compounds. Meanwhile, enzymes in the flour go to work on the gluten, snipping some bonds to make a supremely extensible dough. I'd have to find speedy ways to accomplish both effects. It would be no easy feat.

I started with a test run using my favorite thin-crust pizza recipe: Combine bread flour, a little sugar, and a small amount of yeast in a food processor with water, and then let it sit for 10 minutes; this lets the flour absorb the water, which allows gluten to form. Next, add salt and oil and run the machine until the dough is smooth. After that, you'd normally refrigerate the dough and wait a few days for fermentation to happen. But the clock was ticking, so I divided the dough into two balls and let them proof at room temperature for just 30 minutes. As I expected, when I tried to shape a ball into a round, it stubbornly sprang back. The only way to get the dough near 12 inches in diameter was to strong-arm it with a rolling pin. It baked up flat, bland, and tough.

Clearly, the few pinches of yeast in my original recipe (which do a great job of leavening in 24 hours) weren't enough to make the dough rise much in 30 minutes—not to mention that the rolling pin was pushing out what little air there was. Increasing the yeast was the obvious answer, but it's also the adjustment where most quick pizza recipes fail. Good pizza dough should taste subtly fermented, not just yeasty. So how much more yeast could I add? I ended up with 2 teaspoons, enough to give the dough lift but not so much that it tasted too yeasty. I also started with warm tap water, which activated the yeast more quickly.

The rise was better, but I still needed a rolling pin to shape the highly elastic dough. Furthermore, while the pizza didn't taste overly yeasty, it didn't taste like much else either. Fortunately, for the latter issue I knew of a trick from our recipe for Almost No-Knead Bread: Mix in vinegar and beer. Beer includes many of the same flavorful compounds that are created by yeast during bread fermentation—alcohols, aldehydes, and esters—and vinegar adds the acidity that yeast and bacteria create in slow-fermented dough.

The two quickest ways to improve my dough's extensibility were to increase its moisture and to take a close look at the type of flour I was using. I was only able to increase the liquid from 6.5 to 7 ounces before the dough became too wet to handle. It was a little more yielding, but not enough.

As for the flour, the bread flour that my favorite thin-crust pizza recipe calls for is high in protein. Generally speaking, the more protein a flour has, the more gluten it forms. That's great if you can use a long proof to let that gluten relax. But without the luxury of time, I wondered if lower-protein (less gluten-forming) all-purpose or cake flour might help. Sure enough, doughs made with these flours were easier to work with. But gluten formation is not the only reason bread bakers use bread flour. High-protein flour also helps a dough bake up crisp and light. It holds more water, which forms bubbles throughout the crust when it turns to steam, and an airier crust crisps up much better than a dense one. Without enough protein, these crusts were anything but crisp.

How about using semolina flour? It's unusual in that it's high in protein but forms a dough that's easier to stretch than typical bread doughs. In other words, it was just what my dough needed: A high protein level would help create crispness, and more stretch would make for a more workable dough.

Indeed, when I swapped a portion of the bread flour for semolina, the crust was transformed, with greater extensibility along with the crispness that is a hallmark of a great pizza. But there was a limit to how much semolina I could use: Beyond 50 percent of the total by

NOTES FROM THE TEST KITCHEN

SHORT-CUTTING FERMENTED FLAVOR
Since the yeast in our dough doesn't have enough time to create rich flavors, we add beer, which contains flavor compounds created by yeast fermentation. We also add vinegar, which provides the acetic acid that yeast produces during a slow rise.

weight, the dough didn't have enough structure to hold air bubbles. Even with my modest ½ cup of semolina, it was still too tight to shape without a rolling pin.

At this point, I'd questioned almost everything about the pizza-making process. But there was one question I'd yet to ask: Why proof the dough and then roll it (and push out all those valuable air bubbles)? If I rolled the dough as soon as it was mixed, it could proof in its round shape.

With an eye on the clock, I rolled a ball of dough between sheets of oiled parchment and then let it proof for 30 minutes. I removed the top sheet, sprinkled the puffy round with flour, flipped it onto a peel, and removed the second sheet before topping it with sauce and cheese and baking it on a preheated stone.

Sixty minutes after I'd started, I was enjoying my best quick pizza yet. It had been easy to shape, and the crust was chewy but light since the air bubbles that developed during proofing hadn't been knocked out by shaping. Will it be replacing my three-day pizza recipe? No chance. Will I be making this dough every time I want same-day pizza? Without a doubt.

ANDREW JANJIGIAN, *Cook's Illustrated*

One-Hour Pizza

MAKES TWO 11½-INCH PIZZAS

For the best results, weigh your ingredients. We like the depth anchovies add to the sauce, but you can omit them, if desired. For the mild lager, we recommend Budweiser or Stella Artois. Extra sauce can be refrigerated for up to a week or frozen for up to a month. Some baking stones can crack under the intense heat of the broiler. Our recommended stone from Old Stone Oven won't, but if you're using another stone, check the manufacturer's website. If you don't have a pizza peel, use an overturned rimmed baking sheet instead.

DOUGH

1⅓ cups (7⅓ ounces) bread flour
½ cup (3 ounces) semolina flour
2 teaspoons instant or rapid-rise yeast
2 teaspoons sugar
½ cup plus 2 tablespoons (5 ounces) warm water (115 degrees)
¼ cup (2 ounces) mild lager
2 teaspoons distilled white vinegar

1½ teaspoons extra-virgin olive oil
1 teaspoon salt
    Vegetable oil spray
    All-purpose flour

SAUCE

1 (28-ounce) can whole peeled tomatoes, drained
1 tablespoon extra-virgin olive oil
3 anchovy fillets, rinsed and patted dry (optional)
1 teaspoon salt
1 teaspoon dried oregano
½ teaspoon sugar
¼ teaspoon pepper
⅛ teaspoon red pepper flakes

PIZZA

1 ounce Parmesan cheese, grated fine (½ cup)
6 ounces whole-milk mozzarella, shredded (1½ cups)

1. FOR THE DOUGH: Adjust oven rack 4 to 5 inches from broiler element, set pizza stone on rack, and heat oven to 500 degrees.

2. While oven heats, process bread flour, semolina flour, yeast, and sugar in food processor until combined, about 2 seconds. With processor running, slowly pour warm water, lager, vinegar, and oil through feed tube; process until dough is just combined and no dry flour remains, about 10 seconds. Let dough stand for 10 minutes.

3. Add salt to dough and process until dough forms satiny, sticky ball that clears sides of workbowl, 30 to 60 seconds. Transfer dough to lightly floured counter and gently knead until smooth, about 15 seconds. Divide dough into 2 equal pieces and shape each into smooth ball.

4. Spray 11-inch circle in center of large sheet of parchment paper with oil spray. Place 1 ball of dough in center of parchment. Spray top of dough with oil spray. Using rolling pin, roll dough into 10-inch circle. Cover with second sheet of parchment. Using rolling pin and your hands, continue to roll and press dough into 11½-inch circle. Set aside and repeat rolling with second ball of dough. Let dough stand at room temperature until slightly puffy, 30 minutes.

5. FOR THE SAUCE: Process all ingredients in food processor until smooth, about 30 seconds. Transfer to medium bowl.

ONE-HOUR PIZZA

DETROIT-STYLE PIZZA

6. FOR THE PIZZA: When dough has rested for 20 minutes, heat broiler for 10 minutes. Remove top piece of parchment from 1 disk of dough and dust top of dough lightly with all-purpose flour. Using your hands or pastry brush, spread flour evenly over dough, brushing off any excess. Liberally dust pizza peel with all-purpose flour. Flip dough onto peel, parchment side up. Carefully remove parchment and discard.

7. Using back of spoon or ladle, spread ½ cup sauce in thin layer over surface of dough, leaving ¾-inch border around edge. Sprinkle ¼ cup Parmesan evenly over sauce, followed by ¾ cup mozzarella. Slide pizza carefully onto stone and return oven to 500 degrees. Bake until crust is well browned and cheese is bubbly and beginning to brown, 8 to 12 minutes, rotating pizza halfway through baking.

8. Transfer pizza to wire rack and let cool for 5 minutes before slicing and serving. Repeat steps 6 and 7 to top and bake second pizza.

DETROIT-STYLE PIZZA

✅ **WHY THIS RECIPE WORKS:** Our challenge in creating a recipe for Detroit pizza—a crispy, buttery pizza from the Motor City—was figuring out how to mimic the tender crumb, the mild and melty cheese (which can be found only in Michigan), and the vibrant tomato sauce that covers the pizza. The stand mixer did most of the kneading for us; the rich, hydrated dough required a 15-minute rest and a 2-hour rise to produce the tender, buttery crust we were after. We topped the pizza with handfuls of Monterey Jack cheese, which we found to be the only acceptable substitute for the brick cheese typically used on Detroit pizzas. A combination of dried herbs, sugar, and canned crushed tomatoes gave our sauce authentic flavor and texture.

Detroit pizza, a deep-dish local favorite, is light and airy, with a crunchy, buttery crust. It's topped with soft, stretchy cheese and a slightly sweet tomato sauce full of herbs and spices. But aficionados will tell you that the best part is the crispy, lacy fried edges.

The pizza starts familiarly enough, with mixing and kneading the dough, which is then transferred to a 13 by 9-inch seasoned steel pan and left to rise and fill the pan. Cooks then flip the traditional pizza script, evenly spreading shredded brick cheese—a mild, slightly tangy semisoft cheese that's hard to find outside Michigan—from the dough's middle to its edges before draping ladlefuls of the sweet tomato sauce over the cheese. In the oven, the dough bakes into a soft base with crispy, brown, cheesy edges.

While this style of pizza originated at a Detroit bar named Buddy's in the 1940s, there are now many local experts. I reached out to Shawn Randazzo of Detroit Style Pizza Co. to learn what goes into his dough and how to best reproduce the flavor and texture of brick cheese. After picking his brain for tips, I compiled some recipes and put them to work, producing five pizzas that were purportedly Detroit style. I fed them to my coworkers, including a few Detroit natives. The results? Well, the optimistic take was "promising, but not quite."

I experimented with different types of flour for my dough, ultimately landing on ubiquitous all-purpose flour for its easy availability. To create that soft interior, Randazzo warned me, I'd need a rather wet and sticky dough, so I let the stand mixer do most of the hard work of bringing it together. After a quick 1-minute knead on the counter, I eased the dough into a 13 by 9-inch baking pan that I'd lightly greased. After it proofed for a few hours, the silky dough tripled in volume, nearly filling the pan, and I noticed many large bubbles, a sign that this dough was going to be tender and airy but still chewy.

This was the point at which, if I were making another style of pizza, I'd add sauce. But Detroit pizza takes cheese first, sauce later. I first had to find a good substitute for mild, melty brick cheese. To do so, I held a grand tasting, pitting thirteen types of cheese against brick cheese, which I had mail-ordered. The tasters had a clear preference for Monterey Jack. It was slightly tangy, melted beautifully, and had just enough fat in it to fry those essential crispy edges as it baked.

In Detroit, pizza chefs use canned tomatoes and dried spices for the sauce. I settled on a mixture of canned crushed tomatoes, fresh garlic, fresh basil, dried basil (I needed both to mimic the trademark complexity of the herb mixture), dried oregano, sugar, salt, and pepper.

After baking dozens of pizzas, I was proud to serve my Detroit-born colleagues big squares of their hometown favorite with soft interiors, tangy sauce, melty cheese, and those trademark lacy, crispy edges.

ASHLEY MOORE, *Cook's Country*

SERVES 4

When kneading the dough on medium speed, the mixer can wobble and move on the counter. Place a towel or shelf liner under the mixer to keep it in place, and watch it closely. To add more toppings, such as pepperoni or sausage, to your pizza, press them into the dough before adding the cheese.

PIZZA

- 1 tablespoon extra-virgin olive oil
- 2¼ cups (11¼ ounces) all-purpose flour
- 1½ teaspoons instant or rapid-rise yeast
- 1½ teaspoons sugar
- 1 cup (8 ounces) water, room temperature
- ¾ teaspoon salt
- 10 ounces Monterey Jack cheese, shredded (2½ cups)

SAUCE

- 1 cup canned crushed tomatoes
- 1 tablespoon extra-virgin olive oil
- 1 tablespoon chopped fresh basil
- 1 garlic clove, minced
- 1 teaspoon dried oregano
- 1 teaspoon dried basil
- ½ teaspoon sugar
- ½ teaspoon pepper
- ¼ teaspoon salt

1. FOR THE PIZZA: Spray 13 by 9-inch nonstick baking pan with vegetable oil spray, then brush bottom and sides of pan with oil. Using stand mixer fitted with dough hook, mix flour, yeast, and sugar on low speed until combined, about 10 seconds. With mixer running, slowly add room-temperature water and mix until dough forms and no dry flour remains, about 2 minutes, scraping down bowl as needed. Cover with plastic wrap and let stand for 10 minutes.

2. Add salt to bowl and knead on medium speed until dough forms satiny, sticky ball that clears sides of bowl, 6 to 8 minutes. Turn dough onto lightly floured counter and knead until smooth, about 1 minute.

3. Transfer dough to prepared pan, cover with plastic, and let rest for 15 minutes. Using your well-oiled hands, press dough into corners of pan. (If dough resists stretching, let it rest for another 10 minutes before trying again to stretch.) Cover with plastic and let dough rise at room temperature until nearly

tripled in volume and large bubbles form, 2 to 3 hours. Adjust oven rack to lowest position and heat oven to 500 degrees.

4. FOR THE SAUCE: Combine all ingredients in bowl. (Sauce can be refrigerated for up to 24 hours.)

5. Sprinkle Monterey Jack evenly over dough to edges of pan. Spoon three 1-inch-wide strips of sauce, using ⅓ cup sauce for each, over cheese evenly down length of pan.

6. Bake until cheese is bubbly and browned, about 15 minutes. Let pizza cool in pan on wire rack for 5 minutes. Run knife around edge of pan to loosen pizza. Using spatula, slide pizza onto cutting board. Cut into 8 pieces and serve.

BOOGALOO WONDERLAND SANDWICHES

✓ **WHY THIS RECIPE WORKS:** This beloved Detroit sandwich—a sassier, spicier, cheesier version of a Sloppy Joe—is tied together by a bold sauce. To a base of sautéed ground beef and onion, we added ketchup, dried thyme (a signature ingredient), cider vinegar for tanginess, brown sugar to balance the vinegar, and Worcestershire sauce for added savoriness and complexity. To take our sauce to the next level and give it that Boogaloo oomph, we added chili powder (to bump up the heat and warm spice) and dry mustard (which adds plenty of bite without announcing its own flavor too loudly).

A Boogaloo Wonderland sandwich bears a passing resemblance to the classic Sloppy Joe, but that comparison doesn't really do it justice. It's bigger and bolder, spicier and tangier. It's just as simple to make, but if you ask me, this Detroit original, little known outside the city, has more punch, personality, and oomph. And no one can deny that it has a much, much cooler name.

The Boogaloo's base ingredients aren't surprising; they include ground beef, melted American cheese, and sautéed onion on a sub roll. But what ties this sandwich together—and sets it apart—is its bold, brassy sauce, a glazy mix of sweet and savory flavors that soaks into the bread and makes the Boogaloo a beautiful mess to eat. Unfortunately, the original sauce recipe is top secret. I would have to puzzle out the recipe with my team in the test kitchen.

BOOGALOO WONDERLAND SANDWICHES

The original sauce lies somewhere between tomato sauce and barbecue sauce, so for a first crack at it I tested two versions, one using a canned tomato sauce base and the other a ketchup base. To each I added dried thyme (a signature ingredient), cider vinegar, brown sugar, and Worcestershire sauce to create a complex mix of sweet, tangy, and savory flavors. Tasters crowned the ketchup-based sauce the clear winner, praising its added body and concentrated flavor. But it still lacked the touch of heat, the hint of warm spice, and the oomph that a true Boogaloo requires.

To bump up the heat and spice, I reached for chili powder (a mix containing both chiles and cumin). As for the oomph, after trying some common flavor boosters—soy sauce, Dijon, horseradish, and even anchovy paste—I landed on dry mustard. It adds that bite you'd get from wasabi or horseradish, but rather than announce its own flavor too loudly, it sings in harmony with the rest of the Boogaloo choir.

I got my onion and ground beef (1¼ pounds of 85 percent lean, enough for four sandwiches) going in a skillet to brown. Then, once the onion started to soften and the meat began to sizzle, I stirred in the sauce, saving some to serve with the sandwiches later. I laid out four rolls on a baking sheet, spooned saucy beef over the bottoms, covered each with a couple of slices of cheese, and popped the sandwiches in the oven to toast the buns a touch, melt the cheese, and give the sauce time to get acquainted with the bread. (This step also created lovely browned, faintly crunchy edges on the bread—not quite toasted but leaning in that direction.)

I lined up the finished Boogaloos for my tasters, and we dove in. I asked the assembled crowd for feedback, but they pretended not to hear me. They were too busy devouring the sandwiches.

MATTHEW FAIRMAN, *Cook's Country*

NOTES FROM THE TEST KITCHEN

BUY AMERICAN

Yes, it usually contains stabilizers, but American cheese is deliciously milky and mild. And because it melts better than any other cheese, it's the perfect choice for our Boogaloo Wonderland Sandwiches. Our favorite American cheese is made by **Boar's Head**.

Boogaloo Wonderland Sandwiches
SERVES 4

Heinz Organic Tomato Ketchup and Heinz Filtered Apple Cider Vinegar are our favorites. Both light and dark brown sugar will work in this recipe. Don't be tempted to substitute another kind of cheese for the American; nothing melts like it. Serve with your favorite hot sauce, if desired.

SAUCE

- 1 cup ketchup
- 3 tablespoons cider vinegar
- 2 tablespoons packed brown sugar
- 2 tablespoons Worcestershire sauce
- ¾ teaspoon dried thyme
- ¾ teaspoon dry mustard
- ¾ teaspoon granulated garlic
- ¾ teaspoon chili powder
- ¼ teaspoon pepper

SANDWICHES

- 1 tablespoon vegetable oil
- 1¼ pounds 85 percent lean ground beef
- 1 onion, sliced thin
- 1 teaspoon pepper
- ¾ teaspoon salt
- 4 (6-inch) Italian sub rolls, sliced lengthwise with 1 side intact
- 8 slices American cheese

1. FOR THE SAUCE: Combine all ingredients in small saucepan and bring to boil over medium-high heat. Cook, whisking constantly, until slightly thickened, about 3 minutes.

2. FOR THE SANDWICHES: Adjust oven rack to middle position and heat oven to 350 degrees. Heat oil in 12-inch nonstick skillet over medium-high heat until just smoking. Add beef, onion, pepper, and salt and cook, breaking meat into small pieces with wooden spoon, until liquid has evaporated and meat begins to sizzle, about 10 minutes. Add 1 cup sauce and bring to boil. Reduce heat to medium and simmer until slightly thickened, about 1 minute.

3. Place rolls on rimmed baking sheet. Divide meat mixture evenly among roll bottoms. Top each sandwich with 2 slices American cheese. Bake until cheese is melted and rolls are warmed through, about 5 minutes. Divide remaining sauce equally among sandwiches. Fold roll tops over meat and serve.

GRILLED LAMB-STUFFED PITA

✔ **WHY THIS RECIPE WORKS:** Seasoned with herbs and warm spices, pressed between pita rounds, and grilled, these lamb sandwiches inspired by Middle Eastern *arayes* offer a flavorful, juicy, street food–style alternative to the everyday burger on a bun. Along with traditional cumin, coriander, and onion, we added lemon zest to our meat mixture as well as cayenne for heat and paprika for its complementary pepper flavor. The grill made the pita extra crisp, providing contrast to the texture of the filling. As the sandwiches cooked, the lamb released fat and juices into the bread to help it crisp up. To balance the sandwiches' richness, we serve them with a bright and cooling yogurt-tahini sauce.

Lamb is a staple in Middle Eastern cooking; roasted leg of lamb, shanks braised in heady spice mixtures, flavorful stews, and meatballs are all common. But I recently encountered a whole new application from the estimable Lebanese cookbook author Anissa Helou: ground meat sandwiches known as *arayes*. What makes these sandwiches—a popular street food found across the region—so intriguing is that the meat gets cooked inside the pita. In Helou's version, she seasons ground lamb with parsley, onion, cumin, and cinnamon; spreads it over the pita; and places the sandwich on a hot grill (baking the sandwich is also common). As the lamb cooks, its flavorful juices and fat soak into the pita, which turns crisp and toasty. This sounded like a great alternative to plain grilled burgers; I had to try it.

As I'd hoped, the lamb plus seasonings made for a juicy, flavorful filling. And I loved the thin bread, which let the lamb take center stage but also lent a satisfying crunch where the edges had crisped. The whole thing was definitely a notch above plain ground meat shrouded in a burger bun.

Still, there were aspects that could be rejiggered. First, stuffing the pitas was a challenge: I cut each pita halfway around its circumference, spooned in the meat mixture, and spread it in an even layer from edge to edge. But it was difficult to spread evenly, especially into the edges of the pita pocket; more than one pita tore in my hands. Also, I needed to develop a more detailed grilling process. Helou's version didn't indicate how hot the fire should be but merely said to grill the sandwiches for about 5 minutes per side until the filling was cooked and the bread crisp. The bread cooked up a bit dry and tough toward the center rather than crisp, a problem that I suspected had to do with the heat level and cooking method. Tasters also found the meat a bit thin, and I wondered if, though flavorful, the filling couldn't stand a little bit more seasoning to better balance the lamb's richness.

The first thing I did was work out an easier way to fill the sandwiches. Since it was hard to reach deep into the pocket without tearing the bread, why not separate it into two pieces by running a pair of scissors around the bread's circumference? I worried that creating two pieces might make the bread separate from the filling, but the ground lamb proved sticky enough to hold on to the pita pieces both during cooking and once the sandwiches were done. To further ensure that the bread remained intact, I used the freshest pitas I could find, since older pitas are drier and thus more brittle, and I spread the meat mixture over the less fragile of the two sides since it would be less likely to break.

Next, I dealt with the meat. I upped the ratio of ground lamb to pita so that each sandwich was thicker. And to better balance the lamb's richness, I added a little lemon juice and swapped out more neutral, grassy parsley for brighter, more aromatic cilantro. Bigger pieces of cilantro and onion were distracting, so I pulsed them together in the food processor until they were finely chopped. And paprika and cayenne contributed both pepper flavor and heat that balanced the richness of the lamb.

As for the grill setup, a medium fire didn't toast the bread sufficiently, while a very hot fire burned it before the meat cooked through. A medium-hot fire worked best, but I noticed that the bread tended to dry out rather than toast. To fix this, I needed the meat to render its fat more quickly, as the fat would cause

GRILLED LAMB-STUFFED PITAS WITH YOGURT SAUCE

the bread to fry a bit. To jump-start the rendering process, I started cooking with the grill covered to create an oven-like environment that would heat the filling from the get-go. With these changes, I had a juicy, flavor-packed lamb pita sandwich that might just beat my regular old beef burger.

Now my sandwiches just needed a few accompaniments. Arayes are traditionally served with yogurt, so I created a tart, minty yogurt-tahini sauce to serve alongside. I also made a simple Mediterranean-style parsley salad with cucumber, pomegranate, and feta.

My tasters all loved this Middle Eastern alternative to a burger, with its spicy, flavorful lamb filling and supercrisp pita.

ANDREW JANJIGIAN, *Cook's Illustrated*

Grilled Lamb-Stuffed Pitas with Yogurt Sauce

SERVES 4 TO 6

You can substitute 85 percent lean ground beef for the ground lamb, if desired. This recipe works best with ¼-inch-thick pitas that are fresh and pliable. To determine which side of the pita is thicker, look closely at the pattern of browning across its surface; the thinner side is usually covered with char marks in a dotted-line pattern. Serve with a dressed green salad or with Parsley-Cucumber Salad with Feta, Pomegranate, and Walnuts (recipe follows).

SAUCE
- 1   cup plain Greek yogurt
- ½   cup minced fresh mint
- 2   tablespoons lemon juice
- 2   tablespoons tahini
- 2   tablespoons extra-virgin olive oil
- ½   teaspoon salt

SANDWICHES
- 1   onion, cut into 1-inch pieces
- 1   cup fresh cilantro leaves
- ¼   cup extra-virgin olive oil
- 1   tablespoon grated lemon zest plus 3 tablespoons juice
- 1   tablespoon ground coriander
- 1   tablespoon ground cumin
- 1   tablespoon paprika
- 2   teaspoons salt
- 1½ teaspoons pepper
- ½   teaspoon cayenne pepper
- ¼   teaspoon ground cinnamon
- 2   pounds ground lamb
- 4   (8-inch) pita breads

1. FOR THE SAUCE: Whisk all ingredients together in bowl. Set aside.

2. FOR THE SANDWICHES: Pulse onion and cilantro in food processor until finely chopped, 10 to 12 pulses, scraping down sides of bowl as needed. Transfer mixture to large bowl. Stir in oil, lemon zest and juice, coriander, cumin, paprika, salt, pepper, cayenne, and cinnamon. Add lamb and knead gently with your hands until thoroughly combined.

3. Using kitchen shears, cut around perimeter of each pita and separate into 2 halves. Place 4 thicker halves on counter with interiors facing up. Divide lamb mixture into 4 equal portions and place 1 portion in center of each pita half. Using spatula, gently spread lamb mixture into even layer, leaving ½-inch border around edge. Top each with thinner pita half. Press each sandwich firmly until lamb mixture spreads to ¼ inch from edge of pita. Transfer sandwiches to large plate, cover with plastic wrap, and set aside. (Sandwiches may be held for up to 1 hour before grilling.)

NOTES FROM THE TEST KITCHEN

PERFECTING THE PITA
Didn't know there's a difference between the two halves of a pita? It turns out the side that is against the oven floor as the pita bakes is more fragile. You can identify it by the pattern of dotted lines across it, which is from the metal-chain conveyor belt that the breads sit on as they move through the oven.

Cut around perimeter with scissors to separate bread into 2 pieces and then spread meat mixture on thicker side.

4A. FOR A CHARCOAL GRILL: Open bottom vent completely. Light large chimney starter two-thirds filled with charcoal briquettes (4 quarts). When top coals are partially covered with ash, pour evenly over grill. Set cooking grate in place, cover, and open lid vent completely. Heat grill until hot, about 5 minutes.

4B. FOR A GAS GRILL: Turn all burners to high, cover, and heat grill until hot, about 15 minutes. Turn all burners to medium-high.

5. Clean and oil cooking grate. Place sandwiches on grill, cover, and cook until bottoms are evenly browned and edges are starting to crisp, 7 to 10 minutes, moving sandwiches as needed to ensure even cooking. Flip sandwiches, cover grill, and continue to cook until second sides are evenly browned and edges are crisp, 7 to 10 minutes longer. Transfer sandwiches to cutting board and cut each in half crosswise. Transfer sandwiches to platter and serve, passing sauce separately.

Parsley-Cucumber Salad with Feta, Pomegranate, and Walnuts

SERVES 4 TO 6

Our parsley and cucumber salad is a crisp, refreshing accompaniment to rich grilled meats such as beef kebabs or our Grilled Lamb-Stuffed Pitas with Yogurt Sauce. Use flat-leaf parsley for this salad.

- 1 tablespoon pomegranate molasses
- 1 tablespoon red wine vinegar
  Salt and pepper
  Pinch cayenne pepper
- 3 tablespoons extra-virgin olive oil
- 3 cups fresh parsley leaves
- 1 seedless English cucumber, unpeeled, halved lengthwise and sliced thin
- 1 cup walnuts, toasted and chopped coarse
- ½ cup pomegranate seeds
- 4 ounces feta cheese, sliced thin

Whisk molasses, vinegar, ¼ teaspoon salt, ⅛ teaspoon pepper, and cayenne together in large bowl. Whisking constantly, add oil in thin stream until fully incorporated. Add parsley and cucumber and toss to coat. Add half of walnuts and half of pomegranate seeds and toss to combine. Season with salt and pepper to taste. Transfer to serving platter and top with feta, remaining walnuts, and remaining pomegranate seeds. Serve.

EASY CHICKEN SHAWARMA

✔ WHY THIS RECIPE WORKS: This street-cart and takeout staple is tricky to reproduce at home without installing a rotating spit, layering 30 pounds of meat onto it, and cooking the meat for hours. However, by using the broiler and boneless chicken thighs, we were able to create an authentic-tasting home version. The intense heat generated by the oven's broiler ably bloomed the flavors of the cumin-paprika mixture we applied to the chicken and browned the meat's craggy surface. Opting for a quicker weeknight method, we gained the benefits of marinating by broiling lemon halves alongside the meat. Squeezing the lemon juice over the sliced chicken just before serving lent it brightness and smoky depth. To round out the meal, we serve the shawarma with a cabbage slaw, diced cucumbers, sliced tomatoes, a lemony yogurt sauce, and pita bread.

It's not often that I get the urge to install a rotating spit in my small apartment kitchen. But, putting aside concerns about fire safety, I'd consider it for a good chicken shawarma. Shawarma, a Middle Eastern specialty, is made by layering marinated meats (chicken, lamb, beef, or turkey) into a large mass on a vertical spit that spins for hours in front of an open flame. As the meat rotates, a cook shaves off the beautifully charred exterior pieces, drops them into a fresh pita, and sends it down the line for toppings such as pickles, creamy tahini or yogurt sauces, tomato-cucumber salad, and a good squeeze of lemon juice. I wanted to find a way to make the same deeply seasoned, smoky, and tender meat (and sandwich) in a home kitchen—with bonus points awarded if I could make it fast enough for a weeknight dinner.

I knew a few things from the start: I wasn't going to install a spit, and I wasn't going to stack 30 pounds of chicken into a big torpedo that cooked for days. The broiler made sense here; its direct radiant heat is more like traditional spit-cooking than roasting in the oven or searing on the stove. As for the cut of chicken, boneless, skinless chicken thighs had the best balance of meaty flavor and juicy texture and had a relatively quick cooking time.

The recipes I found for homemade chicken shawarma called for marinating the meat for anywhere from 30 minutes to 24 hours in a mixture of olive oil and spices such as paprika, cumin, coriander, allspice,

CHICKEN SHAWARMA

turmeric, chili powder, and cardamom, plus hard-to-find Middle Eastern seasonings such as sumac and za'atar (a spice blend that includes herbs and sesame seeds). Wanting to keep my recipe not only easy but also pantry-friendly, I did a series of tests to eliminate spices until I was left with just paprika and cumin. These two spices, along with olive oil, salt, and pepper, gave the chicken a bold, aromatic, and smoky profile. And the spices provided plenty of flavor when tossed with the chicken just prior to broiling—no marinating necessary. After 20 minutes of broiling on the upper-middle oven rack, the chicken was cooked perfectly: deeply charred on the outside, moist and tender within.

To finish the shawarma, I let the chicken rest for 5 minutes and then sliced it thin. As I was squeezing lemon over the top, it occurred to me that I could deepen the lemon's flavor by broiling lemon halves with the chicken. This trick worked wonders, lending both brightness and additional smoky depth. With an easy cabbage-parsley slaw, some sliced tomatoes, diced cucumbers, and a lemony yogurt sauce to drizzle over all of it, I finally had the shawarma I'd been so badly craving. And it's fast enough for a weeknight.

ALLI BERKEY, *Cook's Country*

Chicken Shawarma

SERVES 4 TO 6

If you're using table salt, cut the amounts in this recipe in half.

- 1 **small head red cabbage (1¼ pounds), cored and sliced very thin (6 cups)**
- ½ **cup fresh parsley leaves**
- 6 **tablespoons extra-virgin olive oil**
  Kosher salt and pepper
- 1 **cup plain whole-milk yogurt**
- 2 **tablespoons lemon juice plus 1 lemon**
- 2 **garlic cloves, minced**
- 2½ **pounds boneless, skinless chicken thighs, trimmed**
- 2 **teaspoons paprika**
- 2 **teaspoons ground cumin**
- 3 **plum tomatoes, cored and sliced thin**
- ½ **English cucumber, cut into ½-inch dice**
  Pita bread, warmed

1. Combine cabbage, parsley, ¼ cup oil, and 1 teaspoon salt in bowl; set aside. Combine yogurt, lemon juice, garlic, ¾ teaspoon salt, and ½ teaspoon pepper in second bowl; set aside.

2. Adjust oven rack 6 inches from broiler element and heat broiler. Line rimmed baking sheet with aluminum foil and set wire rack in sheet.

3. Pat chicken dry with paper towels. Combine chicken, paprika, cumin, 2 teaspoons salt, ½ teaspoon pepper, and remaining 2 tablespoons oil in large bowl.

4. Place chicken in single layer on prepared wire rack, smooth sides down. Trim ends from lemon, then cut lemon in half. Place lemon halves cut side up on rack. Broil until chicken is well browned and registers at least 175 degrees, 16 to 20 minutes, rotating sheet halfway through broiling. Let rest for 5 minutes.

5. Slice chicken into thin strips and transfer to platter. Squeeze juice from 1 lemon half over chicken. Squeeze juice from remaining lemon half into cabbage mixture and stir to combine. Transfer cabbage mixture to platter with chicken. Arrange tomatoes and cucumber on platter. Serve with yogurt sauce and warm pita.

SHRIMP PO' BOYS

☑ WHY THIS RECIPE WORKS: For a crunchy coating on our shrimp, we relied on a three-step process. First, we tossed them in a dry mixture of flour, cornmeal, and Creole seasoning. Next, we dipped them in beaten eggs with a bit of the dry mixture added. Finally, we again dredged them in the flour mixture. This breading process allowed more batter to stick to the shrimp, maximizing crunchiness. We let the coated shrimp rest in the refrigerator before frying them to ensure that the batter didn't slough off during cooking. Store-bought Creole seasoning gave the coating a subtle spicy kick. Lightly toasting the sub rolls before building our sandwiches gave them the traditional crunch of New Orleans–style French bread.

The first so-called poor boy sandwiches served in New Orleans were made with sliced beef and gravy, but the idea was ripe for improvisation—not just with the name (it was soon shortened to "po' boy") but with the fillings, too. One version, stuffed with crunchy, flavorful fried shrimp and tons of fixings, became especially popular.

SHRIMP PO' BOYS

I set out to create a sandwich that would deliver a satisfying range of spicy-savory New Orleans flavors. The first trick was to nail the shrimp. Simply coating the shrimp using the typical three-step method (tossing them in a bit of seasoned flour to create a dry surface, then dunking them in beaten egg, and then adding another layer of seasoned flour) before frying them in hot oil gave me tender shrimp with lightly crispy exteriors. But I didn't want lightly crispy, I wanted crunchy. We've added cornmeal to similar seasoned-flour coatings on chicken in the past, so I gave it a try here. And it worked—sort of. The shrimp were crunchier, but the coating was now sliding off the shrimp.

A colleague suggested bolstering the beaten egg with a bit of the seasoned flour to create a slightly more paste-like mixture. Doing so—and then giving the fully coated shrimp a 30-minute rest in the refrigerator before frying them—helped the coating adhere to the shrimp. And jazzing up the flour dredge with a Creole spice mix added an extra flavor punch.

No shrimp po' boy is complete without a super-flavorful dressing, so I created a simple rémoulade by stirring mayonnaise together with sharp horseradish, savory Worcestershire sauce, some piquant hot sauce, and ground pepper. I slathered fresh sub rolls with sauce on both sides and piled them high with shrimp, lettuce, tomatoes, and briny pickle chips: These sandwiches won't leave any po' boy hungry.

ALLI BERKEY, *Cook's Country*

Shrimp Po' Boys

SERVES 4

Use refrigerated prepared horseradish, not the shelf-stable kind, which contains preservatives and additives. Frank's RedHot Original Cayenne Pepper Sauce is best here. Use a Dutch oven that holds 6 quarts or more. Do not refrigerate the breaded shrimp for longer than 30 minutes, or the coating will be too wet. It may seem like you're spreading a lot of rémoulade on the rolls, but it will be absorbed by the other ingredients.

RÉMOULADE

- ⅔ cup mayonnaise
- 2 tablespoons prepared horseradish
- 1 tablespoon Worcestershire sauce
- 1 tablespoon hot sauce
- ¼ teaspoon pepper

SHRIMP

- 2 cups all-purpose flour
- ¼ cup cornmeal
- 2 tablespoons Creole seasoning
- 4 large eggs
- 1 pound medium-large shrimp (31 to 40 per pound), peeled, deveined, and tails removed
- 2 quarts peanut or vegetable oil
- 4 (8-inch) Italian sub rolls, split lengthwise and toasted
- 2 cups shredded iceberg lettuce
- 2 large tomatoes, cored and sliced thin
- 1 cup dill pickle chips

1. FOR THE RÉMOULADE: Whisk all ingredients together in bowl. Set aside.

2. FOR THE SHRIMP: Set wire rack in rimmed baking sheet. Whisk flour, cornmeal, and Creole seasoning together in shallow dish. Whisk eggs and ½ cup flour mixture together in second shallow dish.

3. Place half of shrimp in flour mixture and toss to thoroughly coat. Shake off excess flour mixture, dip shrimp into egg mixture, then return to flour mixture, pressing gently to adhere. Transfer shrimp to prepared wire rack. Repeat with remaining half of shrimp. Refrigerate shrimp for at least 15 minutes or up to 30 minutes.

4. Line large plate with triple layer of paper towels. Add oil to large Dutch oven until it measures about 1½ inches deep and heat over medium-high heat to 375 degrees. Carefully add half of shrimp to oil. Cook, stirring occasionally, until golden brown, about 4 minutes. Using slotted spoon or spider skimmer, transfer shrimp to prepared plate. Return oil to 375 degrees and repeat with remaining shrimp.

NOTES FROM THE TEST KITCHEN

CREOLE SEASONING

Recipes for Louisiana spice blends vary in name, but whether called Cajun or Creole (the terms are often used interchangeably), most contain paprika, garlic, thyme, salt, pepper, and cayenne. In taste tests, we preferred saltier, spicier products and those that stuck to traditional paprika-heavy and garlic-forward notes. Our favorite is **Tony Chachere's Original Creole Seasoning**. It's "vibrant" and "zesty," with strong notes of garlic and red pepper, a "punch of heat," and a "slightly sweet" aftertaste.

5. Spread rémoulade evenly on both cut sides of each roll. Divide lettuce, tomatoes, pickle chips, and shrimp evenly among rolls. Serve.

CHORIZO AND POTATO TACOS

✔ **WHY THIS RECIPE WORKS:** Juicy, highly seasoned Mexican chorizo is the key to these classic tacos, but it can be hard to find, so we devised a quick method for making our own. We started by toasting ancho chile powder, paprika, and other spices in oil to intensify their flavors, and then we mixed ground pork into the spiced oil along with some cider vinegar. We cooked the mixture in a skillet and added parboiled diced potatoes to absorb the flavorful juices as they finished cooking. Mashing some of the potatoes and mixing them into the filling made it more cohesive. A bright yet creamy puree of tomatillos, avocado, cilantro, and jalapeños complemented the richness of the filling.

The Mexican tradition of pairing chorizo with potatoes as a taco filling may sound odd to the uninitiated, but it's pretty ingenious. When fried, Mexican chorizo falls into crumbles, producing fragrant red juices that bathe the meat in spice, fat, and vinegar. The potatoes tidily absorb the chorizo drippings, perfectly dispersing and diffusing the flavor, so the effect is pleasantly piquant rather than overpowering.

Mexican chorizo is a rare commodity in my neighborhood, but that didn't mean I couldn't make my own chorizo and potato tacos. It simply meant that I'd have to start by making my own chorizo.

Since I needed only 8 ounces of sausage, I started with ground pork instead of the pork butt often used. For my small batch, store-bought ancho chile powder seemed more sensible than the traditional whole dried chiles. I also added paprika for color, a bit of sugar and salt, garlic, coriander, dried oregano, cinnamon, allspice, and cayenne. Lastly, I mixed in cider vinegar for tartness. The result was almost overwhelming—spicy, salty, and pleasantly sour—just as it's supposed to be.

In anticipation of this moment, I had already parboiled a pound of peeled, diced Yukon Gold potatoes. I mixed them into the chorizo until they were stained red and then let the mixture finish cooking while I focused on the accompaniments.

It was a perfect opportunity to try my hand at *guacamole taquero*, the simple creamy, tangy taco-shop green sauce. I simply pureed raw tomatillos, avocado, jalapeños, cilantro, lime juice, garlic, and salt. I scooped some of the potato and chorizo mixture into a warmed tortilla, spooned on some sauce, and took a bite. One-third of the filling landed on my shoe.

Undeterred, I mashed some of the potatoes in the skillet and stirred them into the mixture, which made it more cohesive. Problem solved. With tacos this good, I was determined not to sacrifice a bit.

ANDREA GEARY, *Cook's Illustrated*

Chorizo and Potato Tacos

SERVES 4

If you can purchase a good-quality Mexican-style chorizo, skip step 2 and cook the chorizo as directed in step 3. The raw onion complements the soft, rich taco filling, so we do not recommend omitting it. For a spicier sauce, use two jalapeño chiles.

FILLING

- 1 pound Yukon Gold potatoes, peeled and cut into ½-inch chunks
- Salt and pepper
- 3 tablespoons vegetable oil
- 1 tablespoon ancho chile powder
- 1 tablespoon paprika
- 1½ teaspoons ground coriander
- 1½ teaspoons dried oregano
- ¼ teaspoon ground cinnamon
- Pinch cayenne pepper
- Pinch ground allspice
- 3 tablespoons cider vinegar
- 1½ teaspoons sugar
- 1 garlic clove, minced
- 8 ounces ground pork

SAUCE

- 8 ounces tomatillos, husks and stems removed, rinsed well, dried, and cut into 1-inch pieces
- 1 avocado, halved, pitted, and cut into 1-inch pieces
- 1–2 jalapeño chiles, stemmed, seeded, and chopped
- ¼ cup chopped fresh cilantro leaves and stems
- 1 tablespoon lime juice
- 1 garlic clove, minced
- ¾ teaspoon salt

CHORIZO AND POTATO TACOS

12 (6-inch) corn tortillas, warmed

Finely chopped white onion

Fresh cilantro leaves

Lime wedges

1. FOR THE FILLING: Bring 4 cups water to boil in 12-inch nonstick skillet over high heat. Add potatoes and 1 teaspoon salt. Reduce heat to medium, cover, and cook until potatoes are just tender, 3 to 5 minutes. Drain potatoes and set aside. Wipe skillet clean with paper towels.

2. Combine oil, chile powder, paprika, coriander, oregano, cinnamon, cayenne, allspice, ¾ teaspoon salt, and ½ teaspoon pepper in now-empty skillet. Cook over medium heat, stirring constantly, until mixture is bubbling and fragrant. Off heat, carefully stir in vinegar, sugar, and garlic (mixture will sputter). Let stand until steam subsides and skillet cools slightly, about 5 minutes. Add pork to skillet. Mash and mix with rubber spatula until spice mixture is evenly incorporated into pork.

3. Return skillet to medium-high heat and cook, mashing and stirring until pork has broken into fine crumbles and juices are bubbling, about 3 minutes.

4. Stir in potatoes, cover, and reduce heat to low. Cook until potatoes are fully softened and have soaked up most of pork juices, 6 to 8 minutes, stirring halfway through cooking. Off heat, using spatula, mash approximately one-eighth of potatoes. Stir mixture until mashed potatoes are evenly distributed. Cover and keep warm.

5. FOR THE SAUCE: Process all ingredients in food processor until smooth, about 1 minute, scraping down sides of bowl as needed. Transfer to serving bowl.

6. FOR THE TACOS: Spoon filling into center of each tortilla and serve, passing sauce, onion, cilantro, and lime wedges separately.

NOTES FROM THE TEST KITCHEN

MAKE A DOUBLE BATCH

Our recipe calls for 8 ounces of ground pork. But since ground pork is often sold in 1-pound packages, we like to make a double batch of chorizo and freeze half for a later batch of tacos. Simply double all the ingredients and let the spice mixture cool fully before stirring it into the pork. The uncooked chorizo can be frozen for up to 6 months.

NEW ENGLAND PORK PIES

WHY THIS RECIPE WORKS: The hallmark of these individual pies is their juicy, soft, and extra-savory pork filling. To achieve this, we combined ground pork with finely ground Ritz Crackers, which bound the pork together, held in moisture to keep it juicy, and added enough fat to give it an ultratender texture. A mixture of melted butter, sour cream, and an egg pulsed into flour yielded a smooth, pliable dough that baked up into a rich, crumbly-yet-sturdy crust. We divided some of the dough into six ⅓-cup portions and then rolled each portion into a round before fitting them into individual ramekins. For the pie tops, we rolled out the remaining dough, stamped out circles, and sealed the pies by rolling the edges up into a rope-like border. We made a quick gravy by thickening our favorite beef broth with a bit of cornstarch; once the pies were baked to golden brown, we poured the gravy in through the vent holes.

The stout little pies from Hartley's Original Pork Pies in Somerset, Massachusetts, cut a charming figure with their straight, sturdy sides and golden crimped crowns. The crumbly crusts contain a deeply seasoned, savory, juicy filling of ground pork and gravy.

Translating the pies to a home kitchen, though, was a tall order. First, I needed a baking vessel to mimic Hartley's 100-year-old individual cast-iron pie tins. Muffin tins were too small and the wrong shape. Larger 6-ounce ceramic ramekins proved perfect in both size and shape, yielding evenly golden-brown sides and bottoms.

For the dough, I processed flour with melted butter to create the crumbly crust I wanted. Sour cream added richness and flavor without compromising texture, and an egg provided structure.

Simply pressing portions of dough into the ramekins didn't work well. Rolling and cutting the dough to fit was a better route. For the bottoms and sides, I measured ⅓ cup of dough for each pie, rolled each portion into a circle of even thickness, and then fit each one into a ramekin. For the tops, I rolled out the remaining dough and stamped out circles with an inverted ramekin. Once the pies were filled, I placed the circles on top and rolled up the overhanging dough to seal the pies.

Grinding my own pork was off the table, but because preground pork is relatively lean, I suspected I'd need a panade (a mixture of bread or bread crumbs and liquid, usually milk) to help it hold on to moisture. After a usually milk) to help it hold on to moisture. After a few unsuccessful tests, a colleague suggested ditching the panade for buttery crushed Ritz Crackers. The extra fat in the crackers helped the meat stay supple.

At Hartley's, cooks pour flavorful pork gravy through the pie's vent holes for a juicy finish. To mimic this step, I thickened our favorite beef broth with a bit of cornstarch.

My pork pies released easily from the greased ramekins. When these proud little packages of ultrasavory, supermoist filling in a buttery crust impressed my tasters, I knew I'd done Hartley's justice.

CECELIA JENKINS, *Cook's Country*

New England Pork Pies

SERVES 6

You will need six 6- to 7-ounce ramekins, measuring 3½ inches wide and about 2 inches deep, for this recipe.

DOUGH

- 12 tablespoons unsalted butter, melted and cooled
- ½ cup sour cream
- 1 large egg, plus 1 lightly beaten large egg for brushing
- 3 cups (15 ounces) all-purpose flour
- ½ teaspoon salt

FILLING

- 22 Ritz Crackers
- 1½ pounds ground pork
- 1¼ teaspoons salt
- 1¼ teaspoons pepper

GRAVY

- 1½ cups beef broth
- 1 tablespoon cornstarch

1. FOR THE DOUGH: Whisk melted butter, sour cream, and 1 egg in bowl until combined. Process flour and salt in food processor until combined, about 3 seconds. Add butter mixture and pulse until dough forms, about 10 pulses, scraping down sides of bowl as needed. Turn out dough onto counter and form into 4-inch disk. Wrap disk tightly in plastic wrap and refrigerate for at least 30 minutes or up to 24 hours. (If chilling longer than 30 minutes, allow dough to soften on counter for 30 minutes before rolling.)

2. FOR THE FILLING: Meanwhile, adjust oven rack to middle position and heat oven to 400 degrees. In clean, dry workbowl, process crackers until finely ground, about 20 seconds. Combine pork, salt, pepper, and cracker crumbs in bowl and knead with your hands until fully combined. Refrigerate until ready to use.

3. Using ⅓ cup dry measuring cup, portion out 6 pieces of dough (3½ ounces each); set aside and cover with plastic. Roll remaining dough into 11-inch circle on well-floured counter. Using inverted 6- to 7-ounce ramekin as guide, cut 6 circles for tops of pies, rerolling scraps if necessary. Set tops aside and cover with plastic.

4. Spray six 6- to 7-ounce ramekins with vegetable oil spray. Roll each ⅓-cup dough portion into 7-inch circle on well-floured counter. Line ramekins with 7-inch dough circles, letting excess dough hang over rims. As dough pleats along insides of ramekins, press pleats flat to even out thickness.

5. Divide filling among dough-lined ramekins, about heaping ½ cup each. Place reserved dough circles over filling. Roll overhanging bottom dough inward and crimp together with top dough.

6. Brush tops of pies generously with beaten egg. Using paring knife, poke hole in center of each pie to create ½-inch-wide vent. Place ramekins on parchment paper–lined rimmed baking sheet. Bake until tops of pies are deep golden brown, 40 to 45 minutes, rotating sheet halfway through baking. Let pies cool for 10 minutes.

7. FOR THE GRAVY: Whisk broth and cornstarch in small saucepan until cornstarch is dissolved. Bring to boil over medium-high heat and cook until thickened, about 30 seconds. Remove from heat and transfer to 2-cup liquid measuring cup.

8. Lift pies out of ramekins, loosening edges with paring knife if necessary (do not invert; juices inside are hot). If vent holes have shrunk during baking, widen with paring knife so gravy can be poured in. Pour gravy into vent hole of each pie until pie is filled (you will have extra gravy for serving). Let pies cool for 20 minutes. Serve, passing remaining gravy separately.

TO MAKE AHEAD: At end of step 5, poke vent holes in pies but do not brush with egg. Wrap pies tightly in plastic wrap and freeze for up to 1 month. When ready to bake, do not thaw pies. Unwrap frozen pies and proceed with step 6, extending baking time to about 1¼ hours.

NEW ENGLAND PORK PIES

ROASTED BEEF TENDERLOIN

✓ **WHY THIS RECIPE WORKS:** We set out to create a foolproof recipe that would lessen the anxiety of cooking this showstopping roast. Salting the trimmed beef tenderloin overnight seasoned it throughout, giving it more intense flavor. Roasting it in a low 250-degree oven ensured even cooking and gave us a larger safety net to prevent overcooking. Cutting the tenderloin in half before searing it in a piping-hot skillet made it easy to fit in the pan and ensured a deep brown crust. With our roast cooked to perfection, we decided to pair it with a bold, complex red wine sauce. Browning beef stew meat added savory, beefy depth to the sauce. Shallot and a bit of sugar balanced some of the tannins from a hefty amount of earthy red wine, and whisking in cornstarch and extra butter to finish gave the sauce an unctuous, velvety texture.

Beef tenderloin's many virtues are well known: It looks impressive on the table, it's luxuriously tender, and it cooks relatively quickly. Plus, with its uniform shape and no bones, it's a breeze to carve. But it's an expensive cut, and there's not much leeway between just right and overcooked. I set out to create a foolproof recipe that would take the anxiety and guesswork out of cooking this showstopping, crowd-pleasing roast.

You can buy a whole beef tenderloin either trimmed or untrimmed; untrimmed tenderloins are cheaper per pound, but the fatty side muscle called the chain, any exterior fat, and the silverskin must all be removed before roasting it (see "Five Steps to Prep a Tenderloin," page 114). I started with a 5-pound trimmed whole beef tenderloin, which provides enough meat to feed a holiday crowd.

Salting the tenderloin overnight seasoned it throughout, giving it more intense flavor. After extensive testing, I opted to roast the meat gently in a low 250-degree oven to ensure that it cooked evenly. The relatively low heat also provided a comforting safety net—an extra 5 unplanned minutes at 250 degrees can do much less damage than those same 5 minutes at 450 degrees. Pulling the roast when the center registered 125 degrees (and letting it rest for 30 minutes before carving) gave me perfectly moist, pink, medium-rare slices. But the outside of the roast was a pale gray—not exactly a festive (or appetizing) holiday color. I wanted a nicely browned, burnished crust that would add flavor and visual appeal.

I tried broiling the roast, but in the time it took to brown, the top third of the meat overcooked. I tested a few tricks to enhance browning during roasting, including coating the roast with butter, sugar, baking soda, or soy sauce. I even rubbed one tenderloin with mayonnaise. But none of these hacks really worked.

I wanted to sear the roast in a hot skillet on the stovetop to brown it after roasting, but a whole tenderloin doesn't fit in a skillet.

The solution? I sliced the roast in half before beginning the cooking process so I could later fit the pieces side by side in a 12-inch skillet. This method also offered an additional advantage: With two pieces, I had more control over how each one was cooked—I could cook one piece to rare and the other to medium-rare, for instance. And cutting the tenderloin in half actually made it easier to bring it to the table but kept it looking impressive.

And there you have it: a simple yet highly refined and foolproof method for a tender and juicy holiday roast tenderloin. To take this roast over the top, I made a rich, glossy red wine sauce that takes a bit of work (and some extra meat if you bought a trimmed tenderloin) but is worth every minute you put into it.

MORGAN BOLLING, *Cook's Country*

Classic Roast Beef Tenderloin

SERVES 12 TO 16

The roast must be salted and refrigerated for at least 12 hours before cooking. If you're buying an untrimmed tenderloin, be sure it weighs 6 to 7 pounds. Serve with Red Wine Sauce (recipe follows), if desired.

- 1 **(5-pound) trimmed whole beef tenderloin**
  Kosher salt and pepper
- 2 **tablespoons vegetable oil**

1. Cut tenderloin crosswise at base of head to make 2 roasts. Using kitchen twine, tie head at 1-inch intervals. Tuck tail end of second roast underneath by 3 to 5 inches to create more even shape. Tie tucked portion with kitchen twine at 1-inch intervals to secure.

2. Place 1 roast on large sheet of plastic wrap and sprinkle all over with 1 tablespoon salt. Wrap tightly in double layer of plastic. Repeat with remaining roast and 1 tablespoon salt. Refrigerate roasts for at least 12 hours or up to 24 hours.

CLASSIC ROAST BEEF TENDERLOIN

FIVE STEPS TO PREP A TENDERLOIN (OR TWO IF YOU PURCHASED A TRIMMED TENDERLOIN)

Buying an untrimmed tenderloin can save you money, but it requires a little more prep work. Trimmed tenderloins are pricier and easier to prep. If you're using an untrimmed tenderloin, start with step 1; if you have a trimmed tenderloin, start with step 4.

1. TRIM FAT Place roast on cutting board with wider end (head) on left. Pat dry with paper towels, then pull away (cutting with boning knife as needed) and discard outer layer of fat.

2. REMOVE CHAIN Starting at thin end (tail) of roast, pull fatty chain away from side of roast, slicing through fat with boning knife as needed to detach it.

3. REMOVE SILVERSKIN Insert boning knife under silverskin on tail end of roast. Angle knife slightly upward and use gentle sawing motion to remove silverskin.

4. CUT IN TWO After removing any excess fat or remaining silverskin, slice tenderloin at base of head into 2 roasts. Tuck end of tail piece under itself.

5. TIE ROASTS Tie head and tail ends at even intervals with twine.

3. Adjust oven rack to middle position and heat oven to 250 degrees. Set wire rack in rimmed baking sheet. Season roasts with pepper and place on prepared wire rack. Roast until meat registers 125 degrees (for medium-rare) or 130 degrees (for medium), 1 hour 20 minutes to 1 hour 40 minutes for tail-end roast and 1 hour 40 minutes to 2 hours for head-end roast. Transfer roasts to carving board, tent with aluminum foil, and let rest for 20 minutes.

4. Pat roasts dry with paper towels. Heat oil in 12-inch nonstick skillet over medium-high heat until just smoking. Add both roasts and sear on all sides until well browned, 5 to 7 minutes. Transfer roasts to carving board, remove twine, and slice ½ inch thick. Serve.

Red Wine Sauce

MAKES ABOUT 2 CUPS

Medium-bodied red wines, such as Côtes du Rhône or Pinot Noir, are best for this recipe. You can substitute chain meat trimmed from a beef tenderloin for the stew meat called for here.

5	tablespoons unsalted butter, cut into 5 pieces and chilled
12	ounces beef stew meat, cut into 1-inch pieces
2	tablespoons tomato paste
2	cups red wine
2	cups beef broth
1	shallot, sliced thin
2	tablespoons soy sauce
1½	tablespoons sugar
6	sprigs fresh thyme
2½	teaspoons cornstarch
1	tablespoon water
	Salt and pepper

1. Melt 1 tablespoon butter in large saucepan over medium-high heat. Add beef and cook, stirring occasionally, until well browned and fond forms on bottom of saucepan, 10 to 12 minutes.

2. Add tomato paste and cook until darkened in color and fragrant, about 1 minute. Stir in wine, broth, shallot, soy sauce, sugar, and thyme sprigs and bring to boil, scraping up any browned bits. Cook until reduced to 4 cups, 12 to 15 minutes.

3. Strain sauce through fine-mesh strainer set over bowl; discard solids. Return sauce to saucepan and bring to boil over medium-high heat. Dissolve cornstarch in water. Whisk cornstarch mixture into sauce and boil until slightly thickened, about 30 seconds. Reduce heat to low and whisk in remaining 4 tablespoons butter, 1 piece at a time. Season with salt and pepper to taste. Remove from heat and cover to keep warm.

GRILLED SKIRT STEAK

✔ **WHY THIS RECIPE WORKS:** For this recipe, we chose the outside skirt steak, which is 3 to 4 inches wide, and avoided the wider, far less tender inside skirt steak. To make the most of this steak's ample surface area, we submerged it in a citrusy, garlicky mojo marinade. Soy sauce in the marinade seasoned the meat, and its glutamates enhanced the meat's beefiness. We rubbed a thin coating of baking soda over the steaks before grilling them over high heat to guarantee great browning. To emphasize the mojo flavor, we boiled the marinade to make it food-safe and turned it into a sauce that we drizzled over the steaks.

Back when I was a line cook at Craigie Street Bistrot in Cambridge, Massachusetts, we had a nightly routine involving skirt steak. The end pieces were never plated because they were too small to show off the beautifully cooked beef, so the chef habitually tossed them into a "meat bucket." At the end of the night, the tidbits were heated up under the broiler for a postshift snack. Trust me when I tell you (after many, many bites) that this fatty cut is intensely beefy, tender, and juicy—a true cook's treat.

Skirt steak is long, narrow, and only ½ to 1 inch thick. Because it's so thin, you need to cook it over high heat to ensure that the outside is well browned by the time the interior is tender and juicy. That makes a grill, which is easy to get blisteringly hot, the best tool for the job. As a bonus, a large grill grate can accommodate all the ribbonlike steaks at the same time instead of in batches.

Skirt steak is also a great candidate for a marinade. In the test kitchen, we often shy away from marinating meat because the flavorings don't penetrate much beyond the surface of a thick, smooth cut. But because skirt steak is so thin, with loose, open fibers and lots of nooks and crannies, a marinade can have a big effect.

I knew exactly what I wanted to bathe my steaks in: a garlicky, citrusy, Cuban-style mojo that would really stand up to the rich, buttery beef. Once I'd perfected the marinade and the steak cookery, I planned on whipping up a complementary sauce to drizzle onto the meat.

Skirt steaks are often rolled up for packaging because when they are unrolled, they can be nearly 2 feet long. I divided 2 pounds of steak (enough to serve four to six people) into 6- to 8-inch lengths.

Then came the marinade: I stirred together ½ cup of orange juice and 2 tablespoons of lime juice (my substitute for the difficult-to-find sour orange juice traditionally used in mojo) and added the usual seasonings: ground cumin, dried oregano, plenty of minced garlic, and a few red pepper flakes. I also made sure to add a good amount of salt—1½ teaspoons for the 2 pounds of meat. The salt would not only season the meat, it would also dissolve some proteins and loosen the bundles of muscle fibers, making the steak more tender, and hold in water to keep the meat moist.

I pulled out a 13 by 9-inch baking dish, which would be a good vessel for soaking the steaks with minimal overlapping. I refrigerated the steaks for an hour, flipping them at the 30-minute mark to make sure both sides got coated with marinade.

When I removed the steaks from the marinade, I thoroughly patted them dry with paper towels since any excess moisture would inhibit browning; I then rubbed them with a light coating of oil. Over a hot fire (created by distributing 6 quarts of lit coals evenly over half the grill) the steaks were cooked to medium (130 degrees) in 6 to 8 minutes. Although we bring most steaks to medium-rare (125 degrees), we have found that the tougher muscle fibers of skirt steak need to hit 130 degrees before they shrink and loosen enough to turn perfectly tender.

I gathered my colleagues grillside to have a taste, and the feedback rolled in: The mojo flavor was coming through beautifully, but the steaks could taste even beefier. Also, the browning was good but not great.

I had ideas about how to address both problems, so I reached for the two skirt steaks that had arrived in that morning's delivery. I was surprised to see that one was almost twice as wide as the other. But they looked similar otherwise, so I carried on.

GRILLED MOJO-MARINATED SKIRT STEAK

This time I added a little soy sauce to the mojo marinade (to compensate, I halved the amount of salt). Soy sauce can be a secret weapon in marinades: Its salt seasons, and its glutamates enhance savory flavor.

Once the steaks were out of the marinade and patted dry, I incorporated an ingredient for better browning: baking soda. Added to the oil I had been rubbing onto the steaks, baking soda would help create more substantial browning by raising the meat's pH. The higher its pH, the better meat is able to hold on to water, so it browns instead of releasing the moisture onto the grill grates and creating steam. A higher pH also speeds up the Maillard reaction, making the treated meat brown even better and more quickly.

I was pleased to see the steaks rapidly develop a deep sear on the grill. This was a signal that they were likely done cooking, so I slid them to the cooler side of the grill to take their temperature (their thinness made temping them on the hotter side risky because they could easily overcook). Sure enough, they registered 130 degrees, so I gave them a 10-minute rest to allow the juices to redistribute throughout the meat. As I sampled a few slices, I was happy to find that the meat was not just deeply seasoned but also had an even beefier flavor than before, thanks to the umami-rich soy sauce.

However, the steaks' texture was a different story: Even though I'd soaked both the narrow and the wide steaks in the same marinade and cooked them on the same grill to precisely 130 degrees, the narrow steak was much more tender than the wide one. It was only after speaking to several butchers that I understood why: It turns out that there are two types of skirt steak—the narrow outside skirt and the wide inside skirt—that come from separate parts of the cow and therefore have markedly different textures.

I prepared one more batch, making sure to use outside skirt steaks. While the meat marinated, I started gathering citrus, garlic, and spices for the mojo sauce I'd been planning. But wait: All the ingredients I needed were already in the leftover marinade. Why not reuse it? I poured it from the baking pan into a saucepan, brought it to a boil to make it food-safe, and took a taste. It needed richness and a little extra acidity to become a sauce, so I stirred in a little lime juice and extra-virgin olive oil. I also tossed in orange and lime zests to give the sauce more of the bright, tropical flavor typical of sour oranges.

Once the steaks were off the grill and had rested, I carefully sliced them against the grain and at an angle before drizzling on the mojo sauce. My favorite steak had now realized its full potential: The beautifully seared meat was rich, well seasoned, juicy, and tender, and the vibrant sauce played off of it beautifully.

LAN LAM, *Cook's Illustrated*

Grilled Mojo-Marinated Skirt Steak
SERVES 4 TO 6

Skirt steaks come from two different muscles and are sometimes labeled as inside skirt steak or outside skirt steak. The more desirable outside skirt steak measures 3 to 4 inches wide and ½ to 1 inch thick. Avoid the inside skirt steak, which typically measures 5 to 7 inches wide and ¼ to ½ inch thick, as it is very chewy. Skirt steak is most tender when cooked to medium (130 to 135 degrees). Thin steaks cook very quickly, so we recommend using an instant-read thermometer for a quick and accurate measurement.

6	garlic cloves, minced
2	tablespoons soy sauce
1	teaspoon grated lime zest plus ¼ cup juice (2 limes)
1	teaspoon ground cumin
1	teaspoon dried oregano
	Salt
½	teaspoon grated orange zest plus ½ cup juice
¼	teaspoon red pepper flakes
2	pounds skirt steak, trimmed and cut with grain into 6- to 8-inch-long steaks
2	tablespoons extra-virgin olive oil
1	teaspoon baking soda

1. Combine garlic, soy sauce, 2 tablespoons lime juice, cumin, oregano, ¾ teaspoon salt, orange juice, and pepper flakes in 13 by 9-inch baking dish. Place steaks in dish. Flip steaks to coat both sides with marinade. Cover and refrigerate for 1 hour, flipping steaks halfway through refrigerating.

2. Remove steaks from marinade and transfer marinade to small saucepan. Pat steaks dry with paper towels. Combine 1 tablespoon oil and baking soda in small bowl. Rub oil mixture evenly onto both sides of each steak.

3. Bring marinade to boil over high heat and boil for 30 seconds. Transfer to bowl and stir in lime zest, orange zest, remaining 2 tablespoons lime juice, and remaining 1 tablespoon oil. Set aside sauce.

4A. FOR A CHARCOAL GRILL: About 25 minutes before grilling, open bottom vent completely. Light large chimney starter filled with charcoal briquettes (6 quarts). When top coals are partially covered with ash, pour evenly over half of grill. Set cooking grate in place, cover, and open lid vent completely. Heat grill until hot, about 5 minutes.

4B. FOR A GAS GRILL: Turn all burners to high, cover, and heat grill until hot, about 15 minutes. Turn off 1 burner (if using grill with more than 2 burners, turn off burner farthest from primary burner) and leave other burner(s) on high.

5. Clean and oil cooking grate. Cook steaks on hotter side of grill until well browned and meat registers 130 to 135 degrees (for medium), 2 to 4 minutes per side. (Move steaks to cooler side of grill before taking temperature to prevent them from overcooking.) Transfer steaks to cutting board, tent with aluminum foil, and let rest for 10 minutes. Cut steaks on bias against grain into ½-inch-thick slices. Arrange slices on serving platter, drizzle with 2 tablespoons sauce, and serve, passing extra sauce separately.

NOTES FROM THE TEST KITCHEN

SKIRT (STEAK) SHOPPING
There are two types of skirt steak: inside and outside. The inside skirt comes from the transverse abdominal muscle and is rather tough; the more desirable outside skirt comes from the diaphragm and is quite tender.

BUY THE OUTSIDE SKIRT
3 to 4 inches wide, ½ to 1 inch thick, quite tender

AVOID THE INSIDE SKIRT
5 to 7 inches wide, ¼ to ½ inch thick, very chewy

SMOKED STEAK

✔ **WHY THIS RECIPE WORKS:** Smoking steaks can lend them complexity, but most recipes overwhelm the meat's delicate flavor with too much smoke. We found that the key was using a small amount of wood chips and cooking the steaks quickly over direct heat so that they were just kissed with smoke. Since wood chips pack differently, we weighed the chips for more control over the smoke quantity. Salting the steaks for an hour before cooking ensured that the seasoning penetrated below the meat's surface, and coating them with an herb-spice rub lent an extra layer of flavor that complemented the smoke. We also grilled lemons to serve with the steaks for a hit of brightness.

I've always wondered why there isn't a tradition of smoking more cuts of beef. We smoke chicken, turkey, pork, and many kinds of fish, but when it comes to beef, not so much. Sure, there are some notable exceptions, such as Texas-style barbecued ribs and brisket. But why don't we smoke quicker-cooking cuts; for example, steak?

It turns out I'm not the only one to have this thought, as I was able to rustle up a few recipes for smoked steaks. While most called for rib eye or porterhouse, I was more intrigued by those calling for flat-iron steak, a cut we haven't used much in the test kitchen. It's a beefy-tasting steak from the shoulder that's decently marbled and tender and also has the advantage of being relatively inexpensive. Its only drawback is that it can have a slightly mineral flavor. To my mind, that made it a perfect candidate for smoking, as the smoke would camouflage any overly metallic notes and give the steak even more dimension. Since blade steaks are cut from the same part of the cow, I'd make sure my recipe also worked with them for those who can't find flat iron.

Most recipes I found for smoked steak, no matter the cut, took a similar approach, essentially treating the steaks like slow-cooked barbecue. They called for setting up the grill with a hotter and a cooler side by arranging the coals over half the grill and putting an aluminum foil packet of soaked wood chips on the coals. They cooked the steak covered (to trap smoke and direct its flow over the meat) on the cooler side of the grill until it neared its target temperature and then moved it to the hotter side, directly over the coals, to give it a good char on the exterior.

GRILL-SMOKED HERB-RUBBED FLAT-IRON STEAKS

I gave this approach a try and immediately hit two snags: First, cooked to the typical medium-rare, the steak was still chewy. It turns out that flat-iron steak needs to be cooked to medium for the muscle fibers to shrink and loosen enough to be tender. Second, tasters felt that the smoke flavor was overwhelming. I realized that while collagen-rich barbecue cuts (such as brisket) that are cooked far beyond well-done benefit from lots of smoke flavor to give them more complexity, steaks cooked to medium-rare or even medium have a more nuanced flavor that is easily lost with too much smoke.

Over the next few tests, I dialed back the smoke, eventually reducing the wood chips to just 1 cup. Since we've found that wood chips can pack very differently depending on their shape and size, I switched to using a set weight (2½ ounces) to better control the amount of smoke. I also raised the grill's temperature by adding more coals so that the steaks would cook through more quickly, thus lessening their exposure to the smoke. And yet, even with these changes, they were too smoky.

Suddenly, the answer seemed obvious. I shouldn't be following the lead of all those recipes by cooking the steaks over indirect heat like barbecue. I should be cooking them how we normally cook steaks—quickly, over direct heat—but with smoke.

With that in mind, I salted another batch of steaks and let them sit for an hour to ensure that the seasoning penetrated below the surface. In the meantime, I set up the grill. I used a full chimney of charcoal, spreading the coals evenly across half the grill as before. But this time, I topped them off with a packet of wood chips I hadn't soaked. Soaking the chips serves only to delay the onset of smoking; now that I would be grilling for such a short period, I needed the chips to begin smoking right away. I dropped the steaks onto the grate and cooked them directly over the coals, covered, until they reached the 130-degree target for medium, which took just 5 minutes per side.

These steaks were just what I wanted: juicy and kissed with a hint of smoke that enhanced rather than overwhelmed. To complement the smoke flavor, I put together a dry rub featuring thyme, rosemary, fennel seeds, black peppercorns, and red pepper flakes to apply to the steaks just before grilling. For some tempered brightness, I grilled lemon wedges alongside the steaks to serve with them. When I tried swapping in blade steaks, they worked perfectly (folks just had to cut around the line of gristle that runs down the middle).

Now my recipe was perfect on a charcoal grill, but what about gas? Gas grills are less efficient at smoking foods than charcoal grills since they aren't as tightly sealed and don't have vents that can be positioned to help draw smoke over the meat. To give the steaks comparable exposure to smoke in such a short amount of time, I increased the amount of chips to 1½ cups.

Whether I used flat-iron or blade steak, I knew I'd deliver an impressive steak dinner.

ANDREW JANJIGIAN, *Cook's Illustrated*

Grill-Smoked Herb-Rubbed Flat-Iron Steaks
SERVES 4 TO 6

This recipe requires rubbing the steaks with salt and letting them sit at room temperature for 1 hour before cooking. You can substitute blade steaks for the flat-iron steaks, if desired. We like both cuts cooked to medium (130 to 135 degrees). We like hickory chips in this recipe, but other kinds of wood chips will work. Gas grills are not as efficient at smoking meat as charcoal grills, so we recommend using 1½ cups of wood chips if using a gas grill.

> 2 teaspoons dried thyme
> 1 teaspoon dried rosemary
> ¾ teaspoon fennel seeds
> ½ teaspoon black peppercorns
> ¼ teaspoon red pepper flakes
> 4 (6- to 8-ounce) flat-iron steaks, ¾ to 1 inch thick, trimmed
> 1 tablespoon kosher salt
> 1-1½ cups (2½-3¾ ounces) wood chips
> Vegetable oil spray
> 2 lemons, quartered lengthwise

1. Grind thyme, rosemary, fennel seeds, peppercorns, and pepper flakes in spice grinder or with mortar and pestle until coarsely ground. Transfer to small bowl. Pat steaks dry with paper towels. Rub steaks evenly on both sides with salt and place on wire rack set in rimmed baking sheet. Let stand at room temperature for 1 hour. (After 30 minutes, prepare grill.)

2. Using large piece of heavy-duty aluminum foil, wrap wood chips (1 cup if using charcoal; 1½ cups if using gas) in 8 by 4½-inch foil packet. (Make sure chips do not poke holes in sides or bottom of packet.) Cut 2 evenly spaced 2-inch slits in top of packet.

3A. FOR A CHARCOAL GRILL: Open bottom vent completely. Light large chimney starter filled with charcoal briquettes (6 quarts). When top coals are partially covered with ash, pour evenly over half of grill. Place wood chip packet on coals. Set cooking grate in place, cover, and open lid vent completely. Heat grill until hot and wood chips are smoking, about 5 minutes.

3B. FOR A GAS GRILL: Remove cooking grate and place wood chip packet directly on primary burner. Set grate in place, turn all burners to high, cover, and heat grill until hot and wood chips are smoking, about 15 minutes. Leave primary burner on high and turn other burner(s) to medium.

4. Clean and oil cooking grate. Sprinkle half of herb rub evenly over 1 side of steaks and press to adhere. Lightly spray herb-rubbed side of steaks with oil spray, about 3 seconds. Flip steaks and repeat process of sprinkling and pressing steaks with remaining herb rub and coating with oil spray on second side.

5. Place lemons and steaks on hotter side of grill, cover (position lid vent over steaks if using charcoal), and cook until lemons and steaks are well browned on both sides and meat registers 130 to 135 degrees (for medium), 4 to 6 minutes per side. (If steaks are fully charred before reaching desired temperature, move to cooler side of grill, cover, and continue to cook.) Transfer lemons and steaks to clean wire rack set in rimmed baking sheet, tent with foil, and let rest for 10 minutes. Slice steaks thin against grain and serve, passing lemons separately.

NOTES FROM THE TEST KITCHEN

THE BEST GRILL TONGS

Good grill tongs let you deftly grab, lift, and turn food without piercing it, and they keep your hands far from the heat. We tested six models, using each to turn asparagus spears, chicken parts, and slabs of ribs. We also used them to open and close hot hinged grill grates and to arrange glowing coals into a banked fire.

Our former winner, the **OXO Good Grips 16" Locking Tongs**, took top marks again. They are light—making them easy to use—and were the shortest in the group, providing good control while still keeping us safe from the heat. Shallow, scalloped pincers with narrow tips securely grasped both large and small items. They performed well in every task and were, simply, a dream to use.

POT ROAST WITH ROSEMARY–RED WINE SIMMERING SAUCE

✓ WHY THIS RECIPE WORKS: Pot roast with a velvety red wine–based sauce is the epitome of a cozy Sunday meal. The sauce that gives pot roast its flavor would usually be made from the meat's braising liquid, but we found that making our flavorful Rosemary–Red Wine Simmering Sauce first and braising the meat right in the sauce had a few benefits. First, the sauce could be made in advance, streamlining the prep. And since the already-flavorful sauce gained even deeper flavor during braising, we found that we could skip the messy step of browning the roasts. Well-marbled chuck-eye roast is our favorite cut for pot roast, and working with two smaller roasts instead of one large one cut down on cooking time. Transferring the covered pot to the oven to braise made for gentle, even, and hands-off cooking. Reserving half of the sauce to stir in at the end of cooking ensured that the concentrated sauce wasn't too potent and provided welcome brightness.

Recently, I've noticed a proliferation of jarred "simmering sauces" or "braising sauces" for sale in markets and specialty stores. The concept behind these sauces is simple: You just pour the sauce into a pot, add whatever meat and vegetables you like, and simmer until everything is cooked through. Sounds easy, right? It is; but many of these sauces are pricey, not readily available at regular supermarkets, and—worst of all—have a dull, one-dimensional flavor. But the idea of a sauce I could make ahead and use later as part of a satisfying one-pot meal was so appealing, I decided to try making my own.

I was particularly intrigued by the comforting American-style sauces that could be used to braise well-marbled cuts of beef. The thought of streamlining a labor-intensive braise by making a sauce ahead of time was too good to pass up. Plus, when it comes to inexpensive stewing and braising cuts, the sauce is what makes the meal, so it was undeniably appealing to have a flavor-packed sauce from the get-go.

Since I wanted a versatile sauce that could be paired with any cut of beef, I opted for a simple yet sophisticated red wine base. I started with the aromatics; onions, carrot, and celery made for a well-rounded backbone. I also added a bit of garlic, a cup and a half each of beef broth and red wine, a bay leaf, and a sprig of rosemary for some earthy notes. I reduced the liquid a bit to soften the vegetables and concentrate the

POT ROAST WITH ROSEMARY–RED WINE SIMMERING SAUCE

flavors, then removed the bay leaf and rosemary sprig before transferring everything to a blender and blitzing it to a velvety smoothness. While pureeing the sauce components might seem like an unusual technique, it was an easy way to make my sauce thick, luxurious, and cohesive—and it meant I could skip the addition of any flavor-dulling flour or the fussy step of straining.

This first attempt was a bit of a disappointment—tasters found the sauce lacking in savoriness, and the wine flavor was a bit harsh. Even though I knew the sauce would reduce more when cooked with the meat, I wanted to make sure it tasted great on its own—I envisioned a versatile sauce that could also be used to dress up simple roasts, mashed potatoes, or root vegetables.

For my next test, I decreased the amount of wine to 1 cup and increased the beef broth to 2 cups to keep the amount of liquid consistent. I also called on two glutamate-rich ingredients we often use in the test kitchen to amp up savory flavor: tomato paste (sautéed briefly with the garlic so that it didn't taste raw) and soy sauce. As I suspected, both gave the sauce more depth.

With the flavor of my sauce perfected, it was now time to incorporate it into a slow-simmering braise. While the possibilities were myriad, I decided to zero in on a perfect pot roast with root vegetables; the complex flavor of the sauce would make it feel composed enough for company but its ready-made ease ensured it was simple enough for a comforting Sunday dinner. I started with a chuck-eye roast, the test kitchen's preferred cut for pot roast, and cut it into two pieces, which would both cut down on cooking time and allow me to remove any large pieces of intramuscular fat. I poured my sauce into a Dutch oven and then nestled in the roasts (since the sauce was so flavorful, I decided to skip the messy and time-consuming step of browning) along with some chunks of carrots, parsnips, and potatoes. I set the oven at 300 degrees and let the pot roast cook in the oven's gentle, even heat for several hours until everything was tender.

The sauce had indeed deepened in flavor with the long braise—so much so that it had overconcentrated and lost much of its pleasant brightness. And despite my trimming the roasts before cooking, the sauce was a bit too greasy.

The greasiness was easy to solve: I simply poured the sauce into a fat separator after braising and let it settle for a few minutes. But what to do about the flavor? In other pot roast recipes, we've reserved some of the wine to stir in at the end of cooking to brighten up the dish. But here, the wine was incorporated into the sauce and taking some out would ruin the sauce's carefully calibrated flavor. I didn't want to do that—the sauce was perfect on its own—but it did give me an idea. What if I waited to add some of the sauce to the pot until after braising?

This worked like a charm. Subsequent tests revealed that I only needed 2 cups of sauce to successfully braise the meat and vegetables. During these tests, I made one more change to the recipe as well: I salted the roasts and let them sit for an hour at room temperature before braising to ensure they were well seasoned throughout. Once the meat and vegetables were cooked, I removed them from the pot so the meat could rest. I brought the defatted braising sauce and the fresh sauce to a quick simmer, added some thyme to reinforce the herbal flavor, and poured it over the sliced beef. With that, my simple yet surprisingly refined braise was a hit.

I ran a few additional storage tests on the sauce by itself, and was thrilled to find that I could keep it in the fridge for up to a week or in the freezer for up to a month. That meant I could have it on hand whenever I wanted it, whether for my new favorite pot roast or any other beef braise I could dream up.

ANNE WOLF, *America's Test Kitchen Books*

Pot Roast with Rosemary–Red Wine Simmering Sauce

SERVES 6 TO 8

Use Yukon Gold potatoes measuring 1 to 2 inches in diameter. If your parsnips are very thick, slice them in half lengthwise first to ensure even cooking.

- 1 (3½- to 4-pound) boneless beef chuck-eye roast, pulled into 2 pieces at natural seam and trimmed of large pieces of fat
  Salt and pepper
- 1 recipe Rosemary–Red Wine Simmering Sauce (recipe follows)
- 1½ pounds small Yukon Gold potatoes, peeled
- 1 pound carrots, peeled and cut into 2-inch lengths
- 1 pound parsnips, peeled and cut into 2-inch lengths
- ¼ teaspoon chopped fresh thyme

1. Season beef with 1½ teaspoons salt, place on wire rack set in rimmed baking sheet, and let sit at room temperature for 1 hour.

2. Adjust oven rack to lower-middle position and heat oven to 300 degrees. Pat beef dry with paper towels and season with pepper. Tie 3 pieces of kitchen twine around each piece of beef to form even roasts.

3. Bring 2 cups sauce to simmer in Dutch oven over medium heat. Nestle roasts in sauce and scatter potatoes, carrots, and parsnips around sides. Cover, transfer pot to oven, and cook until roasts are tender and fork slips easily in and out of meat, 3½ to 4 hours, gently turning roasts over in sauce and stirring vegetables halfway through cooking.

4. Transfer roasts to carving board, tent with aluminum foil, and let rest for 10 to 15 minutes. Using slotted spoon, transfer vegetables to serving dish and cover tightly with foil. Transfer sauce to fat separator and let settle for 5 minutes. Return defatted sauce to now-empty pot. Stir in remaining sauce and bring to simmer over medium heat. Stir in thyme and season with salt and pepper to taste.

5. Remove twine from roasts, slice against grain into ½-inch-thick slices, and transfer to serving dish with vegetables. Spoon half of sauce over beef and serve, passing remaining sauce separately.

Rosemary–Red Wine Simmering Sauce
MAKES ABOUT 4 CUPS

We like to use this sauce in our Pot Roast with Rosemary–Red Wine Simmering Sauce, but you can also use it to braise other cuts of beef such as short ribs. It also works well on its own as a sauce for beef roasts, mashed potatoes, or root vegetables.

- 2 tablespoons unsalted butter
- 2 onions, chopped
- 1 carrot, peeled and chopped
- 1 celery rib, chopped
  Salt and pepper
- 1 tablespoon tomato paste
- 2 garlic cloves, minced
- 2 cups beef broth
- 1 cup dry red wine
- 2 teaspoons soy sauce
- 1 sprig fresh rosemary
- 1 bay leaf

1. Melt butter in medium saucepan over medium heat. Add onions, carrot, celery, and ½ teaspoon salt and cook until vegetables are softened and lightly browned, 8 to 10 minutes. Stir in tomato paste and garlic and cook until fragrant, about 30 seconds. Stir in broth, wine, soy sauce, rosemary sprig, and bay leaf, scraping up any browned bits. Bring to simmer and cook, stirring occasionally, until vegetables are softened and sauce is reduced to about 4 cups, 10 to 15 minutes.

2. Discard rosemary sprig and bay leaf. Transfer sauce to blender and process until smooth, about 1 minute. Season with salt and pepper to taste. (Sauce can be refrigerated for up to 1 week or frozen for up to 1 month.)

WINE-BRAISED SHORT RIBS

✓ **WHY THIS RECIPE WORKS:** To create a short-rib dish with tender meat and a silky, complex sauce, we started with easy-to-find, meaty English-style short ribs. While we loved the deep flavor we got from searing the ribs, we didn't like the extra time and mess. Instead we braised the ribs, uncovered, in the oven. This step allowed the oven to do the browning for us, imparting plenty of meaty, roasted flavor. White wine, as opposed to red wine or port, contributed acidity that contrasted with the richness of the meat. Defatting and reducing the braising liquid concentrated it into an ultraflavorful, rib-coating sauce.

As a veteran of professional kitchens, allow me to let you in on a little secret that restaurant chefs don't want you to know: Those braised short ribs on the menu, served over mashed potatoes or polenta and anointed with a glossy, rich sauce? They are incredibly easy to prepare: Just brown the ribs, add wine and stock, and let the mixture cook in a low oven for a few hours until the ribs are meltingly tender. The ribs are relatively inexpensive, the sauce makes itself, and there's hardly any hands-on prep. What you do need, however, is time for the tough connective tissue to become tender.

I started by preparing a handful of recipes for braised short ribs. My tasters and I were unanimous in our preference for English-style short ribs, which are meatier and much easier to find than flanken-style ribs. The sauces were tasty but leaned toward overly rich. Pulling

WINE-BRAISED SHORT RIBS

in pieces from the better recipes, I landed on a basic method: Sear the ribs, and then remove them and deglaze the pan with red wine. Add the ribs back in along with broth. Cover and cook in the oven until the meat is tender and falling off the bone. Spoon the braising liquid over the ribs and serve. Simple.

Through days of testing I made a few improvements to the recipe. I enhanced the cooking liquid—and thus the sauce—with bay leaves, tomato paste, and fresh thyme. Defatting and reducing the braising liquid after the ribs were done added a little more work, but the payoff was worth it—the sauce was cleaner, more flavorful, and had a velvety texture my tasters loved.

My biggest beef (sorry!) with this method was the browning step. It took 15 minutes and left my stovetop splattered with grease. In the test kitchen, we've learned that you can achieve the complex flavors you get from searing by cooking braises uncovered with the meat standing out of the liquid; the hot oven does the browning for you. So I compared two batches of short ribs: one that I seared and braised covered versus a batch where I skipped the searing and left the pot uncovered.

The uncovered braise had the same deep, rich flavor, but the exteriors of the ribs that had sat above the braising liquid were a bit leathery. Flipping the ribs halfway through cooking provided an easy fix. The last hurdle to clear was that my tasters felt that the dish was plenty flavorful but a little heavy. I tried finishing the sauce with vinegar, but that just covered up the problem.

Nearly every wine-braised short rib recipe I found called for red wine or port. Going out on a limb, I tried a batch using white wine in an attempt to lighten things up. My tasters absolutely loved it. The crisp white wine cut through the richness and made for a fresher, brighter dish that was still plenty rich.

A moist, meaty rib drizzled with this surprisingly lively sauce is a meal fit for a celebration. I may just celebrate how easy it is to make.

MORGAN BOLLING, *Cook's Country*

Wine-Braised Short Ribs

SERVES 4 TO 6

English-style short ribs contain a single rib bone. A crisp, dry white wine such as Sauvignon Blanc is best here. If you're using table salt, reduce the amount called for by half. Use a large Dutch oven with a capacity of 6 quarts or more.

5   pounds bone-in English-style short ribs, bone 4 to 5 inches long, 1 to 1½ inches of meat on top of bone, trimmed
    Kosher salt and pepper
1   tablespoon vegetable oil
1   large onion, chopped
1   tablespoon tomato paste
1   teaspoon all-purpose flour
2   cups dry white wine
3   cups chicken broth
4   garlic cloves, peeled and smashed
4   sprigs fresh thyme
2   bay leaves
2   tablespoons unsalted butter, cut into 2 pieces and chilled

1. Adjust oven rack to lower-middle position and heat oven to 325 degrees. Sprinkle ribs with ¾ teaspoon salt and ½ teaspoon pepper; set aside.

2. Heat oil in large Dutch oven over medium heat until shimmering. Add onion and cook until lightly browned, 4 to 6 minutes. Add tomato paste and flour and cook, stirring constantly, until paste begins to darken, about 45 seconds. Add wine, increase heat to high, and bring to boil. Cook until mixture is slightly thickened, about 3 minutes.

NOTES FROM THE TEST KITCHEN

PICK THE RIGHT RIBS

There are two kinds of bone-in short ribs you might see in your local market: English and flanken. English-style are cut between the ribs, leaving a thick piece of meat atop the bone. Flanken are cut across the bone and are about ½ inch thick; because they have less mass, they're not great for braising. At the meat counter, look for English-style short ribs that are 4 to 5 inches long with 1 to 1½ inches of meat on top. Similar-size ribs will cook more evenly than those that are a jumble of sizes. The meat shrinks back from the bone during cooking.

4 to 5 inches

BONE-IN ENGLISH-STYLE SHORT RIB
Deep marbling = deep flavor

3. Stir in broth, garlic, thyme sprigs, and bay leaves. Nestle ribs into braising liquid, bone side up (ribs may overlap). Bring braising liquid to simmer, transfer pot to oven, and cook, uncovered, for 1½ hours.

4. Remove pot from oven. Flip ribs meat side up so meat is above braising liquid. Return pot to oven and cook, uncovered, until fork slips easily in and out of meat, 1 to 1½ hours longer.

5. Transfer ribs to serving platter and tent with aluminum foil. Strain braising liquid through fine-mesh strainer into fat separator; discard solids. Allow liquid to settle for about 5 minutes.

6. Strain off fat and return defatted braising liquid to now-empty pot. Bring to boil over high heat and cook until reduced to 1 cup, 4 to 7 minutes. Reduce heat to low and whisk in butter, 1 piece at a time. Season sauce with salt and pepper to taste. Pour sauce over meat and serve.

BRAISED BRISKET WITH POMEGRANATE, CUMIN, AND CILANTRO

✓ **WHY THIS RECIPE WORKS:** For braised brisket that would be both tender and moist, we started by salting the meat and letting it sit for at least 16 hours, which helped it retain moisture as it cooked; the salt also seasoned it. From there, we brought the meat to 180 degrees—the sweet spot for the collagen breakdown that is necessary for the meat to turn tender—relatively quickly in a 325-degree oven and then lowered the oven temperature to 250 degrees so that the brisket finished cooking gently and retained as `much moisture as possible. Instead of searing the meat (a messy, unwieldy step), we removed it and then reduced the braising liquid (chicken broth, pomegranate juice, lots of onions and garlic, anchovies, tomato paste, herbs, and spices) in the pan to achieve rich flavor. Reducing the sauce also built body, which we enhanced with flour and gelatin for a velvety consistency.

When brisket is done right, there is perhaps no better cut of beef to braise, especially when serving a crowd. It's beefy, velvety, and moist, and it slices beautifully. The braising liquid can be seasoned with any aromatic vegetable, herb, or spice, and during the long cooking time, it reduces to a rich-tasting jus or full-bodied gravy. The final product is ideal as a Sunday dinner for family or for company.

Most recipes follow more or less the same script. Brown the meat, usually in a Dutch oven; set it aside; and then cook aromatics (usually including loads of onions) until softened and browned. Return the brisket to the pot, add enough liquid (wine, beer, water, stock, tomatoes, etc.) to partially submerge it, and braise it, covered, in the oven until the meat is fork-tender and easily sliced. Many recipes, particularly classic Jewish versions, call for adding vegetables or fruits late in the process to be served alongside the meat.

Anyone who's made brisket knows that producing fork-tender meat takes a long time—upwards of 5 hours, according to the recipes I've tried. But more problematic is the fact that by the time the meat is tender, it's usually dry, too. That's because brisket is loaded with collagen, the main structural protein in meat that makes it tough. Collagen requires long, steady heat exposure to break down, but in that time the meat's muscle fibers are also contracting and squeezing out moisture. So in a sense, braising meat is a balancing act: using enough heat to break down collagen while still keeping the heat low enough to retain moisture.

I was determined to produce brisket that was both tender and moist. And while I was at it, I'd see how I could dress up the flavors so the dish would feel special enough to serve at the holidays.

Butchers typically divide whole briskets into two cuts, the point and the flat. I would go with the flat cut, which is available in most supermarkets and, as its name suggests, is flatter and more uniform and thus easier to slice.

When we want meat to retain moisture, our first move is almost always to apply salt, which not only seasons the meat but also, if left on long enough before cooking, changes the protein structure so that the meat better holds on to moisture. Brisket is particularly dense, so to help the salt penetrate, I halved the brisket lengthwise to create two slabs (doing so would also speed cooking and make for more manageable slices) and poked each slab all over on both sides with a skewer. Even so, after a series of tests, I determined that the meat tasted juicier and better seasoned when the salt had at least 16—or up to 48—hours to work its magic.

On to the cooking. For the time being, I skipped searing the meat, which is messy and time-consuming, and focused on enlivening the braising liquid instead. I started by sautéing onions and garlic in a Dutch oven, and I made an unconventional choice for the braising liquid: pomegranate juice. Its acidity would balance the unctuous meat, and its fruity flavor would be a nod to traditional Jewish versions. I added some chicken broth and bay leaves along with the juice and brought the liquid to a simmer. I then added the brisket with the fat cap facing up so that the bulk of the meat would be submerged and the exposed part would be protected by the fat. I covered the pot and placed it in a 325-degree oven. After about 5 hours, it was tender but—despite having been salted for 48 hours—still too dry.

I reasoned that reducing the oven temperature would prevent the meat from drying out as much, even though I knew that it would add to the cooking time. I dropped the temperature from 325 degrees to 250 degrees—but now the brisket took far longer to cook than I would ever have expected. In fact, after 6 hours, the brisket still wasn't even remotely tender, and when I took its temperature, I was surprised to see that it never exceeded 165 degrees. That wasn't hot enough for significant collagen breakdown, which happens most rapidly above 180 degrees, so the meat never tenderized.

Puzzled as to why the meat's temperature had plateaued, I did some research and discovered that this issue is familiar to anyone who has barbecued large pieces of meat. As meat gets hot enough for moisture to be driven off, its surface cools, preventing the interior of the meat from getting any hotter. Known as evaporative cooling, it's the same process that happens when you perspire: As water on your skin evaporates, your skin's temperature decreases, which in turn keeps your internal body temperature stable.

There are only two ways to overcome evaporative cooling in meat: Prevent moisture from being driven off by wrapping it tightly in aluminum foil, as is often done when barbecuing large cuts (not an option when braising), or limit how much the meat can cool by turning up the heat. If the meat can't cool too much on the outside, it can continue to heat up on the inside.

Since evaporative cooling starts to kick in at about 160 degrees and collagen breakdown happens fastest above 180 degrees, my charge was clear: I needed to hurry the meat into that rapid collagen breakdown zone (180 to 200 degrees) and hold it there long enough for the collagen to completely break down.

I started my next braise in a 325-degree oven, as I had before, but this time I waited until the meat's temperature hit 180 degrees, about 1½ hours into cooking, and then lowered the oven to 250 degrees. At this point, any evaporative cooling on the exterior of the meat wasn't enough to lower the meat's internal temperature, and it continued to climb slowly. After another 2 full hours, the brisket's temperature hit 200 degrees, at which point the meat was both fork-tender and still wonderfully moist.

Things were looking good: Instead of producing a dry brisket in 5-plus hours, I now had a method that cooked it perfectly in about 4 hours. All I needed to do was polish the sauce.

The curious thing was that the sauce was thin, not velvety and full-bodied. At first I didn't understand why, since all that collagen in the brisket was supposedly breaking down and converting to gelatin, which typically gives the braising liquid a luscious, silky body. But then I did some more research on the collagen in

NOTES FROM THE TEST KITCHEN

BUYING BRISKET
Butchers typically divide whole briskets into two cuts, the point and the flat. Though the point cut cooks nicely because it contains more intramuscular fat, it's hard to find and irregularly shaped. We prefer the flat cut because it is available in most markets and, as its name suggests, is flatter and more uniform and thus easier to slice.

POINT CUT
Knobby shape, good marbling, but hard to find

FLAT CUT
More uniform shape, thick fat cap that adds flavor and protection, widely available

GIVE IT A TRIM

TRIM FAT CAP TO ¼ INCH
Leaving some fat on the surface protects the exposed top of the meat from drying out.

BRAISED BRISKET WITH POMEGRANATE, CUMIN, AND CILANTRO

brisket and made a surprising discovery: Most of the collagen in brisket doesn't actually break down and convert to gelatin; it merely softens enough to make the brisket tender.

That being the case, I needed to find other ways to add body to the sauce. I started with the onions, some of which had practically dissolved during the long cooking time. To coax more of them into breaking down and thickening the sauce, I sautéed them from the start with a small amount of baking soda, which helps break down their cell walls. Then I strained the liquid to get a smooth consistency. I also stirred in some flour when I sautéed the onions and some powdered gelatin when I added the liquid to the pot, just to give the sauce more body.

The combination produced a velvety sauce, but I wanted the liquid to taste even more meaty. I could get that by browning the meat, but I wanted to avoid this splattery step if possible and had a couple of ideas that would be less labor-intensive. First, I moved the braise from a Dutch oven to a large roasting pan, figuring that the broader surface would allow the braising liquid to reduce further and create more flavor-packed fond. To mimic the pot's tight-fitting lid, I covered the roasting pan with aluminum foil. Next, I removed the foil cover partway through cooking so that the braising liquid at the edges of the pan and the portion of the meat that wasn't submerged were able to brown. That worked, but it also slowed the cooking.

I fully cooked the meat without worrying about the sauce. I then set aside the meat, strained and defatted the sauce, and returned the sauce alone to a 400-degree oven. After 30 minutes or so, the sauce had reduced nicely and a dark ring of fond had formed on the sides of the pan. Once I'd stirred it into the sauce, this fond contributed the flavor of a well-seared brisket with none of the hassle. To polish those flavors, I added cumin, cardamom, cayenne pepper, and black pepper, plus glutamate-rich tomato paste and anchovies (the anchovies don't turn the sauce the least bit fishy if minced fine).

The results were my ideal brisket: tender and moist meat and a lush but well-balanced gravy. A handful of pomegranate seeds and chopped cilantro scattered across the top added tangy, fresh bursts and jewel-like color, turning this typically humble braise into a holiday-worthy centerpiece. I also created two variations, one in which I braised the meat in beer and paired it with

prunes (which are often seen in classic Jewish versions), ginger, and Dijon mustard, and another, more classic version with red wine and thyme. Whether for company or family, this is a foolproof brisket recipe I'll return to again and again.

ANDREW JANJIGIAN, *Cook's Illustrated*

Braised Brisket with Pomegranate, Cumin, and Cilantro

SERVES 6 TO 8

This recipe requires salting the brisket for at least 16 hours; if you have time, you can salt it for up to 48 hours. We recommend using a remote probe thermometer to monitor the temperature of the brisket. Serve with boiled or mashed potatoes or buttered noodles.

1	(4- to 5-pound) beef brisket, flat cut, fat trimmed to ¼ inch
	Kosher salt and pepper
2	tablespoons vegetable oil
2	large onions, chopped
¼	teaspoon baking soda
6	garlic cloves, minced
4	anchovy fillets, rinsed, patted dry, and minced to paste
1	tablespoon tomato paste
1	tablespoon ground cumin
1½	teaspoons ground cardamom
⅛	teaspoon cayenne pepper
¼	cup all-purpose flour
2	cups pomegranate juice
1½	cups chicken broth
3	bay leaves
2	tablespoons unflavored gelatin
1	cup pomegranate seeds
3	tablespoons chopped fresh cilantro

1. Place brisket, fat side down, on cutting board and cut in half lengthwise with grain. Using paring knife or metal skewer, poke each roast 20 times, pushing all the way through roast. Flip roasts and repeat on second side.

2. Sprinkle each roast evenly on all sides with 2½ teaspoons salt (5 teaspoons salt total). Wrap each roast in plastic wrap and refrigerate for at least 16 hours or up to 48 hours.

3. Adjust oven rack to middle position and heat oven to 325 degrees. Heat oil in large roasting pan over medium heat until shimmering. Add onions and baking soda and cook, stirring frequently, until onions have started to soften and break down, 4 to 5 minutes. Add garlic and cook until fragrant, about 30 seconds. Stir in anchovies, tomato paste, cumin, cardamom, cayenne, and ½ teaspoon pepper. Add flour and cook, stirring constantly, until onions are evenly coated and flour begins to stick to pan, about 2 minutes. Stir in pomegranate juice, broth, and bay leaves, scraping up any browned bits. Stir in gelatin. Increase heat to medium-high and bring to boil.

4. Unwrap roasts and place in pan. Cover pan tightly with aluminum foil, transfer to oven, and cook until meat registers 180 to 185 degrees at center, about 1½ hours. Reduce oven temperature to 250 degrees and continue to cook until fork slips easily in and out of meat, 2 to 2½ hours longer. Transfer roasts to baking sheet and wrap sheet tightly in foil.

5. Strain braising liquid through fine-mesh strainer set over large bowl, pressing on solids to extract as much liquid as possible; discard solids. Let liquid settle for 10 minutes. Using wide, shallow spoon, skim fat from surface and discard. Wipe roasting pan clean with paper towels and return defatted liquid to pan.

6. Increase oven temperature to 400 degrees. Return pan to oven and cook, stirring occasionally, until liquid is reduced by about one-third, 30 to 40 minutes. Remove pan from oven and use wooden spoon to draw liquid up sides of pan and scrape browned bits around edges of pan into liquid.

7. Transfer roasts to carving board and slice against grain ¼ inch thick; transfer to wide serving platter. Season sauce with salt and pepper to taste and pour over brisket. Tent platter with foil and let stand for 5 to 10 minutes to warm brisket through. Sprinkle with pomegranate seeds and cilantro and serve.

TO MAKE AHEAD: Follow recipe through step 6 and let sauce and brisket cool completely. Cover and refrigerate sauce and roasts separately for up to 2 days. To serve, slice each roast against grain ¼ inch thick and transfer to 13 by 9-inch baking dish. Heat sauce in small saucepan over medium heat until just simmering. Pour sauce over brisket, cover dish with aluminum foil, and cook in 325-degree oven until meat is heated through, about 20 minutes.

VARIATIONS

Beer-Braised Brisket with Prunes and Ginger

Omit ground cumin and ground cardamom. Stir in 1 teaspoon five-spice powder with anchovies in step 3. Substitute 1½ cups beer for pomegranate juice and increase chicken broth to 2 cups. Stir in 2 tablespoons Dijon mustard and 1 (3-inch) piece ginger, peeled and sliced thin, with chicken broth in step 3. Stir 1½ cups pitted prunes into braising liquid before returning roasting pan to oven in step 6. Omit pomegranate seeds and substitute parsley for cilantro.

Braised Brisket with Red Wine and Thyme

Omit ground cumin and ground cardamom. Increase chicken broth to 2 cups and substitute 1 cup red wine for pomegranate juice. Add 6 thyme sprigs with bay leaves in step 3. Omit pomegranate seeds and cilantro.

SICHUAN BRAISED TOFU WITH BEEF

WHY THIS RECIPE WORKS: Our version of *mapo* tofu is bold in flavor, with a balanced spiciness. We started with cubed soft tofu, poaching it gently in chicken broth to help the cubes stay intact in the braise. For the sauce base, we used plenty of ginger and garlic along with four Sichuan pantry powerhouses: Asian broad bean chili paste (*doubanjiang*), fermented black beans, Sichuan chili powder, and Sichuan peppercorns. A small amount of ground beef acted as a seasoning, not as a primary component of the dish. In place of the chili oil often called for, we used a generous amount of vegetable oil, extra Sichuan chili powder, and toasted sesame oil. We finished the dish with just the right amount of cornstarch to create a velvety thickness.

Spicy, rich, and savory, *mapo* tofu is the most renowned dish from China's Sichuan province and serves as comfort food for chili fans everywhere. But even die-hard fans tend to order it in restaurants rather than make it at home. Perhaps they imagine that making something so deeply flavorful would take a long time and many steps. But in fact, mapo tofu—soft cubes of tofu and a modest amount of ground beef or pork swimming in a glossy red sauce with loads of garlic and ginger, multiple fermented bean seasonings, numbing Sichuan

SICHUAN BRAISED TOFU WITH BEEF (MAPO TOFU)

peppercorns, and fiery Sichuan chili powder—is fast and easy to make. And despite its potential cacophony of flavors, a good version somehow manages to blend them all into a harmonious whole that is spicy but never overwhelming and entirely satisfying when ladled over heaps of steamed white rice.

Traditionally, the first step is to simmer or steep cubes of tofu in hot salted water or broth. Odd as this sounds, experts say that this step firms the tofu so it holds its shape during braising. Meanwhile, ground beef or pork (recipes use either, though beef is traditional and is what I chose) is cooked in a pot or wok until it begins to brown and is then set aside. Next, minced garlic, ginger, Asian broad bean chili paste, Sichuan peppercorns, Sichuan chili powder, and fermented black beans (more on these ingredients later) are sizzled in oil. Some recipes also call for drizzling in Sichuan chili oil for yet another layer of fiery flavor; others add sweetness via hoisin sauce or sugar. Once the oil has taken on a deep red color from the chili powder, the browned meat is returned to the pot along with the tofu and its simmering liquid and scallions (or leeks). The mixture braises for a few minutes until the tofu starts to absorb the flavor of the sauce. Finally, a cornstarch slurry is stirred in to add body before the tofu is served with a garnish of toasted, ground Sichuan peppercorns for a final layer of floral, citrusy, buzzing crunch.

My first task was figuring out what kind of tofu to use. Styles differ mainly in how thoroughly the soybean curds have been drained and pressed to remove moisture and firm up their structure. The best texture for mapo tofu, I found, is one that holds its shape when cubed yet is still soft and custard-like.

After buying out the tofu section at the supermarket, I found two styles to avoid. Undrained silken tofu is usually so fragile that it falls apart with the slightest disturbance, producing a gloppy dish, while extra-firm" tofu typically has a dense, bouncy texture and doesn't absorb the flavors of the sauce. I got the best results with the kind of tofu typically labeled soft.

As for how to prepare the tofu, simmering or steeping it in hot salted water turned out to be essential to getting its texture right. Heat shrinks the proteins in the outer layers of the cubes, tightening them and helping them stay intact during cooking while still allowing for a yielding, custardy texture. To simplify the process, I microwaved the tofu and water until the water was steaming. I also used this as an opportunity to gently wilt the scallions. Chicken broth and salted water worked equally well to set the tofu, but ultimately I liked the depth that broth contributed.

As a contrast to the neutral, clean-tasting tofu, the sauce should be deeply savory, spicy, and rich. That meant using plenty of garlic (nine cloves) and ginger (a 3-inch knob), along with four Chinese pantry staples: Asian broad bean chili paste, Sichuan peppercorns, Sichuan chili powder, and fermented black beans. The broad bean chili paste (*doubanjiang*) lends the dish tremendous savory depth for which there is no substitute. Since some chili bean pastes are a little too coarse to use straight from the jar, and because I needed to mince lots of garlic and ginger, I whizzed everything with the oil in a food processor to form a smooth paste.

Sichuan peppercorns are nutty, floral, and citrusy and deliver a pleasant (and temporary), mild tingling sensation. There's no substitute for them either, and I found that toasting them in the microwave drew out their robust personality. Sichuan chili powder packs heat and subtle fruitiness, and fermented black beans provide salty umami flavor.

Finally, I liked how a bit of sugar helped round out the flavors of the dish, but I preferred hoisin sauce— yet another fermented bean product, this one made from soybeans—because it contributed another layer of complexity in addition to sweetness.

Lastly, mapo tofu should contain a good amount of oil—that's why it's rich and always served with plenty of rice. But instead of buying chili oil, which is traditionally prepared by steeping dried red chiles and Sichuan peppercorns in very hot oil, straining them out, and adding a little toasted sesame oil, I realized I could re-create its flavor and red glow by simply increasing the amounts of Sichuan chili powder, Sichuan peppercorns, and vegetable oil in my recipe and incorporating a few teaspoons of sesame oil.

And there I had it: a version of mapo tofu that was bold, intricately seasoned, and as fiery as it was satisfying. Plus, now that I had the Sichuan staples on hand, I could quickly throw this dish together any night of the week—instead of ordering takeout.

ANDREW JANJIGIAN, *Cook's Illustrated*

Sichuan Braised Tofu with Beef (Mapo Tofu)
SERVES 4 TO 6

Ground pork can be used in place of beef, if desired. Asian broad bean chili paste (or sauce) is also known as *doubanjiang* or *toban djan*; our favorite, Pixian, is available online. Lee Kum Kee Chili Bean Sauce is a good supermarket option. If you can't find Sichuan chili powder, an equal amount of Korean red pepper flakes (*gochugaru*) is a good substitute. In a pinch, use 2½ teaspoons of ancho chile powder and ½ teaspoon of cayenne pepper. If you can't find fermented black beans, you can use an equal amount of fermented black bean paste or sauce or 2 additional teaspoons of Asian broad bean chili paste. Serve with steamed white rice.

- 1 tablespoon Sichuan peppercorns
- 12 scallions
- 28 ounces soft tofu, cut into ½-inch cubes
- 2 cups chicken broth
- 9 garlic cloves, peeled
- 1 (3-inch) piece ginger, peeled and cut into ¼-inch rounds
- ⅓ cup Asian broad bean chili paste
- 1 tablespoon fermented black beans
- 6 tablespoons vegetable oil
- 1 tablespoon Sichuan chili powder
- 8 ounces 85 percent lean ground beef
- 2 tablespoons hoisin sauce
- 2 teaspoons toasted sesame oil
- 2 tablespoons water
- 1 tablespoon cornstarch

1. Place peppercorns in small bowl and microwave until fragrant, 15 to 30 seconds. Let cool completely. Once cool, grind in spice grinder or mortar and pestle (you should have 1½ teaspoons).

2. Using side of chef's knife, lightly crush white parts of scallions, then cut scallions into 1-inch pieces. Place tofu, broth, and scallions in large bowl and microwave, covered, until steaming, 5 to 7 minutes. Let stand while preparing remaining ingredients.

3. Process garlic, ginger, chili paste, and black beans in food processor until coarse paste forms, 1 to 2 minutes, scraping down sides of bowl as needed. Add ¼ cup vegetable oil, chili powder, and 1 teaspoon peppercorns and continue to process until smooth paste forms, 1 to 2 minutes longer. Transfer spice paste to bowl.

4. Heat 1 tablespoon vegetable oil and beef in large saucepan over medium heat; cook, breaking up meat with wooden spoon, until meat just begins to brown, 5 to 7 minutes. Transfer beef to bowl.

5. Add remaining 1 tablespoon vegetable oil and spice paste to now-empty saucepan and cook, stirring frequently, until paste darkens and oil begins to separate from paste, 2 to 3 minutes. Gently pour tofu with broth into saucepan, followed by hoisin, sesame oil, and beef. Cook, stirring gently and frequently, until dish comes to simmer, 2 to 3 minutes. Whisk water and cornstarch together in small bowl. Add cornstarch mixture to saucepan and continue to cook, stirring frequently, until thickened, 2 to 3 minutes longer. Transfer to serving dish, sprinkle with remaining peppercorns, and serve. (Mapo tofu can be refrigerated for up to 24 hours.)

VARIATION

Sichuan Braised Tofu with Shiitakes (Mapo Tofu)
SERVES 4 TO 6

Serve with steamed white rice.

- 2 cups water
-   Salt
- ½ ounce dried shiitake mushrooms, rinsed
- 1 tablespoon Sichuan peppercorns
- 12 scallions
- 28 ounces soft tofu, cut into ½-inch cubes
- 9 garlic cloves, peeled
- 1 (3-inch) piece ginger, peeled and cut into ¼-inch rounds
- ⅓ cup Asian broad bean chili paste
- 1 tablespoon fermented black beans
- ½ cup vegetable oil
- 1 tablespoon Sichuan chili powder
- 4 ounces fresh shiitake mushrooms, stemmed, or oyster mushrooms, trimmed
- 2 tablespoons hoisin sauce
- 2 teaspoons toasted sesame oil
- 2 tablespoons soy sauce
- 1 tablespoon cornstarch

1. Microwave water, ½ teaspoon salt, and dried mushrooms in covered large bowl until steaming, about 1 minute. Let sit until softened, about 5 minutes. Drain mushrooms in fine-mesh strainer, reserving liquid; set aside soaked mushrooms and return liquid to large bowl.

2. Place peppercorns in small bowl and microwave until fragrant, 15 to 30 seconds. Let cool completely. Once cool, grind in spice grinder or mortar and pestle (you should have 1½ teaspoons).

3. Using side of chef's knife, lightly crush white parts of scallions, then cut scallions into 1-inch pieces. Place tofu and scallions in bowl with reserved mushroom liquid and microwave until steaming, 5 to 7 minutes. Let stand while preparing remaining ingredients.

4. Process garlic, ginger, chili paste, and black beans in food processor until coarse paste forms, 1 to 2 minutes, scraping down sides of bowl as needed. Add ¼ cup vegetable oil, chili powder, and 1 teaspoon peppercorns and continue to process until smooth paste forms, 1 to 2 minutes longer. Transfer spice paste to bowl.

5. Place reserved soaked mushrooms and fresh shiitake mushrooms in now-empty processor and pulse until finely chopped, 15 to 20 pulses (do not overprocess). Heat 2 tablespoons vegetable oil and mushroom mixture in large saucepan over medium heat, breaking up mushrooms with wooden spoon, until mushrooms begin to brown and stick to bottom of saucepan, 5 to 7 minutes. Transfer mushroom mixture to bowl.

6. Add remaining 2 tablespoons vegetable oil and spice paste to now-empty saucepan and cook, stirring frequently, until paste darkens and oil begins to separate from paste, 2 to 3 minutes. Gently pour tofu with mushroom liquid into saucepan, followed by hoisin, sesame oil, and mushroom mixture. Cook, gently stirring frequently, until dish comes to simmer, 2 to 3 minutes. Whisk soy sauce and cornstarch together

in small bowl. Add cornstarch mixture to saucepan and continue to cook, stirring frequently, until thickened, 2 to 3 minutes longer. Transfer to serving dish, sprinkle with remaining peppercorns, and serve. (Mapo tofu can be refrigerated for up to 24 hours.)

BROWN SUGAR–ORANGE PORK TENDERLOIN

☑ **WHY THIS RECIPE WORKS:** Mildly flavored pork tenderloin is a blank canvas to which home cooks can apply many flavor choices. Deeply sweet with earthy undertones, brown sugar paired wonderfully with the pork when combined with fresh thyme, orange, and sweet-sharp cider vinegar, but we found that the sugar burned easily over high heat. To get around that and to avoid overcooking the pork, we seared the tenderloins before applying the sugar rub and pulled the skillet from the oven when the pork registered 135 degrees, allowing carryover cooking to bring it to our target temperature of 145 degrees.

A pork tenderloin holds the promise of delivering an appealingly tender roast to the table with a minimal investment of time, effort, and expense. But how do you add pizzazz to this mild-tasting cut? How about pairing it with brown sugar, an ingredient that our test kitchen matchmakers have proven goes exceedingly well with many cuts of pork? The combination of brown sugar and quick-cooking pork tenderloin seemed like it would result in a blissful union.

But when I experimented with existing recipes for brown sugar pork tenderloin, it was a dysfunctional marriage at best. Most of these recipes called for seasoning the pork with salt and brown sugar, searing it on the stovetop, and then moving it to the oven to finish cooking. Almost without fail, the pork was overcooked and the sugar burnt.

Fixing the first problem—overcooked pork—was a simple matter of adjusting the target temperature. Recipes suggested roasting the seared tenderloins until they reached between 145 and 160 degrees, but this gave me dense, chewy meat. I lowered that bar to 135 degrees, knowing that carryover cooking (the

---

NOTES FROM THE TEST KITCHEN

PARCOOK YOUR TOFU

The tofu on the left wasn't simmered in broth prior to being incorporated into the sauce; the tofu on the right was. Heat shrinks the proteins in the outer layers of the tofu, which tightens them and helps the pieces stay intact in the sauce.

cooking that happens while the meat rests after coming out of the oven) would bring it to about 145 degrees, just the right temperature for perfectly cooked pork.

As for the acrid, burnt sugar crust, I knew that both searing and roasting with the crust in place was too much. But how could I avoid burning while still cooking the roast quickly? For my next test, I tried something unusual and seasoned the pork with only salt and pepper before searing it. Once the exterior was nicely browned, I spooned the brown sugar on top of the pork and placed it in the preheated 375-degree oven. In the relatively gentle heat, the sugar that sat atop the tenderloins didn't burn; instead, it was transformed into a crunchy, flavorful, faintly sweet crust.

With this success under my belt, I turned to the task of adding extra flavor to the brown sugar topping. After experimenting, I landed on a simple mixture of minced fresh thyme, grated orange zest, salt, and a pinch of cayenne pepper stirred together with the brown sugar, which gave the dish a savory complexity and a balanced sweetness that accentuated but didn't overwhelm the pork. Adding a touch of orange juice to the pan while the pork rested dissolved the sugary fond left behind, creating a luscious sauce that made a happy match with the tender pork. A couple of teaspoons of apple cider vinegar kept the sweetness in check.

At our final tasting of this juicy, brightly flavored, and supereasy dish, my tasters and I agreed: Pork and brown sugar belong together—on our plates.

MATTHEW FAIRMAN, *Cook's Country*

Brown Sugar–Orange Pork Tenderloin

SERVES 4

The Microplane Premium Classic Zester/Grater is our winning zesting tool. Do not use dark brown sugar here, as it is too strong-tasting for this sauce.

¼ cup packed light brown sugar

2 teaspoons minced fresh thyme

½ teaspoon grated orange zest plus 1 tablespoon juice
    Kosher salt and pepper

⅛ teaspoon cayenne pepper

2 (1-pound) pork tenderloins, trimmed

2 tablespoons vegetable oil

2 tablespoons water

2 teaspoons cider vinegar

1. Adjust oven rack to upper-middle position and heat oven to 375 degrees. Combine sugar, thyme, orange zest, ⅛ teaspoon salt, and cayenne in bowl; set aside. Pat tenderloins dry with paper towels and sprinkle with 1 tablespoon salt and ½ teaspoon pepper.

2. Heat oil in 12-inch nonstick skillet over medium-high heat until just smoking. Add tenderloins and cook until browned on all sides, 5 to 7 minutes.

3. Off heat, sprinkle sugar mixture evenly over tops of tenderloins, pressing to adhere (it's OK if some falls off). Transfer skillet to oven and roast until meat registers 135 degrees, 10 to 14 minutes. Transfer tenderloins to plate, tent with aluminum foil, and let rest for 10 minutes.

4. Add water, vinegar, orange juice, and any accumulated pork juices to liquid left in skillet. Place skillet over medium heat (skillet handle will be hot) and cook until sauce is slightly thickened, about 2 minutes, pressing on any solid bits of sugar with spatula to dissolve. Slice tenderloins ½ inch thick and serve with sauce.

MAKE-AHEAD CIDER-BRAISED PORK CHOPS

✓ **WHY THIS RECIPE WORKS:** Pork and apples are a tried and true pairing, but the apple flavor in cider-braised pork chops can be fleeting, and recipes often skimp on the time necessary for the pork to become fall-off-the-bone tender. We wanted tender, juicy chops infused with deep apple flavor. Patting the chops dry before searing them helped develop a flavorful crust. To boost apple flavor, we supplemented the cider with apple butter, which thickened the sauce and made it rich and glossy. Garlic and thyme offered aromatic notes. To further reinforce the apple flavor and brighten the sauce, we whisked in more apple butter and some cider vinegar just before serving.

Of all the ways to cook pork chops, nothing compares with the fall-off-the-bone tenderness produced by slow braising. The test kitchen has developed several recipes for braised pork chops over the years, and while they're all fantastic, my favorite is a version that uses apple cider as the braising liquid. This recipe plays up the natural affinity between pork and apples and produces beautifully tender pork chops blanketed in a sweet-savory sauce that's packed with autumnal flavor.

MAKE-AHEAD CIDER-BRAISED PORK CHOPS

There's just one problem: Slow braising doesn't exactly lend itself to everyday cooking. Sure, I can make this cozy meal on a lazy weekend, but more often than not, the hour of hands-on time plus the 1½- to 2-hour cooking time puts braised pork chops out of my reach on a typical weeknight. I wondered if there was a way to get this dish onto my table more often.

I started by analyzing the recipe itself, which starts with thick bone-in blade-cut pork chops. These chops have a couple of advantages over other types: They have a higher fat content, which allows them to stay moist through the long cooking time and gives the braise rich flavor. Also, the bones enrich the sauce with gelatin, giving it a silkier texture. Browning the chops builds flavorful fond in the pot, and transferring the pot to the oven to braise allows for more even cooking—no risk of scorching on the bottom as in stovetop recipes.

But it's the sauce that's the real key to the dish's bold flavor: Rather than apple cider alone, we also stir in a couple tablespoons of apple butter, which provides concentrated apple flavor and gives the sauce more body. Once the pork is done cooking, we strain and defat the sauce, then whisk in more apple butter to reinforce the flavor, along with a bit of apple cider vinegar for brightness and some parsley for a little freshness.

My task now: To figure out the most efficient way to prepare this recipe ahead of time without losing any of the great flavor that makes it so worthwhile. As with most braises, I figured it would keep fine in the fridge for a day or two—and it might even improve, since the flavors would have more time to meld. I ran a simple test to confirm my theory: I made the recipe straight through, but stopped short of straining the sauce and adding the vinegar, parsley, and extra apple butter. After reheating, all I had to do was strain and defat the sauce and stir in those final ingredients. I invited tasters to test batches prepared this way after being stored in the fridge for one, two, and three days. The decision was unanimous: They all tasted great.

But what if I wanted to store the chops for longer? I don't always have the time for Sunday cooking marathons, so the ability to freeze the chops and save them for a future busy night would be invaluable. I made another batch, this time freezing the cooked chops and braising liquid and leaving only the last step of the

recipe for serving day. A few days later, I took the container out of the freezer and put it in the fridge to thaw completely. In the meantime, I started on a fresh batch of chops so that my tasters would be able to taste both versions side by side—there's no ignoring flaws when you've got a direct comparison.

Once the frozen chops had thawed, I placed them in a pot and brought the sauce to a simmer, covering the pot to keep in moisture. The sauce was on the thick side, but adding a bit of apple cider returned it to the proper consistency. Once everything was warmed through, I finished up the last step of the recipe. When I presented both the previously frozen and freshly made batches to my tasters, I didn't tell them which was which—and not one person could identify them. To make sure that the chops and sauce could withstand a longer stay in the freezer, I ran the same test twice more with a batch that I froze for two weeks and a batch that I froze for a month. Both times, I got the same feedback: The frozen braised pork chops were very nearly identical to those that I had just made.

Now that I know I can make this warming braise on my schedule, it will be making much more regular appearances in my fall dinner rotation.

NICOLE KONSTANTINAKOS WITH KELLEY BAKER,
America's Test Kitchen Books

Make-Ahead Cider-Braised Pork Chops
SERVES 4

Be sure to buy chops of equal thickness to ensure they all cook at the same rate.

4	(10- to 12-ounce) bone-in blade-cut pork chops, about 1 inch thick, trimmed
	Salt and pepper
2	tablespoons vegetable oil
1	onion, chopped
¼	cup apple butter
2	tablespoons all-purpose flour
3	garlic cloves, minced
1	cup apple cider
1	sprig fresh thyme
1	tablespoon cider vinegar
1	tablespoon minced fresh parsley

1. Adjust oven rack to lower-middle position and heat oven to 300 degrees. Cut 2 slits, about 2 inches apart, through outer layer of fat and silverskin on each chop. Pat chops dry with paper towels and season with salt and pepper. Heat 1 tablespoon oil in Dutch oven over medium-high heat until just smoking. Brown 2 chops well on 1 side, about 4 minutes; transfer to plate. Repeat with remaining 1 tablespoon oil and remaining 2 chops.

2. Pour off all but 1 tablespoon fat left in pot, add onion, and cook over medium heat until softened, about 5 minutes. Stir in 2 tablespoons apple butter, flour, and garlic and cook until fragrant, about 1 minute. Stir in cider and thyme sprig, scraping up any browned bits, and bring to boil.

3. Nestle chops into pot along with any accumulated juices, cover, and transfer to oven. Cook until chops are completely tender, 1½ to 2 hours.

4. Transfer chops to serving platter. Strain sauce; discard solids. Let liquid settle for 5 minutes, then skim excess fat from surface. Whisk in vinegar, parsley, and remaining 2 tablespoons apple butter and season with salt and pepper to taste. Serve.

TO MAKE AHEAD: Braised pork chops, prepared through step 3, can be refrigerated for up to 3 days or frozen for up to 1 month; if frozen, thaw completely in refrigerator. To reheat, bring chops, covered, to gentle simmer and cook until hot throughout, adjusting consistency with hot water or cider as needed, and continue with step 4.

NOTES FROM THE TEST KITCHEN

PREVENTING CURLED PORK CHOPS

To prevent pork chops from buckling and curling when cooked, cut 2 small slits, about 2 inches apart, through outer layer of fat and silverskin on each chop.

SLOW-ROASTED DEVILED PORK CHOPS

WHY THIS RECIPE WORKS: Most recipes call for pan-searing or broiling pork chops, but here we opted to slow-roast them in a low oven. This way, they retained as much moisture as possible—a must for lean cuts to taste juicy—and cooked evenly from edge to edge, no flipping required. To punch up their mild flavor, we deviled them by painting the tops and sides of the chops with a bold, balanced, complex-tasting paste of spicy, sharp Dijon mustard mixed with dry mustard, minced garlic, and cayenne and black peppers. A bit of brown sugar and salt balanced the paste's heat and acidity. For textural contrast and visual appeal, we coated the tops of the chops with crispy panko bread crumbs, which we toasted in butter to render them deep golden brown and make them water-resistant so that they didn't absorb too much moisture from the mustard coating and turn soggy.

You wouldn't usually call upon the devil to save a weeknight dinner, but that's exactly what Mr. Micawber does in Charles Dickens's novel *David Copperfield* (1850) when he covers undercooked mutton with mustard, salt, and black and cayenne peppers. It is a classic example of deviling, the practice of seasoning food with some combination of mustard, pepper, and/or vinegar, which dates back to at least the 18th century. Nowadays, the term refers to any treatment that uses those components to punch up mild-mannered foods such as hard-cooked eggs, deli ham, or bland chicken breasts and pork chops.

The ease and bold flavors of deviling appeal to me, particularly when applied to boneless pork chops, which I often make for weeknight dinners. But recipes vary widely when it comes to the type and intensity of heat—from a weak sprinkle of black pepper to a thick slather of sharp mustard, neither of which offers the complex, balanced spiciness and acidity that I would want in this dish. Plus, mustard-coated pork chops are often covered in bread crumbs, but I've found that the fine crumbs soak up moisture from the mustard and turn soggy.

But those are just the surface issues related to deviling, and they would be relatively simple to fix. The bigger problem with most deviled pork chops is how they're cooked: They're usually coated with mustard and then seared or broiled, the goal being to develop a deeply browned, flavorful crust. But inevitably, the lean meat dries out and toughens.

To fix these issues, I would start by finding a cooking technique that produced tender, juicy chops. Then I would need to fine-tune a mustard-based deviling paste that would be assertive and vibrant enough to perk up the pork without overwhelming it. Once those elements were in place, I'd see about adding a bread-crumb crust.

The more I thought about the role of well-browned meat on deviled pork chops, the more I wondered if it was necessary. Once the chops were covered with the punchy mustard paste and, potentially, a crunchy bread-crumb coating, would you really miss the flavor and texture of the seared meat? I did a quick test and confirmed that the answer was no; the mustard-based paste I'd used to coat the meat more or less camouflaged the flavor of the sear. Searing was out.

Instead, I would try to slow-roast the chops, as we often do with large roasts and thick steaks. The benefit is twofold: Lower heat keeps the temperature of the meat's outermost layers low, which prevents them from squeezing out moisture and promotes more even cooking by reducing the temperature differential between the meat's exterior and interior. Lower heat also encourages enzymes within the pork to break down some of the muscle protein, leading to more tender meat.

I placed four boneless, 1-inch-thick chops on a wire rack set in a rimmed baking sheet so that air could circulate around them for even cooking. Then I slid the sheet into a 275-degree oven and left them alone until they hit 140 degrees. That took about 40 minutes, which was longer than I'd ever waited for pork chops to cook. But the juicy, tender results were worth it. The only hiccup was that the chops stuck to the rack, so the next time I coated it with vegetable oil spray to ensure that the meat released cleanly.

On to the mustard paste. I followed the lead of other recipes and started with Dijon, which offered an assertive punch of clean heat and acidity along with a creamy texture that clung well to the chops. Then I took a cue from the Dickensian formula and seasoned the mustard with salt as well as black and cayenne peppers; each type of pepper lent its own distinct heat, and both enhanced the mustard's burn. For savory flavor, I worked in a small amount of garlic that I had minced to a paste (which resulted in even flavor distribution) and balanced the fiery concoction with a couple of teaspoons of brown sugar. After patting a new batch of chops dry, I brushed the entire surface of each one with the paste, set them on the rack, and popped them into the oven.

The paste was nicely seasoned and packed decent punch, but now that I was tasting it with the pork, I wanted even more of that nasal bite. A heavier coat of the paste wasn't the way to go; for one thing, I wanted more heat but not more acidity. Plus, it would be messy to both slather more paste on the meat and clean it off the wire rack after cooking; the baked-on coating from the underside of the chops was already sticking to the rack. Instead, I tried adding dry (also known as English) mustard, a variety of hot mustard that's sold in powdered form. In many cases, the powder is reconstituted in a little water before being used, but that wouldn't be necessary here since the Dijon contained plenty of moisture. I ran a few tests and worked my way up to a hefty 1½ teaspoons of dry mustard, so that the paste's heat was potent but still layered—a sharp punch that tingled on the tongue and tapered off into a slow, satisfying burn.

I ran two more quick tests. The first was to see if I could get away with coating just the top and sides of the chops now that the paste was so potent. I could, which cut back considerably on the mess before and after roasting. The second test—whether to brush the chops with the paste before or after cooking—confirmed that we preferred the drier consistency and more rounded flavor of the cooked paste. The only downside was the visual: a dull, mottled, ocher coating. It was time to consider that bread-crumb crust.

Besides visual appeal, a crust would offer nice textural contrast to the meat, and the mustard paste would be the glue I'd need to help the crumbs adhere to the chops. To keep the coating process simple, I decided to cover just the top surfaces.

To prevent the crumbs from soaking up moisture from the paste and turning mushy, I employed a two-pronged solution. First, I used panko: pretoasted

DEVILED PORK CHOPS

coarse bread crumbs that we always turn to when we want a craggy texture and great crunch. Second, I sautéed the panko crumbs in butter so that they would turn golden brown; they wouldn't get any color in the low oven. I pressed about 2 tablespoons of crumbs onto the top of each chop and slid them into the oven.

This batch was golden and crispy on top and moist and juicy throughout and boasted a fiery but balanced flavor that kept you going back for more. Best of all, the method was dead simple; once the chops were in the oven, I didn't have to flip them or tend to them in any way until they were done.

I never thought I'd get so excited about a boneless pork chop. I guess you could say the devil made me do it.

ANNIE PETITO, *Cook's Illustrated*

Deviled Pork Chops

SERVES 4

For the best results, be sure to buy chops of similar size. This recipe was developed using natural pork; if using enhanced pork (injected with a salt solution), do not add salt to the mustard paste in step 2. Serve the pork chops with mashed potatoes, rice, or buttered egg noodles.

  2 **tablespoons unsalted butter**
  ½ **cup panko bread crumbs**
     Kosher salt and pepper
  ¼ **cup Dijon mustard**
  2 **teaspoons packed brown sugar**
  1½ **teaspoons dry mustard**
  ½ **teaspoon garlic, minced to paste**
  ¼ **teaspoon cayenne pepper**
  4 **(6- to 8-ounce) boneless pork chops, ¾ to 1 inch thick**

1. Adjust oven rack to middle position and heat oven to 275 degrees.

2. Melt butter in 10-inch skillet over medium heat. Add panko and cook, stirring frequently, until golden brown, 3 to 5 minutes. Transfer to bowl and sprinkle with ⅛ teaspoon salt. Stir Dijon, sugar, dry mustard, garlic, cayenne, 1 teaspoon salt, and 1 teaspoon pepper in second bowl until smooth.

3. Set wire rack in rimmed baking sheet and spray with vegetable oil spray. Pat chops dry with paper towels. Transfer chops to prepared wire rack, spacing them 1 inch apart. Brush 1 tablespoon mustard mixture over top and sides of each chop (leave bottoms uncoated). Spoon 2 tablespoons toasted panko evenly over top of each chop and press lightly to adhere.

4. Roast until meat registers 140 degrees, 40 to 50 minutes. Remove from oven and let rest on rack for 10 minutes before serving.

NOTES FROM THE TEST KITCHEN

CALIBRATING THE BEST BURN

Our deviled paste draws its complex fiery flavor from a combination of spicy components: Dijon mustard, dry mustard, and cayenne and black peppers. Each of these ingredients activates pain receptors in your mouth—TRPV1, which is the same nerve channel that responds to the pain of piping hot liquid, and TRPA1, a close relative. But the different ingredients stimulate the nerves in different ways, so the combination adds up to a much more complex experience of spiciness. The stimulation of pain and other tactile nerves in the mouth, called chemesthesis, can take many forms—a quick jolt of heat, a lingering burn, the sensation of a pinprick—and can even affect different parts of your mouth and nose. Here's what each deviling component brings to the mix.

DIJON MUSTARD
Compound:
Allyl isothiocyanate
Sensory effect:
Sharp nasal sting

DRY MUSTARD
Compound:
Allyl isothiocyanate
Sensory effect:
Sharp nasal sting

CAYENNE PEPPER
Compound:
Capsaicin
Sensory effect:
Burning on the tongue
and in the throat

BLACK PEPPER
Compound:
Piperine
Sensory effect:
Burning and
tingling on the tongue

OVEN-ROASTED JERK RIBS

✓ **WHY THIS RECIPE WORKS:** Although many American cooks employ jerk seasoning as a spicy coating for grilled chicken, it was originally used in Jamaican cooking to season pork. As a nod to this, we developed a recipe for boldly seasoned jerk pork ribs. We chose St. Louis–style spareribs for their uniform shape, a quality that helps them cook evenly. Letting the ribs marinate in our jerk paste for at least 1 hour infused them with fiery yet fruity flavor. Roasting them in a low 275-degree oven for 4 hours turned them meltingly tender. And brushing them with another coat of jerk paste cut with tangy vinegar gave them a bright, fresh crust.

The foundation of most great jerk recipes is the combination of fiery Scotch bonnet chiles, warm allspice, and fragrant thyme; these elements combine to create a flavor that's bold, yes, but also deeply complex—hot, sweet, savory, herbal, and fruity. Although Americans may know jerk best as a spicy coating for grilled chicken, in Jamaica it was originally used to season pork. As a nod to this history—and, to be honest, because I love ribs—I set out to develop a recipe for oven-cooked jerk ribs that could brighten up any table with big flavors and a little Jamaican heat.

The first order of business was to determine what type of ribs to use. I tried coating St. Louis–style spareribs, baby back ribs, and country-style pork ribs with store-bought jerk paste and roasted them in a low 275-degree oven. About 4 hours later, I pulled out the now-tender ribs and called my team to taste. We liked the St. Louis–style ribs best; their meaty, almost sweet flavor was a perfect vehicle for the bold jerk seasoning.

The next order of business was improving on the jarred jerk paste. I prepared six promising jerk recipes I'd found in various Caribbean and barbecue cookbooks. They all had their merits, but some called for as many as 23 ingredients—excessive for what should be a simple dish. After several days of trial and error, I created my own version using the most essential ingredients: habanero chiles (a close relative of Scotch bonnets, which can be hard to find), ground allspice, dried thyme, scallions, garlic, ginger, brown sugar,

salt, and—to create the right consistency—vegetable oil. I roasted a few racks that I'd slathered with this homemade jerk paste and called the troops in to taste. "Pretty good," my colleagues opined, "but not yet great."

I headed back into the test kitchen and set about tweaking the recipe. Letting the ribs marinate for a few hours in the intense jerk paste made them more flavorful. Using molasses in place of the brown sugar added more depth to the mix. But the ribs were still missing something, and my tasters helped me pinpoint it: acid. Following the lead of a few recipes I'd seen, I tried both brushing the ribs with cider vinegar and squeezing some lime juice over them before serving, but the raw acids were too sharp and masked the nuanced jerk flavor. Instead, I mixed a little vinegar with some reserved marinade and brushed it over the ribs for the last 10 minutes of cooking. This created a bright, fresh, deeply flavorful crust that took the ribs from good to great.

We suggest serving these spicy, punchy ribs with a reggae soundtrack and plenty of ice-cold Red Stripe beer.

MORGAN BOLLING, *Cook's Country*

NOTES FROM THE TEST KITCHEN

WHICH RIBS WORK BEST FOR JERK?

Three cuts of pork ribs are commonly offered at supermarkets: St. Louis–style, baby back, and country-style ribs. Country-style ribs aren't ribs at all but are more like long, irregular chops cut from where the loin meets the shoulder; they contain a mix of dark and light meat. Baby back ribs are cut from the loin area and are smaller and leaner than St. Louis–style spareribs. For this recipe, we opted for St. Louis–style, as their big flavor (they're cut from near the belly, where bacon comes from) stood up to the jerk's bold spices. If you see spareribs not called "St. Louis–cut," they probably have extra meat and bone attached—this gives them an irregular shape and makes them hard to cook evenly.

ST. LOUIS–STYLE RIBS
meaty flavor, uniform shape

JERK PORK RIBS

Jerk Pork Ribs

SERVES 4 TO 6

This recipe requires letting the coated ribs sit for at least 1 hour. We recommend wearing rubber gloves when handling the habaneros—they're hot! If you are spice-averse, remove the seeds and ribs from the habaneros or substitute jalapeños, which are less spicy.

8	scallions, chopped coarse
¼	cup vegetable oil
¼	cup molasses
3	tablespoons chopped fresh ginger
2	tablespoons ground allspice
1–2	habanero chiles, stemmed
3	garlic cloves, peeled
1	tablespoon dried thyme
1	tablespoon salt
2	(2½- to 3-pound) racks St. Louis–style spareribs, trimmed
3	tablespoons cider vinegar
	Lime wedges

1. Process scallions, oil, 3 tablespoons molasses, ginger, allspice, habaneros, garlic, thyme, and salt in blender until smooth, 1 to 2 minutes, scraping down sides of blender jar as needed. Transfer ¼ cup jerk paste to bowl, cover, and refrigerate until needed. Place ribs on rimmed baking sheet and brush all over with remaining paste. Cover sheet tightly with plastic wrap and refrigerate for at least 1 hour or up to 24 hours.

2. Adjust oven rack to middle position and heat oven to 275 degrees. Line second rimmed baking sheet with aluminum foil and set wire rack in sheet. Unwrap ribs and place, meat side up, on prepared wire rack. Roast until tender and fork inserted into meat meets no resistance, 4 to 4½ hours.

3. Stir vinegar and remaining 1 tablespoon molasses into reserved jerk paste. Brush meat side of racks with vinegar mixture. Return ribs to oven and roast until sauce sets, about 10 minutes. Transfer ribs to carving board, tent with foil, and let rest for 20 minutes. Slice racks between ribs. Serve with lime wedges.

CHINESE BARBECUED SPARERIBS

✔ WHY THIS RECIPE WORKS: Chinese-style barbecued ribs are usually marinated for several hours and then slow-roasted and basted repeatedly to build up a thick crust. We skipped both of those time-consuming steps and instead braised the ribs, cut into individual pieces to speed cooking and create more surface area, in a highly seasoned liquid, which helped the flavor penetrate thoroughly and quickly. Then we strained, defatted, and reduced the braising liquid to make a full-bodied glaze in which we tossed the ribs before roasting them on a rack in a hot oven to color and crisp their exteriors.

Chinese barbecued spareribs are typically associated with Cantonese buffets and pupu platters, those medleys of vaguely authentic finger food that have been fixtures in Chinese American and Polynesian restaurants for decades. But unlike the questionable provenance of platter mates such as crab rangoon and chicken fingers, spareribs have real roots in Chinese cuisine. Their lurid red glow, lacquered sheen, and flavors redolent of hoisin and soy sauces, ginger, garlic, and five-spice powder indicate they are a form of *char siu*, the Cantonese-style barbecued pork you can find hanging in the windows of meat shops in any Chinatown. Their appeal is obvious—the meat is salty and sweet, with a deeply caramelized exterior and a satisfying, resilient chew—and recipes for them have appeared in American newspapers, magazines, and cookbooks since the mid-20th century.

The distinct chew of Chinese barbecued spareribs sets them apart from the fall-off-the-bone tenderness of most American styles. They're also cooked very differently, since they're not actually barbecued. Like all forms of char siu, the ribs are marinated and then slow-roasted. In restaurants, this happens in large, boxy ovens where the meat hangs from hooks—a setup that allows fat to drip and hot air to circulate all around the meat so that it achieves its hallmark burnished finish. But this method also makes Chinese ribs tricky to replicate in a home oven, something I've always wanted to do in the winter months when I take a hiatus from the grill or when I don't feel like trekking to Chinatown for the real deal.

Spareribs are cut close to the belly of the pig, and a whole rack can weigh more than 5 pounds since it includes the brisket bone and surrounding meat. To make smaller, evenly rectangular racks that are easier to fit on a grill or in the oven, butchers lop off the brisket portion and call this more svelte cut St. Louis–style spareribs. They're meaty and flavorful and are our go-to cut for most rib recipes.

I started with two racks and mixed up a char siu marinade: soy and hoisin sauces, Chinese rice wine, garlic, ginger, five-spice powder, white pepper, and red food coloring (traditionally this color came from fermented rice or bean paste).

The recipes I found recommended marinating the ribs for hours or even for days. We typically find that marinating meat for anything longer than an hour is overkill, since very few flavors penetrate much beyond the meat's surface, no matter how long it soaks. But here a longer marinade might actually be worthwhile, since the char siu marinade contains soy and hoisin sauces—powerhouse ingredients packed with salt and glutamates, both of which penetrate deep into meat.

Since the layer of meat on ribs is thin, a 2-hour soak seemed like plenty of time. I went with that and tried three common cooking methods. The first re-creates the conditions of a Chinese barbecue oven by cooking a whole slab of ribs on a rack in a low oven, flipping it and basting it with a reduction of the marinade so that all sides of the rack get good exposure to the marinade and the heat. The results were chewy yet tender and had a lacquered coat, but this method required 3 to 4 hours of closely attended cooking in addition to marinating time—more of a commitment than I wanted.

The second, a speedier variation on that method, turns up the heat to about 350 degrees so that the ribs cook in 1 to 1½ hours. Unfortunately, the time savings came at the expense of the meat, which was dry. And the third, more common approach is to cut the rack into individual ribs and roast them in two stages: covered for 1 to 1½ hours so that they steam and tenderize and then brushed with a reduction of the marinade and roasted (or broiled) uncovered for about 15 minutes to dry out and color their exteriors.

The third method, moist heat followed by dry, was the most promising. Cutting the racks into single ribs speeds cooking and creates lots of surface area for painting on the flavor-packed glaze. And moist heat is a very efficient way to cook meat, since water conducts energy faster than air does. The drawback is that you don't want to baste ribs that you cover—the steamy environment doesn't allow the first coat to dry and set, so you never get a substantial buildup of glaze. I'd have to get all my glazing done after I uncovered them.

My next move was to intensify the marinade so that when it reduced, a single coat of glaze would taste robust. I mixed up another batch with more soy and hoisin, more garlic and ginger, and more spices. I also added honey, another typical char siu component that would lend the basting liquid more body.

But as I mixed up my new marinade, something occurred to me: If the ribs needed to soak in the marinade and moist heat was the most efficient way to cook them, why not do both at once by braising the ribs in the marinade before roasting them? Heat would also help the flavors penetrate the meat more quickly, so the cooking time wouldn't need to be long for the flavors to soak in. Then I could further reduce the braising liquid and use that to baste the ribs.

I made another batch of my marinade but this time thinned it with a little water and placed it in a Dutch oven. I added the ribs and let them simmer on the stovetop until they were just tender, which took about 1 hour and 15 minutes. After straining and defatting the braising liquid, I returned it to the pot to simmer until it had reduced to a thick glaze; at this point, I also added some toasted sesame oil for further complexity. In the meantime, I heated the oven to 425 degrees and set a wire rack inside a rimmed baking sheet that I'd lined with aluminum foil and partially filled with water to catch the drips of fat and glaze that would otherwise cause the sheet to smoke. I tossed the ribs in the glaze and then placed them bone side up on the rack.

After 15 minutes, with a flip halfway through, they were done. The braising liquid's salty-sweet flavor had penetrated the meat, and the glaze created a lacquered sheen that gave way to the meat's satisfying chew. It was char siu to rival the best I'd had in Chinatown, but it was easy to make in my own kitchen.

ANDREW JANJIGIAN, *Cook's Illustrated*

Chinese-Style Barbecued Spareribs

SERVES 6 TO 8 AS AN APPETIZER OR 4 TO 6 AS A MAIN COURSE

It's not necessary to remove the membrane on the bone side of the ribs. These ribs are chewier than American-style ribs; if you prefer them more tender, cook them for an additional 15 minutes in step 1. Adding water to the baking sheet during roasting helps prevent smoking. Serve the ribs alone as an appetizer or with vegetables and rice as a main course. You can serve the first batch immediately or tent them with foil to keep them warm.

- 1 (6-inch) piece fresh ginger, peeled and sliced thin
- 8 garlic cloves, peeled
- 1 cup honey
- ¾ cup hoisin sauce
- ¾ cup soy sauce
- ½ cup Chinese rice wine or dry sherry
- 2 teaspoons five-spice powder
- 1 teaspoon red food coloring (optional)
- 1 teaspoon white pepper
- 2 (2½- to 3-pound) racks St. Louis–style spareribs, cut into individual ribs
- 2 tablespoons toasted sesame oil

1. Pulse ginger and garlic in food processor until finely chopped, 10 to 12 pulses, scraping down sides of bowl as needed. Transfer ginger-garlic mixture to Dutch oven. Add honey; hoisin; soy sauce; ½ cup water; rice wine; five-spice powder; food coloring, if using; and white pepper and whisk until combined. Add ribs and stir to coat (ribs will not be fully submerged). Bring to simmer over high heat, then reduce heat to low, cover, and cook for 1¼ hours, stirring occasionally.

2. Adjust oven rack to middle position and heat oven to 425 degrees. Using tongs, transfer ribs to large bowl. Strain braising liquid through fine-mesh strainer set over large container, pressing on solids to extract as much liquid as possible; discard solids. Let cooking liquid settle for 10 minutes. Using wide, shallow spoon, skim fat from surface and discard.

3. Return braising liquid to pot and add sesame oil. Bring to boil over high heat and cook until syrupy and reduced to 2½ cups, 16 to 20 minutes.

4. Set wire rack in aluminum foil–lined rimmed baking sheet and pour ½ cup water into sheet. Transfer half of ribs to pot with braising liquid and toss to coat. Arrange ribs, bone sides up, on prepared rack, letting excess glaze drip off. Roast until edges of ribs start to caramelize, 5 to 7 minutes. Flip ribs and continue to roast until second side starts to caramelize, 5 to 7 minutes longer. Transfer ribs to serving platter; repeat process with remaining ribs. Serve.

TO MAKE AHEAD: At end of step 3, refrigerate ribs and glaze separately, covered, for up to 2 days. When ready to serve, bring glaze and half of ribs to simmer in Dutch oven over medium heat, then proceed with step 4. Repeat with remaining ribs.

NOTES FROM THE TEST KITCHEN

FLAVOR-PACKED INDOOR RIBS IN 2 HOURS
American barbecued ribs require you to spend the better part of a day tending a live fire. Our version of the Chinese approach uses the oven and takes 2 hours from start to finish.

CUT RACK INTO RIBS
Individual ribs have more surface area than an uncut rack, which means each one is exposed to heat and to the marinade on all sides. (It's not necessary to remove the rack's membrane before slicing.)

BRAISE IN MARINADE
Moist heat quickly tenderizes the meat and accelerates the penetration of flavorful compounds, so the cooking time doesn't need to be long for the flavors to soak in.

ROAST IN HOT OVEN
Just 10 to 15 minutes in a hot oven dries the ribs' exteriors so that the glaze can set and caramelize.

HARISSA-RUBBED BONELESS LEG OF LAMB

✓ **WHY THIS RECIPE WORKS:** The robust, fragrant flavor profile of North African cuisine is a perfect pairing with rich, meaty lamb. We took advantage of the broad surface area of a boneless leg of lamb by rubbing it with Tunisian-inspired harissa paste. We bloomed paprika, coriander, Aleppo pepper, cumin, caraway, and garlic in oil in the microwave and applied our quick homemade harissa to the inside of the leg before rolling it up and tying it to make a compact roast. We seared the exterior of the meat before moving the lamb to the oven where it finished roasting to a juicy medium-rare. We also applied more of the harissa to the outside of the roast in between the two cooking steps. We prepared a quick vegetable side while the roast rested by tossing cauliflower florets with the pan drippings and roasting them until they were tender and browned. Combining the warm cauliflower with shredded carrots, sweet raisins, cilantro, and toasted almonds produced a side that paired perfectly with the fragrant, richly spiced lamb.

Boneless leg of lamb may not be what springs to mind when you plan to host a Sunday supper, but perhaps it should be. Not only does this cut boast plenty of rich flavor, but the butchering has already been done for you; and unlike cumbersome bone-in leg of lamb, a boneless leg is more easily translated into a tidy, simple-to-serve roast. I decided to focus my efforts on a half leg, a moderately sized cut that's perfect for feeding a small group. And because the meat is so flavorful on its own, I hoped all I'd need was an impactful spice blend to turn my roast into a satisfying centerpiece.

But before tinkering with flavor, I first needed to nail down a suitable roasting technique. This ragged, uneven cut of meat is best served rolled up, a shape that allows for even cooking and thorough seasoning. After pounding the half leg to even thickness and seasoning it with salt, I rolled it up and secured the shape with twine. In a perfect world, all I'd need to do next would be to slide the lamb into a hot oven, which would deeply brown the exterior and gradually cook the meat to a juicy medium-rare. Unfortunately, what emerged after this first round was a tough, chewy roast accompanied by billows of smoke. Worse yet, that smoke had infused the meat with an off-putting flavor.

Clearly, oven searing wouldn't deliver the crisp, tasty crust I sought; I needed a more direct approach. To achieve deep browning before the fat had a chance to burn and smoke, I decided to try searing the roast on the stovetop. This worked beautifully: With just a light coating of oil on the outside of the roast, the lamb developed a perfectly burnished exterior in a matter of minutes. I then propped the seared lamb on a rack in my roasting pan and slid it into the oven where it took about an hour to reach a perfect medium-rare.

This salt-seasoned leg was tasty, but I wanted something bolder for my roast. As I flipped through cookbooks looking for inspiration, I was drawn to a few North African recipes, which used an intriguing array of spices and condiments to flavor the lamb. Rather than call for a litany of hard-to-find spices, I decided to give harissa a try. This smoky chile paste is ubiquitous in North African cuisine, but as I sampled different jarred products, I discovered just how varied this condiment can be. Some were incredibly spicy, while others were puzzlingly bland; some were chunky and thick, others were thin and watery. I decided the only way to guarantee a perfectly spreadable, moderately spicy paste was to make my own. Since chiles are harissa's backbone, I chose a mix of ground dried varieties. Paprika gave the paste a mild, sweet flavor and Aleppo pepper contributed a complex fruitiness and slow-building heat. To the ground chiles I added plenty of minced garlic, aromatic spices—coriander, cumin, and caraway seeds—and peppery olive oil to turn it into a thick paste. To bloom the spices without pulling out an extra skillet, I simply microwaved them for a minute. My homemade harissa couldn't have been easier.

I spread harissa all over the inside of the pounded leg to ensure that its deep flavor would be present in every tender bite of lamb. I once again tied the roast and proceeded with my recipe, brushing a layer of harissa on the seared exterior to help build a spiced crust as the leg roasted in the oven. After about an hour of roasting, I was met with a beautifully fragrant, deeply flavorful, juicy leg of lamb. But as I let it rest—a step critical to keeping the meat juicy—I eyed the juices pooled in the bottom of my roasting pan. What if I used this harissa-spiked fat to flavor a simple side to round out my roast? I decided to use the meat's 15-minute rest to prepare a quick North African–inspired vegetable to accompany the lamb.

I tossed cauliflower florets with a few tablespoons of the fat in the roasting pan and sealed them under a sheet of foil, roasting them at 475 degrees to soften and steam them before removing the foil to encourage flavorful browning. Sliced onion offered lightly caramelized bites. Tossed with shredded carrots and raisins for some subtle sweetness, cilantro and lemon juice for freshness, and some toasted almonds for crunch, this speedy salad was the perfect complement to the meaty lamb, subtly echoing its flavors and turning my Sunday roast into an impressive (and easy) one-pan supper.

RUSSELL SELANDER, *America's Test Kitchen Books*

Harissa-Rubbed Roast Boneless Leg of Lamb with Warm Cauliflower Salad

SERVES 6 TO 8

If you can't find Aleppo pepper, you can substitute ¾ teaspoon paprika and ¾ teaspoon finely chopped red pepper flakes. Leg of lamb is often sold in elastic netting that must be removed.

- ½ cup extra-virgin olive oil
- 6 garlic cloves, minced
- 2 tablespoons paprika
- 1 tablespoon ground coriander
- 1 tablespoon ground dried Aleppo pepper
- 1 teaspoon ground cumin
- ¾ teaspoon caraway seeds
  Salt and pepper
- 1 (3½- to 4-pound) boneless half leg of lamb, trimmed and pounded to ¾-inch thickness
- 1 head cauliflower (2 pounds), cored and cut into 1-inch florets
- ½ red onion, sliced ¼ inch thick
- 1 cup shredded carrots
- ½ cup raisins
- ¼ cup fresh cilantro leaves
- 2 tablespoons sliced almonds, toasted
- 1 tablespoon lemon juice, plus extra for seasoning

1. Combine 6 tablespoons oil, garlic, paprika, coriander, Aleppo pepper, cumin, caraway seeds, and 1 teaspoon salt in bowl and microwave until bubbling and very fragrant, about 1 minute, stirring halfway through microwaving. Let cool to room temperature.

2. Adjust oven rack to lower-middle position and heat oven to 375 degrees. Set V-rack in large roasting pan and spray with vegetable oil spray. Lay roast on cutting board with rough interior side (which was against bone) facing up and rub with 2 tablespoons spice paste. Roll roast and tie with kitchen twine at 1½-inch intervals, then rub exterior with 1 tablespoon oil.

3. Heat remaining 1 tablespoon oil in 12-inch skillet over medium-high heat until just smoking. Brown lamb on all sides, about 8 minutes. Brush lamb all over with remaining spice paste and place fat side down in prepared V-rack. Roast until thickest part registers 125 degrees (for medium-rare), 50 to 70 minutes, flipping lamb halfway through roasting. Transfer lamb to carving board, tent with aluminum foil, and let rest while making salad.

4. Increase oven temperature to 475 degrees. Pour all but 3 tablespoons fat from pan; discard any charred drippings. Add cauliflower, ½ teaspoon salt, and ½ teaspoon pepper to pan and toss to coat. Cover with aluminum foil and roast until cauliflower is softened, about 5 minutes.

5. Remove foil and spread onion evenly over cauliflower. Roast until vegetables are tender and cauliflower is golden brown, 10 to 15 minutes, stirring halfway through roasting. Transfer vegetable mixture to serving bowl, add carrots, raisins, cilantro, almonds, and lemon juice and toss to combine. Season with salt, pepper, and lemon juice to taste. Slice leg of lamb into ½-inch-thick slices and serve with salad.

NOTES FROM THE TEST KITCHEN

PREPARING A BONELESS LEG OF LAMB

Place the rough side of the meat (the side that was closest to the bone) facing up on a counter or cutting board. Pound the meat to ¾-inch thickness to ensure even cooking.

POULTRY AND SEAFOOD

FRIED CHICKEN TENDERS

✔ **WHY THIS RECIPE WORKS:** The chicken tenders served at the Puritan Backroom in Manchester, New Hampshire, are hard to resist: crunchy on the outside and almost impossibly juicy, mildly sweet, and deeply seasoned throughout. To replicate the recipe, we marinated chicken tenderloins in a savory-sweet mixture of duck sauce, water, and salt. We then tossed the tenders in a seasoned breading right after pulling them from the marinade so that the viscous marinade mingled with the breading, coating the tenders in craggy, batter-like bits. The sugar in the marinade had the added effect of aiding browning, allowing the tenders to become crispy and golden brown after just 4 minutes of frying.

At the Puritan Backroom Restaurant in Manchester, New Hampshire, the owners know what the people want: chicken tenders. In fact, the restaurant, located in the biggest city in a political battleground state, is so popular for its tenders that the Backroom is now considered a must-stop spot for presidential nominees seeking to press some flesh.

To see why, a couple of colleagues and I paid the Backroom a visit. Frankly, I was worried about making a special trip for chicken tenders, which are so often an underwhelming afterthought for restaurants. It's as if they assume chicken fingers are just kids'-menu food and refuse to waste their time making them well.

This was decidedly not the case at the Puritan Backroom. The tenders we tried were crunchy on the outside, almost impossibly juicy inside, and deeply seasoned throughout, with a mild sweetness. Served in a heap alongside a dish of sweet and sour duck sauce, they were indeed fit for a POTUS.

If one thing sets the Backroom's tenders apart, it's that subtle sweetness. The Puritan cooks marinate their tenders overnight, but they wouldn't say what was in the marinade. Since the tenders they serve are so juicy, I was willing to bet that the marinade had a healthy dose of salt, which would flavor and season the chicken and help it retain moisture, as well as some sugar. However, when I tried soaking the chicken in a salt and sugar solution, it tasted great, but the coating—a classic combination of flour and cornstarch—emerged from the oil powdery and pale rather than crunchy, golden, and substantial.

I had a hunch why this might be. At Puritan, I noticed that the marinade was slightly viscous and the cooks breaded the tenders right after pulling them from the marinade so that the marinade mingled with the breading and coated the chicken in craggy bits. My marinade was watery by comparison, and I was shaking off any excess liquid before breading. I needed a new, thicker marinade.

Looking at my ingredient list, it hit me. Could the cooks at Puritan be marinating their tenders in the same duck sauce they use as a dipping sauce? That would explain both the sweetness and the thickness of the marinade.

I grabbed some duck sauce, thinned it with water to the consistency I remembered, and then bumped up the salt until it was brine strength. After giving the chicken an overnight soak, I tossed it straight from the marinade into the breading. I then let the breaded chicken rest in the fridge (on a wire rack set in a rimmed baking sheet) for an hour to ensure that the breading would cling to the tenders rather than slough off during frying. I slid the chicken into the hot oil with high hopes.

To my delight, in just 4 minutes, the tenders had turned a gorgeous shade of deep golden brown and the breading clung beautifully. What's more, the sugar in the duck sauce had the unexpected advantage of enhancing the browning in the breading.

As my colleagues devoured the tenders, I was reminded of the Puritan Backroom and its throngs of happy customers. This was food good enough to persuade all hungry people, no matter what their political leanings, to set aside differences and share a meal.

MATTHEW FAIRMAN, *Cook's Country*

Puritan Backroom-Style Chicken Tenders
SERVES 4

For the best results, we prefer to let the chicken marinate overnight, but just 1 hour works if you are short on time. Plan ahead: The chicken needs to chill for at least 1 hour after coating. Use a Dutch oven with at least a 6-quart capacity. Serve the tenders with one of our dipping sauces (recipes follow).

PURITAN BACKROOM–STYLE CHICKEN TENDERS

1 cup water

½ cup duck sauce

Salt and pepper

2 pounds chicken tenderloins, trimmed

1¾ cups all-purpose flour

¼ cup cornstarch

2 teaspoons baking powder

1½ teaspoons garlic powder

¼ teaspoon cayenne pepper

3 quarts peanut or vegetable oil

1. Whisk water, duck sauce, and 1 tablespoon salt in bowl until salt is dissolved. Add chicken to marinade, cover, and refrigerate for at least 1 hour or overnight.

2. Whisk flour, cornstarch, baking powder, garlic powder, cayenne, 1½ teaspoons pepper, and 1 teaspoon salt together in large bowl. Set wire rack in rimmed baking sheet. Remove half of chicken from marinade, add to flour mixture, and toss to coat, pressing to adhere. Transfer chicken to prepared rack. Repeat with remaining chicken and remaining flour mixture. Refrigerate for at least 1 hour or up to 2 hours.

3. Line large plate with triple layer of paper towels. Add oil to large Dutch oven until it measures about 2 inches deep and heat over medium-high heat to 350 degrees. Add half of chicken to hot oil and fry until deep golden brown and registering 160 degrees, about 4 minutes, stirring occasionally. Transfer chicken to prepared plate. Season with salt and pepper to taste. Return oil to 350 degrees and repeat with remaining chicken. Serve.

Puritan Backroom–Style Sweet-and-Sour Sauce

MAKES ABOUT ½ CUP

Since the consistency of duck sauce can vary significantly from product to product, we call for a range for the amount of water.

½ cup duck sauce

4 teaspoons distilled white vinegar

1 teaspoon soy sauce

¼ teaspoon salt

Pinch ground ginger

Pinch cayenne pepper

1–2 tablespoons water

Combine duck sauce, vinegar, soy sauce, salt, ginger, and cayenne in bowl. Add 1 tablespoon water and check consistency; sauce should cling to spoon but should not be gloppy or runny. Adjust consistency with up to 1 additional tablespoon water as needed.

Chipotle-Barbecue Dipping Sauce

MAKES ABOUT 1 CUP

Our preferred liquid smoke product is Wright's Liquid Smoke, which contains only smoke and water.

¾ cup ketchup

3 tablespoons molasses

1 tablespoon cider vinegar

1 tablespoon minced canned chipotle chile in adobo sauce

⅛ teaspoon liquid smoke (optional)

Salt and pepper

Whisk ketchup, molasses, vinegar, chipotle, and liquid smoke, if using, in bowl until combined. Season with salt and pepper to taste.

Honey-Dijon Dipping Sauce

MAKES ¾ CUP

Yellow mustard can be substituted for the Dijon, if desired.

½ cup Dijon mustard

¼ cup honey

Salt and pepper

Whisk mustard and honey in bowl until combined. Season with salt and pepper to taste.

NOTES FROM THE TEST KITCHEN

WHAT IS DUCK SAUCE?

No, it's not a sauce made from ducks. This thick, sweet sauce is also called plum sauce, and it's made with plums and/or apricots, plenty of sugar, and seasonings (often including vinegar). And the name? The sauce is traditionally served alongside roast duck in Chinese cuisine.

Many of us are familiar with the clear plastic packets of the orangy, corn syrup–sweetened stuff that come with our Chinese takeout orders, but higher-quality versions can be found in the international section of most supermarkets.

MAKE-AHEAD CHICKEN PARMESAN

✔ **WHY THIS RECIPE WORKS:** Traditional chicken Parmesan is a minefield of potential problems: dry meat, soggy crust, and a chewy blanket of mozzarella. To keep the meat moist, we salted the cutlets for 20 minutes, and to keep the exterior crunchy, we replaced more than half of the bread crumbs with grated Parmesan cheese. Mixing the usual shredded mozzarella with creamy fontina helped ensure that the cheese stayed smooth and melty, not congealed, and we placed the mixture directly on the fried cutlet so that it formed a waterproof layer between the crust and the sauce. A simple homemade sauce made with plenty of aromatics and fresh basil was the perfect finishing touch to this improved classic.

Great chicken Parmesan is hard to beat: Crispy breaded chicken cutlets, gooey melted cheese, and a zesty tomato sauce come together in symphonic harmony. Quite simply, it is comfort food at its most comforting. The test kitchen has a fantastic recipe for chicken Parmesan, but it takes about an hour and a half from start to finish, and most weeknights I simply don't have the bandwidth to manage the preparation involved. So when I started working on a collection of make-ahead recipes for an upcoming book project, I turned my attention to translating this beloved classic into a make-ahead possibility.

The recipe is broken down into three basic parts: make a simple, thick tomato sauce; bread and fry the cutlets; then broil the cutlets with the cheese before topping with sauce (the sauce is added at the end to avoid a soggy crust). I decided to look at each piece of the recipe to identify potential opportunities for cooking in advance.

First up for examination: the sauce. The sauce gets its flavor from canned crushed tomatoes and plenty of punchy ingredients such as minced garlic, dried oregano, red pepper flakes, and fresh basil. The mixture is cooked until slightly thickened, which eliminates excess water and prevents the sauce from making the chicken soggy. It's easy to make, but it still requires about 25 minutes to prep and cook. Fortunately, I figured the sauce would be an ideal candidate for making ahead; from past testing I knew that tomato-based sauces can be kept in the fridge for a few days and

usually freeze beautifully. Some quick storage tests revealed that the sauce could be refrigerated for up to three days and frozen for up to a month.

But preparing only the sauce in advance wouldn't save me a ton of kitchen time. I needed to take my make-ahead approach further, so I turned my attention to the other parts of the recipe: the breading, frying, and broiling of the chicken. The biggest questions I wanted to answer were: Should the chicken be stored before or after frying? Would the breaded cutlets keep better in the fridge or the freezer? Could the cheese be added in advance? And finally: How best to cook (or reheat) the chicken on serving day?

In the original recipe, chicken breasts are sliced in half horizontally, gently pounded to an even ½-inch thickness, and salted for a few minutes (to enhance flavor and help the lean meat hold on to moisture). The cutlets are then dipped into a mixture of egg and flour (most recipes call for dipping in flour and then egg, but we found that combining the two worked just as well and cut down on dishes) before being coated with panko bread crumbs and Parmesan cheese. Because this coating is key to the texture and flavor of the dish, I knew I needed to maintain all of its appeal in order for my make-ahead version to be viable.

For my initial tests, I prepared several batches of cutlets, breading them all but frying only half. I stored one fried and one uncooked batch in the fridge, and transferred another fried and another uncooked batch to the freezer. Over the next few days, I cooked my way through the remaining steps of the recipe for all four batches.

From these first attempts, I got some clear results. The fried, refrigerated cutlets were a nonstarter; the coating was sodden and unsalvageable. The unfried refrigerated batch, however, was nearly indistinguishable from a freshly made batch; the coating crisped up nicely in the pan and could then be broiled with the cheese per the usual recipe.

The frozen versions were a slightly different story. The unfried frozen cutlets didn't work well; they needed to be defrosted before frying (putting the frozen cutlets straight into the pan resulted in either a burnt coating or undercooked meat), but during defrosting the chicken exuded moisture that made the crust decidedly less crisp. However, the fried-then-frozen cutlets held promise. I knew that the brief stint under the

MAKE-AHEAD CHICKEN PARMESAN

broiler to melt the cheese wouldn't be enough to warm them through, and, as with the unfried cutlets, defrosting wasn't a good option. But what about simply baking the fried, frozen cutlets? I hoped this approach would simultaneously heat the cutlets, drive off moisture and re-crisp the crust, and melt the cheese.

I arranged the cutlets (cheeseless for now) on a baking sheet and popped them into a 400-degree oven. After 20 minutes, the top crusts were golden and crunchy, but the melting ice crystals had caused the bottoms to steam slightly. Placing the cutlets on a wire rack fixed the problem; air could circulate around the cutlets as they baked, producing a uniformly crisp crust.

Now I needed to circle back to the cheese. I tested adding it at the beginning of baking and partway through, and found that it melted more thoroughly—without negatively affecting the crust—if I topped the cutlets at the outset. I wondered if I could take my make-ahead option one step further and freeze the fried cutlets with the cheese on top, but the cheese didn't adhere to the frozen cutlets very well and it was easy enough to sprinkle the cheese on before baking.

Now that I had three avenues to make my favorite chicken Parmesan ahead of time (refrigerating or freezing the sauce, refrigerating the breaded raw cutlets, or freezing the cutlets after frying), each of which produced a dish that was just as good as freshly made, I knew this comforting favorite would be spotted on my table a lot more often.

KATHRYN CALLAHAN WITH ANDREA GEARY,
America's Test Kitchen Books

Make-Ahead Chicken Parmesan

SERVES 4

This recipe makes enough sauce to top the cutlets as well as four servings of pasta.

SAUCE

- 2 tablespoons extra-virgin olive oil
- 2 garlic cloves, minced
  Kosher salt and pepper
- ¼ teaspoon dried oregano
  Pinch red pepper flakes
- 1 (28-ounce) can crushed tomatoes
- ¼ teaspoon sugar
- 2 tablespoons chopped fresh basil

CHICKEN

- 2 (6- to 8-ounce) boneless, skinless chicken breasts, trimmed, halved horizontally, and pounded ½ inch thick
- 1 teaspoon kosher salt
- 2 ounces whole-milk mozzarella cheese, shredded (½ cup)
- 2 ounces fontina cheese, shredded (½ cup)
- 1 large egg
- 1 tablespoon all-purpose flour
- 1½ ounces Parmesan cheese, grated (¾ cup)
- ½ cup panko bread crumbs
- ½ teaspoon garlic powder
- ¼ teaspoon dried oregano
- ¼ teaspoon pepper
- ⅓ cup vegetable oil
- ¼ cup torn fresh basil

1. FOR THE SAUCE: Heat 1 tablespoon oil in medium saucepan over medium heat until shimmering. Stir in garlic, ¾ teaspoon salt, oregano, and pepper flakes and cook until fragrant, about 30 seconds. Stir in tomatoes and sugar, increase heat to high, and bring to simmer. Reduce heat to medium-low and simmer until thickened, about 20 minutes. Off heat, stir in basil and remaining 1 tablespoon oil. Season with salt and pepper to taste, and cover to keep warm.

2. FOR THE CHICKEN: Sprinkle each side of each cutlet with ⅛ teaspoon salt and let stand at room temperature for 20 minutes. Combine mozzarella and fontina in bowl and set aside.

3. Adjust oven rack 4 inches from broiler element and heat broiler. Whisk egg and flour together in shallow dish until smooth. Combine Parmesan, panko, garlic powder, oregano, and pepper in second shallow dish. Pat chicken dry with paper towels. Working with 1 cutlet at a time, dredge in egg mixture, allowing excess to drip off, then coat with Parmesan mixture, pressing gently to adhere; transfer to large plate.

4. Heat oil in 10-inch nonstick skillet over medium-high heat until shimmering. Carefully place 2 cutlets in skillet and cook until crispy and deep golden, 1½ to 2 minutes per side. Transfer to paper towel–lined plate and repeat with remaining 2 cutlets.

5. Place cutlets on rimmed baking sheet and sprinkle cheese mixture evenly over top. Broil until cheese is melted and beginning to brown, 2 to 4 minutes.

6. Transfer chicken to serving platter and top each cutlet with 2 tablespoons sauce. Sprinkle with basil and serve immediately, passing additional sauce separately.

TO MAKE AHEAD: Sauce can be refrigerated for up to 3 days or frozen for up to 1 month; if frozen, thaw completely in refrigerator. Breaded chicken, prepared through step 3, can be refrigerated for up to 24 hours.

Alternatively, cooked chicken, prepared through step 4, can be frozen for up to 1 month. To reheat, place frozen cutlets on wire rack set in rimmed baking sheet, top with cheese, bake in 400-degree oven on middle rack until crisp and hot throughout, 20 to 30 minutes, and continue with step 6.

SLOW-COOKER CHICKEN TIKKA MASALA

✓ WHY THIS RECIPE WORKS: We wanted to create a flavorful take on chicken tikka masala that had tender, moist pieces of chicken napped with a robustly spiced creamy tomato sauce. While traditionally this dish calls for marinating the chicken overnight and cooking the sauce separately, we turned to our slow cooker for an easy hands-off version that would infuse big flavor into the chicken while cooking the entire dish to perfection. For a tikka masala recipe with assertive flavor, we needed the perfect sauce. Fresh tomatoes and canned sauce both released too much liquid during cooking, which created a thin sauce made worse by the juices released by the chicken. Switching to drained canned diced tomatoes along with flavor-packed tomato paste proved to be the answer, and when we added just the right mix of aromatics plus garam masala, our sauce had the bold, zesty tomato flavor that is the hallmark of this dish. To finish, we tempered yogurt and added it after cooking to ensure a velvety rich sauce.

When I'm in the mood for takeout, it's not pizza or lo mein that I crave; chicken tikka masala is always the first thing on my list. This rich dish of chicken in a creamy, spiced tomato sauce is one I've always wanted to master at home, but most recipes are elaborate and feature many tedious elements—a lengthy marinating time, a finicky cream sauce, and the delicate task of grilling or broiling cubes of lean chicken breast—as well as an exhaustive list of hard-to-source spices. I wanted a recipe that would be delicious yet doable and yield reliably moist pieces of chicken in an indulgent sauce. With these goals in mind, my thoughts immediately turned to the slow cooker. Its steady, even heat is ideal for quick-cooking proteins, and the moist cooking environment promised tender, juicy pieces of chicken flavored by the surrounding sauce. So, with visions of a simple, foolproof tikka masala in my future, I pulled out my slow cooker and got to work.

First, I needed to review the standard tikka masala components and steps. Its signature sauce features the brightness of tomatoes, a little spicy heat, and the richness of heavy cream. I wanted to maintain the classic heat and complexity, but I also wanted my ingredient list to be supermarket-friendly. Instead of playing around with endless combinations of spices I went with the simplest choice: commercial garam masala. With a warm, fragrant blend of cardamom, black pepper, cinnamon, and coriander, it put me on the fast track to a complex, aromatic sauce. Chopped onion and minced serrano chile promised a fresh, spicy, balanced base. I avoided dirtying another pan by blooming my aromatics along with a little oil in the microwave. I knew canned crushed tomatoes were an easy route to bright, fresh tomato flavor so I emptied a can into my slow cooker, stirring it in along with some heavy cream. With my sauce at the ready, it was time to tackle the chicken.

Traditional tikka masala recipes call for marinating the meat in yogurt, based on the long-standing belief that this step tenderizes the meat and allows it to absorb the flavors of the spices and aromatics. But I knew better than to try this, as previous attempts at yogurt marinades have shown us that this process often leads to mushy meat. I hoped that slowly simmering the chicken in my punched-up sauce would serve the same purpose, infusing it with flavor as it gently cooked through. To test this idea, I cut boneless, skinless chicken breasts into generous chunks, stirred them into the creamy sauce, and let the slow cooker work its magic.

SLOW-COOKER CHICKEN TIKKA MASALA

This first batch made it clear that I had some work to do. As the hours ticked by, the chicken slowly cooked through, but the resulting pieces were a little tough and dry. Also, the sauce was a disappointment: Not only had the tomatoes left the sauce watery and thin, but the cream had curdled. Speeding up the cooking process would resolve the first issue, so for my next batch I cut the breasts into smaller, quicker-cooking pieces. As for the sauce, I eliminated some liquid by giving drained diced tomatoes a try; I also held off on adding the cream until just before serving.

This sauce showed improvement, emerging more concentrated and tomatoey, but it still lacked tikka masala's characteristic complexity. The addition of a few cloves of garlic, some grated fresh ginger, and a little sugar balanced the sauce's heat and provided welcome depth, and a couple tablespoons of tomato paste contributed the dish's signature deep red color and intensified the tomato flavor. Tempering the cream with some of the sauce—in addition to stirring it in at the end—effectively prevented curdling, but it also thinned out my sauce's hard-earned texture. Thinking back to the traditional recipes I'd studied, I decided to give yogurt a try. Bingo: Not only did yogurt add just

the right creamy dimension to the thick sauce, it also introduced a sophisticated balance of richness and tang that the cream had lacked.

I finally had it: an easy, three-step tikka masala that was a true hands-off, fuss-free success. With incredible depth of flavor, perfectly tender chicken, and a luxurious sauce, my slow-cooker chicken tikka masala now rivaled the best takeout has to offer.

LEAH COLINS, *America's Test Kitchen Books*

Slow-Cooker Chicken Tikka Masala

SERVES 4

COOKING TIME: 2 TO 3 HOURS ON LOW
SLOW COOKER SIZE: 4 TO 7 QUARTS

For a spicier dish, do not remove the ribs and seeds from the chile.

- 1   onion, chopped fine
- 3   tablespoons vegetable oil
- 1   serrano chile, stemmed, seeded, and minced
- 2   tablespoons tomato paste
- 4   teaspoons garam masala
- 3   garlic cloves, minced
- 1   tablespoon grated fresh ginger
- 2   teaspoons sugar
     Salt and pepper
- 1   (14.5-ounce) can diced tomatoes, drained
- 2   pounds boneless, skinless chicken breasts, trimmed and cut into 1½-inch pieces
- ¾   cup plain whole-milk yogurt
- ¼   cup minced fresh cilantro

1. Microwave onion, oil, serrano, tomato paste, garam masala, garlic, ginger, sugar, and ½ teaspoon salt in bowl, stirring occasionally, until onion is softened, about 5 minutes; transfer to slow cooker. Stir in tomatoes. Season chicken with salt and pepper and stir into slow cooker. Cover and cook until chicken is tender, 2 to 3 hours on low.

2. Whisk ½ cup sauce and yogurt together in bowl (to temper), then stir mixture back into slow cooker and let sit until heated through, about 5 minutes. Stir in cilantro and season with salt and pepper to taste. Serve.

NOTES FROM THE TEST KITCHEN

SHOPPING FOR GARAM MASALA

Garam masala is a northern Indian combination of up to 12 dry-roasted, ground spices and is used in a wide range of dishes. The most common ingredients include black peppercorns, cinnamon, cloves, cardamom, coriander, cumin, dried chiles, fennel, mace, nutmeg, and bay leaves. (Ginger and caraway seeds also make frequent appearances.) In search of a good-tasting, commercially available garam masala, we tested a handful of top products. Tasters' favorite was **McCormick Gourmet Collection Garam Masala**, chosen for its ability to both blend into dishes and round out their acidic and sweet notes. It also won praise for adding a mellow, well-balanced aroma to most dishes.

INDOOR PULLED CHICKEN

✓ **WHY THIS RECIPE WORKS:** Our Indoor Pulled Chicken mimics the texture and flavor of outdoor slow-smoked pulled chicken in just a fraction of the time. We started by braising boneless, skinless chicken thighs in a mixture of chicken broth, salt, sugar, molasses, gelatin, and liquid smoke, which simulated the flavor of traditional smoked chicken. The gelatin and broth helped replicate the unctuous texture and intense chicken flavor of whole chicken parts. To mimic the richness of skin-on chicken, we skipped trimming the fat from the thighs and added the rendered fat back to the finished pulled chicken. Finally, we mixed the shredded meat with some of the barbecue sauce and cooked it briefly to drive off excess moisture.

Traditional pulled chicken is a true labor of love: First you brine bone-in, skin-on parts for an hour or so. Then you cook them slowly over coals and wood chunks until the meat is moist and tender within and kissed with smoke flavor throughout. With the skin burnished to a deep mahogany, smoked chicken is a beautiful thing—making it feel almost like a crime to pull off the skin, shred the richly flavored meat, and douse it in barbecue sauce for sandwiches.

I had already developed a killer recipe for smoked chicken, and if I make it for friends, you'd better believe I'm going to get full credit for all the work by showing off its burnished parts. But for those times when I need a quick weeknight meal or when my grill is covered with 16 inches of snow, I had a hunch that I could make some really good pulled chicken by simply braising chicken parts in a smoky barbecue sauce. It wouldn't give me burnished skin, but I wouldn't need that anyway.

My smoked chicken recipe calls for whole breasts and leg quarters; I pull the white meat off the fire early since it cooks faster than the dark meat. But in the interest of keeping things as simple as possible, I decided to use only thighs for my indoor pulled chicken. They are our preferred cut for braising since they have lots of collagen, which turns to gelatin and gives the meat a moist, tender texture. Using the boneless, skinless type was one more way to streamline things.

I arranged 2 pounds of thighs (enough to make six to eight sandwiches) in a Dutch oven along with the makings of a tangy barbecue sauce—ketchup, molasses,

Worcestershire sauce, hot sauce, and salt and pepper—and enough water to comfortably cover the chicken. I also stirred in a couple of teaspoons of liquid smoke. I know what you might be thinking, but stick with me: Liquid smoke is an all-natural ingredient made from real woodsmoke and would replicate the flavor achieved via wood chips (see "Don't Shy Away from Liquid Smoke" on page 162).

I brought the pot to a simmer and let it bubble until the thighs were tender, about 25 minutes. To shred the chicken, I found that our usual method of pulling it apart with a pair of forks was overkill for meat so fall-apart tender. It was also slow. Putting the thighs in the bowl of a stand mixer and using the paddle attachment—which we sometimes use to shred large quantities—worked, but it was a big piece of equipment to haul out for 10 seconds of use. In the end, shredding the meat with a pair of tongs was the most efficient way to get the job done.

I stirred some of the braising liquid into the shredded chicken and piled it onto buns. Between bites, my colleagues offered critiques. One was that the meat was washed out: It lacked seasoning and had none of the concentrated chicken-y taste that you get in real smoked chicken. Also, the sauce was thin.

I changed up my method, this time simmering the thighs in a much smaller amount of liquid, hoping it would produce better-tasting meat. I used only 1 cup of water mixed with sugar, salt, molasses, and liquid smoke. Sugar and salt are common brine components and would flavor the meat, molasses would add bittersweet notes, and liquid smoke would, of course, contribute the smoky element. I separately prepared a thick barbecue sauce to coat the chicken in before serving.

NOTES FROM THE TEST KITCHEN

A NEW WAY TO SHRED CHICKEN

Instead of using two forks to shred the chicken, we squeeze it gently with tongs. The meat is so tender that it falls apart easily into bite-size pieces.

Sure enough, the salty-sweet braising liquid had infused the meat with the taste of a brined, slowly smoked bird. Still, it was lacking the deep poultry flavor and unctuous meatiness of real smoked chicken. But aside from the cooking method, the only other difference between this recipe and my outdoor recipe was the lack of skin and bones.

Chicken skin contains fat that renders and bastes the meat as it cooks. Chicken skin, bones, and tendons offer collagen, which breaks down during cooking to form gelatin, giving the meat a rich, luxurious texture. How could I get more of these missing elements—fat and gelatin—into my recipe?

As I prepped my next batch, I thought about how we normally trim and discard the fat attached to boneless, skinless chicken thighs. This time around, I decided to leave it. Once the chicken was cooked, I strained the braising liquid, skimmed off the fat (2 pounds of thighs yielded about 3 tablespoons), and added it to the chicken. I also swapped the braising water for chicken broth and stirred in some powdered gelatin. The extra fat, along with the broth and gelatin, greatly improved the flavor and overall unctuousness of the meat.

The chicken needed to be reheated after shredding, so I mixed it with some of the braising liquid and a little barbecue sauce and heated it until it absorbed all the liquid and appeared dry, which took about 5 minutes. (Since the liquid smoke flavor seemed to diminish during braising, I added a bit more at this point.) After this step, the chicken was meaty and dense, ready for extra sauce to be added at the table.

For some variety, I mixed up two more sauces: a mustardy South Carolina–style sauce and a vinegary North Carolina–style option. Now when I crave pulled chicken, will I head outside? Maybe, if the sun is shining and I have time to burn. Otherwise, I'm staying in.

ANDREW JANJIGIAN, *Cook's Illustrated*

Indoor Pulled Chicken

SERVES 6 TO 8

Do not trim the fat from the chicken thighs; it contributes to the flavor and texture of the pulled chicken. If you don't have 3 tablespoons of fat to add back to the pot in step 3, add melted butter to make up the difference. We like mild molasses in this recipe; do not use blackstrap. Serve the pulled chicken on white bread or hamburger buns with pickles and coleslaw.

1 cup chicken broth

2 tablespoons molasses

1 tablespoon sugar

1 tablespoon liquid smoke

1 teaspoon unflavored gelatin

Salt and pepper

2 pounds boneless, skinless chicken thighs, halved crosswise

1 recipe barbecue sauce (recipes follow)

Hot sauce

1. Bring broth, molasses, sugar, 2 teaspoons liquid smoke, gelatin, and 1 teaspoon salt to boil in large Dutch oven over high heat, stirring to dissolve sugar. Add chicken and return to simmer. Reduce heat to medium-low, cover, and cook, stirring occasionally, until chicken is easily shredded with fork, about 25 minutes.

2. Transfer chicken to medium bowl and set aside. Strain cooking liquid through fine-mesh strainer set over bowl (do not wash pot). Let liquid settle for 5 minutes; skim fat from surface. Set aside fat and defatted liquid.

3. Using tongs, squeeze chicken until shredded into bite-size pieces. Transfer chicken, 1 cup barbecue sauce, ½ cup reserved defatted liquid, 3 tablespoons reserved fat, and remaining 1 teaspoon liquid smoke to now-empty pot. Cook mixture over medium heat, stirring frequently, until liquid has been absorbed and exterior of meat appears dry, about 5 minutes. Season with salt, pepper, and hot sauce to taste. Serve, passing remaining barbecue sauce separately.

NOTES FROM THE TEST KITCHEN

DON'T SHY AWAY FROM LIQUID SMOKE

Until we did some research years ago, we assumed (as many people do) that there must be some kind of synthetic chemical chicanery going on in the making of liquid smoke. But that's not the case.

Liquid smoke is made by channeling smoke from smoldering wood chips through a condenser, which quickly cools the vapors, causing them to liquefy. The water-soluble flavor compounds in the smoke are trapped within this liquid, while the insoluble tars and resins are removed by a series of filters, resulting in a clean, all-natural smoke-flavored liquid. Some manufacturers add other flavorings to liquid smoke, but our top-rated product, **Wright's Liquid Smoke**, contains nothing but smoke and water.

Lexington Vinegar Barbecue Sauce

MAKES ABOUT 2 CUPS

For a spicier sauce, add hot sauce to taste.

- 1 cup cider vinegar
- ½ cup ketchup
- ½ cup water
- 1 tablespoon sugar
- ¾ teaspoon salt
- ¾ teaspoon red pepper flakes
- ½ teaspoon pepper

Whisk all ingredients together in bowl.

South Carolina Mustard Barbecue Sauce

MAKES ABOUT 2 CUPS

You can use either light or dark brown sugar in this recipe.

- 1 cup yellow mustard
- ½ cup distilled white vinegar
- ¼ cup packed brown sugar
- ¼ cup Worcestershire sauce
- 2 tablespoons hot sauce
- 1 teaspoon salt
- 1 teaspoon pepper

Whisk all ingredients together in bowl.

Sweet and Tangy Barbecue Sauce

MAKES ABOUT 2 CUPS

We like mild molasses in this recipe.

- 1½ cups ketchup
- ¼ cup molasses
- 2 tablespoons Worcestershire sauce
- 1 tablespoon hot sauce
- ½ teaspoon salt
- ½ teaspoon pepper

Whisk all ingredients together in bowl.

CAST-IRON BAKED CHICKEN

WHY THIS RECIPE WORKS: In the pursuit of roast chicken with juicy meat and golden-brown skin that we could make on a weeknight, we turned to the cast-iron skillet, which retains heat well and, once hot, distributes that heat evenly across the skillet's surface. To avoid having to cut up a whole chicken and to reduce the cooking time, we started with chicken parts. To aid in getting a burnished color on the skin, we added paprika to a spice rub of onion powder, granulated garlic, and plenty of salt and pepper. For a finishing touch, we added six sprigs of thyme and a couple of tablespoons of butter to the skillet, which combined with the chicken juices to create a complementary sauce.

There is a reason we've developed so many recipes for roast chicken in the test kitchen over the years: We love the stuff. Nothing's more comforting or satisfying.

On its face, baking chicken is as easy as this: You put seasoned chicken in a hot oven, and later you take it out and eat it. While this can work if the planets align in your favor, the devil may lurk in the details. Get the temperature or timing wrong and your chicken can emerge from the oven either with flabby, pale skin and dry meat or, in a misguided pursuit of crispy skin, completely overcooked.

But policing the details takes time and, really, on a weeknight, who has time? I wanted an easy, dead-simple recipe for perfectly cooked and deeply flavorful baked chicken to serve four people. And I wanted it all in a skillet.

In the interest of ease, I started with chicken parts rather than a whole chicken. Parts cook through slightly faster than a whole bird and, more important, they're much easier to serve—no carving.

NOTES FROM THE TEST KITCHEN

THE BEST CAST-IRON SKILLET
Our favorite cast-iron skillet is the **Lodge Classic Cast Iron Skillet, 12"**. With a slick, preseasoned interior and plenty of room, it browns foods deeply. It also has a convenient helper handle for managing heavy loads.

I grabbed a jar of sweet paprika—in part for its flavor but mostly for the burnished color it lends to the skin. To the paprika, I added onion powder, granulated garlic, and, of course, plenty of salt and pepper, and I seasoned the chicken pieces all over with this mixture.

For my first few experiments, I simply arranged the chicken in a traditional skillet and slid it into a hot oven. After a half-hour or so, it emerged looking just fine—but not great. The paprika added a bit of color, but the skin wasn't nearly as evenly rendered and crispy as I wanted.

I wondered if I was using the right skillet. For my next round, I decided to switch to cast iron, which retains heat better and, once hot, distributes that heat evenly across the surface of the skillet. I slipped my cast-iron skillet into the oven while it preheated. Once the oven and skillet were hot, I carefully added the seasoned chicken parts, skin side down. They immediately began to sizzle—the sound of rendering skin. After 15 minutes, I removed the skillet from the oven and flipped the pieces. After another 15 minutes of baking, the skin, which had taken on a beautiful brown color, crunched faintly against the juicy, seasoned meat.

One last touch was missing: some herb flavor. I added six sprigs of thyme and a couple of tablespoons of butter to the pan. When the chicken was done, I found that the butter, thyme, and pan juices had mingled to create a lovely, flavorful sauce. I spooned this pan sauce over the chicken parts for a final herby finish. My tasters were happy, and so was I.

Perfectly cooked, moist chicken? Yup. Gorgeous brown skin? Yes. This simple, weeknight-ready method was good to go.

BRYAN ROOF, *Cook's Country*

Cast-Iron Baked Chicken

SERVES 4

Note that the cast-iron skillet should be preheated along with the oven; this is key to getting crispy, well-browned skin. You will not achieve the same type of browning with a conventional skillet. A 4-pound whole chicken will yield the 3 pounds of parts called for in the recipe.

- 2 teaspoons paprika
- 2 teaspoons salt
- 1 teaspoon pepper
- ½ teaspoon onion powder
- ½ teaspoon granulated garlic
- 3 pounds bone-in chicken pieces (2 split breasts, 2 drumsticks, 2 thighs, and 2 wings with wingtips discarded), trimmed
- 2 tablespoons unsalted butter
- 6 sprigs fresh thyme

1. Adjust oven rack to middle position, place 12-inch cast-iron skillet on rack, and heat oven to 450 degrees. Combine paprika, salt, pepper, onion powder, and granulated garlic in bowl. Pat chicken dry with paper towels and sprinkle all over with spice mixture.

2. When oven is heated, carefully remove hot skillet. Add butter, let it melt, and add thyme sprigs. Place chicken in skillet skin side down, pushing thyme sprigs aside as needed. Transfer skillet to oven and bake for 15 minutes.

3. Remove skillet from oven and flip chicken. Return skillet to oven and bake until breasts register 160 degrees and drumsticks/thighs register at least 175 degrees, about 15 minutes longer.

4. Let chicken rest in skillet for 10 minutes. Transfer chicken to platter and spoon pan juices over top. Serve.

NOTES FROM THE TEST KITCHEN

SUCCESS STARTS WITH A HOT SKILLET

GET SKILLET RIPPING HOT Cast iron preheats evenly in the oven.

START CHICKEN SKIN SIDE DOWN This initial browning imparts deep flavor.

ONE-BATCH FRIED CHICKEN

✓ **WHY THIS RECIPE WORKS:** Inspired by the pressure-frying machine in which Colonel Sanders created his famous fried chicken, we set out to find a faster way to fry that would get all the chicken on the table at the same time. To season the meat and keep it moist, we soaked bone-in chicken pieces in a mixture of buttermilk and salt. To the flour dredge, we added Italian seasoning blend, along with granulated garlic, ground ginger, and celery salt for savory notes. Both black and white peppers added pleasant, mild heat, and a bit of baking powder ensured a crunchy, not tough, exterior. A few tablespoons of buttermilk rubbed into the seasoned flour created a shaggy coating that, after a rest in the refrigerator, adhered nicely to the skin and fried up into a satisfying crunchy crust. For fast frying, we cooked the chicken all in one batch and covered the pot for the first half of cooking. We let the pieces fry undisturbed so the coating set almost entirely around each piece before flipping and frying the chicken uncovered for the second half of cooking.

Colonel Sanders famously touted the "11 secret herbs and spices" in his fast-food fried chicken, but the real secret to its success wasn't his flavorings—it was how he cooked it. Lore of the secret recipe overshadowed the little-known fact that Harland Sanders, the famous bow-tied Colonel, used a covered pressure-frying machine to consistently produce juicy, deep-fried chicken in a fraction of the time traditionally required—a speedy technology still used today.

While I didn't have a pressure fryer, I was excited by the idea of faster frying. What's more, I wanted to find a way to fry a full cut-up chicken (except the wings): two breasts (cut in half), two thighs, and two drumsticks in just one batch. Could I come up with a method that fried all the pieces together so they all were ready to eat at the same time? Inspired by the Colonel's inventiveness, I went into the kitchen to find out.

As we often do with fried chicken, I started by soaking bone-in chicken pieces in a mixture of buttermilk and salt to season the meat and help it stay moist. Then, using my fingers, I rubbed a few tablespoons of buttermilk into some seasoned flour (I'd experiment more with the exact seasonings later) to create a shaggy coating, which I knew would fry up into an extra-crunchy exterior. I let the coated chicken rest in the fridge for a spell to help the coating adhere.

To fit all the chicken pieces into my pot, I had to significantly decrease the amount of oil typically used in deep frying so it didn't overflow—just 6 cups did the trick. I heated the oil and then carefully added the chicken to the pot. It was a snug fit, and with so many pieces going in at once, the oil temperature dropped dramatically.

I covered the pot for the first half of the frying time to create a closed environment, which, while not the same as a pressure fryer, did echo the technology in one regard: It held in the heat.

This was a good start. But more chicken in the pot also meant more moisture to deal with. (Nearly all fried foods release moisture when cooked in oil; this is why the oil bubbles.) The good news? Because there was already so much moisture in the pot, the condensation accumulating on the lid didn't cause any extra splatter when it dripped off the lid as I lifted it. The bad news? The moisture trapped in the oil was encouraging the coating to slip off the chicken before it had set up and cooked through, especially when I went to flip the chicken halfway through the cooking time.

Hot spots in the pot also posed a problem, but since I didn't want to move the chicken during the frying process to alleviate them, I instead moved the pot, rotating it 180 degrees on the burner after the first 5 minutes of cooking.

Adjusting my timing to allow the chicken to fry mostly undisturbed for at least 10 minutes was the key; this allowed the coating to set almost entirely around each piece before I disturbed the chicken with my tongs. What's more, the pieces shrank a bit during this undisturbed cooking time due to loss of moisture, so I had more room to flip them. I left the lid off for the second half of the cooking time to allow excess moisture to escape and to allow me to watch the chicken's coating set fully into a crunchy, deep golden-brown exterior.

With the frying technique finally settled, I started noodling around to create my own seasoned flour inspired by the Colonel's famous flavor mix. Rather than call for a long list of dried herbs, I reached for a jar of Italian seasoning blend (a mix of dried herbs: oregano, thyme, basil, rosemary, and sage). Granulated garlic, ground ginger, and celery salt added lively savory notes, and both black and white peppers produced a pleasant, mild heat. A bit of baking powder added to the dredge helped ensure a crunchy but not tough exterior.

The final analysis from my tasters? While my entry-level one-batch technique was fast and easy enough for a beginner, the chicken tasted like it'd been fried by a pro.

CECELIA JENKINS, *Cook's Country*

One-Batch Fried Chicken

SERVES 4

Use a Dutch oven that holds 6 quarts or more. To take the temperature of the chicken pieces, take them out of the oil and place them on a plate; this is the safest way and provides the most accurate reading.

BRINE AND CHICKEN

- 2 cups buttermilk
- 1 tablespoon salt
- 3 pounds bone-in chicken pieces (2 split breasts cut in half crosswise, 2 drumsticks, and 2 thighs), trimmed
- 1½ quarts peanut or vegetable oil

COATING

- 3 cups all-purpose flour
- 3 tablespoons white pepper
- 1 tablespoon pepper
- 1 tablespoon celery salt
- 1 tablespoon granulated garlic
- 1 tablespoon ground ginger
- 1 tablespoon Italian seasoning
- 1 tablespoon baking powder
- ½ teaspoon salt
- 6 tablespoons buttermilk

1. FOR THE BRINE AND CHICKEN: Whisk buttermilk and salt in large bowl until salt is dissolved. Submerge chicken pieces in buttermilk mixture. Cover with plastic wrap and refrigerate for at least 1 hour or up to 24 hours.

2. FOR THE COATING: Whisk flour, white pepper, pepper, celery salt, granulated garlic, ginger, Italian seasoning, baking powder, and salt together in large bowl. Add buttermilk and, using your fingers, rub flour mixture and buttermilk together until craggy bits form throughout.

3. Set wire rack in rimmed baking sheet. Working with 2 pieces of chicken at a time, remove from buttermilk mixture, allowing excess to drip off, then drop into flour mixture, turning to coat thoroughly and pressing to adhere. Transfer to prepared rack, skin side up. Refrigerate, uncovered, for at least 1 hour or up to 2 hours.

NOTES FROM THE TEST KITCHEN

MAKING FRIED CHICKEN

1. USE BUTTERMILK TWO WAYS Buttermilk and salt create a brine that seasons the chicken and keeps it moist. We also add buttermilk to our seasoned flour; the liquid creates small lumps that fry up extra-crunchy.

2. DREDGE AND LET SIT Chilling the chicken for at least an hour helps the coating set up and stick.

3. START FRYING Put all the chicken into the hot oil, cover the pot, and fry for 10 minutes. Rotating the pot after 5 minutes ensures even heating.

4. UNCOVER AND FLIP Some pieces might have "bald" uncooked tops. Flip all of the pieces and fry for 8 minutes.

5. DRAIN AND LET REST Paper towels soak up excess oil. Let the chicken rest for 10 minutes before serving.

4. Set second wire rack in second rimmed baking sheet and line with triple layer of paper towels. Add oil to large Dutch oven until it measures about 1 inch deep and heat over medium-high heat to 350 degrees. Add all chicken to oil, skin side down in single layer (some slight overlap is OK), so that pieces are mostly submerged. Cover and fry for 10 minutes, rotating pot after 5 minutes. Adjust burner, if necessary, to maintain oil temperature around 300 degrees.

5. Uncover pot (chicken will be golden around sides and bottom but unset and gray on top) and carefully flip chicken. Continue to fry, uncovered, until chicken is golden brown and breasts register 160 degrees and drumsticks/thighs register 175 degrees, 7 to 9 minutes longer. Transfer chicken to paper towel–lined rack and let cool for 10 minutes. Serve.

ROAST CHICKEN WITH BREAD SALAD

✔ **WHY THIS RECIPE WORKS:** For our own take on Zuni Café's roast chicken with bread salad, we started by butterflying a whole chicken and salting it overnight so it would cook quickly and evenly and be juicy and well seasoned. Before roasting the chicken in a 475-degree oven, we covered the bottom of a skillet with bread cubes that we had moistened with oil and broth and then draped the chicken on top. The bread cubes toasted and browned beneath the bird while absorbing its juices to create a mix of moistened, crispy-fried, and chewy pieces all packed with savory flavor. To finish the dish, we built a vinaigrette of champagne vinegar, oil, currants, thinly sliced scallions, Dijon mustard, and chicken drippings that we tossed with peppery arugula, and the toasted bread. We served the salad alongside the carved chicken so the greens didn't wilt.

Few dishes are as beloved and crowd-pleasing as roast chicken. Perhaps no one knew this better than the late, renowned chef Judy Rodgers of Zuni Café in San Francisco. When she put her roast chicken with warm bread salad on the menu in the late '80s, it was a real hit. Now, some 30 years later, it still is.

I recently prepared Rodgers's recipe from *The Zuni Café Cookbook* (2002). The chicken was beautifully executed: the skin deeply bronzed, the meat juicy and well seasoned. And the salad? The bread itself was a lovely mix of crunchy, fried, chewy, and moist pieces, all tossed with savory chicken drippings. Currants, pine nuts, just-softened scallions and garlic, salad greens, and a sharp vinaigrette completed the salad. Served with the chicken, it was a perfect meal.

But the recipe for this rustic dish is anything but simple. It's a meticulously detailed four-page essay that calls for preparing the chicken and bread separately (the latter in two stages), so their cooking has to be coordinated, as do the salad's many components, including vinegar-soaked currants, sautéed aromatics, and toasted nuts. This could all be tackled easily in a professional kitchen, but at home it seemed taxing.

Before I did anything else, I wanted to nail the chicken cookery. I butterflied a chicken by snipping out the backbone and then pressing down on its breastbone to help the bird lie flat.

Rodgers called for salting her chicken overnight, which is a trick we often use as well. The salt draws moisture from the flesh, forming a concentrated brine that is eventually reabsorbed, seasoning the meat and keeping it juicy. I lifted up the skin and rubbed kosher salt onto the flesh; I then refrigerated the bird for 24 hours. This would give the salt time to penetrate the flesh as well as dry the skin so it would brown and crisp more readily.

The next day, I placed the bird skin side up in a 12-inch skillet (rather than a large roasting pan, so the juices could pool without risk of scorching) and slid it, brushed with oil to encourage deep browning, into a 475-degree oven. Because the chicken was butterflied, I was pretty sure I could roast it at a high temperature without the breast and thigh meat cooking unevenly. Sure enough, 45 minutes later I had a mahogany-brown, crispy-skinned, succulent chicken.

On to my favorite part: the bread. What makes Rodgers's bread salad unique is its mix of crispy chewy textures, achieved by removing the crusts from a rustic loaf, cutting the bread into large chunks, coating the chunks with oil, and broiling them. The bread chunks are then torn into smaller pieces and tossed with currants, pine nuts, cooked scallions and garlic, broth, and vinaigrette. Finally, the mixture is baked in a covered dish so that the bread emerges, as Rodgers described it, "steamy hot, a mixture of soft, moist wads, crispy-on-the-outside-but-moist-in-the-middle wads, and a few downright crispy ones."

ROAST CHICKEN WITH WARM BREAD SALAD

I wondered if I could streamline things by cooking the bread with the chicken, which would also allow the bread to directly soak up all the bird's juices and fat. The test kitchen has recipes that call for butterflying poultry and draping it over stuffing prior to roasting, and I thought a similar technique could work well here. The pieces touching the skillet would crisp just like Rodgers's broiled bread, and the chicken juices would keep the remaining pieces moist.

Rodgers called for an open-crumbed loaf such as ciabatta; I wanted something sturdier to hold up under the chicken, so I opted for a denser country-style loaf, which I cut into 1-inch pieces and placed in the skillet before arranging the butterflied bird on top. When I removed it from the oven, I was pleased: The bread beneath the chicken was saturated with savory chicken juices on one side and was deeply golden, crispy, and fried on the other side where it had been in contact with the pan. The only problem was that the pieces around the edges of the pan had dried out and burned slightly. Plus, a lot of the bread had stuck to the pan.

For my next batch, I moistened the bread with ¼ cup of chicken broth. I also spritzed the skillet with vegetable oil spray and stirred a little olive oil into the bread before arranging it in the skillet. I hoped this would help the edge pieces fry and crisp without sticking. Finally, I didn't trim away any of the bird's excess fat or skin. This way, I would be capturing every last drop of the drippings—arguably the most flavorful element a chicken has to offer. These were good moves: The bread boasted a mix of textures and tasted intensely chicken-y, and nothing burned or dried out. That said, the crusted pieces were still tough.

I started anew, this time removing all the crust so I was left with only the soft inner crumb. This eliminated the tough parts, but now the bread had no structure and collapsed into a single mass.

I prepared another loaf but this time removed only the thick bottom crust. So they would be sure to soften, I arranged the remaining crusted pieces directly under the bird, crust side up. To say it worked well would be an understatement: This bread offered a little of everything: crunchy, fried, chewy, and moist pieces. There wasn't a tough piece in the mix. It was time to pull the dish together.

As I examined the salad components, I decided to make a couple of adjustments: Instead of sautéing thinly sliced scallions with garlic, I decided to skip the garlic and keep the scallions raw, which I mixed, along with sweet currants, into a sharp dressing of champagne vinegar and extra-virgin olive oil. For body and more punch to cut the dish's richness, I added a spoonful of Dijon mustard. And because the bread would provide plenty of crunch and richness, I left out the pine nuts, too. Finally, I poured the accumulated chicken juices into the dressing before tossing it with the bread and a heap of peppery arugula. Instead of arranging the carved chicken on top of the salad, which caused the greens to wilt, I served it alongside.

My streamlined rendition of the Zuni chicken and bread salad hit all the right notes: salty, savory, sweet, fresh, and bright. I only hope that it will be as memorable and enduring as the original.

ANNIE PETITO, *Cook's Illustrated*

Roast Chicken with Warm Bread Salad

SERVES 4 TO 6

Note that this recipe requires refrigerating the seasoned chicken for 24 hours. This recipe was developed and tested using Diamond Crystal kosher salt. If you have Morton kosher salt, which is denser than Diamond Crystal, put only ½ teaspoon of salt onto the cavity. Red wine or white wine vinegar may be substituted for champagne vinegar, if desired. For the bread, we prefer a round rustic loaf with a chewy, open crumb and a sturdy outer crust.

1   (4-pound) whole chicken, giblets discarded
    Kosher salt and pepper

4   (1-inch-thick) slices country-style bread (8 ounces), bottom crust removed, cut into ¾- to 1-inch pieces (5 cups)

¼   cup chicken broth

6   tablespoons plus 2 teaspoons extra-virgin olive oil

2   tablespoons champagne vinegar

1   teaspoon Dijon mustard

3   scallions, sliced thin

2   tablespoons dried currants

5   ounces (5 cups) baby arugula

1. Place chicken, breast side down, on cutting board. Using kitchen shears, cut through bones on either side of backbone; discard backbone. Do not trim off any excess fat or skin. Flip chicken over and press on breastbone to flatten.

2. Using your fingers, carefully loosen skin covering breast and legs. Rub ½ teaspoon salt under skin of each breast, ½ teaspoon under skin of each leg, and 1 teaspoon salt onto bird's cavity. Tuck wings behind back and turn legs so drumsticks face inward toward breasts. Place chicken on wire rack set in rimmed baking sheet or on large plate and refrigerate, uncovered, for 24 hours.

3. Adjust oven rack to middle position and heat oven to 475 degrees. Spray 12-inch skillet with vegetable oil spray. Toss bread with broth and 2 tablespoons oil until pieces are evenly moistened. Arrange bread in skillet in single layer, with majority of crusted pieces near center, crust side up.

4. Pat chicken dry with paper towels and place, skin side up, on top of bread. Brush 2 teaspoons oil over chicken skin and sprinkle with ¼ teaspoon salt and ¼ teaspoon pepper. Roast chicken until skin is deep golden brown and thickest part of breast registers 160 degrees and thighs register 175 degrees, 45 to 50 minutes, rotating skillet halfway through roasting.

5. While chicken roasts, whisk vinegar, mustard, ¼ teaspoon salt, and ¼ teaspoon pepper together in small bowl. Slowly whisk in remaining ¼ cup oil. Stir in scallions and currants and set aside. Place arugula in large bowl.

6. Transfer chicken to carving board and let rest, uncovered, for 15 minutes. Run thin metal spatula under bread to loosen from bottom of skillet. (Bread should be mix of softened, golden-brown, and crunchy pieces.) Carve chicken and whisk any accumulated juices into vinaigrette. Add bread and vinaigrette to arugula and toss to evenly coat. Transfer salad to serving platter and serve with chicken.

NOTES FROM THE TEST KITCHEN

SKIP THE TRIMMING

Most of our chicken recipes call for trimming away any excess fat and skin. But since those elements produce hugely flavorful drippings, we decided to leave them intact for our Roast Chicken with Warm Bread Salad. This meant that more savory, chicken-y drippings would be available for the bread to absorb. An untrimmed 4-pound chicken exudes about ½ cup of drippings.

ROAST TURKEY BREAST WITH GRAVY

☑ WHY THIS RECIPE WORKS: For an impressive roast turkey breast, we removed the backbone so the breast sat flat in the oven for even browning and more stability during carving. Salting the breast for 24 hours seasoned it and helped it retain moisture as it cooked. Roasting it in a 12-inch skillet instead of a roasting pan helped contain drippings underneath the bird so they didn't scorch. Starting the breast at 325 degrees helped gently cook the white meat, while finishing it at 500 degrees ensured a deeply bronzed exterior. While the turkey cooked, we used the backbone to make a flavorful stock to use as the base for a gravy, which we built directly in the skillet.

Here's a Thanksgiving secret: You don't have to roast a whole turkey to get all the glory. A bone-in, skin-on turkey breast can be a great option when hosting a smaller crowd or if your guests simply prefer white meat. Other benefits: A breast requires less cooking time, which frees up your oven for other dishes, and it's much easier to carve than a whole bird.

But to produce a true holiday centerpiece, you must overcome a few turkey breast hurdles. White meat is notorious for emerging from the oven dry and chalky, and the skin is rarely adequately browned and crispy. What's more, since a breast doesn't offer much in the way of pan drippings, making gravy isn't always a given. I resolved to deliver an impressive roast turkey breast boasting juicy, well-seasoned meat; crispy, deeply browned skin; and a savory gravy to serve alongside.

First on my list: salt, which would keep the turkey juicy. When rubbed over the flesh, salt draws out moisture. The moisture then mixes with the salt and forms a concentrated solution, which, over time, migrates back into the meat, seasoning it and altering its proteins so that they retain moisture during cooking.

Using my fingers, I carefully peeled back the turkey breast's skin and rubbed salt onto the flesh and then on the bone side. I then smoothed the skin back into place and refrigerated the turkey for 24 hours. The next day, I placed the turkey breast, skin side up, in a V-rack set inside a roasting pan, brushed it with butter (its milk solids would encourage browning), sprinkled it with a bit more salt, and roasted it in a 450-degree oven. After

ROAST WHOLE TURKEY BREAST WITH GRAVY

about an hour, the breast reached the target temperature of 160 degrees. However, the meat was somewhat dry despite the salting, and browning was patchy. Plus, because the fat didn't have enough time to fully render, the skin wasn't particularly crispy. Finally, the breast itself was rather unwieldy and difficult to keep upright.

Removing the turkey's backbone would make it sit flat and would also encourage even browning since the breast would be more level. Fortunately, this was easily accomplished with the help of kitchen shears. I set the backbone aside—I would use it later to make gravy.

As I prepared to arrange the breast in the roasting pan, it struck me that the pan was excessively large. Plus, the minimal drippings tended to scorch. I switched to a 12-inch ovensafe skillet. Freed of its backbone, the breast rested securely on its flat underside and fit snugly in the skillet so juices could collect directly beneath it with no risk of scorching.

Now, about that dry meat and the skin that never fully rendered. Substantially lowering the oven temperature helped with the former problem: When roasted at 325 degrees, the meat stayed moist. Unfortunately, the skin was now pale, though much of its fat had rendered. I decided to try a reverse-sear technique, a method in which we cook the meat in a low oven until it reaches the desired temperature and then sear it on the stovetop. The interior stays juicy while the exterior browns quickly. In this case, I'd use a hot oven for the final "sear" rather than move the pan to the stovetop.

Eager to try this approach, I roasted the breast at 325 degrees until it reached an internal temperature of 145 degrees. Then I took it out of the oven and cranked the heat to 500 degrees. Once the oven was up to temperature, I returned the breast to the oven and roasted it until it hit 160 degrees, which happened faster than I expected. I hadn't accounted for carryover cooking while the breast sat in the hot skillet between oven stints, so it came to temperature before it could get much color. I tried again, removing the breast from the oven when the meat registered just 130 degrees, so it would have more time to brown in the hotter oven. This was my best turkey breast yet: The skin was a deep mahogany and beautifully crispy, and the well-seasoned meat was juicy.

While my turkey breast was in the oven roasting, I used the reserved turkey back to make a simple broth that would be the gravy base. I browned the back; added onion, celery, carrot, fresh herbs, and water; and then simmered and strained the mixture. When I transferred the breast to a carving board to rest, I built the gravy right in the skillet, which was full of flavorful fat and drippings. I made a roux, added white wine followed by my broth, and let the gravy simmer to reduce. After about 20 minutes, the gravy was nicely thickened and the breast was ready to carve.

I served up my impressive platter of turkey—burnished and crispy on the outside, moist and well seasoned within—and its flavorful gravy, without missing the dark meat at all.

ANNIE PETITO, *Cook's Illustrated*

Roast Whole Turkey Breast with Gravy

SERVES 6 TO 8

Note that this recipe requires refrigerating the seasoned breast for 24 hours. This recipe was developed using Diamond Crystal kosher salt. If you use Morton kosher salt, reduce the salt in step 2 to 2½ teaspoons, rubbing 1 teaspoon of salt into each side of the breast and ½ teaspoon into the cavity. If you're using a self-basting (such as a frozen Butterball) or kosher turkey breast, do not salt in step 2. If your turkey breast comes with the back removed, you can skip making the gravy or substitute 1 pound of chicken wings for the turkey back.

- 1 (5- to 7- pound) bone-in turkey breast
  Kosher salt and pepper
- 2 tablespoons unsalted butter, melted
- 2 teaspoons extra-virgin olive oil, plus extra as needed
- 1 small onion, chopped
- 1 small carrot, chopped
- 1 small celery rib, chopped
- 5 cups water
- 2 sprigs fresh thyme
- 1 bay leaf
- ¼ cup all-purpose flour
- ¼ cup dry white wine

1. Place turkey breast on counter skin side down. Using kitchen shears, cut through ribs, following vertical line of fat where breast meets back, from tapered end of breast to wing joint. Using your hands, bend back away from breast to pop shoulder joints out of sockets. Using paring knife, cut through joints between bones to separate back from breast. Reserve back for gravy. Trim excess fat from breast.

2. Place turkey breast, skin side up, on counter. Using your fingers, carefully loosen and separate turkey skin from each side of breast. Peel back skin, leaving it attached at top and center of breast. Rub 1 teaspoon salt onto each side of breast, then place skin back over meat. Rub 1 teaspoon salt onto underside of breast cavity. Place turkey on large plate and refrigerate, uncovered, for 24 hours.

3. Adjust oven rack to middle position and heat oven to 325 degrees. Pat turkey dry with paper towels. Place turkey, skin side up, in 12-inch ovensafe skillet, arranging so narrow end of breast is not touching skillet. Brush melted butter evenly over turkey and sprinkle with 1 teaspoon salt. Roast until thickest part of breast registers 130 degrees, 1 to 1¼ hours.

4. Meanwhile, heat oil in large saucepan over medium-high heat. Add reserved back, skin side down, and cook until well browned, 6 to 8 minutes. Add onion, carrot, and celery and cook, stirring occasionally, until vegetables are softened and lightly browned, about 5 minutes. Add water, thyme sprigs, and bay leaf and bring to boil. Reduce heat to medium-low and simmer for 1 hour. Strain broth through fine-mesh strainer into container. Discard solids; set aside broth (you should have about 4 cups). (Broth can be refrigerated for up to 24 hours.)

5. Remove turkey from oven and increase oven temperature to 500 degrees. When oven reaches 500 degrees, return turkey to oven and roast until skin is deeply browned and thickest part of breast registers 160 degrees, 15 to 30 minutes. Using spatula, loosen turkey from skillet; transfer to carving board and let rest, uncovered, for 30 minutes.

6. While turkey rests, pour off fat from skillet. (You should have about ¼ cup; if not, add extra oil as needed to equal ¼ cup.) Return fat to skillet and heat over medium heat until shimmering. Sprinkle flour evenly over fat and cook, whisking constantly, until flour is coated with fat and browned, about 1 minute. Add wine, whisking to scrape up any browned bits, and cook until wine has evaporated, 1 to 2 minutes. Slowly whisk in reserved broth. Increase heat to medium-high and cook, whisking occasionally, until gravy is thickened and reduced to 2 cups, about 20 minutes. Season with salt and pepper to taste. Carve turkey and serve, passing gravy separately.

THAI GRILLED CHICKEN

✔ WHY THIS RECIPE WORKS: For our take on Thai grilled chicken, we started with Cornish hens, which are similar in size to the hens traditionally used by chicken vendors in Thailand. Butterflying and flattening the hens helped them cook more quickly and evenly on the grill. We created a marinade consisting of cilantro leaves and stems (a substitute for hard-to-find cilantro root), lots of garlic, white pepper, ground coriander, brown sugar, and fish sauce; thanks to its pesto-like consistency, it clung to the hens instead of sliding off. We set up a half-grill fire and started cooking the hens skin side up over the cooler side of the grill so the fatty skin had time to slowly render while the meat cooked; we then finished them over the hotter side to crisp the skin. We whipped up a version of the traditional sweet-tangy-spicy dipping sauce by combining equal parts white vinegar and sugar and simmering the mixture until it was slightly thickened and would cling nicely to the chicken. Plenty of minced garlic and Thai chiles balanced the sauce with savory, fruity heat.

I can't think of a cuisine that doesn't lay claim to a grilled chicken dish, but the Thai version might be my favorite. Called *gai yang*, it's street food that originated in Thailand's northeastern Isan region but has become ubiquitous throughout the country. Countless variations exist, but the most popular features small whole chickens that are butterflied, flattened, and marinated in a garlic-herb paste. To keep the hens flat, cooks position them between bamboo clips that look like giant clothespins; they then grill the hens over a low charcoal fire so that their fat renders and their skin crisps. What you get is the best version of grilled chicken—juicy meat, bronzed skin, and smoky char—made extraordinary by the flavor-packed marinade. The chicken is cut into pieces and served with a tangy-sweet-spicy dipping sauce and sticky rice, which soaks up the assertive flavors.

As a bonus, this dish can be prepared using mostly pantry staples. The only ingredient I'd have to work around was the bird itself. Thai chickens typically weigh between 1 and 3 pounds, so I'd have to find an alternative. After that, it would be a matter of ironing out the marinade and the fire setup, as many recipes are vague on the grill instructions.

I discovered that the Thai chickens are often replaced with whole conventional chickens, while other recipes call for parts or Cornish hens. Cornish hens offer a few unique benefits that make them ideal for this recipe: They have a high ratio of skin to meat, so both the dark and white portions cook up juicy; they weigh 1¼ pounds or so (about the same size as the Thai chickens) and cook in about 30 minutes when butterflied; and they're convenient and elegant for portioning—one bird per person.

Gai yang vendors typically butterfly chickens along the breastbone, but I found that this method caused the skin to pull away from the breast, leaving the lean white meat exposed and at greater risk of drying out. Butterflying by cutting out the backbones with kitchen shears and flattening the birds was the better approach. The skin stayed intact on one side, so it browned evenly, and the hens were uniformly flat, so they cooked at the same rate. As for the bamboo "clothespins," they flatten the birds and function as handles that make them easier to flip. But as long as I handled the hens carefully with tongs, I could move them on the grill without skewering.

I marinated the hens overnight in a paste made from garlic, cilantro stems (a substitute for the traditional cilantro root), white pepper, and fish sauce—the four marinade components I found in every recipe. Then I grilled the hens skin side up over the cooler side of a half-grill fire. Just before the meat was done, I placed them over the coals to crisp the skin.

They cooked up juicy and savory, thanks in large part to the salty fish sauce, which essentially brined the meat, seasoning it and helping it retain moisture during cooking. To bolster that effect, I added a couple of teaspoons of salt. But many recipes further season the marinade with soy sauce, ginger, lemon grass, ground coriander, or sugar (usually Thai palm sugar or brown sugar). When I added some of these to the base ingredients for evaluation, I liked the nutty, citrusy flavor of ground coriander (made from the seeds of the cilantro plant) and the malty sweetness of brown sugar, so these were in. I also thickened the marinade, which tended to slide off the meat, to a clingy, pesto-like consistency by adding cilantro leaves along with the stems.

On to fixing the flavor and consistency of the dipping sauces, which ranged from sticky and cloyingly sweet to thin and fiery. I wanted a balance of sweetness and tang, so I simmered white vinegar and sugar until the mixture thickened to a light syrup. Minced raw garlic and Thai chiles gave the sauce a fruity burn that red pepper flakes just couldn't match.

I set out the hens and sauce along with sticky rice, which I made by mimicking the equipment used in Thailand. As my colleagues tore into the burnished hens, sweet-tangy sauce dripping from their fingers, they joked (sort of) that I should set up a gai yang stand of my own.

ANNIE PETITO, *Cook's Illustrated*

Thai Grilled Cornish Hens with Chili Dipping Sauce (Gai Yang)

SERVES 4

The hens need to marinate for at least 6 hours before cooking (a longer marinating time is preferable). If your hens weigh 1½ to 2 pounds, grill three hens instead of four and extend the initial cooking time in step 6 by 5 minutes. If you can't find Thai chiles, substitute Fresno or red jalapeño chiles. Serve with Thai-Style Sticky Rice (recipe follows) or steamed white rice.

HENS

- 4 (1¼- to 1½-pound) Cornish game hens, giblets discarded
- 1 cup fresh cilantro leaves and stems, chopped coarse
- 12 garlic cloves, peeled
- ¼ cup packed light brown sugar
- 2 teaspoons white pepper
- 2 teaspoons ground coriander
- 2 teaspoons salt
- ¼ cup fish sauce

THAI GRILLED CORNISH HENS

DIPPING SAUCE

- ½ cup distilled white vinegar
- ½ cup granulated sugar
- 1 tablespoon minced Thai chiles
- 3 garlic cloves, minced
- ¼ teaspoon salt

1. FOR THE HENS: Working with 1 hen at a time, place hens breast side down on cutting board and use kitchen shears to cut through bones on either side of backbones; discard backbones. Flip hens and press on breastbones to flatten. Trim any excess fat and skin.

2. Pulse cilantro leaves and stems, garlic, sugar, white pepper, coriander, and salt in food processor until finely chopped, 10 to 15 pulses; transfer to small bowl. Add fish sauce and stir until marinade has consistency of loose paste.

3. Rub hens all over with marinade. Transfer hens and any excess marinade to 1-gallon zipper-lock bag and refrigerate for at least 6 hours or up to 24 hours, flipping bag halfway through marinating.

4. FOR THE DIPPING SAUCE: Bring vinegar to boil in small saucepan. Add sugar and stir to dissolve. Reduce heat to medium-low and simmer until vinegar mixture is slightly thickened, about 5 minutes. Remove from heat and let vinegar mixture cool completely. Add chiles, garlic, and salt and stir until combined. Transfer sauce to airtight container and refrigerate until ready to use. (Sauce can be refrigerated for up to 2 weeks. Bring to room temperature before serving.)

5A. FOR A CHARCOAL GRILL: Open bottom vent completely. Light large chimney starter filled with charcoal briquettes (6 quarts). When top coals are partially covered with ash, pour evenly over half of grill. Set cooking grate in place, cover, and open lid vent completely. Heat grill until hot, about 5 minutes.

5B. FOR A GAS GRILL: Turn all burners to high, cover, and heat grill until hot, about 15 minutes. Leave primary burner on high and turn off other burner(s). Adjust primary burner (or, if using three-burner grill, primary burner and second burner) as needed to maintain grill temperature between 400 and 450 degrees.

6. Clean and oil cooking grate. Remove hens from bag, leaving any marinade that sticks to hens in place. Tuck wingtips behind backs and turn legs so drumsticks face inward toward breasts. Place hens, skin side up, on cooler side of grill (if using charcoal, arrange hens so that legs and thighs are facing coals). Cover and cook until skin is browned and breasts register 145 to 150 degrees, 30 to 35 minutes, rotating hens halfway through cooking.

7. Using tongs, carefully flip hens skin side down and move to hotter side of grill. Cover and cook until skin is crisp, deeply browned, and charred in spots and breasts register 160 degrees, 3 to 5 minutes, being careful to avoid burning.

8. Transfer hens, skin side up, to cutting board; tent with aluminum foil and let rest for 10 minutes. Slice each hen in half or into 4 pieces and serve, passing dipping sauce separately.

Thai-Style Sticky Rice (Khao Niaw)

SERVES 4

This recipe requires letting the rice soak in water for at least 4 hours before cooking. When shopping, look for rice labeled "Thai glutinous rice" or "Thai sweet rice"; do not substitute other varieties. Thai glutinous rice can be found in Asian markets and some supermarkets or online.

- 2 cups Thai glutinous rice

1. Place rice in medium bowl and pour enough water over rice to cover by 2 inches. Let stand at room temperature for at least 4 hours or up to 8 hours.

2. Cut 18-inch square of double-thickness cheesecloth. Line large fine-mesh strainer with cheesecloth, letting excess hang over sides. Drain rice in prepared strainer, then rinse under running water until water runs clear. Fold edges of cheesecloth over rice and pat surface of rice smooth.

3. Bring 1½ inches water to boil in large saucepan. Set strainer in saucepan (water should not touch bottom of strainer), cover with lid (it will not form tight seal), reduce heat to medium-high, and steam rice for 15 minutes. Uncover and, using tongs, flip cheesecloth bundle (rice should form sticky mass) so side that was closer to bottom of saucepan is now on top. Cover and continue to steam until rice is just translucent and texture is tender but with a little chew, 15 to 20 minutes longer, checking water level occasionally and adding more if necessary.

4. Remove saucepan from heat, drain excess water from saucepan, and return strainer to saucepan. Cover and let rice stand for 10 to 15 minutes before serving.

PAN-SEARED SALMON STEAKS

✔ **WHY THIS RECIPE WORKS:** In this recipe, we prepared salmon steaks in a way that encouraged a well-browned, crisp crust; promoted even cooking; and delivered a beautiful presentation. Deboning and then tying each steak into a round produced a structurally sound parcel that cooked evenly and resulted in two large surfaces on which to develop a well-browned crust. A light coating of cornstarch enhanced the crispness of the crust.

Salmon steaks have a lot going for them. Because neither side of a steak has skin, its fleshy surface area is greater than that of a fillet, promising plenty of crisp exterior to contrast with the silky interior. Also, whereas a fillet has a thick end and a tapered end, which can lead to uneven cooking, a steak is uniformly thick and thus (with some creative tying) can deliver a more evenly cooked piece of fish.

I set about forming a salmon steak into a shape that would not only promote even cooking but also make it structurally sound. Using a paring knife, I removed the spine bones and interior membrane, which made room to peel back the skin from one of the belly flaps and tuck the flap into the gap I'd created. I wrapped the second flap around the first and used kitchen twine to secure the salmon into a medallion—an elegant step up from the common fillet.

A 15-minute brine helped keep the salmon juicy when cooked over medium-high heat in an oiled nonstick skillet, and the steaks developed a moderate crust as long as I patted them dry after brining. But I wasn't entirely satisfied with the color and texture of the medallions' crust. Perhaps a coating of flour would help? A quick dredge made the crust crispier, but coverage was spotty. How about finer cornstarch? Simply shaking off the excess left too much starch on the fish and produced an unpleasantly thick coating; instead, I used a pastry brush to gently sweep away the excess so that only a translucent dusting remained. These medallions emerged with perfectly even and beautifully crisp, browned exteriors encasing moist, buttery flesh. To accompany these top-notch medallions, I crafted several vibrant toppings that would complement the rich salmon.

STEVE DUNN, *Cook's Illustrated*

Pan-Seared Salmon Steaks
SERVES 4

You can serve the salmon steaks topped with our Tarragon Chimichurri, Dried Cherry Mostarda, or Kalamata Olive Relish (recipes follow).

> Salt and pepper
> 4 (8- to 10-ounce) salmon steaks, ¾ to 1 inch thick
> ¼ cup cornstarch
> 2 tablespoons vegetable oil
> Lemon wedges

1. Dissolve ¼ cup salt in 2 quarts cold water in large container. Submerge salmon in brine and let stand at room temperature for 15 minutes. Remove salmon from brine and pat dry with paper towels.

2. Place 1 salmon steak on counter with belly flaps facing you. Locate white line at top of salmon steak. Using paring knife, cut along 1 side of white line, around spine, then along membrane inside belly flap. Repeat process on other side of white line.

3. Using kitchen shears, cut out spine and membrane; discard. Run your fingers along each steak where spinal structure was removed and locate any pinbones; remove pinbones using tweezers. Remove 1½ inches of skin from 1 flap of steak. Tuck skinned portion into center of steak. Wrap other flap around steak and tie with kitchen twine. Repeat with remaining steaks.

4. Lightly season both sides of salmon with salt and pepper. Spread cornstarch in even layer on large plate. Lightly press both sides of salmon into cornstarch. Using pastry brush, remove excess cornstarch.

5. Heat oil in 12-inch nonstick skillet over medium-high heat until shimmering. Place salmon in skillet and cook until first side is browned, about 3 minutes. Flip salmon and cook until second side is browned, about 3 minutes. Continue to cook, flipping salmon every 2 minutes, until centers are still translucent when checked with tip of paring knife and register 125 degrees, 2 to 6 minutes longer. Transfer salmon to serving platter, discard twine, and serve with lemon wedges.

PAN-SEARED SALMON STEAKS

Tarragon Chimichurri

MAKES ABOUT 1 CUP

½ cup minced fresh parsley
¼ cup extra-virgin olive oil
2 tablespoons minced fresh tarragon
2 tablespoons white wine vinegar
2 garlic cloves, minced
¼ teaspoon red pepper flakes
　 Salt and pepper

Combine all ingredients in bowl and season with salt and pepper to taste.

Kalamata Olive Relish

MAKES ABOUT 1 CUP

1 cup pitted kalamata olives, chopped fine
1 tablespoon capers, rinsed and minced,
　 plus 1 teaspoon brine
1 tablespoon chopped fresh basil
1 tablespoon lemon juice
1 tablespoon extra-virgin olive oil
1 garlic clove, minced
　 Salt and pepper

Combine all ingredients in bowl and season with salt and pepper to taste.

Dried Cherry Mostarda

MAKES ABOUT 1½ CUPS

¾ cup plus 1 tablespoon water
½ cup dried cherries
1 teaspoon minced fresh thyme
¼ cup sugar
2 tablespoons whole-grain mustard
1 tablespoon white wine vinegar
1 tablespoon lemon juice
　 Salt and pepper
1 teaspoon cornstarch

Bring ¾ cup water, cherries, and thyme to simmer in small saucepan over high heat. Reduce heat to medium-low and cook until liquid has reduced to about ¼ cup, 8 to 10 minutes. Stir in sugar, mustard, vinegar, and lemon juice and season with salt and pepper to taste. Continue to cook, stirring frequently, for 5 minutes. Combine cornstarch and remaining 1 tablespoon water in small bowl. Stir cornstarch mixture into sauce and continue to cook until thickened, about 2 minutes. Off heat, season with salt and pepper to taste. Let cool before serving.

BLACK RICE BOWLS WITH SALMON

✓ **WHY THIS RECIPE WORKS:** Black rice is an ancient grain that was once reserved for the emperors of China. Its dark color signifies the presence of anthocyanins, and it contains more protein, fiber, and iron than other rice varieties. We decided to use it as the base for a Japanese-style rice bowl. To ensure well-seasoned grains with a bit of chew, we boiled the rice like pasta and then drizzled it with a mix of rice vinegar, mirin, miso, and ginger. We roasted wild salmon fillets until medium-rare and arranged them atop the rice before garnishing our bowls with radishes, avocado, cucumber, nori, and scallions.

After long days testing recipes at work, I almost always come home craving something nutritious, satisfying, and above all, easy. I usually find myself cobbling together a bowl of whatever vegetables, grains, and proteins I have on hand. My go-to template is simple enough—I like topping a bed of rice or grain with a protein, drizzling on a simple dressing, and finishing it off with a smattering of fresh vegetables. But for those nights when I'm not cooking on the fly, I wanted a recipe that upgraded my basic dinner bowl, bringing in generous portions of flavorful, nutrient-rich salmon and a mix of bold accompanying tastes and textures.

I decided to begin with a flavorful rice base, and sought an option to get my bowl on strong nutritional footing. Unlike white rice, which is stripped of its natural fiber, brown rice and red rice have great chew and contain a healthy dose of hearty fiber and vitamins. While either rice would make a good choice, I was also intrigued by a third option: black rice. With deep purple grains and plenty of protein, iron, and fiber, this striking rice—sometimes called "forbidden rice"—seemed like an ideal base layer for my bowl.

I'd never cooked black rice before, so to start I took my cues from the test kitchen's recipe for brown rice. Like brown rice, black rice is unpolished, meaning that the hull of the grain is still intact, which requires an entirely different cooking approach than what we would use for white rice. By stirring the rice into a pot of boiling water—essentially cooking it like pasta—each grain absorbs liquid from every angle, so the starches gelatinize uniformly and become evenly tender. This method worked beautifully for my black rice, creating perfectly tender grains with a distinctly roasty, nutty flavor that had me hooked instantly.

With the grain portion of my bowl established, I moved on to the salmon. Unlike milder proteins, this rich fish requires little adornment. I opted for wild salmon over farm-raised and figured that roasting it would be a good option. But when I prepared the fish following the test kitchen's oven-roasting method—cooking seasoned fillets on a preheated baking sheet in a gradually cooling oven—I was met with four drastically overcooked pieces of fish. A little research explained why: Because wild salmon is leaner and more abundant in collagen than the farm-raised variety, the muscle fibers contract more, thus expelling moisture more quickly. For the next round I kept my oven temperatures the same—preheating it to 500 degrees and then dropping it to 275 just before adding the fish—but this time I checked on the salmon periodically during roasting so I could monitor its doneness. When the fillets hit 120 degrees, they were juicy, tender, and perfectly cooked.

Now that I had my two key components in place, it was time to play with flavor. The combination of rice and salmon inspired me to make a sushi-style bowl. I started by assembling a rice vinegar–based dressing. Aiming for bright, punchy flavors, I added mirin (a salty-sweet Japanese rice wine), soy sauce, ginger, and both orange and lime zest. I tossed the rice with my dressing, topped the bowl with flaked pieces of salmon, and drizzled on some extra dressing for good measure. My tasters were impressed, but wondered if the dressing could have even more pop. Swapping umami-rich white miso paste for the soy sauce added the oomph my bowl was lacking, and eliminating the orange zest allowed the lime to really shine brightly. To double down on my bowl's Japanese ties, I crumbled some nori—the dried seaweed used to wrap sushi—over the warm flaked salmon, which added a toasty, green flavor to the mix. To finish, I wanted to top my bowl with some vegetables for extra color and texture (as well as bonus nutrients), so I garnished each serving with a mix of bright, contrasting components. For some lively crunch and freshness, I sliced up radishes, cucumbers, and scallions. Avocado complemented the salmon and added a buttery richness. (It also provided a dose of heart-healthy monounsaturated fat.)

With a final drizzle of dressing, my assembled bowl was complete. Featuring a top-notch cast of taste-good, feel-good ingredients, this satisfying meal had it all: big, robust flavors, vibrant colors, and a mix of crunch and creaminess to keep me interested right to the last bite.

AFTON CYRUS, *America's Test Kitchen Books*

Black Rice Bowls with Salmon

SERVES 4

Skin-on salmon fillets hold together best during cooking, and the skin helps keep the fish moist. If your salmon is less than 1 inch thick, start checking for doneness early. If using farmed salmon, cook until the thickest part registers 125 degrees. Nori is seaweed that has been dried and pressed into sheets for rolling sushi; you can find it in the international foods aisle of the supermarket.

RICE AND DRESSING

- 1½ cups black rice
- Salt and pepper
- ¼ cup rice vinegar
- ¼ cup mirin
- 1 tablespoon white miso
- 1 teaspoon grated fresh ginger
- ½ teaspoon grated lime zest plus 2 tablespoons juice

SALMON AND VEGETABLES

- 4 (4- to 6-ounce) skin-on wild-caught salmon fillets, 1 inch thick
- 1 teaspoon vegetable oil
- Salt and pepper
- 1 (8- by 7½-inch) sheet nori, crumbled (optional)
- 4 radishes, trimmed, halved, and sliced thin
- 1 avocado, halved, pitted, and sliced thin
- 1 cucumber, halved lengthwise, seeded, and sliced thin
- 2 scallions, sliced thin

BLACK RICE BOWLS WITH SALMON

1. FOR THE RICE AND DRESSING: Bring 4 quarts water to boil in Dutch oven over medium-high heat. Add rice and 1 teaspoon salt and cook until rice is tender, 20 to 25 minutes. Drain rice and transfer to large bowl.

2. Whisk vinegar, mirin, miso, ginger, and lime zest and juice together in small bowl until miso is fully incorporated. Season with salt and pepper to taste. Measure out ¼ cup vinegar mixture and drizzle over rice. Let rice cool to room temperature, tossing occasionally, about 20 minutes. Set remaining dressing aside for serving.

3. FOR THE SALMON AND VEGETABLES: While rice is cooking, adjust oven rack to lowest position, place aluminum foil–lined rimmed baking sheet on rack, and heat oven to 500 degrees. Pat salmon dry with paper towels, rub with oil, and season with salt and pepper.

4. Once oven reaches 500 degrees, reduce oven temperature to 275 degrees. Remove sheet from oven and carefully place salmon skin side down on hot sheet. Roast until center is still translucent when checked with tip of paring knife and registers 120 degrees (for medium-rare), 4 to 6 minutes.

5. Portion rice into 4 individual serving bowls and sprinkle with some of nori, if using. Flake salmon into large 3-inch pieces. Top rice with salmon, radishes, avocado, and cucumber. Sprinkle with scallions and drizzle with reserved dressing. Serve, passing remaining nori separately.

NOTES FROM THE TEST KITCHEN

ALL ABOUT WILD SALMON

Salmon's appealingly rich flavor is due to how its fat is stored: Unlike the fat in white fish, which is mostly stored in the liver, the fat in salmon is spread throughout the flesh. And much of it takes the form of omega-3 fatty acids, an essential polyunsaturated fat that is linked with a reduced risk of heart disease in adults and promotes brain development and healthy vision in infants. Wild salmon is rich in omega-3 fats but lower in total fat than farm-raised. Because wild salmon is leaner than farmed, it can be prone to overcooking, so we cook it to a slightly lower temperature.

EASY FISH AND CHIPS

✔ **WHY THIS RECIPE WORKS:** Crispy fish and chips can usually be found only at a proper English pub, but we wanted to create an authentic version for the home cook. We used a mixture of equal parts all-purpose flour and cornstarch plus a teaspoon of baking powder to mimic that familiar crispy, shell-like coating. Whisking in some beer created a coating that stuck well to the tender pieces of cod and added a malty flavor to each bite. Yukon Gold potatoes worked best for our chips—they were less starchy and more crispy once fried than other potato varieties.

In Detroit, people have been flocking to Scotty Simpson's restaurant for crispy, golden-brown fish and chips since the 1950s. After hearing about executive food editor Bryan Roof's trip to the restaurant, I wanted to find a way to make this light, perfectly crunchy version of fish and chips at home. A tall feat, sure. But I was up for a challenge.

I began my research with a phone call to Harry Barber, the owner of Scotty Simpson's. Barber began working at the restaurant as a dishwasher on his first day of high school decades ago; he purchased the restaurant, as well as the recipe for its famous fish and chips, in 2002. I asked Barber how he made the batter for the fish, but I didn't get very far (trust me—I tried all the tricks up my sleeve to get the information out of him). The recipe is a closely guarded secret. Instead, I needed to rely on Roof's excellent food memory, the pictures from the trip, and the various videos I found online to try to re-create this dish.

As the restaurant does, I chose to use cod because of its firm texture and wide availability. After trying precut fillets from the fish counter at the grocery store, which tended to be inconsistently sized, I found that I got better results when I bought a large fillet and portioned it myself.

I knew that the coating needed to be light and crispy, and after making six batches using existing fish and chips recipes, I narrowed my ingredient list to include just beer, flour, cornstarch, and a leavener. The beer not only provided a subtle sweetness that tasters preferred but also made the coating slightly more acidic, which helped prevent it from getting too tough. (If you prefer, you can substitute seltzer for the beer; it, too, provides the right balance.)

Equal parts all-purpose flour and cornstarch produced the ideal light, golden-brown, shell-like coating I was after. I found that letting the batter rest for 20 minutes before coating the fish helped it adhere better. And a bit of baking powder in the mix helped give the coating a light, airy texture.

For the French fries, I relied on our almost hands-off test kitchen method, which is a cold-fry technique. I simply put my sliced Yukon Gold potatoes into room-temperature oil in a large Dutch oven, brought the oil up to temperature, and cooked the fries, stirring just once, until they were done. Then I realized that to get the hot fish and chips on the table at the same time, I'd need to tweak this method slightly. I cooked the potatoes until they were just golden, removed them to make room for the fish, and then returned them to the hot oil for just 1 minute to finish cooking after the fish was ready.

I called over my coworkers for one final taste. We were thrilled with the crispy, tender, savory results.

ASHLEY MOORE, *Cook's Country*

Fish and Chips

SERVES 4

Try to find large Yukon Gold potatoes, 10 to 12 ounces each, that are similar in size. We prefer peanut or vegetable oil for frying and do not recommend using canola oil since it can impart off-flavors. Use a Dutch oven that holds 6 quarts or more. A light-bodied American lager, such as Budweiser, works best here. If you prefer to cook without alcohol, substitute seltzer for the beer. We prefer to use cod for this recipe, but haddock and halibut will also work well. Serve with Tartar Sauce (recipe follows), if desired.

  1 **cup (5 ounces) all-purpose flour**
  1 **cup (4 ounces) cornstarch**
     Salt and pepper
  1 **teaspoon baking powder**
1½ **cups beer**
  1 **(2-pound) skinless cod fillet, about 1 inch thick**
2½ **pounds large Yukon Gold potatoes, unpeeled**
  8 **cups peanut or vegetable oil**
     Lemon wedges

1. Whisk flour, cornstarch, 1½ teaspoons salt, and baking powder together in large bowl. Add beer and whisk until smooth. Cover with plastic wrap and refrigerate for at least 20 minutes.

2. Cut cod crosswise into 8 equal fillets (about 4 ounces each). Pat cod dry with paper towels and season with salt and pepper; refrigerate until ready to use.

3. Square off each potato by cutting ¼-inch-thick slice from each of its 4 long sides. Cut potatoes lengthwise into ¼-inch-thick planks. Stack 3 or 4 planks and cut into ¼-inch fries. Repeat with remaining planks. (Do not place potatoes in water.)

4. Line rimmed baking sheet with triple layer of paper towels. Combine potatoes and oil in large Dutch oven. Cook over high heat until oil has reached rolling boil, about 7 minutes. Continue to cook, without stirring, until potatoes are limp but exteriors are beginning to firm, about 15 minutes longer. Using tongs, stir potatoes, gently scraping up any that stick, and continue to cook, stirring occasionally, until just lightly golden brown, about 4 minutes longer (fries will not be fully cooked at this point). Using spider skimmer or slotted spoon, transfer fries to prepared sheet. Skim off any browned bits left in pot.

5. Set wire rack in second rimmed baking sheet. Transfer fish to batter and toss to evenly coat. Heat oil over medium-high heat to 375 degrees. Using fork, remove 4 pieces of fish from batter, allowing excess batter to drip back into bowl, and add to hot oil, briefly dragging fish along surface of oil to prevent sticking. Adjust burner, if necessary, to maintain oil temperature between 350 and 375 degrees.

6. Cook fish, stirring gently to prevent pieces from sticking together, until deep golden brown and crispy, about 4 minutes per side. Using spider skimmer or slotted spoon, transfer fish to prepared rack and skim off any browned bits left in pot. Return oil to 375 degrees and repeat with remaining 4 pieces of fish.

7. Return oil to 375 degrees. Add fries to oil and cook until deep golden brown and crispy, about 1 minute. Using spider skimmer or slotted spoon, transfer fries back to prepared sheet and season with salt. Transfer fish and chips to platter. Serve with lemon wedges.

FISH AND CHIPS

Tartar Sauce

MAKES ABOUT 1 CUP

The test kitchen's favorite mayo is Blue Plate Real Mayonnaise, which is not available in all areas of the country. Hellmann's Real Mayonnaise, which is available nationwide, was a close second and is a great option.

¾ cup mayonnaise

¼ cup dill pickle relish

1½ teaspoons distilled white vinegar

½ teaspoon Worcestershire sauce

½ teaspoon pepper

⅛ teaspoon salt

Combine all ingredients in small bowl. Cover with plastic wrap and refrigerate until flavors meld, about 15 minutes.

ROASTED STUFFED LOBSTER TAILS

✔ **WHY THIS RECIPE WORKS:** Roasting is a great way to heighten and concentrate the delicate flavor of lobster. By stuffing and roasting readily available lobster tails (often sold frozen), we capitalized on this technique's strengths and took the dish's flavor over the top. Lobster tails have a tendency to become chewy if overcooked, so after splitting the shell's underside and loosening the meat to make room for the stuffing, we kept the rest of the protective shell intact. For the filling, we combined chopped shrimp and buttery, toasted panko to mirror the rich, sweet flavor of the lobster; chopped parsley, grated lemon zest, and dry sherry offered a fresh, well-rounded profile. After mounding the stuffing into the tails, we roasted them in a baking dish until both the lobster and the filling were gently cooked through for a full-flavored, indulgent lobster feast we could enjoy any day of the year.

Growing up in New England, I've prepared and enjoyed lobster in many forms: steamed whole, doused in butter and tucked into a toasted roll, stirred into a creamy bisque, and even swirled into ice cream. Where I live, there is no shortage of ways for lobster lovers to get their fix in the summertime, but in the colder months (and in places farther afield), the pickings get slim. One ever-present option: lobster tails. Sold both fresh and frozen and available coast to coast, they are certainly a convenient way to serve up a luxe lobster dinner. But while the tail yields the most meat of any single lobster part, it's not nearly enough to constitute a meal. I wanted to come up with a year-round lobster tail recipe that was substantial enough to serve as an impressive main course.

I began by trying a few existing lobster tail recipes. After steaming, boiling, and roasting my way through several batches of tails, I was surprised by the results. While steaming is the most traditional approach and boiling was totally easy, roasting the tails yielded the sweetest, most intense lobster flavor I'd ever encountered. Additionally, the shells offered just enough protection from the dry heat of the oven to keep the tails tender. Lobster tails in the 5- to 6-ounce range were tender and sweet and moderately priced compared with larger ones, so I decided to use this midsize option.

I knew I needed to find a way to make the tails more substantial, and a stuffing seemed like the obvious choice. But many of the recipes I found offered complicated shell-splitting techniques (some even called for whole lobsters, which was a nonstarter for me) and leaned heavily on bready, bland fillings. I wanted a simple technique to match the convenience of working with just tails and an aromatic, nuanced filling that wouldn't overwhelm the sweet, delicate flavor of the lobster.

A few recipes I found called for brining the lobster to boost flavor and ensure moist, tender meat, so I followed suit and then got to work on my splitting technique. After a few test runs, I determined that cutting the bottom (rather than the top) of the shell was best, making it easy to open up the tail and allowing plenty of room for my stuffing. To determine the best roasting technique, I cooked split tails in ovens set to 250, 350, and 450 degrees and at each oven rack height, finally determining that the middle of the road—350 degrees on the middle rack—offered just the right amount of heat to yield sweet, tender lobster in about 20 minutes.

Before moving on to the stuffing, I decided to test whether brining was actually making much of a difference given the brief roasting time. I roasted two more batches, one brined and one not, and gathered my tasters. We determined that the differences were barely noticeable, so I decided to streamline my recipe and eliminate the brining step.

ROASTED STUFFED LOBSTER TAILS

Now for the all-important stuffing. I started with some simple aromatics, softening celery and shallot in butter before stirring in plenty of crunchy panko bread crumbs. When I pulled the baking dish from the oven, however, I was met with soggy, bland stuffing. To fix this, I toasted the panko first, browning the crumbs in butter and letting them cool while I readied the aromatics. This was an improvement, but my stuffing still wasn't substantial enough.

I thought something meaty might bulk up the filling, and seafood seemed to be the obvious choice. I gathered a few possible options—lobster meat, scallops, crabmeat, and shrimp—and incorporated them into separate batches of stuffing. Added raw, each cooked on pace with the roasted tails; and while they all worked well, offering a tender texture and adding plenty of heft to the filling, I decided to go with the less expensive, more readily available shrimp. To ensure their sweetness didn't overwhelm the flavor of the aromatics, I added a splash of sherry to keep the filling balanced.

And finally, I had it: A lobster feast that was simple yet impressive. With a substantial filling and the convenience of lobster tails, I could now enjoy my favorite seafood well beyond the summer months.

RUSSELL SELANDER, *America's Test Kitchen Books*

1. Adjust oven rack to middle position and heat oven to 350 degrees. Melt 4 tablespoons butter in 10-inch skillet over medium heat. Add panko and cook, stirring often, until crumbs are dark golden brown, about 2 minutes. Transfer panko to large bowl and let cool slightly. Wipe skillet clean with paper towels.

2. Melt remaining 2 tablespoons butter in now-empty skillet over medium heat. Add celery, shallot, and salt and cook until softened, 3 to 5 minutes. Stir in sherry and cook until reduced slightly, about 30 seconds. Transfer vegetable mixture to bowl with panko. Stir in shrimp, parsley, and lemon zest until well combined.

3. Using kitchen shears, cut lengthwise through soft shell on underside of lobster tail. Cut meat in half using paring knife, taking care not to cut through outer shell. With lobster tail cut side up, grasp each side with your hands and crack outer shell, opening cut side to expose meat. Lift meat from shell to loosen, then tuck back into shell.

4. Arrange lobster tails cut side up in 13 by 9-inch baking dish, alternating tails front to back. Spoon stuffing evenly into tails, mounding stuffing slightly. Roast until stuffing is golden brown and lobster registers 140 degrees, 20 to 25 minutes. Serve with lemon wedges.

Roasted Stuffed Lobster Tails

SERVES 4

To thaw frozen lobster tails, let them sit either in the refrigerator for 24 hours or submerged in cold water for 30 minutes to 1 hour.

- 6 tablespoons unsalted butter
- ½ cup panko bread crumbs
- 2 celery ribs, chopped fine
- 1 shallot, minced
- ¼ teaspoon salt
- 3 tablespoons dry sherry
- 8 ounces medium-large shrimp (31 to 40 per pound), peeled, deveined, tails removed, and chopped
- ¼ cup chopped fresh parsley
- 1½ teaspoons grated lemon zest, plus lemon wedges for serving
- 4 (5- to 6-ounce) lobster tails

NOTES FROM THE TEST KITCHEN

BUTTERFLYING A LOBSTER TAIL

1. Using kitchen shears, cut lengthwise through soft shell on underside of lobster tail. Cut meat in half using paring knife; do not cut through outer shell.

2. With lobster tail cut side up, grasp each side with your hands and crack outer shell, opening cut side to expose meat.

Substitute 1 finely chopped fennel bulb (about 1 cup) for celery. Substitute minced fennel fronds, if available, for parsley and Pernod for sherry.

SLOW-COOKER PAELLA

✓ **WHY THIS RECIPE WORKS:** We thought the opportunity to try making paella in a slow cooker was too good to be missed. Clam juice, water, and sherry gave us a complex-tasting yet simple base in which to cook the rice, while a hefty amount of garlic, tomato paste, and spices bolstered the flavor of our dish. Boneless, skinless chicken thighs remained tender and moist even after extended cooking, and chorizo provided a smoky meatiness. After a few hours in the slow cooker the meat was cooked perfectly, but the rice was mushy in some places and undercooked in others. Fully covering the rice with a layer of chicken and placing a parchment shield on top of the assembled paella helped trap steam, resulting in perfectly cooked rice and tender chicken. We added quick-cooking shrimp during the last 20 minutes of cooking, followed by peas and roasted red peppers for a bright finish.

Paella is one of my favorite Spanish dishes, and while it has a standard template—rice, saffron, broth, sometimes wine, and a jumble of meat and seafood—the preparation and embellishments vary from recipe to recipe. In pursuit of the perfect paella, I've prepared versions on the grill, in the oven, on the stovetop—you name it—and although the results have all been delicious, the recipes were a project, each calling for a laundry list of prep-heavy ingredients and complicated techniques requiring a watchful eye. Paella originated in the Valencia region of Spain as a way to feed large numbers of people working in the fields, so why are modern recipes so complicated? To bring this dish back to its humble roots, I decided to try to make a pared-down, totally hands-off paella in the gentle heat of the slow cooker.

While typical recipes for paella pile in everything from mussels and clams to pork to poultry, translating this large-scale dish to the confines of my slow cooker meant I needed to select my ingredients with care. Chorizo is a traditional component, and the low-and-slow approach meant I could coax out even more of its smoky, spicy flavor, so it was a keeper. Boneless, skinless chicken thighs promised plenty of meaty richness, and their dark meat could easily handle the lengthy cooking time without drying out. I definitely wanted a seafood component and decided that shrimp would be my surest bet; quick-cooking and subtly sweet, they could be added toward the end.

With the meat and seafood portion of my paella in place, I turned my attention to building the flavor base. *Sofrito*—a sautéed blend of finely chopped onion, bell pepper, and tomato—is traditional, but I knew that softening and browning this mixture in the slow cooker wasn't a possibility. Not wanting to pull out a separate pan, I microwaved chopped onion, sliced red bell pepper, and, for an umami boost, tomato paste along with some oil, garlic, and a few select spices: paprika, cayenne, and crumbled saffron threads. This step effectively softened the onion and unlocked the spices' flavors, but the bell pepper was still a bit crunchy. I didn't want to chop it so fine that it lost its structure or eliminate it altogether, so I decided to swap in jarred roasted red bell peppers, which would require only a few minutes to warm through. I transferred the sofrito to the slow cooker, stirred in the rice, and evenly distributed the chicken thighs and chorizo before pouring in water, clam juice, and some dry sherry. Now I could let my slow cooker do the rest of the work.

The chicken was fully cooked after 2 hours' time, and though I was pleased with the complex array of flavors at play, the rice needed some work. The grains beneath the chicken had absorbed far too much liquid and were mushy, while those on the surface had not fully cooked through. In traditional recipes, the crispy bits of rice along the sides of the pan are the most prized part of the dish (an element known as *socarrat*), but my rice was simply undercooked. To remedy the situation, I tried everything from tinkering with liquid amounts to toasting the rice in the microwave, but nothing worked.

Not willing to admit defeat, I arrived the next morning with an idea: Since the rice below the chicken was cooking through, what if I fully sealed the grains below a more carefully laid layer of chicken? I stirred another batch of sofrito into uncooked rice, poured in the hot liquid to jump-start cooking, and then layered on enough chicken thighs to completely cover the rice. Scattering the chorizo over the thighs meant that its smoky, spicy flavor would season the chicken—and the rice below—as its fat render slowly rendered. With my paella assembled, I covered the slow cooker and waited.

My new approach was a huge step in the right direction: The layer of chicken had contained escaping steam, and as a result, the texture of the rice was vastly improved. For one final test I placed a sheet of parchment atop the layers, thus confining the steam to an even smaller space. With that small adjustment, I was rewarded with perfectly cooked rice as well as the juiciest, most flavorful chicken yet.

Before taking a victory lap, I needed to bring in the shrimp. Scattering a pound of peeled shrimp over the chorizo for the last 20 minutes of cooking did the trick; the steam cooked them to tender, juicy perfection just as the paella finished up. And I hadn't forgotten my roasted red peppers: I added the soft, sweet strands—along with frozen peas for some bright, fresh bursts—with just enough time left to warm them through.

And there it was: the perfect, pared-down paella with all of the classic flavors and none of the fuss.

JOSEPH GITTER, *America's Test Kitchen Books*

Slow-Cooker Paella

SERVES 6 TO 8

COOKING TIME: 2 TO 3 HOURS ON HIGH
SLOW COOKER SIZE: 5 TO 7 QUARTS

You will need an oval slow cooker for this recipe. If using smaller or larger shrimp, be sure to adjust the cooking time as needed. For more information on making a foil collar, see page 75.

 1 onion, chopped fine
 2 tablespoons extra-virgin olive oil
 6 garlic cloves, minced
 2 tablespoons tomato paste
 1 teaspoon smoked paprika
 ¼ teaspoon cayenne pepper
    Pinch saffron threads, crumbled
    Salt and pepper
 2 cups long-grain white rice, rinsed
 1 (8-ounce) bottle clam juice
 ⅔ cup water

 ⅓ cup dry sherry
 1½ pounds boneless, skinless chicken thighs, trimmed and halved
 8 ounces Spanish-style chorizo sausage, cut into ½-inch pieces
 1 pound extra-large shrimp (21 to 25 per pound), peeled, deveined, and tails removed
 ½ cup frozen peas, thawed
 ½ cup jarred roasted red peppers, rinsed, patted dry, and sliced thin
 2 tablespoons chopped fresh parsley
    Lemon wedges

1. Line slow cooker with aluminum foil collar and lightly coat with vegetable oil spray. Microwave onion, oil, garlic, tomato paste, paprika, cayenne, saffron, and 1 teaspoon salt in bowl, stirring occasionally, until onion is softened, about 5 minutes; transfer to prepared slow cooker. Stir in rice.

2. Microwave clam juice, water, and sherry in now-empty bowl until steaming, about 5 minutes; transfer to slow cooker. Season chicken with salt and pepper and arrange in even layer on top of rice. Scatter chorizo over chicken. Gently press 16 by 12-inch sheet of parchment paper onto surface of chorizo, folding down edges as needed. Cover and cook until liquid is absorbed and rice is just tender, 2 to 3 hours on high.

3. Discard parchment and foil collar. Season shrimp with salt and pepper and scatter on top of paella. Cover and cook on high until shrimp is opaque throughout, 20 to 30 minutes.

4. Sprinkle peas and red peppers over shrimp, cover, and let sit until heated through, about 5 minutes. Sprinkle with parsley and serve with lemon wedges.

NOTES FROM THE TEST KITCHEN

CREATING A PARCHMENT SHIELD

Press 16 by 12-inch sheet of parchment paper firmly onto layer of chorizo, folding down edges as needed.

CHAPTER 7

BREAKFAST, BRUNCH, AND BREADS

MIGAS

✔ **WHY THIS RECIPE WORKS:** This classic Tex-Mex breakfast combines scrambled eggs with chiles, onion, and crisp-chewy tortillas. We fried the tortillas in oil before adding the eggs, which infused the scramble with toasted-corn flavor. A mix of onion, red bell pepper, and briny pickled jalapeños gave the dish a pleasant Tex-Mex backbone. For soft, fluffy egg curds, we started the eggs over medium-high heat to create steam to puff up the curds, and then turned the heat to low to ensure that the eggs didn't overcook. Shredded Monterey Jack cheese, folded in at the end, made for creamy, cohesive eggs.

Some say the breakfast of champions is a bowl of Wheaties. But after a trip to Austin, Texas, I call shenanigans. There, I ate a plate of *migas*—fluffy scrambled eggs cooked with chiles and onion and studded with pleasantly chewy strips of corn tortillas. The tortilla pieces infused the eggs with a deep, sweet toasted-corn flavor that made the dish a knockout. I set out to make a great homemade version.

Most recipes for migas (its name translates literally as "crumbs") call for either store-bought tortilla chips or fresh corn tortillas that are cut into strips, deep- or pan-fried, and stirred into scrambled eggs. I made a couple of versions with each. The chips added mostly saltiness and very little corn flavor. The fresh corn tortillas that I fried myself, on the other hand, took me right back to Texas.

As I cobbled together a working recipe, the first order of business was to make frying the tortilla strips as easy as possible. Deep frying was a little much at breakfast time. A shallow fry in a skillet, with just a few tablespoons of oil, was much easier. I set the strips aside, willing myself not to eat them all before I got my eggs going.

After sautéing some onion, red bell pepper, and fresh jalapeños, I followed our tried-and-true company method for preparing scrambled eggs, starting them in a hot pan and then quickly reducing the heat while gently folding the eggs to ensure fluffy curds. I added my tortilla strips during the final seconds of cooking and dug in. Disappointment: The tortillas added precious little flavor.

For my next batch, I fried the tortilla strips and then, instead of removing them, left them in the skillet, adding the vegetables to soften and then scrambling the eggs.

A win. The crispy strips (and the oil they were fried in) offered tons of toasted-corn flavor to the eggs.

Briny jarred jalapeños (an easy substitute for fresh) added welcome heat and acidity, and a little Monterey Jack helped create a creamy, cohesive scramble.

MORGAN BOLLING, *Cook's Country*

Migas

SERVES 4

It's important to follow the visual cues when making the eggs, as your pan's thickness will affect the cooking time. If you're using an electric stove, heat a second burner on low and move the skillet to it when it's time to adjust the heat. For a spicier dish, use the larger amount of jarred jalapeños.

- 8 large eggs
  Salt and pepper
- 3 tablespoons vegetable oil
- 6 (6-inch) corn tortillas, cut into 1 by ½-inch strips
- 1 onion, chopped fine
- 1 small red bell pepper, stemmed, seeded, and chopped fine
- 1–2 tablespoons minced jarred jalapeños
- 1½ ounces Monterey Jack cheese, shredded (⅓ cup), plus extra for serving
- 1 tablespoon chopped fresh cilantro
  Salsa

1. Whisk eggs, ¼ teaspoon salt, and ¼ teaspoon pepper in bowl until thoroughly combined, about 1 minute; set aside.

2. Heat oil in 12-inch nonstick skillet over medium-high heat until shimmering. Add tortillas and ¼ teaspoon salt and cook, stirring occasionally, until golden brown, 4 to 6 minutes. Add onion, bell pepper, and jalapeños and cook, stirring occasionally, until vegetables are softened, 5 to 7 minutes.

3. Add egg mixture and, using heat-resistant rubber spatula, constantly and firmly scrape along bottom and sides of skillet until eggs begin to clump and spatula leaves trail on bottom of skillet, 30 to 60 seconds.

4. Reduce heat to low and gently but constantly fold egg mixture until clumped and still slightly wet, 30 to 60 seconds. Off heat, gently fold in Monterey Jack and cilantro. Serve immediately, passing salsa and extra Monterey Jack separately.

MIGAS

BLUEBERRY-OAT PANCAKES

✔ WHY THIS RECIPE WORKS: To give classic pancakes a nutrition boost, we turned to whole grains and zeroed in on oats for their nutty flavor, hearty texture, and high fiber content. We created a smooth base for our batter using mostly oat flour, with a small amount of all-purpose flour to provide structure and lift. The addition of whole rolled oats, presoaked until just softened, gave our pancakes a satisfying, nubby texture. Fresh blueberries, cinnamon, and nutmeg paired nicely with the toasty oats, and switching from whole milk to buttermilk kept our pancakes light and fluffy.

Pancakes are the perfect weekend treat—simple to prepare, fluffy, and just sweet enough—but a recent brunch outing opened my eyes to a new twist on the standard version: oat pancakes. Unlike the classic stacks I've made for years, these cakes were complex, boasting a nutty, subtly spiced flavor and a hearty yet surprisingly light texture. I knew right away that these irresistible, wholesome, and supersatisfying pancakes would offer a welcome change of pace and make eating nutritious, fiber- and protein-rich whole grains a pleasure, so I set out to craft a recipe of my own.

After a little research, I determined there were a few different approaches for incorporating the oats. Some recipes used cooked oatmeal; some swapped all-purpose flour for oat flour; and others struck a balance between the two, incorporating softened whole oats into an oat flour batter. This third option appealed to me, as it promised both plenty of oat flavor and a satisfying texture. But while I welcomed the heartiness that whole oats would provide, I still wanted my cakes to be light and fluffy. To get there, I had some questions to tackle: Could I use oats and oat flour alone, or would some all-purpose flour be necessary? And given that oat flour is naturally gluten-free, how would I get the proper rise? Finally, which dairy product would impart the best flavor and texture? I knew had my work cut out for me, but I was excited to get started.

I began with a few side-by-side tests to learn how oat flour and rolled oats (the test kitchen's pick over quick, instant, and thick-cut oats for their hearty flavor and texture in baked goods) behaved in pancakes. Soaking the oats rather than cooking them into an oatmeal seemed the most efficient route, and one that

promised a nubby, distinct chew. To determine what volume of oats I could use without weighing down my pancakes, I soaked ½ cup, 1 cup, and 1½ cups of oats in milk for about 15 minutes. I readied three batches of batter while I waited, using oat flour in place of all-purpose and folding everything together before adding in the milk-oat mixture. I cooked a few pancakes from each batch and took a taste. The batch made with 1 cup of oats was the best of the three, yielding pancakes with decent chew and a good distribution of oats, but the overall texture was a bit leaden. To give them a little more lightness, I gradually replaced some of the oat flour with all-purpose flour, which would boost the pancakes' gluten structure and open up the crumb. Small amounts made little difference, while a 50/50 split between all-purpose and oat flours diminished the nutty oat flavor. But when I paired ½ cup all-purpose flour with 1½ cups oat flour I finally flipped out a batch with a light, tender crumb and a distinct oat taste.

With the flour question settled, I turned my attention to other ingredients—egg and leavener—to further perfect my pancakes' texture. A single egg didn't yield enough structure, but whisking in a second egg along with 2½ teaspoons of baking powder made a big difference, giving the high-protein oat flour remarkable lift.

Aside from the step of soaking the oats, my recipe was shaping up to be pretty similar to that of classic pancakes, but I wondered if there was any merit to using home-ground flour. I pulsed rolled oats in my food processor until they were as finely ground as I could manage, but the resulting flour simply wasn't as fine as store-bought and the resulting pancakes were noticeably denser.

With my recipe's technique in the bag, I was ready to play around with flavor. Up to this point I had been using whole milk, but I when I tried replacing it with buttermilk and then with plain yogurt (with water as my oats' soaking liquid), I was quickly won over by the buttermilk version. Subtly tangy with a smooth, light texture, these pancakes offered the best of classic buttermilk flapjacks but with the added nuance of hearty oat taste. I also sampled a few simple spice combinations and settled on nutmeg and cinnamon balanced with a touch of vanilla. As I readied my final batch I decided these satisfying cakes could do with a few juicy bursts of sweetness, so I grabbed a carton of blueberries and, after ladling a few portions into the hot pan, sprinkled some berries onto each round.

After flipping over 800 pancakes in pursuit of perfection, I finally had it: fluffy, beautifully golden-brown cakes that are a wholesome, feel-good treat.

AFTON CYRUS, *America's Test Kitchen Books*

Blueberry-Oat Pancakes

MAKES 18 PANCAKES; SERVES 6

An electric griddle set at 350 degrees can be used in place of a skillet. We prefer using store-bought oat flour, but you can make your own in a pinch: Grind 1½ cups (4½ ounces) old-fashioned rolled oats in a food processor to a fine meal, about 2 minutes; note pancakes will be denser if using ground oats. Do not use toasted oat flour, or quick, instant, or thick-cut oats in this recipe. Serve with maple syrup and additional blueberries if desired.

2 cups low-fat buttermilk, plus extra as needed
1 cup (3 ounces) old-fashioned rolled oats
1½ cups (4½ ounces) oat flour
½ cup (2½ ounces) all-purpose flour
2½ teaspoons baking powder
1 teaspoon ground cinnamon
¼ teaspoon salt
⅛ teaspoon ground nutmeg
2 large eggs
3 tablespoons plus 2 teaspoons vegetable oil
3 tablespoons sugar
2 teaspoons vanilla extract
7½ ounces (1½ cups) blueberries

1. Adjust oven rack to middle position and heat oven to 200 degrees. Set wire rack in rimmed baking sheet and place in oven. Combine 1 cup buttermilk and oats in bowl and let sit at room temperature until softened, about 15 minutes.

2. Whisk oat flour, all-purpose flour, baking powder, cinnamon, salt, and nutmeg together in large bowl. In separate bowl, whisk remaining 1 cup buttermilk, eggs, 3 tablespoons oil, sugar, and vanilla together until frothy, about 1 minute. Whisk buttermilk mixture into flour mixture until smooth. Using rubber spatula, fold in oat-buttermilk mixture.

3. Heat 1 teaspoon oil in 12-inch nonstick skillet over medium heat until shimmering, 3 to 5 minutes. Using paper towels, wipe out oil, leaving thin film

in pan. Using ¼-cup measure, portion batter into pan, spreading each into 4-inch round using back of spoon. Sprinkle each pancake with about 1 tablespoon blueberries. Cook until edges are set and first side is golden, 2 to 3 minutes.

4. Flip pancakes and cook until second side is golden, 2 to 3 minutes. Serve or transfer to wire rack in oven. Repeat with remaining batter, whisking additional buttermilk into batter as needed to loosen, and adding remaining oil to pan as necessary.

CHEESE BLINTZES

✓ **WHY THIS RECIPE WORKS:** To bring a streamlined version of this Eastern European specialty to the home kitchen, we started by nixing the hard-to-find, gritty-textured farmer's cheese in favor of smoother ricotta cheese. A little cream cheese boosted the ricotta's creaminess and gave it a pleasant tang, while confectioners' sugar provided just enough sweetness and body. We found no need for a crêpe pan; a traditional skillet worked just fine, turning out larger crêpes that were easier to fill and fold. To simplify our cooking method, we cooked the crêpes on only one side. After browning the blintzes in butter, we topped them with a bright, quick-cooking raspberry sauce.

I've never understood the appeal of blintzes, having only known them as eggy crêpes stuffed with gritty, sweetened cheese and topped with a cloying fruit sauce. But after a recent trip to New York City, our executive food editor Bryan Roof couldn't stop talking about the beautiful blintzes he'd eaten and I was intrigued.

The reasons so few people make blintzes were revealed by the recipes I found. They called for specialty pans and for flipping the giant crêpes halfway through cooking. And each recipe produced a gritty, not creamy, filling. I had work to do.

First I'd tackle the filling. I wanted it smooth, creamy, and just sweet enough. While blintzes are often made with farmer's cheese—a mild fresh cheese with a lovely flavor but a tendency toward grittiness—I found that ricotta made a much smoother filling. A little cream cheese added tanginess, and confectioners' sugar gave it just enough sweetness and body.

For the crêpes, I started with the test kitchen's favorite recipe, a simple batter that produces light, pliable crêpes about 6 inches in diameter. But because I'd eventually be folding these into rectangular packets stuffed with cheese filling, I needed them to be bigger than usual. I made a few alterations to the ingredient amounts and, rather than reach for a small crêpe pan, grabbed a 12-inch nonstick skillet. Scooping ⅓ cup of the batter into my hot, lightly buttered pan, I slowly swirled it to cover the surface and cooked it for about 1 minute, until it was lightly golden on the bottom.

While regular crêpes must be flipped at this point to achieve a lovely browned color on both sides, crêpes for blintzes need to cook through only long enough to firm up for filling and folding; after all, one side is invisible on the plate. I could simply remove the crêpes one by one as they cooked and pile them onto a plate.

Once filled, these blintzes would make a second visit to the skillet to brown and warm through. To guard against any filling oozing out into the skillet, I had to fold them up very carefully: After spooning the filling onto each crêpe, I folded over the bottom edge and then the sides. I finished rolling the crêpe around the filling to form a neat, tidy blintz. I could nestle six of these blintzes at a time into my skillet to finish cooking.

A bright, quick-cooking sauce of tart raspberries balanced the rich, lightly sweetened blintz filling. My bad blintz memories were banished.

CECELIA JENKINS, *Cook's Country*

Cheese Blintzes with Raspberry Sauce

MAKES 12 BLINTZES, SERVES 4 TO 6

Don't worry if you lose a few crêpes along the way; the batter makes about 15 to account for any mistakes. If the batter doesn't stick to the skillet when swirling, that means the skillet is too greased and/or not hot enough. Return the skillet to the heat and cook 10 seconds longer; then try again to swirl the batter. With the next try, use less butter to brush the skillet. If the filled and rolled blintzes split on the sides, be careful while searing them because the filling may sputter. You do not need to thaw the raspberries before making the sauce.

FILLING

- 11 ounces (1¼ cups plus 2 tablespoons) whole-milk ricotta cheese
- ½ cup (2 ounces) confectioners' sugar
- 1 ounce cream cheese, softened
- ¼ teaspoon salt

SAUCE

- 10 ounces (2 cups) frozen raspberries
- ¼ cup (1¾ ounces) granulated sugar
- ¼ teaspoon salt

CRÊPES

- 2 cups (10 ounces) all-purpose flour
- 2 teaspoons granulated sugar
- ½ teaspoon salt
- 3 cups whole milk
- 4 large eggs
- 4 tablespoons unsalted butter, melted and cooled, plus 4 tablespoons unsalted butter

1. FOR THE FILLING: Whisk all ingredients in bowl until no lumps of cream cheese remain. Refrigerate until ready to use. (Filling can be refrigerated for up to 2 days.)

2. FOR THE SAUCE: Combine raspberries, sugar, and salt in small saucepan. Cook over medium heat, stirring occasionally, until slightly thickened, 8 to 10 minutes. (Sauce can be refrigerated for up to 2 days.)

3. FOR THE CRÊPES: Whisk flour, sugar, and salt together in medium bowl. Whisk milk and eggs together in separate bowl. Add half of milk mixture to flour mixture and whisk until smooth. Whisk in 3 tablespoons melted butter until incorporated. Whisk in remaining milk mixture until smooth. (Batter can be refrigerated for up to 2 days before cooking. It will separate; rewhisk it before using.)

4. Brush bottom of 12-inch nonstick skillet lightly with some of remaining 1 tablespoon melted butter and heat skillet over medium heat until hot, about 2 minutes. Add ⅓ cup batter to center of skillet and simultaneously lift and rotate skillet in circular motion to swirl batter, allowing batter to run and fully cover bottom of skillet. Cook crêpe until edges look dry and start to curl and bottom of crêpe is light golden, about 1 minute. Using rubber spatula, lift edge of crêpe and slide it onto plate. Repeat with remaining batter, stacking crêpes and brushing skillet with melted butter every other time. (Adjust burner between medium-low and medium heat as needed toward end of crêpe-making process.)

CHEESE BLINTZES WITH RASPBERRY SAUCE

5. Working with 1 crêpe at a time, spoon 2 tablespoons filling onto crêpe about 2 inches from bottom edge and spread into 4-inch line. Fold bottom edge of crêpe over filling, then fold sides of crêpe over filling. Gently roll crêpe into tidy package about 4 inches long and 2 inches wide. Repeat with remaining crêpes and filling. (Assembled blintzes can be transferred to plate, covered with plastic wrap, and refrigerated for up to 24 hours.)

6. Melt 2 tablespoons butter in now-empty skillet over medium heat. Add half of blintzes, seam sides down, and cook until golden brown, 2 to 4 minutes, gently moving blintzes in skillet as needed for even browning. Using spatula, gently flip blintzes and continue to cook until golden brown on second side, 2 to 4 minutes longer. Transfer blintzes to platter, seam sides down, and wipe skillet clean with paper towels. Repeat with remaining 2 tablespoons butter and remaining blintzes. Serve with raspberry sauce.

TO MAKE AHEAD: At end of step 5, transfer blintzes to rimmed baking sheet and freeze. Transfer frozen blintzes to zipper-lock bag and freeze for up to 1 month. When ready to cook, do not thaw blintzes. Reduce heat in step 6 to medium-low and cook blintzes, covered, until golden brown, 6 to 9 minutes per side.

LEMON-BLUEBERRY MUFFINS

✔ **WHY THIS RECIPE WORKS:** We were after big, bold lemon-blueberry muffins. A tablespoon of lemon zest in the batter added plenty of vibrant citrus flavor. Sour cream made the muffins' crumb more tender and enhanced the lemon tang. Rather than dipping each muffin in melted butter and sugar (as is done with the muffins made at the Hotel Iroquois, which inspired this recipe), we took an easier route: We brushed the batter with butter and sprinkled lemon sugar over the top before baking.

Lemon and blueberry are a power couple in the baking world. That's because the vibrant freshness of lemon plays well with the tart sweetness of blueberries. For many years, the Hotel Iroquois in Mackinac Island, Michigan, has capitalized on this fruity affinity with its signature mini lemon-blueberry muffins. Full of rich, buttery flavor; ample amounts of both lemon and blueberries; and a crunchy top resulting from a quick

dip in a mixture of melted butter and sugar right after baking, these muffins have earned legions of fans.

Inspired to make a similar recipe in full-size form, I turned first to the test kitchen's archive of blueberry muffin recipes. After making a few, I put together a basic lineup of dry ingredients: flour, salt, and baking powder. I mixed in melted butter, milk, eggs, sugar, and 1 teaspoon of lemon zest before folding in frozen wild blueberries—a test kitchen favorite for year-round quality. Twenty minutes later I had beautiful muffins, but they barely tasted of lemon, and dipping full-size muffins in the butter-sugar mixture was a messy affair.

For the next batch, I amped up the lemon flavor by tripling the amount of zest in the batter. And I switched out the milk for sour cream, which made the muffins more tender and enhanced their lemony tang. These tweaks helped, but I needed that crunchy sugar top.

Rather than dip each muffin in melted butter and sugar, I simply brushed the tops of the uncooked muffins with melted butter and sprinkled them with sugar. In the oven, the sugar gently caramelized into a sweet, crunchy shell.

For my final batch, I measured my dry ingredients the night before and baked the muffins in the morning. An inviting aroma filled the kitchen as we gathered around to taste. The warm, lemony flavors were almost as good as crawling back into bed for a snooze.

MORGAN BOLLING, *Cook's Country*

Mackinac Lemon-Blueberry Muffins
MAKES 12 MUFFINS

To prevent streaks of blue in the batter, leave the blueberries in the freezer until the last possible moment. Frozen blueberries make this a year-round recipe; fresh blueberries may be substituted, if desired. If your lemons are small, buy an extra one to ensure that you're able to get 5 teaspoons of zest.

1½ cups (10½ ounces) sugar

5 teaspoons grated lemon zest (2 lemons)

2½ cups (12½ ounces) all-purpose flour

4 teaspoons baking powder

¾ teaspoon salt

1½ cups sour cream

7 tablespoons unsalted butter, melted

2 large eggs

7½ ounces (1½ cups) frozen blueberries

1. Adjust oven rack to middle position and heat oven to 400 degrees. Generously spray 12-cup muffin tin, including top, with vegetable oil spray. Combine ¼ cup sugar and 2 teaspoons lemon zest in small bowl; set aside.

2. Whisk flour, baking powder, and salt together in bowl. Whisk sour cream, 5 tablespoons melted butter, eggs, remaining 1¼ cups sugar, and remaining 1 tablespoon lemon zest together in large bowl.

3. Using rubber spatula, fold flour mixture into sour cream mixture until just combined. Fold in blueberries until just evenly distributed; do not overmix. Using greased ⅓-cup dry measuring cup or #12 portion scoop, portion batter among cups in prepared muffin tin; evenly distribute any remaining batter among cups. Brush batter with remaining 2 tablespoons melted butter and sprinkle with sugar-zest mixture (about 1 teaspoon per muffin cup).

4. Bake until muffins are golden brown and toothpick inserted in center comes out with few crumbs attached, 20 to 25 minutes, rotating muffin tin halfway through baking. Let muffins cool in muffin tin on wire rack for 10 minutes. Transfer muffins to rack and let cool for 5 minutes. Serve warm.

HOT CROSS BUNS

✓ **WHY THIS RECIPE WORKS:** For a light and airy, slightly sweet Easter bun, we added plumped raisins to a simple, water-based yeasted dough and gave it plenty of time to rise. Butter and eggs added richness, and an egg wash gave the buns a gorgeous golden-brown sheen once baked. To decorate our baked buns, we opted for a simple confectioners' sugar and milk icing, which we piped in long continuous stripes across the rows to create a traditional cross atop each bun.

One legend says that if you hang a hot cross bun from your kitchen rafter, it will expel bad spirits. Another promises protection from shipwrecks if you carry a bun on your boat. While these ends sound nice, I wasn't looking for magical intervention; I just wanted a warm, slightly sweet, dried fruit–studded bun for Easter or any other time.

The trick with hot cross buns is achieving the right structure. The airy buns are richer than most breads but not buttery like a brioche. And the lean icing on top of the buns whets my sweet tooth, but only just.

I used a stand mixer to knead together a basic dough from flour, water, yeast, sugar, and salt. I knew a nice long knead would help develop gluten and build structure in the dough, trapping air and allowing the buns to rise to lofty heights. I also added some butter and eggs to make the dough richer and more flavorful—but not so much that it would weigh things down.

My next move was to look through cookbooks for traditional bells and whistles to embellish my hot cross buns. A colleague suggested including warm spice in the dough, so I added a bit of ground cinnamon to my next batch of buns.

I loved the aroma of the cinnamony baking bread wafting from the oven. But when I inspected my baked buns, my optimism deflated. They were dense and compact, a far cry from the pillowy rolls I'd baked before. I assumed I had simply mismeasured something, so I made a couple more batches of buns, measuring extra carefully, to check my work. Still bad.

What gives? A chat with our science editor shed light: He taught me that cinnamon contains a flavor compound called cinnamaldehyde, which can inhibit yeast activity and prevent bread from fully rising. What's fine for a relatively dense cinnamon swirl bread can prove fatal to a soft, airy bun. I ditched the cinnamon and moved on to the dried fruit. I made batches with both currants and raisins, and my tasters much preferred the bigger, sweeter flavor of raisins plumped in warm water.

The real signature of a hot cross bun is its top. I tried the old English technique of making crosses from ropes of flour paste dough that are then draped over each bun and baked, but these were a pain to make. Besides, my tasters wanted icing. A simple confectioners' sugar and milk icing did the trick, piped in long, continuous stripes across the rows of baked buns in the pan to create a series of crosses.

My final task was to make sure I could have freshly baked buns for breakfast without having to get out of bed at the crack of dawn. After testing a few make-ahead methods, I found a winner: Make the dough the day before, form it into buns, tuck them into their pan, and let them proof as usual. Then refrigerate them overnight. Come morning, pop them into the oven to bake. Hot cross buns, with an emphasis on the hot.

KATIE LEAIRD, *Cook's Country*

HOT CROSS BUNS

Hot Cross Buns

MAKES 12 BUNS

You can use either regular or golden raisins in this recipe. The buns can be served warm or at room temperature. Plan ahead: The dough will need to rise in two stages for a total of 3½ to 4½ hours.

BUNS

¾ cup raisins

2 tablespoons water, plus ¾ cup warm water (110 degrees)

3 large eggs, plus 1 large egg, lightly beaten

6 tablespoons unsalted butter, melted

4 cups (20 ounces) all-purpose flour

½ cup (3½ ounces) granulated sugar

2¼ teaspoons instant or rapid-rise yeast

1¼ teaspoons salt

ICING

1 cup (4 ounces) confectioners' sugar

4 teaspoons milk

⅛ teaspoon vanilla extract

Pinch salt

1. FOR THE BUNS: Combine raisins and 2 tablespoons water in small bowl; cover and microwave until steaming, about 1 minute. Let sit until softened, about 15 minutes. Drain raisins and discard liquid.

2. Whisk warm water, 3 eggs, and melted butter together in 4-cup liquid measuring cup. Using stand mixer fitted with dough hook, mix flour, sugar, yeast, and salt on low speed until combined, about 30 seconds. With mixer running, add egg mixture and mix until dough comes together, about 2 minutes.

3. Increase speed to medium and knead until dough is smooth and elastic, about 10 minutes. Reduce speed to low, add raisins, and knead until combined, about 2 minutes (dough will be sticky and some raisins may not be fully incorporated into dough at this point; this is OK).

4. Turn out dough and any errant raisins onto lightly floured counter and knead by hand to evenly incorporate raisins into dough, about 1 minute. Form dough into smooth, taut ball; transfer to greased large bowl and cover with plastic wrap. Let rise until doubled in size, 2 to 2½ hours.

5. Grease 13 by 9-inch baking pan. Turn out dough onto lightly floured counter and divide into 12 equal pieces. Form each piece into rough ball by pinching

and pulling dough edges under so that top is smooth. On clean counter, cup each ball with your palm and roll into smooth, tight ball. Arrange in prepared pan in 3 rows of 4 and cover loosely with plastic. Let buns rise until nearly doubled in size and starting to press against one another, 1½ to 2 hours.

6. Adjust oven rack to middle position and heat oven to 350 degrees. Brush buns with beaten egg. Bake until golden brown and centers register at least 190 degrees, 24 to 26 minutes. Transfer pan to wire rack and let buns cool until just warm, about 1 hour.

7. FOR THE ICING: Combine all ingredients in bowl until smooth (icing will be very thick). Transfer icing to small zipper-lock bag. Cut off very tip of 1 corner of bag. Pipe continuous line of icing across center of each row of buns, then pipe icing in lines perpendicular to first to form cross in center of each bun. Serve.

TO MAKE AHEAD: Make dough through step 5 and let rise until doubled in size. Cover tightly with plastic wrap and refrigerate for up to 24 hours. Proceed with recipe from step 6, extending baking time by 5 minutes.

COFFEE CAKE

✓ **WHY THIS RECIPE WORKS:** Our streusel-topped coffee cake recipe makes use of a food processor for mixing both the cake and the streusel topping. To ensure a tender cake, we opted to use the reverse-creaming method (combining the butter and flour before adding the wet ingredients). This mixing method coated the flour's proteins with fat and prevented them from linking up and forming gluten when water was added. Building a thick batter kept it from rising over and covering the streusel at the edges of the pan. Finally, baking the cake in a springform pan instead of the typical round cake pan allowed for fuss-free unmolding that kept the streusel intact.

The custom of sipping a hot beverage while enjoying a sweet cake or bread goes back to 17th-century Europe, when German, Dutch, and Scandinavian cooks were habitual pastry makers and coffee was fast becoming part of the daily routine. Eventually, the practice spread to the United States, and today, three types of coffee cake are common: the yeasted kind, featuring a sweet cheese and/or fruit filling; the rich sour cream Bundt version that shows off elegant bands of crumb filling when sliced; and the streusel-topped type, with a nutty crunch highlighting a moist cake. It is this last cake that appeals to me the most. Instead of drawing attention with graceful swirls of filling or the dramatic curves of a Bundt shape, its focus is on the contrasting textures and complementary flavors of the cake and topping.

The trouble is, many such coffee cake recipes are relatively complicated, requiring multiple bowls and appliances. I wanted a simpler method that produced the same tender cake and crunchy, flavorful topping.

The cake portion of this treat is commonly made by creaming butter and sugar using a mixer and then alternately incorporating the flour and liquid ingredients. Since I like to use a food processor to chop nuts for streusel and I wanted to avoid dirtying a second appliance, my first instinct was to adapt this method to a food processor. But while the food processor deftly whipped the butter and sugar into a pale, aerated state, its powerful motor was incapable of gently folding in flour and liquids. The result of those aggressively whizzing blades was one seriously tough cake. That's because flour contains proteins, which, in the presence of water, link up to form gluten. While some gluten is necessary to give baked goods structure, cakes with too much gluten are unpleasantly tough.

Luckily, there was another method to consider. Reverse creaming—the method of working butter into the dry ingredients until the flour is mostly coated in fat before adding the wet ingredients—limits gluten formation by "waterproofing" the gluten-forming proteins. Without access to water, gluten can't develop, so the method virtually guarantees a soft, tender crumb. It seemed like the technique would adapt well to a food processor, so it was definitely worth trying.

Since I planned to use the food processor for both components of my coffee cake, I started by making the streusel. I prepared a standard topping by processing toasted pecans and brown sugar until the nuts were finely ground. Then it was a simple matter of incorporating flour, cinnamon, salt, and some melted butter.

After setting aside the streusel, I prepared the cake batter using a recipe I'd cobbled together from my research. First, I whizzed together flour, sugar, baking soda, baking powder, salt, and cinnamon. Then I added softened butter and pulsed until only very small pieces of the butter remained. Finally, I pulsed in milk, an egg, an egg yolk (for extra richness), and vanilla extract

to form a thick batter. After scraping the batter into a greased and floured round cake pan, I smoothed the top with a rubber spatula, sprinkled the streusel evenly over the top, and baked the cake in a 350-degree oven.

An hour later, as I was flipping the cake out of the pan and inverting it onto a wire rack to cool, I could see that my streusel—though wonderfully nutty and delicately spiced—needed some help. It was sinking into the batter at the edge, losing its crunch and marring the cake's appearance. What's more, it was too fine and rained down from the pan when I inverted the cake. The good news was that the reverse-creaming method had worked: The cake itself was tender as could be.

But back to the streusel. It didn't make sense to invert a cake with a crumbly topping, so I decided to try switching from the typical cake pan to a springform pan, which would allow me to remove the collar without dislodging the topping. Once the springform pan was prepared, I set it on a rimmed baking sheet to catch any batter that oozed out. To help the streusel cling together, I added 1 teaspoon of water. After just a couple of pulses, I could see that this seemingly minor addition made this batch much more cohesive.

Now I just needed to prevent the streusel from disappearing into the edges of the cake. To better understand the problem, I peered into the oven to monitor a batter-filled pan during baking. I realized that the streusel wasn't sinking at all. Rather, the cake batter at the edges was heating up first and thus thinning out, filling with bubbles from the leavener, and climbing the sides of the pan, where it flowed over onto the streusel.

At first I thought I needed to reduce the amount of leavener in the cake, but this didn't stop the cake from rising up and over onto sections of the streusel. It did, however, result in a dense, heavy crumb.

What worked was increasing the viscosity of the batter to make it less prone to climbing. I had been using 1½ cups of flour and decided to bump the amount up to 1⅔ cups. This slight addition didn't make the crumb noticeably drier, but it did thicken and firm the batter just enough to keep it and the streusel in place at the edges as it heated up.

Each bite of this coffee cake offered an appealing combination of crunchy cinnamon-pecan streusel and rich, tender cake. And I could make it quickly, using a single kitchen appliance.

LAN LAM, *Cook's Illustrated*

Coffee Cake with Pecan-Cinnamon Streusel

SERVES 8 TO 10

For the best results, we recommend weighing the flour. Do not use a skewer to test for doneness until the center appears firm when the pan is shaken. If you do, the weight of the streusel may squeeze out air and the cake may sink. The baked cake can be stored at room temperature, wrapped in plastic wrap, for up to 24 hours.

STREUSEL

- 1 cup pecans, toasted
- ⅓ cup packed (2⅓ ounces) brown sugar
- ½ cup (2½ ounces) all-purpose flour
- ¾ teaspoon ground cinnamon
- ¼ teaspoon salt
- 4 tablespoons unsalted butter, melted and cooled
- 1 teaspoon water

CAKE

- 1⅔ cups (8⅓ ounces) all-purpose flour
- 1 cup (7 ounces) granulated sugar
- 1 teaspoon ground cinnamon
- 1 teaspoon baking powder
- ½ teaspoon baking soda
- ¾ teaspoon salt
- 7 tablespoons unsalted butter, cut into 7 pieces and softened
- ¾ cup milk
- 1 large egg plus 1 large yolk
- 1 teaspoon vanilla extract

1. Adjust oven rack to lower-middle position and heat oven to 350 degrees. Grease and flour 9-inch springform pan and place on rimmed baking sheet.

2. FOR THE STREUSEL: Process pecans and sugar in food processor until finely ground, about 10 seconds. Add flour, cinnamon, and salt and pulse to combine, about 5 (1-second) pulses. Add melted butter and water and pulse until butter is fully incorporated and mixture begins to form clumps, 8 to 10 (1-second) pulses. Transfer streusel to bowl and set aside.

3. FOR THE CAKE: In now-empty processor, process flour, sugar, cinnamon, baking powder, baking soda, and salt until combined, about 10 seconds. Add butter and pulse until very small but visible pieces of butter remain, 5 to 8 (5-second) pulses. Add milk, egg and yolk, and vanilla; pulse until dry ingredients are moistened, 4 to 5 (1-second) pulses. Scrape down sides

of bowl. Pulse until mixture is well combined, 4 to 5 (1-second) pulses (some small pieces of butter will remain). Transfer batter to prepared pan and smooth top with rubber spatula. Starting at edges of pan, sprinkle streusel in even layer over batter.

4. Bake cake on sheet until center is firm and skewer inserted into center of cake comes out clean, 45 to 55 minutes. Transfer pan to wire rack and let cake cool in pan for 15 minutes. Remove side of pan and let cake cool completely, about 2 hours. Using offset spatula, transfer cake to serving platter. Using serrated knife, cut cake into wedges and serve.

TO MAKE AHEAD: Coffee cake can be prepared through step 3, wrapped in plastic wrap, and refrigerated for up to 24 hours. To bake, continue with the recipe from step 4, increasing the baking time by 15 to 20 minutes.

SLOW-COOKER MONKEY BREAD

✓ WHY THIS RECIPE WORKS: We wanted a slow-cooker recipe for monkey bread that didn't compromise on its sticky, sweet appeal. To expedite the rising and proofing process we used a generous amount of instant yeast and added sugar to the dough. Rolling the balls of dough in melted butter and sugar gave them a thick, caramel-like coating. We found we didn't need to wait for a second proofing of the dough after it was shaped and assembled in the slow cooker; the gentle heat of the slow cooker properly proofed the dough as it came up to temperature. To prevent uneven cooking, and to make the monkey bread easy to remove, we placed both a foil collar and double-layered sling in the slow cooker.

Baking in the slow cooker is the ultimate challenge. While this low-and-slow vessel is perfect for simmering stews and chilis or gradually turning a tough cut of meat supremely tender, harnessing its strengths in baked applications takes some creative rethinking. When our team of test cooks began work on a new collection of slow-cooker recipes, I set my sights on a sweet and sticky loaf that might benefit from the slow cooker's strengths: monkey bread. This tempting, knotty loaf of tender, sugar-coated bread balls is usually assembled in a Bundt pan and baked, emerging as a caramelized, pull-apart delight. I wanted to see if I could reach similar (if not simpler) ends right on my countertop, ideally in a single afternoon.

In my research, I found a number of monkey breads that were two-day affairs: The dough was started the night before, refrigerated, and then shaped and baked the next day. I wanted my recipe to be faster and easier, so I sought out a dough I could proof and bake the same day. A quick-rising bread seemed like the right move, so I cobbled together a white sandwich-style bread dough made with yeast. I kneaded the dough together by hand, let it rise, and then puzzled over how to arrange the dough in the slow cooker.

I knew that rolling the dough balls in butter and sugar was the best way to ensure a rich, caramelized coating on each little round—but how many balls did I need and how large should I make them? I decided to start small, which would not only maximize the surface area for my sweet coating, but also hopefully allow the pieces to cook through more quickly. I eked out 64 pieces from my batch of dough and rolled them into rough balls before dunking them in melted butter and a sweet, spiced blend of sugar and cinnamon. Coating the slow cooker with nonstick spray seemed like a wise move, as it would prevent the sweet coating from fusing to the insert as it heated up. I wanted to give each ball some exposure to the warm sides of the slow cooker, so rather than piling them in, I carefully nestled them into the bottom where I let them rise once more before setting the slow cooker to high and waiting.

This first batch showed just how far I had to go. Despite the coating of nonstick spray, most of the balls stuck to the liner, forcing me to scrape them out in messy wads. And even though I'd cut the dough into small pieces, the balls emerged with one side over-cooked and the other gummy and raw. I tasted the few pieces that were cooked through and found the flavor to be lean and the texture crumbly.

Wondering if baking my bread on the high setting was the best choice, I decided to prepare two batches—one I'd bake on low and the other I'd try on high again. For richer flavor, I decided to switch the dough to a sweet roll instead of sandwich bread, bringing in a couple tablespoons of melted butter, replacing most of the water with whole milk, and sweetening the dough with a generous ¼ cup of sugar. To remedy the texture, I moved the kneading process to my stand mixer, which I hoped would create a stronger, more even gluten structure.

Since the oil spray had done little to protect against sticking, I decided to try lining the insert with aluminum foil. Along with this protective foil collar, I also created a foil sling—a common test kitchen trick for making light work of lifting sticky, sweet baked goods out of their pans.

My updated dough needed an hour and a half or so to double in size, after which I rolled and coated the individual balls and arranged them in the bottom of the slow cooker. But before leaving them to proof again, I wondered: What if I skipped the second proofing period and allowed the monkey bread to rise right as it began baking? Enriched breads often demand a longer proofing time, but the gradual warming of the slow cooker might just do the trick, allowing the dough to rise before the slow-building heat actually began cooking the bread.

With my twin batches at the ready, I set one slow cooker to high, the other to low, and waited. Periodically taking the loaves' temperatures was a surefire way to determine doneness, and I removed each loaf when it reached 190 degrees. Tasting the breads side by side, it was clear that the high setting was the way to go: The bread baked at low heat had proofed too slowly and emerged gummy and squat, while the batch baked on high was well risen with a tender texture and rich flavor. The foil liner and sling had done their parts as well, providing insulation against the high heat and allowing the bread to be removed with ease.

Skipping the second proofing had saved time, but I was hoping to identify a few more shortcuts. In traditional recipes, the perk of having dozens of little balls is the ultracaramelized coating (thanks to the oven's intense heat), but here only the insert-facing side of the balls deepened in color and much of the caramel

---

NOTES FROM THE TEST KITCHEN

ASSEMBLING MONKEY BREAD

Place coated pieces in prepared slow cooker, staggering seams where dough balls meet as you build layers.

SLOW-COOKER MONKEY BREAD

flavor was coming from the cinnamon–brown sugar mixture itself. I decided to see what kind of outcome I'd get from larger balls of dough, so for my next batch, I divided the dough into 32 pieces—a much quicker endeavor. I was about to roll them into spheres once more when I paused—this monkey bread bakes into a flat oval, not a dome, so why was I rolling my dough into balls anyhow? This time, after slicing the dough into even amounts, I went straight for the coating and arranged the unrolled pieces in the lined insert. This was the simplest and most successful batch yet: On top of the intoxicating aromas of cinnamon and sugar, I was rewarded with big, fluffy, tender mouthfuls of rich, sweet bread.

A generous drizzle of glaze was the perfect finish to my monkey bread, and at last I had proof that rich, yeasted bread was not only possible in the slow cooker—it was easy and downright delicious.

LEAH COLINS, *America's Test Kitchen Books*

Slow-Cooker Monkey Bread

SERVES 6 TO 8

COOKING TIME: 2 TO 4 HOURS ON HIGH
SLOW COOKER SIZE: 5 TO 7 QUARTS

You will need an oval slow cooker for this recipe. For more information on making a foil collar, see page 75.

DOUGH

3¼ cups (16¼ ounces) all-purpose flour

2¼ teaspoons instant or rapid-rise yeast

2 teaspoons salt

1 cup whole milk, room temperature

⅓ cup water, room temperature

¼ cup (1¾ ounces) granulated sugar

2 tablespoons unsalted butter, melted

BROWN SUGAR COATING

1 cup packed (7 ounces) light brown sugar

2 teaspoons ground cinnamon

8 tablespoons unsalted butter, melted and cooled

GLAZE

1 cup (4 ounces) confectioners' sugar

2 tablespoons whole milk

1. FOR THE DOUGH: Whisk flour, yeast, and salt together in bowl of stand mixer. Whisk milk, water, sugar, and melted butter in 4-cup liquid measuring cup until sugar has dissolved. Using dough hook on low speed, slowly add milk mixture to flour mixture and mix until cohesive dough starts to form and no dry flour remains, about 2 minutes, scraping down bowl as needed. Increase speed to medium-low and knead until dough is smooth and elastic and clears sides of bowl but sticks to bottom, 8 to 10 minutes.

2. Transfer dough to lightly floured counter and knead by hand to form smooth, round ball, about 30 seconds. Place dough, seam side down, in lightly greased large bowl or container, cover tightly with plastic wrap, and let rise until doubled in size, 1½ to 2 hours. (Unrisen dough can be refrigerated for at least 8 hours or up to 16 hours; let sit at room temperature for 1 hour before shaping in step 4.)

3. FOR THE BROWN SUGAR COATING: Line slow cooker with aluminum foil collar, then press 2 double-layered large sheets of foil into slow cooker perpendicular to one another, with extra foil hanging over edges. Lightly coat prepared slow cooker with vegetable oil spray. Combine sugar and cinnamon in bowl. Place melted butter in second bowl.

4. Transfer dough to lightly floured counter and press into rough 8-inch square. Using pizza cutter or chef's knife, cut dough into 6 even strips. Cut each strip into 6 pieces (36 pieces total). Cover dough pieces loosely with greased plastic.

5. Working with a few pieces of dough at a time (keep remaining pieces covered), dip pieces in melted butter, then roll in sugar mixture to coat. Place coated pieces in prepared slow cooker, staggering seams where dough balls meet as you build layers. Once dough is layered, sprinkle remaining sugar mixture on top.

6. Cover and cook until dough is set and registers 190 degrees, 2 to 4 hours on high. (Top of monkey bread will be pale and slightly tacky to touch.) Using foil sling, transfer monkey bread to wire rack and let cool for 20 minutes.

7. FOR THE GLAZE: Whisk sugar and milk in bowl until smooth. Invert monkey bread onto serving dish; discard foil. Drizzle glaze over bread, letting it run down sides. Serve warm.

GOUGÈRES

✓ WHY THIS RECIPE WORKS: Cheesy, crisp, and delicate gougères are ideal for entertaining, as they come together quickly and can be prepared in advance and recrisped. We began with a traditional choux paste, made by cooking water, butter, and flour until a dough formed. Then we used the food processor to beat in two eggs plus an extra egg white. The added white improved crispness and provided more water, which turned to steam and helped the gougères puff even more, and its proteins provided better structure for more airiness. We packed an extra ounce of Gruyère into our gougères for plenty of cheese flavor.

While some French classics feel stodgy, I'm willing to bet that gougères will never go out of style. It's not just that their crisp, browned exteriors and airy, popover-like interiors flavored with nutty Gruyère cheese give them huge appeal. These two-bite puffs also look impressive and can be made in advance and reheated.

The foundation for gougères is *pâte à choux*, or choux pastry. The most classic versions involve cooking butter, water, and flour in a saucepan until the loose batter stiffens and turns into a dough. Eggs then get beaten in, one at a time, for structure and flavor. To make the choux into gougères, the next steps are to stir in grated cheese, pipe the dough into little rounds, and bake. Starting in a hot oven ensures that the puffs expand dramatically. The temperature is then lowered to finish cooking them through.

Following a few such recipes, I found room for improvement. Fresh out of the oven, the best puffs were crisp outside and just custardy enough inside to provide contrast—but if they sat around for even 20 minutes, they softened. I also found that, depending on the oven, the puffs could overbrown. They weren't nearly cheesy enough, and beating in the eggs by hand was a chore.

I cooked a paste of ½ cup of water, 5 tablespoons of butter, and ½ cup of flour along with a little salt and cayenne for depth. But instead of beating in the eggs by hand, I worked them into the dough in a food processor, along with an extra egg white. The proteins in the white would boost crispness and provide structure for more airiness. The water in the white would provide steam to help the dough puff.

I also adjusted the baking process. With the help of a probe thermometer, I confirmed that when I turned the dial on my well-insulated oven from 425 to 375 degrees, the temperature didn't always drop much, depending on where the oven was in its heating cycle. When the temperature didn't drop much, the puffs browned and dried out on their exteriors by the time the interiors were done. But when I pulled them earlier, the interiors were gummy and dense. I wondered if I could get more consistent results by simply shutting off the oven. I gave this approach a shot: After 15 minutes at 425 degrees, I turned off the oven and left the puffs inside with the door closed for another 15 minutes. This batch came out just right: perfectly browned with the ideal airy centers.

With the choux settled, it was time to bring in the cheese. I made another batch of choux, but this time after adding the eggs to the processor I added 4 ounces of grated Gruyère—a full ounce more than other recipes—and then piped and baked my rounds as before.

When I removed my gougères from the oven, I could see that they were overbrowned on the bottoms and a little greasy. But the bigger problem was the interiors, which were dense and doughy. Upon inspection, I noticed that most of the air bubbles had tears in their walls. The addition of such a hefty amount of cheese was preventing the bubbles from expanding fully.

To find a solution, I first considered the gluten-forming proteins in the flour. Gluten creates a stretchy network that provides structure to baked goods, so it seemed logical that more gluten would provide more strength so that the bubbles could expand properly without tearing. To that end, I switched from using all-purpose flour to higher-protein bread flour. Second, since fat inhibits gluten formation, I reduced the amount of butter from 5 tablespoons to 2; this would mitigate greasiness. To my disappointment, these changes brought only marginal improvement.

I wondered if I could do better by manipulating the egg proteins. Raw egg proteins are coiled up in tight bundles. When heated, they uncoil and form strong, springy networks. I ran a series of tests: more whole eggs, more whites, and more yolks in varying amounts. But in all cases, the dough became too wet, making it hard to work with. Was there some way to get the two eggs and one white I'd been using all along to set up and establish some structure more quickly?

Egg proteins unwind not only when heated but also when beaten well. After a chat with our science editor, I discovered another way to make them unwind more quickly: Combine them with salt. For my next batch

I added the salt to the eggs instead of the dough. What a difference one little change made. When I tore open these gougères, I found the airy centers I was after.

Still, the puffs were browning too much on their bottoms. Baking them on the upper-middle rack helped, but the real fix was nesting my rimmed baking sheet in a second baking sheet; this created a thin air gap between the two, which insulated the pastry bottoms.

Now I took a closer look at portioning the dough. Piping the dough with a pastry bag was of course an option, but two spoons worked almost as well. (This dough is too stiff to use a zipper-lock bag with the corner snipped off.) Whether I used a pastry bag or spoons, I only had to smooth away any creases or large peaks with the back of a spoon.

From here, I came up with a couple of variations, picking cheeses that are similar in age and texture—and, thus, moisture content—to Gruyère so as not to alter my puffs' perfect texture. Manchego and black pepper paired well, as did Gouda and smoked paprika.

These cheesy, delicately crisp bites are sure to make an appearance at my next party. Though they'll stay crisp for a full hour, I don't expect they'll last that long.

LAN LAM, *Cook's Illustrated*

Gougères

MAKES 24 PUFFS

Use a Gruyère that has been aged for about one year. The doubled baking sheets prevent the undersides of the puffs from overbrowning. Alternatively, loosely roll up an 18 by 12-inch piece of aluminum foil, unroll it, and set it in a rimmed baking sheet. Cover the foil with a sheet of parchment paper and proceed with the recipe. In step 4, the dough can be piped using a pastry bag fitted with a ½-inch plain tip.

- 2 large eggs plus 1 large white
- ¼ teaspoon salt
- ½ cup water
- 2 tablespoons unsalted butter, cut into 4 pieces
  Pinch cayenne pepper
- ½ cup (2½ ounces) all-purpose flour
- 4 ounces Gruyère cheese, shredded (1 cup)

1. Adjust oven rack to upper-middle position and heat oven to 425 degrees. Line rimmed baking sheet with parchment paper and nest it in second rimmed baking sheet. In 2-cup liquid measuring cup, beat eggs and white and salt until well combined. (You should have about ½ cup egg mixture. Discard excess.) Set aside.

2. Heat water, butter, and cayenne in small saucepan over medium heat. When mixture begins to simmer, reduce heat to low and immediately stir in flour using wooden spoon. Cook, stirring constantly, using smearing motion, until mixture is very thick, forms ball, and pulls away from sides of saucepan, about 30 seconds.

3. Immediately transfer mixture to food processor and process with feed tube open for 5 seconds to cool slightly. With processor running, gradually add reserved egg mixture in steady stream, then scrape down sides of bowl and add Gruyère. Process until paste is very glossy and flecked with coarse cornmeal–size pieces of cheese, 30 to 40 seconds. (If not using immediately, transfer paste to bowl, press sheet of greased parchment directly on surface, and store at room temperature for up to 2 hours.)

4. Scoop 1 level tablespoon of dough. Using second small spoon, scrape dough onto prepared sheet into 1½-inch-wide, 1-inch-tall mound. Repeat, spacing mounds 1 to 1¼ inches apart. (You should have

---

NOTES FROM THE TEST KITCHEN

FOR AIRY PUFFS, SALT IS KEY

The salt in our gougères enhances flavor and improves their structure. But rather than add it to the dough, we beat the salt with the eggs before they are combined with the flour mixture. Why? The salt changes the electrical charges on the egg proteins so they uncoil at a lower temperature, allowing them to set up into a strong network earlier in the baking time. This prevents the rising dough from collapsing under the added weight of the cheese. The result? Airy gougères with large interior bubbles.

PERFECTLY HOLLOW
Salting the eggs before incorporating them into the dough makes a strong puff that inflates well.

POORLY INFLATED
Mixing salt directly into the dough makes for a weaker puff that doesn't inflate well.

24 mounds.) Using back of spoon lightly coated with vegetable oil spray, smooth away any creases and large peaks on each mound.

5. Bake until gougères are puffed and upper two-thirds of each are light golden brown (bottom third will still be pale), 14 to 20 minutes. Turn off oven; leave gougères in oven until uniformly golden brown, 10 to 15 minutes (do not open oven for at least 8 minutes). Transfer gougères to wire rack and let cool for 15 minutes. Serve warm. (Cooled gougères can be stored in airtight container at room temperature for up to 24 hours or frozen in zipper-lock bag for up to 1 month. To serve, crisp gougères in 300-degree oven for about 7 minutes.)

VARIATIONS

Gougères with Aged Gouda and Smoked Paprika
Substitute aged gouda for Gruyère and ½ teaspoon smoked paprika for cayenne.

Gougères with Manchego and Black Pepper
Substitute Manchego for Gruyère and ½ teaspoon pepper for cayenne.

IRISH BROWN SODA BREAD

✔ **WHY THIS RECIPE WORKS:** Our take on Irish brown soda bread combines a high proportion of whole-wheat flour with extra wheat germ and bran to produce a rustic loaf with nutty flavor and a coarse crumb. We balanced the strong wheat flavor with white flour and a bit of sugar. Baking powder guaranteed a nicely risen loaf, while baking soda added the tang that's characteristic of soda breads. Buttermilk also contributed welcome flavor. To produce a loaf with pleasing stature, we baked the soft dough in a cake pan rather than free-form.

Compared with the white soda bread strewn with raisins and caraway seeds that makes its annual appearance in the United States around St. Patrick's Day, Ireland's rustic brown soda bread might seem austere. It's traditionally made with just four ingredients: wholemeal flour, baking soda, salt, and buttermilk. But those minimal ingredients make a crusty bread with a savory, nutty flavor that pairs well with everything from soups, cheese, and cured fish to beer and hard cider—and it's equally good with a smear of salted butter. Considering its versatility, it's little wonder that brown soda bread is the preferred version in Ireland.

The other appeal of soda bread is that it's dead simple to make—it can be mixed by hand in a single bowl. The mixture forms a thick dough, not a batter, which immediately gets shaped into a round: There's no kneading or proofing. Then it's scored on the top and baked, either free-form or in a pan, until it's risen, brown, and crusty.

What you get is a homemade whole-grain, multi-purpose bread in less than an hour. But the main ingredient, Irish wholemeal flour, is hard to come by in the States. I hoped that the closest equivalent, American whole-wheat flour, would suffice.

I was optimistic that it would, since both domestic whole-wheat and Irish wholemeal flours consist of entire wheat kernels that have been dried and ground to a powder. So I followed a traditional recipe, combining 3 cups of whole-wheat flour (a straight substitution for wholemeal), 1½ teaspoons of baking soda, and 1 teaspoon of salt in a bowl. Then I stirred in 2 cups of buttermilk to make a shaggy dough. I turned it out onto the counter, shaped it into a round, and, as most recipes instruct, cut a shallow cross in the top before baking it to allow for expansion in the oven. The process was indeed simple, but the loaf was disappointing.

Granted, lightness is not a characteristic attribute of brown soda bread, but this loaf hardly rose at all in the oven, so it was dense. It also lacked the rustic crumb of Irish breads, and it spread too much, so it was quite flat. Wondering if I had underestimated the importance of using authentic Irish flour, I ordered some.

Side by side, the two flours actually looked quite different. The American whole-wheat flour, which does contain bran and germ, was uniformly ground very fine and had a deep-tan hue. The Irish flour was lighter in color, but it contained discrete pieces of bran and germ and felt rough when I rubbed it between my fingers. Those distinct bits, I guessed, were necessary to produce the coarser crumb I was after, and I proved it by making the same recipe again using the Irish flour. This bread was still as dense and flat as the previous loaf, but it had a nicely rustic texture.

The obvious way to replicate the bran and germ presence of the Irish flour? Add bran and germ to domestic whole-wheat flour. Doing so didn't make the loaf any less dense or flat, but it did create the rustic consistency I was after.

IRISH BROWN SODA BREAD

I tend to scoff when people talk in terms of anything more than 100 percent. But as I did the math, I realized that by adding bran and germ to whole-wheat flour, I had created a loaf that was roughly 150 percent whole wheat. That extra jolt actually made the bread taste too wheaty, but I'd worry about that later and stay focused on the texture for now.

In this bare-bones recipe, the lift is dependent upon the acidic buttermilk reacting with the alkaline baking soda to create carbon dioxide gas, which gets trapped in the dough. When the dough heats up in the oven, the trapped gas expands and the bread rises. At least, that's what is supposed to happen.

But that reaction between buttermilk and baking soda is both instant and fleeting. Lacking the deftness and muscle memory of a lifelong soda bread baker, I was probably taking too long to get the bread into the oven and possibly also knocking air out of the dough as I shaped it. Either way, there wasn't enough air left to lighten the loaf. Luckily, I found salvation in the pantry. Actually, I found baking powder, but it amounted to the same thing.

Baking powder came late to Ireland, so really old soda bread recipes don't call for it, but it's a far more reliable leavener than baking soda. It contains both acid and alkaline components, so it's a complete leavening system, but here's the really clever bit: Some of the acids don't dissolve until they warm up, so the chemical reaction is delayed until the dough is safely in the oven. The upshot: When you have baking powder in your recipe, you don't have to be as speedy or as gentle when handling the dough.

I made another loaf with American whole-wheat flour, wheat germ, and bran, this time substituting baking powder for the baking soda. I still mixed and shaped the dough minimally to preserve its craggy, rustic look. I slashed the top, and into the oven it went.

The baking powder did the trick, as I finally produced a risen loaf with the nubbly, coarse, tender crumb I was after. But while I no longer needed the baking soda for lift, I was surprised to discover that I missed its flavor: This loaf didn't have the tang of a yeast bread or the distinctive flavor of a soda bread. What's more, the crust looked a bit wan, since alkaline baking soda raises the pH of the dough and encourages browning. I'd add baking soda back to the recipe.

Since the wheat bran and germ were making the loaf too wheaty, I made some adjustments to my next loaf:

I combined whole-wheat and white flour in a ratio of 2 to 1, and I added 2 teaspoons of sugar. I mixed in bran and germ for texture and baking powder for leavening. After adding baking soda and salt for flavor, I stirred in the buttermilk. This time I baked the dough in a cake pan instead of on a baking sheet. The pan gently corralled the soft dough in the oven, preventing too much spread, so the loaf expanded up as well as out.

Crusty and risen, with a coarse, tender crumb and slightly tangy flavor, this loaf finally checked all the boxes.

ANDREA GEARY, *Cook's Illustrated*

Irish Brown Soda Bread

MAKES ONE 8-INCH LOAF

Our favorite whole-wheat flour is King Arthur Premium. To ensure the best flavor, use fresh whole-wheat flour. Wheat bran can be found at natural foods stores or in the baking aisle of your supermarket. This bread is best when served on the day it is made, but leftovers can be wrapped in plastic wrap for up to 2 days.

- 2 cups (11 ounces) whole-wheat flour
- 1 cup (5 ounces) all-purpose flour
- 1 cup wheat bran
- ¼ cup wheat germ
- 2 teaspoons sugar
- 1½ teaspoons baking powder
- 1½ teaspoons baking soda
- 1 teaspoon salt
- 2 cups buttermilk

1. Adjust oven rack to middle position and heat oven to 375 degrees. Lightly grease 8-inch round cake pan. Whisk whole-wheat flour, all-purpose flour, wheat bran, wheat germ, sugar, baking powder, baking soda, and salt together in medium bowl.

2. Add buttermilk and stir with rubber spatula until all flour is moistened and dough forms soft, ragged mass. Transfer dough to counter and gently shape into 6-inch round (surface will be craggy). Using serrated knife, cut ½-inch-deep cross about 5 inches long on top of loaf. Transfer to prepared pan. Bake until loaf is lightly browned and center registers 185 degrees, 40 to 45 minutes, rotating pan halfway through baking.

3. Invert loaf onto wire rack. Reinvert loaf and let cool for at least 1 hour. Slice and serve.

GARLIC BREAD

✓ **WHY THIS RECIPE WORKS:** Garlic bread is simple to make but is often a disappointment to eat. For an evenly toasted version with just-right garlic flavor, we briefly microwaved fresh garlic (minced to a paste) and butter and combined it with garlic powder, which provided sweet, roasty notes. We then combined the melted garlic butter with solid butter to make a spreadable paste that could be smeared evenly onto the bread. We baked the bread cut side up on a baking sheet and then flipped it and compressed it with a second baking sheet. The panini-like setup pressed the cut side onto the hot sheet so that it evenly crisped and browned while also compressing the bread for a better balance of crust to crumb.

Everyone takes shortcuts in the kitchen, including buying aluminum foil–wrapped garlic bread from the supermarket. And yet once that steamy, squishy, greasy loaf is revealed, regret is inevitable. But even when you take the time to make garlic bread from scratch, success is far from guaranteed. The bread rarely gets perfectly crisp, and most recipes miss the mark with the garlic itself—it's either muted or too in-your-face. I wanted a toasty, golden-brown loaf with a pleasantly crisp crust and a moist interior. There would be a generous amount of butter, and the garlic flavor would be prominent but not harsh.

I decided to work with supermarket Italian bread. Its fine, plush crumb would hold on to butter, and its soft, thin crust could crisp without toughening.

As for the garlic, I knew that it wasn't just a matter of how much to use but how to treat it. Since heat tames garlic's harshness, I minced a tablespoon's worth of cloves and microwaved them with a stick of butter until the garlic lost some of its bite.

Evenly brushing the melted garlic butter onto a halved loaf proved to be challenging: The soft crumb was too good at soaking up the butter and pulled it in like a sponge, leaving some areas saturated and others barely moistened. I decided to melt half the butter with the garlic and then whisk it with the remaining solid butter to make a soft mixture that I could evenly spread—rather than brush—onto the bread.

After being baked with the cut sides facing up, the bread was spotty brown, but the larger garlic chunks jutting up from the surface had darkened and become bitter. A rasp-style grater transformed the cloves into a fine paste that blended smoothly into the butter.

Next, I wanted to add depth with the sweet, toasty flavor of roasted garlic. Roasting a head of garlic was out of the question, so I tried garlic powder. It's made by grinding and drying garlic cloves, a process that gives it a mild roasted flavor. The freeze-dried powder contains the active enzyme alliinase, which, when mixed with water, produces allicin, the compound responsible for the characteristic garlic taste. One teaspoon provided just the right amount of roasty flavor.

But I didn't stop there. I wanted even browning from edge to edge—the kind you get in a grilled sandwich. Well, then why not cook the bread like a grilled sandwich? I slid another halved loaf into the oven, cut sides up, and once the butter had fully soaked in, I flipped the halves cut sides down. I pressed a second baking sheet on top of the bread, panini press style, and returned the assembly to the oven. The top sheet held the bread flat against the bottom sheet, ensuring even browning and crisping.

ANNIE PETITO, *Cook's Illustrated*

Really Good Garlic Bread

SERVES 8

A 12 by 5-inch loaf of supermarket Italian bread, which has a soft, thin crust and fine crumb, works best here. Do not use a rustic or crusty artisan-style loaf. A rasp-style grater makes quick work of turning the garlic into a paste. The amount of time needed to brown the bread after flipping it in step 3 depends on the color of your baking sheet. If using a dark-colored sheet, the browning time will be on the shorter end of the range.

- 1 teaspoon garlic powder
- 1 teaspoon water
- 8 tablespoons unsalted butter
- ½ teaspoon salt
- ⅛ teaspoon cayenne pepper
- 4–5 garlic cloves, minced to paste (1 tablespoon)
- 1 (1-pound) loaf soft Italian bread, halved horizontally

1. Adjust oven rack to lower-middle position and heat oven to 450 degrees. Combine garlic powder and water in medium bowl. Add 4 tablespoons butter, salt, and cayenne to bowl; set aside.

2. Place remaining 4 tablespoons butter in small bowl and microwave, covered, until melted, about 30 seconds. Stir in garlic and continue to microwave, covered, until mixture is bubbling around edges, about 1 minute, stirring halfway through microwaving. Transfer melted butter mixture to bowl with garlic powder–butter mixture and whisk until homogeneous loose paste forms. (If mixture melts, set aside and let solidify before using.)

3. Spread cut sides of bread evenly with butter mixture. Transfer bread, cut sides up, to rimmed baking sheet. Bake until butter mixture has melted and seeped into bread, 3 to 4 minutes. Remove sheet from oven. Flip bread cut sides down, place second rimmed baking sheet on top, and gently press. Return sheet to oven, leaving second sheet on top of bread, and continue to bake until cut sides are golden brown and crisp, 4 to 12 minutes longer, rotating sheet halfway through baking. Transfer bread to cutting board. Using serrated knife, cut each half into 8 slices. Serve immediately.

BROOKLYN PROSCIUTTO BREAD

✔ WHY THIS RECIPE WORKS: To make our prosciutto bread extra-meaty, it all came down to the cut of prosciutto. Thinly sliced deli meat got swallowed by the dough; thicker slabs cut into ½-inch pieces proved to be just right. Using a combination of meats—prosciutto, capicola, and pepperoni—gave each bite a satisfying, savory mix of flavors. We added beer to boost the yeasty, fermented flavor of the bread and opted for bread flour, with its high protein content, to form a strong gluten structure.

Among a Brooklyn butcher shop's hanging salami and shelves of imported Italian canned tomatoes, sitting on a deli counter covered with cured meats, I found an unlikely provision—a loaf of homemade bread. Bread? In a butcher shop? Why?

The answer appeared when I tore into the bread and discovered that it was studded with tiny chunks of prosciutto and salami and flavored throughout with bracing black pepper. A dream come true.

Back at the test kitchen, I set out to re-create this bread, starting with the dough. I needed a substantial base with plenty of structure—one that wouldn't collapse under the weight of the chunks of meat. I settled on a test kitchen recipe for rustic Italian-style bread, using bread flour, yeast, and water, as my canvas.

Bread takes time to rise and grow into a happy, sturdy home for meat add-ins. To build plenty of gluten, I kneaded the dough in a stand mixer until it became elastic. Then I let the dough rise until it doubled in size (this took nearly an hour and a half), formed it into a loaf, and let it proof—a second, shorter rise to let the bread grow to its near-final size before baking.

This bread was structurally sound, but it didn't have much yeasty flavor. I knew that if I let the dough rise longer, the yeast would ferment and develop flavor. But we have a secret weapon in the test kitchen to get around the wait: beer. Adding some to my dough gave it fermented flavor without hours of waiting.

Since cured meats are already salty, I took a restrained approach with the salt in the dough. But, taking a cue from the Brooklyn butchers, I loaded up the dough with 1½ teaspoons of pepper.

Now for the really fun part: adding the meat. First, I tried to knead thinly sliced prosciutto into the dough using the stand mixer, but the thin sheets of meat simply mashed together. Next, I tried tearing the meaty slices into smaller pieces, hoping they would more evenly incorporate into the dough, but the thin strands just got lost in the bread.

It was time to think outside the package of presliced prosciutto. I went to the deli counter and asked for ¼-inch-thick slabs, which I cut into ½-inch pieces and kneaded into the dough. Everyone loved the satisfying pockets of prosciutto this move created.

Now that I had established the best dimensions for the meat morsels, the deli case was my oyster. I experimented with all kinds of Italian cured meats—*soppressata*, mortadella, Genoa salami, and pancetta, to name a few. I then tried combinations of them until I found a winning lineup: equal parts prosciutto, pepperoni, and capicola. The zippy pepperoni added spice to the pork-forward prosciutto, and the capicola contributed a pleasantly peppery sweetness. And to raise the stakes one more notch, I added some provolone for a cheesy variation.

Butcher shop bread? Believe it. This one's a keeper.

KATIE LEAIRD, *Cook's Country*

Prosciutto Bread

MAKES 2 LOAVES

We love the combination of prosciutto, pepperoni, and capicola in this bread, but you can use 9 ounces of any combination of cured meats; just be sure to have each sliced ¼ inch thick at the deli counter. Do not use thinly sliced deli meats, as they will adversely affect the bread's texture. Use a mild lager, such as Budweiser; strongly flavored beers will make this bread taste bitter.

- 3 cups (16½ ounces) bread flour
- 1½ teaspoons instant or rapid-rise yeast
- 1 teaspoon salt
- 1 cup mild lager, room temperature
- 6 tablespoons water, room temperature
- 3 tablespoons extra-virgin olive oil
- 3 ounces (¼-inch-thick) sliced prosciutto, cut into ½-inch pieces
- 3 ounces (¼-inch-thick) sliced pepperoni, cut into ½-inch pieces
- 3 ounces (¼-inch-thick) sliced capicola, cut into ½-inch pieces
- 1½ teaspoons coarsely ground pepper
  Cornmeal

1. Whisk flour, yeast, and salt together in bowl of stand mixer. Whisk beer, room-temperature water, and oil together in 2-cup liquid measuring cup.

2. Fit mixer with dough hook. Mix flour mixture on low speed while slowly adding beer mixture until cohesive dough starts to form and no dry flour remains, about 2 minutes, scraping down bowl as needed. Increase speed to medium and knead until dough is smooth and elastic and clears sides of bowl, about 8 minutes.

3. Reduce speed to low and add prosciutto, pepperoni, capicola, and pepper. Continue to knead until combined, about 2 minutes longer (some meats may not be fully incorporated into dough at this point; this is OK). Transfer dough and any errant pieces of meats to lightly floured counter and knead by hand to evenly incorporate meats into dough, about 1 minute.

4. Form dough into smooth, round ball and place seam side down in lightly greased large bowl. Cover tightly with plastic wrap and let dough rise at room temperature until doubled in size, about 1½ hours.

5. Line baking sheet with parchment paper and lightly dust with cornmeal. Turn out dough onto counter and gently press down to deflate any large air pockets. Cut dough into 2 even pieces. Press each piece of dough into 8 by 5-inch rectangle with long side parallel to counter's edge.

6. Working with 1 piece of dough at a time, fold top edge of rectangle down to midline, pressing to seal. Fold bottom edge of rectangle up to midline and pinch to seal. Flip dough seam side down and gently roll into 12-inch loaf with tapered ends. Transfer loaf to 1 side of prepared sheet. Repeat shaping with second piece of dough and place loaf about 3 inches from first loaf on sheet. Cover with greased plastic and let rise at room temperature until puffy and dough springs back slowly when pressed lightly with your finger, about 45 minutes.

7. Adjust oven rack to middle position and heat oven to 450 degrees. Using sharp paring knife in swift, fluid motion, make ½-inch-deep lengthwise slash along top of each loaf, starting and stopping about 1½ inches from ends. Bake until loaves register 205 to 210 degrees, 22 to 25 minutes. Transfer loaves to wire rack and let cool completely, about 3 hours. Serve.

TO MAKE AHEAD: Make dough through step 3, form into ball, and place seam side down in lightly greased large bowl. Cover tightly with plastic wrap and refrigerate for at least 16 hours or up to 24 hours. Let dough come to room temperature, about 3 hours, before proceeding with step 5.

VARIATION

Prosciutto Bread with Provolone
Add 5 ounces provolone cheese, sliced ¼ inch thick and cut into ½-inch pieces, with meat in step 3.

NOTES FROM THE TEST KITCHEN

SHAPING THE LOAF

After patting half of dough into rectangle, fold top down and bottom up, pressing to seal as you go. Flip it seam down and roll into 12-inch loaf.

PROSCIUTTO BREAD

DESSERTS

BETTER HOLIDAY SUGAR COOKIES

✓ **WHY THIS RECIPE WORKS:** Our holiday roll-and-cut sugar cookies taste as great as they are easy to make. For a crisp and sturdy texture with no hint of graininess, we made superfine sugar by grinding granulated sugar briefly in the food processor, and we added small amounts of baking powder and baking soda to the dough. We skipped creaming softened butter and sugar in favor of whizzing cold butter with sugar in the food processor, which let the dough come together quickly. The just-made dough was cold enough to be rolled out immediately. We then chilled it after rolling. For an even, golden color; minimal browning; and a crisp texture from edge to edge, we baked the cookies at a gentle 300 degrees on a rimless cookie sheet.

Are roll-and-cut sugar cookies a fun, festive project? Not in my kitchen: They've always been a maddening chore with nothing but floury, shapeless disappointments to show for the effort. Most recipes require you to haul out a stand mixer to cream sugar and softened butter before mixing in the remaining ingredients and then to refrigerate the dough before rolling, cutting, and baking. The lump of dough is always stiff after chilling, so it's challenging to roll. Many of the cookies puff during baking, which leaves them uneven or with indistinct outlines. What's more, they're often hard and dense rather than simply sturdy.

I wanted to turn things around with a dough that would be easy—maybe even fun—to work with. It would be firm enough to shape with cookie cutters and to carry frosting and other decorations after baking. The cookies would bake up crisp and flat, with sharp edges, and they would have a satisfying, buttery flavor.

I began with a recipe that had decent flavor. It called for beating two sticks of softened butter with 1 cup of sugar; mixing in 2½ cups of flour, an egg, salt, and vanilla; and then chilling the dough before rolling, cutting, and baking. The resulting cookies were buttery, with just enough sweetness. However, they had a slightly granular texture and a tendency to puff in the oven, which left them bumpy and uneven.

Graininess can come from an excess of sugar, but reducing the sugar by ⅓ cup upset the flavor. Instead, I tried replacing the granulated sugar with confectioners' sugar, but this made the cookies somewhat chalky and hard rather than crisp. However, superfine sugar,

which is granulated sugar that has been ground to a fine—but not powdery—consistency, was just the ticket: fine enough to smooth out any graininess but coarse enough to maintain a slightly open crumb.

To address the cookies' puffiness, I examined the creaming step, the goal of which is to incorporate air. It makes sense for a soft, cakey cookie, but was it detrimental to one that I wanted to be flat and even? To find out, I made another batch in which I briefly mixed the sugar and butter until just combined. Sure enough, these cookies baked up entirely flat.

But they were now a little dense, begging for a tiny amount of air. I turned to baking soda and baking powder; ¼ teaspoon of each produced flat cookies with a crisp yet sturdy texture.

Now it was time to address my other issue with roll-and-cut cookies—the need to chill the dough before rolling it, which inevitably leads to strong-arming a cold, hardened lump into submission. Refrigerating the dough for a shorter time wasn't an option, since it wouldn't have time to chill evenly. And rolling the dough straightaway was out of the question because I was using softened butter, which produced a soft dough that would cling to a rolling pin. I needed a dough made with cold butter.

That meant I would need to "plasticize" the butter, or soften it while keeping it cold, so that my dough would roll out without ripping or sticking. Croissant bakers plasticize blocks of butter by pounding them with a rolling pin. I certainly didn't want to beat butter by hand, but I realized that the solution was already on the counter: the food processor. Unlike the paddle of a stand mixer, which would struggle to soften cold butter quickly, the fast, ultrasharp blades of a food processor could make it malleable.

I processed the sugar and then added chunks of cold butter. Thirty seconds later, the two had combined into a smooth paste. I whizzed in the egg and vanilla, plus a smidge of almond extract for an unidentifiable flavor boost, and then added the dry ingredients. The dough was pliable but not soft or sticky.

This dough rolled out like a dream. To ensure easy cutting and clean, well-defined edges, I still needed to chill the dough, so I placed it in the refrigerator for 1½ hours. By eliminating the need to bring the butter to room temperature, skipping creaming, and making the dough easy to roll, I'd shaved off some time—and plenty of effort—from the recipe.

EASY HOLIDAY COCOA SUGAR COOKIES

I'd been baking the cookies at 350 degrees on the middle rack, but the edges of the cookies around the perimeter of the sheet were dark brown by the time the center ones were golden. The fix was three-pronged. One: I reduced the oven temperature to 300 degrees; more-gradual baking evened the color. Two: I lowered the oven rack, so the cookies baked from the bottom up. This meant that they browned nicely on their undersides (for hidden flavor) while remaining lighter on top. Three: I swapped the rimmed baking sheet I had been using for a rimless cookie sheet. This promoted air circulation, so the cookies baked more evenly.

All that remained was to come up with an icing that tasted good and firmed up nicely. It was the perfect opportunity for a classic royal icing, in which a mix of whipped egg whites and sugar sets into a dry, matte surface. Piped or poured onto the cooled cookies, it was a joyful finish to the best—and easiest—cutout cookies I'd ever made.

ANDREW JANJIGIAN, *Cook's Illustrated*

Easy Holiday Sugar Cookies

MAKES ABOUT FORTY 2½-INCH COOKIES

For the dough to have the proper consistency when rolling, make sure to use cold butter directly from the refrigerator. In step 3, use a rolling pin and a combination of rolling and a pushing or smearing motion to form the soft dough into an oval. A rimless cookie sheet helps achieve evenly baked cookies; if you do not have one, use an overturned rimmed baking sheet. Dough scraps can be combined and rerolled once, though the cookies will be slightly less tender. If desired, stir one or two drops of food coloring into the icing. For a pourable icing, whisk in milk, 1 teaspoon at a time, until the desired consistency is reached. You can also decorate the shapes with sanding sugar or sprinkles before baking.

COOKIES

- 1 large egg
- 1 teaspoon vanilla extract
- ¾ teaspoon salt
- ¼ teaspoon almond extract
- 2½ cups (12½ ounces) all-purpose flour
- ¼ teaspoon baking powder
- ¼ teaspoon baking soda

- 1 cup (7 ounces) granulated sugar
- 16 tablespoons unsalted butter, cut into ½-inch pieces and chilled

ROYAL ICING

- 2⅔ cups (10⅔ ounces) confectioners' sugar
- 2 large egg whites
- ½ teaspoon vanilla extract
- ⅛ teaspoon salt

1. FOR THE COOKIES: Whisk egg, vanilla, salt, and almond extract together in small bowl. Whisk flour, baking powder, and baking soda together in second bowl.

2. Process sugar in food processor until finely ground, about 30 seconds. Add butter and process until uniform mass forms and no large pieces of butter are visible, about 30 seconds, scraping down sides of bowl as needed. Add egg mixture and process until smooth and paste-like, about 10 seconds. Add flour mixture and process until no dry flour remains but mixture remains crumbly, about 30 seconds, scraping down sides of bowl as needed.

3. Turn out dough onto counter and knead gently by hand until smooth, about 10 seconds. Divide dough in half. Place 1 piece of dough in center of large sheet of parchment paper and press into 7 by 9-inch oval. Place second large sheet of parchment over dough and roll dough into 10 by 14-inch oval of even ⅛-inch thickness. Transfer dough with parchment to rimmed baking sheet. Repeat pressing and rolling with second piece of dough, then stack on top of first piece on sheet. Refrigerate until dough is firm, at least 1½ hours (or freeze for 30 minutes). (Rolled dough can be wrapped in plastic wrap and refrigerated for up to 5 days.)

4. Adjust oven rack to lower-middle position and heat oven to 300 degrees. Line rimless cookie sheet with parchment. Working with 1 piece of rolled dough, gently peel off top layer of parchment. Replace parchment, loosely covering dough. (Peeling off parchment and returning it will make cutting and removing cookies easier.) Turn over dough and parchment and gently peel off and discard second piece of parchment. Using cookie cutter, cut dough into shapes. Transfer shapes to prepared cookie sheet, spacing them about ½ inch apart. Bake until cookies are lightly and evenly browned around edges, 14 to 17 minutes, rotating sheet halfway through baking. Let cookies cool on sheet for 5 minutes. Using wide metal spatula, transfer cookies to wire rack and let cool completely. Repeat cutting and baking with remaining dough. (Dough scraps can be patted together, rerolled, and chilled once before cutting and baking.)

5. FOR THE ROYAL ICING: Using stand mixer fitted with whisk attachment, whip all ingredients on medium-low speed until combined, about 1 minute. Increase speed to medium-high and whip until glossy, soft peaks form, 3 to 4 minutes, scraping down bowl as needed.

6. Spread icing onto cooled cookies. Let icing dry completely, about 1½ hours, before serving.

VARIATION

Easy Holiday Cocoa Sugar Cookies
MAKES ABOUT FORTY 2½-INCH COOKIES

COOKIES

1	large egg
1½	teaspoons instant espresso powder
¾	teaspoon salt
½	teaspoon vanilla extract
2½	cups (12½ ounces) all-purpose flour
⅓	cup (1 ounce) Dutch-processed cocoa powder
¼	teaspoon baking powder
¼	teaspoon baking soda
1	cup (7 ounces) granulated sugar
16	tablespoons unsalted butter, cut into ½-inch pieces and chilled

ROYAL ICING

2⅔	cups (10⅔ ounces) confectioners' sugar
2	large egg whites
½	teaspoon vanilla extract
⅛	teaspoon salt

1. FOR THE COOKIES: Whisk egg, espresso powder, salt, and vanilla together in small bowl. Whisk flour, cocoa, baking powder, and baking soda together in second bowl.

2. Process sugar in food processor until finely ground, about 30 seconds. Add butter and process until uniform mass forms and no large pieces of butter are visible, about 30 seconds, scraping down sides of bowl as needed. Add egg mixture and process until smooth and paste-like, about 10 seconds. Add flour mixture and process until no dry flour remains but mixture remains crumbly, about 30 seconds, scraping down sides of bowl as needed.

3. Turn out dough onto counter; knead gently by hand until smooth, about 10 seconds. Divide dough in half. Place 1 piece of dough in center of large sheet of parchment paper and press into 7 by 9-inch oval. Place second large sheet of parchment over dough and roll dough into 10 by 14-inch oval of even ⅛-inch thickness. Transfer dough with parchment to rimmed baking sheet. Repeat pressing and rolling with second piece of dough, then stack on top of first piece on sheet. Refrigerate until dough is firm, at least 1½ hours (or freeze for 30 minutes). (Rolled dough can be wrapped in plastic wrap and refrigerated for up to 5 days.)

4. Adjust oven rack to lower-middle position and heat oven to 300 degrees. Line rimless cookie sheet with parchment. Working with 1 piece of rolled dough, gently peel off top layer of parchment. Replace parchment, loosely covering dough. (Peeling off parchment and then returning it will make cutting and removing cookies easier.) Turn over dough and parchment and gently peel off and discard second piece of parchment. Using cookie cutter, cut dough into shapes. Transfer shapes to prepared cookie sheet, spacing them about ½ inch apart. Bake until cookies show slight resistance to touch, 14 to 17 minutes, rotating sheet halfway through baking. Let cookies cool on sheet for 5 minutes. Using wide metal spatula, transfer cookies to wire rack and let cool completely. Repeat cutting and baking with remaining dough. (Dough scraps can be patted together, rerolled, and chilled once before baking.)

5. FOR THE ROYAL ICING: Using stand mixer fitted with whisk attachment, whip all ingredients on medium-low speed until combined, about 1 minute. Increase speed to medium-high and whip until glossy, soft peaks form, 3 to 4 minutes, scraping down bowl as needed.

6. Spread icing onto cooled cookies. Let icing dry completely, about 1½ hours, before serving.

NOTES FROM THE TEST KITCHEN

COOKIE-SHEET WORKAROUND

The lack of a rim on a cookie sheet (versus a rimmed baking sheet) leads to better air circulation, resulting in more even baking across the sheet and on the tops and bottoms of the cookies. No cookie sheet? No problem. Simply flip over your rimmed baking sheet.

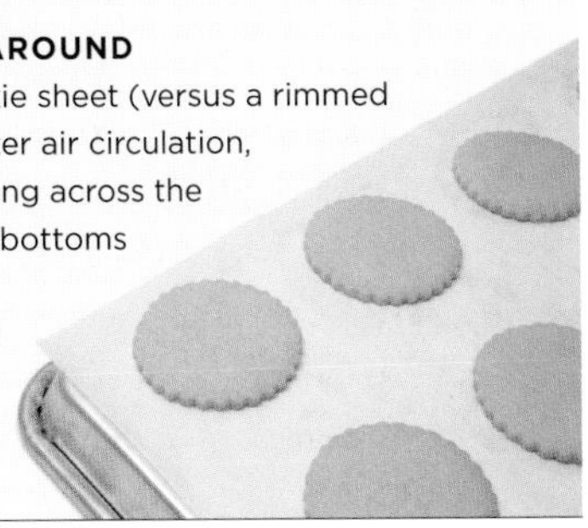

BERGERS-STYLE COOKIES

BERGERS-STYLE COOKIES

✓ **WHY THIS RECIPE WORKS:** This Baltimorean cookie has gained a cult following thanks to the ½-inch layer of fudgy chocolate frosting perched on its cakey, lightly sweet vanilla cookie base. For our version, we creamed butter with sugar and used cake flour instead of all-purpose to create a soft, fluffy cookie base. For the signature sweet-yet-ultrachocolaty frosting, a combination of milk chocolate chips and Dutch-processed cocoa gave us the best chocolate flavor; heavy cream and confectioners' sugar helped us nail the correct texture. Keeping the frosting between 90 and 100 degrees (which makes it the texture of thick brownie batter) ensured that it was easy to mound a hefty 2-tablespoon helping onto each cookie.

Until third grade, I was as picky as kids come. So my mother—who is a doctor but, more important, is also a mom who was afraid that her tiny daughter would shrivel away—fed me a steady diet of the only foods I would eat: breakfast cereal, plain hot dogs (no ketchup or bun), and, because we were in Baltimore, Bergers cookies.

Those who aren't from Baltimore may not be familiar with the glorious Bergers cookie. Its base is a lightly sweet, softly crumbly, dome-shaped vanilla cookie. But the real draw is the ½-inch layer of fudgy chocolate frosting that sits proudly on top. The cookie gets its name from Henry Berger, a German immigrant who opened his bakery in Baltimore in the 1800s. The bakery still churns out cookies by the truckload, and true Baltimoreans know that the *s* in "Bergers" is silent.

Though I've since left Baltimore, I've never stopped loving these treats from my youth. Since they're rarely found outside of Maryland, I decided to make them myself.

To get my bearings, I ordered a batch of Bergers cookies directly from the bakery to share and discuss with my team in the test kitchen. After some recipe research, the few existing recipes I found left me unsatisfied—they tried to clean up the cookie and make it fancy, which it's not—so I baked a handful of similar-sounding vanilla cookies, as well as five options for chocolate frosting and ganache.

The closest cookie replica came from a simple recipe for grocery store–style sugar cookies: It called for butter and sugar to be creamed together before adding an egg, some cream, plenty of vanilla, cake flour (for a softer texture), baking powder, and salt. The cookies were simple in flavor, with just a hint of vanilla, but they were a bit too tender to hold up to the heavy helmet of fudgy frosting. Switching to all-purpose flour wasn't the answer, as it made the cookies too tough.

Egg yolks contain fat, which can add tenderness to cookies. Because I was after a sturdier cookie, I decided to nix the yolk and just use the egg white. The resulting batch of cookies was firm but still fluffy. With the cookie part of my recipe settled, I turned my attention to the chocolate.

I knew that the topping should be thicker than cake frosting but softer than fudge; it should be just supple enough that you leave teeth marks when you bite through it. I started with a ganache recipe that called for melting semisweet chocolate chips and cream together and then whisking in confectioners' sugar. My tests proved that as long as I spread this mixture while it was warm, it would naturally cascade over the cookies and set up into a smooth, dense frosting as it cooled. Now the topping was the right texture, but it was a tad too bitter.

A switch to milk chocolate chips was the answer, especially after I figured out that I also could swap some of the confectioner's sugar for cocoa powder to maintain the frosting's texture while adding a smidge of complexity. With some vanilla and salt to intensify the chocolate flavor, I had a dead ringer for the original Bergers frosting.

Flipping the cookies over before spooning the chocolate onto their flatter bottom sides made it easier to pile it on thick and create their signature domed tops. Until I can make it back to Baltimore, I have a cookie to tide me over.

MORGAN BOLLING, *Cook's Country*

Bergers-Style Cookies
MAKES 24 COOKIES

The consistency of the frosting should resemble that of a thick brownie batter. It should mound and slowly spread over the cookies. It's OK if some of the frosting drips down the sides of the cookies. If the frosting's temperature drops below 90 degrees, it may become too thick to spread. To bring it back to its proper consistency, simply microwave it at 50 percent power in 5-second intervals, whisking after each interval.

COOKIES

2 cups (8 ounces) cake flour

1½ teaspoons baking powder

¼ teaspoon salt

8 tablespoons unsalted butter, softened

¾ cup (5¼ ounces) granulated sugar

1 large egg white

1½ tablespoons heavy cream

1½ teaspoons vanilla extract

FROSTING

3 cups (18 ounces) milk chocolate chips

1¼ cups heavy cream

¼ teaspoon salt

1⅔ cups (5 ounces) Dutch-processed cocoa powder

1¼ cups (5 ounces) confectioners' sugar

1½ teaspoons vanilla extract

1. FOR THE COOKIES: Adjust oven rack to middle position and heat oven to 350 degrees. Line 2 baking sheets with parchment paper. Whisk flour, baking powder, and salt together in bowl; set aside. Using stand mixer fitted with paddle, beat butter and sugar on medium-high speed until pale and fluffy, about 3 minutes.

2. Add egg white, cream, and vanilla and beat until combined. Reduce speed to low and add flour mixture in 3 additions until incorporated, scraping down bowl as needed.

3. Working with 1 heaping tablespoon dough at a time, roll into balls and space 2 inches apart on prepared sheets, 12 per sheet. Using your moistened fingers, press dough balls to form disks about ¼ inch thick and 2 inches in diameter. Bake, 1 sheet at a time, until cookies are just beginning to brown around edges, 8 to 10 minutes, rotating sheet halfway through baking. Let cookies cool completely on sheet.

4. FOR THE FROSTING: Once cookies have cooled, combine chocolate chips, cream, and salt in large bowl. Microwave chocolate mixture at 50 percent power, stirring occasionally, until melted and smooth, 1 to 3 minutes. Whisk cocoa, sugar, and vanilla into chocolate mixture until smooth. (Frosting should be texture of thick brownie batter and register about 95 degrees.)

5. Flip cookies on sheets. Spoon 2 tablespoons frosting over flat side of each cookie to form mound. Let cookies sit at room temperature until frosting is set, about 3 hours. Serve. (Cookies can be stored in airtight container at room temperature for up to 2 days.)

THE LEMONIEST LEMON BARS

✔ **WHY THIS RECIPE WORKS:** For lemon bars with sweet-tart flavor and a crisp, well-browned crust, we started at the bottom. Using melted butter for our pat-in-the-pan crust allowed us to stir it together and eliminated the need for a food processor. For a truly crisp texture, we used granulated sugar instead of the usual confectioners' sugar and baked the crust until it was dark golden brown to ensure that it retained its crispness even after we topped it with the lemon filling. We cooked our lemon filling on the stove to shorten the oven time and keep it from curdling or browning at the edges when it baked. The combination of lemon juice and lemon zest provided complex flavor, and a couple of teaspoons of cream of tartar gave it a bright, lingering finish.

If tart, citrusy flavors are the rays of sunshine that brighten lemon bars, then thickeners are the storm clouds that cover them up. And therein lies a culinary catch-22: For bars with lots of lemon zing, you need lots of lemon juice. But the more juice you use, the more flavor-dulling binders—such as eggs and starch—are required to keep the filling firm and sliceable. My task was to find a way around this problem.

With lemon bars, it's easy to overlook the crust and focus on the wobbly, creamy, lemony layer. And that's exactly what most recipes do. But not mine. Instead of a nondescript platform for the filling, I wanted a crisp crumb with buttery sweetness.

The typical crust is modeled on a British shortbread cookie. I made a classic version, using the food processor to cut cold butter into a mixture of flour, confectioners' sugar, and salt. To ensure that every bite would have the same ratio of crust to filling, I did my best to evenly press the crumbly mixture into an aluminum foil–lined 8-inch square pan. I had to work carefully because, once compressed, the mixture stayed put, and it became difficult to fill in thinner areas or level out thicker spots. I popped the pan into a 350-degree oven and let the crust bake for 25 minutes. This is longer than most recipes specify, but I hoped that deeper browning would produce an especially crisp, full-flavored crust.

When a buttery scent filled the kitchen, the crust was dark brown, so I pulled the pan from the oven. I topped the baked crust with a placeholder filling

BEST LEMON BARS

made by whisking lemon juice and eggs together with sugar and salt before returning the pan to the oven for 30 more minutes.

The longer baking time had indeed helped develop a rich taste. Unfortunately, it didn't make the crust any crispier. After brainstorming with my colleagues, I realized why: The powdery sugar was producing a fine, delicate crumb that melted on my tongue. For a coarser, crunchier consistency, I needed coarser, crunchier granulated sugar.

Finally, to make the dough easier to work with, I melted the butter in the microwave and stirred it into the flour. This created a pliable mass that was much easier to distribute evenly—with no adverse effect on the finished product. As a bonus, I no longer needed a food processor.

I now had a good base on which to showcase a bright, sweet-tart lemon filling. After my initial tests, I concluded that a filling that was twice as deep as the crust was most pleasant to eat; now I just needed to perfect the filling itself. I'd already fiddled with the simplest approach: whisking together lemon juice, sugar, salt, and a thickener—some combination of eggs, flour, and/or cornstarch—and baking until set. Unfortunately, by the time this filling was cooked at the center, its edges were curdled, as evidenced by pockmarks. A liberal dusting of confectioners' sugar disguised the unevenness, but nothing could camouflage the lumpy consistency. No matter how I tweaked the ingredients, oven temperature, and baking time, I couldn't fix this style of filling.

A more promising method required only marginally more work—the filling is precooked, poured over the crust, and baked until set. I gave it a try, cooking ⅔ cup of lemon juice, 6 eggs, 1 cup of sugar, and ¼ teaspoon of salt over medium heat. As soon as it reached a pudding-like consistency, I stirred in 4 tablespoons of butter for richness. I poured the filling over my baked crust and returned the pan to the oven. After 10 minutes, the curd barely jiggled when I shook the pan.

Less time in the oven had solved the textural issues since the edges and center of the filling now finished cooking at the same time: These bars boasted an incredibly smooth surface. However, their flavor was marred by egginess, and they lacked the requisite lemony punch. Reducing the number of whites (the sulfur compounds in egg whites are the source of eggy flavor) took care of any egginess, but it also left the filling runny. That's because the proteins in the egg whites were providing structure when they set. After some experimentation, I found that I could replace that protein with the starch in 2 tablespoons of flour. This would dull the lemon flavor, but I'd get to that next.

As I'd known from the start, the flavor issue would be a challenge. Increasing the lemon juice was out of the question—I'd have to add even more flavor-dulling thickeners, which would defeat the purpose.

I took a step back to consider how flavor in lemon juice (and all foods) works: When you take a bite, you encounter taste with your tongue and aroma through a channel in the back of your mouth that leads directly to your nose. With lemon juice specifically, you taste only the tartness of its citric and malic acids on the tongue, while all the fruity, lemony flavors come from volatile compounds that shoot into that back door to your nasal passage when you exhale. So to add more lemon flavor without more lemon juice, I'd have to consider both taste and aroma.

Incorporating lemony aroma would be easy: I could add lemon zest. Zest has even more volatile flavor chemicals than the juice, which is why it is so often added to foods to enhance lemony flavor. I found that 2 teaspoons of grated zest cooked into the filling (and later strained out) boosted its fruity flavor significantly. The trickier task was increasing that acidic punch in the filling without adding more liquid. What ingredient would help with that?

I flirted with the idea of purchasing powdered citric acid or grinding up vitamin C tablets (ascorbic acid). But then I realized I already had a truly sour-tasting powder in my pantry: cream of tartar. I whipped up two more batches of bars, one of which contained 2 teaspoons of cream of tartar. This was the magic ingredient: Tasters loved the bold sharpness of the bars containing cream of tartar, claiming they were unlike any others they'd tasted. And when they raved about the interplay of the tart, silky filling and the crisp, buttery crust, I knew I had a winner.

LAN LAM, *Cook's Illustrated*

Best Lemon Bars

MAKES 12 BARS

Do not substitute bottled lemon juice for fresh here.

CRUST

  1 cup (5 ounces) all-purpose flour

  ¼ cup (1¾ ounces) granulated sugar

  ½ teaspoon salt

  8 tablespoons unsalted butter, melted

FILLING

  1 cup (7 ounces) granulated sugar

  2 tablespoons all-purpose flour

  2 teaspoons cream of tartar

  ¼ teaspoon salt

  3 large eggs plus 3 large yolks

  2 teaspoons grated lemon zest plus ⅔ cup juice (4 lemons)

  4 tablespoons unsalted butter, cut into 8 pieces

     Confectioners' sugar (optional)

1. FOR THE CRUST: Adjust oven rack to middle position and heat oven to 350 degrees. Make foil sling for 8-inch square baking pan by folding 2 long sheets of aluminum foil so each is 8 inches wide. Lay sheets of foil in pan perpendicular to each other, with extra foil hanging over edges of pan. Push foil into corners and up sides of pan, smoothing foil flush to pan.

2. Whisk flour, sugar, and salt together in bowl. Add melted butter and stir until combined. Transfer mixture to prepared pan and press into even layer over entire bottom of pan (do not wash bowl). Bake crust until dark golden brown, 19 to 24 minutes, rotating pan halfway through baking.

3. FOR THE FILLING: While crust bakes, whisk sugar, flour, cream of tartar, and salt together in now-empty bowl. Whisk in eggs and yolks until no streaks of egg remain. Whisk in lemon zest and juice. Transfer mixture to saucepan and cook over medium-low heat, stirring constantly, until mixture thickens and registers 160 degrees, 5 to 8 minutes. Off heat, stir in butter. Strain filling through fine-mesh strainer set over bowl.

4. Pour filling over hot crust and tilt pan to spread evenly. Bake until filling is set and barely jiggles when pan is shaken, 8 to 12 minutes. (Filling around perimeter of pan may be slightly raised.) Let bars cool completely, at least 1½ hours. Using foil overhang, lift bars out of pan and transfer to cutting board. Cut into bars, wiping knife clean between cuts as necessary. Before serving, dust bars with confectioners' sugar, if using.

EASY ONE-BOWL BROWNIES

✓ **WHY THIS RECIPE WORKS:** Box mixes seem to produce the perfect combination of chewy and moist in brownies. We wanted the same results without all the processing and questionable ingredients, and we wanted it to be easy. For one-bowl brownies with the proper level of chewiness, we used both butter and oil. Using both cocoa and unsweetened chocolate added to the intense chocolaty richness and created a platform of flavor for any add-ins. By being strategic with the addition of ingredients, we saved dishes and combined the batter all in one large bowl. Baked on the lowest rack in the oven, the brownies cooked nicely on the bottom and edges without overcooking and drying out. Folding bittersweet chocolate chunks into the batter gave our chewy brownies gooey pockets of melted chocolate and rounded out their complex flavor.

Here's a rather uncontroversial admission: I love brownies. And here's a controversial one: I've made a few batches using box mixes and found myself relatively satisfied. But all things being equal, I'd rather make brownies from scratch, for the deeper, more complex flavor they deliver.

A typical box mix consists of measured dry ingredients (flour, cocoa powder, sugar, salt, leavening agent, and in some cases artificial ingredients to enhance flavor or ensure even baking). You add oil, eggs, and sometimes water and then stir together and bake.

I knew that I'd have to measure my own ingredients, but beyond that, I wanted my recipe to be as simple as possible and require just one bowl, like the mixes do.

Brownies made with cocoa powder alone will do, but I prefer the richness produced by a combination of cocoa and melted chocolate, so I started by roughly chopping two squares of unsweetened chocolate and whisking them together with boiling water and cocoa powder until everything was evenly melted. I quickly added the sugar and whisked to fully incorporate it. Next, eggs for structure, oil for moistness, and butter for added richness.

Only then did I stir in the flour—and gently: Overworking the batter would overdevelop the gluten and turn my brownies gummy. A bit of salt and 6 ounces of bittersweet chocolate chunks for a final chocolate boost and my brownies were ready for the oven. And I'd dirtied only one bowl.

These superchocolaty brownies make an excellent backdrop for a range of add-ins. I created four variations: a Nutella and hazelnut version, a minty variation, a version featuring white chocolate and raspberry jam, and a peanut butter and marshmallow option. Each addition brought something to the party without blocking the main event—chocolate.

ALLI BERKEY, *Cook's Country*

Easy Chocolate Chunk Brownies

SERVES 8 TO 10

For an accurate measurement of boiling water, bring a full kettle to a boil and then measure out the desired amount.

½ cup plus 2 tablespoons boiling water
2 ounces unsweetened chocolate, chopped fine
⅓ cup (1 ounce) Dutch-processed cocoa powder
2½ cups (17½ ounces) sugar
½ cup plus 2 tablespoons vegetable oil
2 large eggs plus 2 large yolks
4 tablespoons unsalted butter, melted
2 teaspoons vanilla extract
1¾ cups (8¾ ounces) all-purpose flour
¾ teaspoon salt
6 ounces bittersweet chocolate, cut into ½-inch pieces

1. Adjust oven rack to lowest position and heat oven to 350 degrees. Make foil sling for 13 by 9-inch baking pan by folding 2 long sheets of aluminum foil; first sheet should be 13 inches wide and second sheet should be 9 inches wide. Lay sheets of foil in pan perpendicular to each other, with extra foil hanging over edges of pan. Push foil into corners and up sides of pan, smoothing foil flush to pan. Spray foil with vegetable oil spray.

2. Whisk boiling water, unsweetened chocolate, and cocoa in large bowl until chocolate is melted. Whisk in sugar, oil, eggs and yolks, melted butter, and vanilla until combined. Gently whisk in flour and salt until just incorporated. Stir in bittersweet chocolate.

3. Transfer batter to prepared pan. Bake until toothpick inserted in center comes out with few moist crumbs attached, 30 to 35 minutes, rotating pan halfway through baking. Transfer pan to wire rack and let cool for 1½ hours.

4. Using foil overhang, lift brownies out of pan. Return brownies to wire rack and let cool completely, about 1 hour. Cut into 2-inch squares and serve.

VARIATIONS

Easy Nutella-Hazelnut Brownies

Omit bittersweet chocolate. Fold ⅓ cup toasted, skinned, and chopped hazelnuts into batter at end of step 2. Dollop ⅓ cup Nutella evenly over top of batter in pan. Using tip of paring knife, swirl Nutella into batter before baking.

Easy Chocolate-Mint Brownies

Omit bittersweet chocolate. Fold 4 ounces Andes Mints, cut into ½-inch pieces, into batter at end of step 2. Scatter 2 ounces Andes Mints, cut into ½-inch pieces, over top of batter before baking.

Easy White Chocolate–Raspberry Brownies

Omit bittersweet chocolate. Fold 1 cup white chocolate chips into batter at end of step 2. Dollop ⅓ cup raspberry jam evenly over top of batter in pan. Using tip of paring knife, swirl jam into batter before baking.

Easy Peanut Butter–Marshmallow Brownies

Omit bittersweet chocolate. Fold 1 cup peanut butter chips into batter at end of step 2. Dollop ½ cup marshmallow crème evenly over top of batter in pan. Using tip of paring knife, swirl marshmallow crème into batter before baking.

LAZY STRAWBERRY SONKER

✓ **WHY THIS RECIPE WORKS:** Not quite a pie and not quite a cobbler, sonker is a juicy, fruit-filled deep-dish dessert rarely found outside Surry County, North Carolina. A subset of sonker recipes dub themselves "lazy" sonkers, in which the fruit is cooked into a sweet stew and topped with a pancake batter that bakes into a distinct, lightly crisp layer of cake. For our version, we tossed strawberries with sugar, salt, water, and cornstarch and then baked them until they bubbled and thickened. We then poured the batter over the filling and returned it to the oven, where the hot filling baked the batter from underneath into a tender-yet-crisp raft of cake.

In the shadow of North Carolina's Blue Ridge Mountains lies Surry County, where, if you're lucky, you'll cross paths with a fruit sonker. Not quite a pie, not quite a cobbler, and not quite a betty, crisp, or pandowdy, the sonker is a sweet, juicy, comforting, fruit-filled North Carolina dessert rarely found farther afield.

Supremely juicy, with a cakey, sweet crust on top, sonkers are traditionally made deep-dish style to feed crowds and use up surplus summertime fruit on its way out. This is simple country cooking, and my research uncovered more family heirloom recipes than formally published ones.

What's more, each recipe was bewilderingly different from the next. Most of the variance lay in the top crust. Some versions were rectangular variations on pie, with bottom and top crusts, the top sometimes latticed to allow for evaporation. Others dolloped the filling with spoonfuls of biscuit dough, which baked into a pleasing, cobbler-like topping.

But I was most intrigued by a subset of sonker recipes made with a batter topping instead, called "lazy" sonkers. In these, the fruit is cooked into a sweet stew and topped with a pancake batter that bakes into a distinct, lightly crisp layer of cake with juice bubbling up around the edges. My tasters helped me settle on strawberries for the filling, for their ruby-red color and summery sweetness.

It wasn't long before I realized that the lane I'd picked was full of potholes. In some instances, the batter sank into and mixed with the cooked strawberries, preventing the top layer from baking properly. This left soggy pockets of batter and turned the filling into a chalky, Pepto-pink gravy. I tried an even lazier method, simply pouring batter over raw berries, but this version was bereft of the signature juice, and because the surface was bumpy, the batter flowed into spaces between the fruit, giving me gummy spots throughout.

I needed a filling that was superjuicy but still capable of supporting the batter on top as it baked. Rather than cook the berries in a pot, I tossed them with sugar and put them in the baking dish to stew. Stewed berries would give the batter a uniform, level surface on which to bake, and their heat would help bake the batter from underneath. To give the filling just a bit of structure to help it support the batter, I added cornstarch to the berries once they had stewed. The cornstarch thickened the juice a bit as the filling baked, helping it withstand the batter's weight without sacrificing too much moisture.

For further insurance against a sinking top, I looked for ways to create a lighter, more floatable batter. The answer was fat. Fat floats, and since there's more fat in butter than in milk, I replaced some of the milk in my batter with melted butter—which had the bonus of providing a flavor boost as well.

I poured my new batter over a pan of cooked fruit and, to my relief, it floated happily on top of the bubbling berries. Once it had baked into a beautiful layer of golden cake, I gathered my tasters. Their response to this sweet, fruity, juicy dessert was nothing short of enthusiastic.

CECELIA JENKINS, *Cook's Country*

Lazy Strawberry Sonker
SERVES 6

If you're using frozen strawberries in this recipe, there's no need to let them thaw. In steps 2 and 3, be sure to stir the strawberry filling as directed, scraping the bottom of the dish to incorporate the cornstarch so that it evenly and thoroughly thickens the mixture. In step 3, add the butter to the batter while it is still hot so it remains pourable, and be sure to mix the batter only right before pouring it over the filling. Serve with vanilla ice cream.

2 pounds fresh strawberries, hulled (6½ cups), or 2 pounds (7 cups) frozen whole strawberries

1 cup (7 ounces) sugar

Salt

¼ cup water

3 tablespoons cornstarch

1 cup (5 ounces) all-purpose flour

1 teaspoon baking powder

½ cup whole milk

8 tablespoons unsalted butter, melted and hot

¼ teaspoon vanilla extract

1. Adjust oven rack to middle position and heat oven to 350 degrees. Line rimmed baking sheet with parchment paper. Combine strawberries, ¼ cup sugar, and ¼ teaspoon salt in bowl. Whisk water and cornstarch together in second bowl; add to strawberry mixture and toss until strawberries are evenly coated.

2. Transfer strawberry mixture to 8-inch square baking dish and place dish on prepared sheet. Bake until filling is bubbling around sides of dish, 35 to 40 minutes (1 hour if using frozen strawberries), stirring and scraping bottom of dish with rubber spatula halfway through baking.

3. Remove sheet from oven and stir filling, scraping bottom of dish with rubber spatula. Whisk flour, baking powder, remaining ¾ cup sugar, and ¼ teaspoon salt together in bowl. Whisk in milk, melted butter, and vanilla until smooth. Starting in corner of dish, pour batter evenly over filling.

4. Bake until surface is golden brown and toothpick inserted in center comes out with no crumbs attached, 35 to 40 minutes, rotating dish halfway through baking. Let sonker cool on wire rack for 15 minutes. Serve.

VARIATIONS

Lazy Blueberry Sonker

Substitute 2 pounds (6½ cups) fresh or frozen blueberries for strawberries.

Lazy Peach Sonker

Substitute 2½ pounds peaches, peeled, halved, pitted, and cut into ½-inch-thick wedges, or 2 pounds frozen sliced peaches (break up any slices that are frozen together) for strawberries.

BEET-CHOCOLATE CUPCAKES

✓ **WHY THIS RECIPE WORKS:** Taking a cue from Victorian-era cakes, which used beets for their natural sweetness and moisture, we turned to the nutrient-packed root vegetable to add a complementary flavor and color to our unique cupcakes. Whole-wheat flour underscored the beets' delicate earthiness. We opted for a lightly sweetened Greek yogurt–based frosting; its cooling tang paired perfectly with the cupcakes' deep chocolate flavor.

As I see it, beets are incredibly versatile: They're sweet yet earthy and crunchy when raw but temptingly tender when roasted. Beets are great in everything from salads to slaws to juices, but one category I've never explored is desserts. Incorporating beets into a dessert makes sense in a way; they have plenty of natural sugar and we don't hesitate to add other naturally sweet vegetables, such as carrots, to a cake. I set my sights on developing a recipe for a party-perfect cupcake featuring the flavors of rich chocolate and sweet, earthy beets.

I started by giving a few existing recipes a spin, selecting cupcakes that incorporated beets in different ways (grated raw or cooked and then pureed) and in different amounts (from 8 ounces to nearly 2 pounds) and gathered my fellow test cooks to have a taste.

The raw beets were a nonstarter. Even when shredded fine, they added an unpleasant crunch and their flavor was overpowering. The pureed cooked beets were subtler, seamlessly disappearing into the batter and lending the finished cakes a nuanced beet flavor. The cupcakes with the fewest beets had unadulterated chocolate flavor and familiar cake texture, but if I was going to bring beets into my cupcakes, I wanted them to have an unmistakable—though not overwhelming—presence.

Using a test kitchen recipe for rich dark chocolate cupcakes as my starting place, I began my work. While the cooked beets in my trial recipes had good texture and flavor, the work of boiling or roasting them was a turnoff. I tried canned and vacuum-packed beets, but their tinny flavor and wet, heavy texture proved that fresh beets were the only option. What about cooking the beets in the microwave? This did the trick, softening the beets in no time and making for a speedy, smooth puree in the food processor. A few more tests determined that 12 ounces of beets was just right; this amount packed plenty of beet presence into each little cake while still allowing the chocolate flavor to shine.

BEET-CHOCOLATE CUPCAKES

Since I was already using my food processor to puree the softened beets, I wondered if I could also use it to shred them. Not only was this quicker and neater, but the thinner pieces softened even more quickly. To streamline my recipe further, I decided to assemble the entire batter right in the processor's bowl.

It was time to turn my attention back to the base recipe for my cupcakes. Tasty as they were, the cupcakes' tops had a somewhat craggy appearance—not a deal breaker, but also not ideal for applying a smooth layer of frosting. I played around with leaveners, and discovered that eliminating baking powder produced cakes with beautifully rounded domes. Incrementally increasing the amount of milk in my batter also helped, with 3 tablespoons producing a moist, tender crumb.

For bold, intense chocolate flavor that balanced the beets' sweet earthy notes, I needed a combination of cocoa powder and dark chocolate. After trying various combinations and cacao levels, I settled on 70 percent dark chocolate, which imparted a deep, sultry chocolate flavor without overpowering the beets. Dutched cocoa powder doubled down on the chocolate's intensity.

To build the batter, I melted the chocolate in the microwave, boosted it with cocoa powder, and smoothed the mixture out with some melted butter before whirring it in the food processor with the beets. From there, I continued to pulse in the standard cupcake ingredients. This was my best batch yet, but now I had a new concern: If I was boosting my dessert's nutrition with beets, should I also be taking a look at the nutrition of the other ingredients? I tried substituting whole-wheat flour for the all-purpose and found that this swap actually improved the outcome—the slightly nutty, toasty taste of the whole-wheat flour mirrored the earthiness of the beets. Replacing the butter with vegetable oil and the whole milk with 1 percent offered further improvements, reeling in the cakes' richness and allowing the chocolate-beet pairing to truly shine.

My cupcakes were calling out for a tangy, creamy frosting, but rather than stirring together a rich, sugar-laden topping, I focused on keeping things light. Greek yogurt—along with a little cream cheese—offered plenty of tang and a light texture, and a modest ½ cup of confectioners' sugar provided just enough sweetness.

I could have stopped there, but I decided my cupcakes could use a festive touch to make them party-ready. After pulsing more beets in my food processor, I patted out their moisture and then baked them in a low oven to create vibrant beet "sprinkles." Was making my own sprinkles flying in the face of the simplified recipe I was shooting for? Perhaps, but every other step was so effortless that I decided this little flourish was worthwhile and provided the perfect finish.

AFTON CYRUS, *America's Test Kitchen Books*

Beet-Chocolate Cupcakes

MAKES 12 CUPCAKES

Do not substitute natural cocoa powder. We prefer the flavor of 70 percent dark chocolate; higher percentages are too bitter. If the frosting becomes too soft to work with, let it chill in the refrigerator until firm. These cupcakes are best eaten the day they're made. Once frosted, they should be served immediately. Top with Beet "Sprinkles" (recipe follows), if desired.

YOGURT–CREAM CHEESE FROSTING

- ½ cup plain 2 percent Greek yogurt
- 4 ounces cream cheese, softened
- ¼ teaspoon vanilla extract
- Pinch salt
- ½ cup (2 ounces) confectioners' sugar

CUPCAKES

- 12 ounces beets, trimmed, peeled, and quartered
- 2 ounces 70 percent dark chocolate, chopped
- ½ cup (1½ ounces) Dutch-processed cocoa powder
- ⅓ cup vegetable oil
- ¾ cup (5¼ ounces) sugar
- 2 large eggs
- 3 tablespoons 1 percent low-fat milk
- 1 teaspoon vanilla extract
- ½ teaspoon baking soda
- ½ teaspoon salt
- ¾ cup (4⅛ ounces) whole-wheat flour

1. FOR THE YOGURT-CREAM CHEESE FROSTING: Process yogurt, cream cheese, vanilla, and salt in food processor until smooth, about 25 seconds, scraping down sides of bowl as needed. Add sugar and process until incorporated and frosting is creamy and glossy, about 20 seconds. Refrigerate for at least 30 minutes or up to 24 hours until firm but spreadable.

2. FOR THE CUPCAKES: Adjust oven rack to lower-middle position and heat oven to 350 degrees. Line 12-cup muffin tin with paper liners.

3. Working in batches, use food processor fitted with shredding disk to process beets until shredded. Transfer to bowl and microwave, covered, until beets are tender and have released their juices, about 4 minutes, stirring halfway through microwaving. Fit now-empty processor with chopping blade and transfer cooked beets to processor.

4. Microwave chocolate in separate bowl at 50 percent power, stirring occasionally, until melted, about 2 minutes. Whisk in cocoa and oil until smooth and transfer chocolate mixture to food processor with beets; let cool slightly.

5. Process beets and chocolate mixture until smooth, about 45 seconds, scraping down sides of bowl as needed. Add sugar, eggs, milk, vanilla, baking soda, and salt and process until sugar is mostly dissolved and mixture is emulsified, about 15 seconds. Add flour and pulse until just incorporated, about 5 pulses; do not overmix.

6. Divide batter evenly among muffin cups. Bake cupcakes until toothpick inserted in center comes out clean, 20 to 22 minutes, rotating tin halfway through baking. Let cupcakes cool in muffin tin on wire rack for 15 minutes. Remove cupcakes from muffin tin and let cool completely, about 1 hour.

7. Mound 1 tablespoon frosting in center of each cupcake. Using small icing spatula or butter knife, spread frosting to edge of cupcake, leaving slight mound in center. Serve immediately.

Beet "Sprinkles"
MAKES ABOUT ¼ CUP

> 4 ounces beets, trimmed, peeled, and cut
> into 1-inch pieces

Adjust oven rack to middle position and heat oven to 200 degrees. Process beets in food processor until finely ground, about 20 seconds, scraping down sides of bowl as needed. Place ground beets in triple layer of cheesecloth and wring out as much liquid as possible. Transfer drained beets to rimmed baking sheet lined with parchment paper and spread into single layer. Bake, stirring occasionally, until dry and crisp, 45 to 55 minutes. Let cool completely before serving. (Beet sprinkles can be stored in airtight container at room temperature for up to 2 days.)

SALTED CARAMEL CUPCAKES

✓ **WHY THIS RECIPE WORKS:** The pairing of savory salt and sweet caramel is a hard one to resist, and we wanted to create a cupcake that highlighted this combo. For caramel flavor in every bite, we started by giving our cupcakes a core of salted caramel sauce. To ensure the sauce didn't ooze out of the cupcakes at first bite, we added extra butter to help it set up. Since we were already putting in the effort to prepare a homemade caramel sauce, we decided to add some to our base of vanilla frosting as well for a double hit of caramel flavor.

Salt: It's both the most basic seasoning and the most important one. It not only tastes, well, salty, it also heightens the flavor of pretty much anything else—savory or sweet. Salty sweets are popular, and the modern-classic pairing of salt and caramel is a particular favorite. The salt cuts through the caramel's sweetness while also enhancing its rich, buttery flavor. I wanted to create a cupcake that highlighted this irresistible combination in shareable dessert form. I imagined a cupcake that both kids and adults would love, one that would be a hit at birthday parties yet still appropriate for other special occasions.

Cupcakes are so often all about the frosting, but I wanted the cake itself to be the star of the show; I also desired salted caramel flavor in every bite. To start, I settled on a yellow cake base; its buttery richness would highlight the caramel flavor without overpowering it. For the most caramel impact, I decided to create a caramel filling for my cupcakes. But I didn't want a filling that would ooze out of the cupcake at first bite, so I needed to get the consistency just right. I started by cooking sugar, a bit of corn syrup (to prevent crystallization), and water (to help the sugar melt evenly without burning) until it reached a medium amber color to ensure complexity. Then I added cream to give the sauce the requisite richness, vanilla for dimension, and, of course, salt, and cooked it until it registered about 240 degrees, the sweet spot for a sauce with a bit of stiffness. Or so I thought. Caramel cooked to this temperature still oozed out of the cake. Cooking it any further, though, made a too-thick caramel that stuck to tasters' teeth. I found that by swirling in another common caramel addition—butter—I got a sauce with just the right viscosity. Why? Butter is solid but soft at room temperature, so it firmed up the caramel just enough, without making it hard. The butter boost added great flavor to boot.

Now that I'd made the caramel, I had to figure out how to get it inside the cupcake. Many filled cupcakes are injected with their filling through a small concealed hole in the bottom of the cake. I filled a pastry bag with my salted caramel sauce, stuck the tip into the cupcake, and squeezed. Unfortunately, when I cut a cupcake in half I saw that very little caramel had actually made it in—and what had simply blended in with the cake. It was clear that some of the cake would have to go to make room for the caramel, so I removed a cone-shaped section of cake with a paring knife and then filled the space with caramel. (Once the frosting was piped on, the caramel core would be hidden.)

While my caramel sauce was just the right consistency to prevent oozing, it did still seep into the cake a bit and overwhelmed the delicate crumb. I wanted a tender cupcake, but it was clear I needed a base that could better support the filling. Instead of the traditional creaming method I had been using, in which the butter and sugar are creamed together before blending in the wet and dry ingredients, I switched to the reverse creaming method: The butter is mixed into the blended dry ingredients before the eggs, milk, and vanilla are added. The traditional creaming method, which relies on aerating the butter with the sugar, creates air pockets that result in a coarser crumb. In the reverse creaming method, the butter coats the flour before the batter is aerated, keeping the cake tender and fine-crumbed—perfect for holding a core of caramel in place without crumbling apart.

All my cupcakes needed now to be party-ready was a top hat. A brown sugar buttercream was nice and boasted a mild caramel flavor from the molasses in the brown sugar, but since I had already put in the effort to prepare a delicious homemade caramel sauce, it made sense to add it to the frosting for a double hit. I started with an easy vanilla frosting—just butter, confectioners' sugar, vanilla, salt, and a lick of heavy cream to give it the perfect creamy consistency—and then I simply whipped in ¼ cup of my caramel sauce. To finish the cupcakes with flair, I piped the frosting into swirls before drizzling it with more caramel sauce. And, of course, my cupcakes wouldn't be complete without one final touch: a sprinkle of flaky sea salt. Not only did these cupcakes taste amazing with their complex flavor, generous core of caramel, buttery tender cake, and creamy frosting, but they were also some of the prettiest cupcakes I'd seen. Bring them to any celebration and you'll need to convince your friends that they didn't come from a boutique cupcake shop.

AFTON CYRUS, *America's Test Kitchen Books*

Salted Caramel Cupcakes

MAKES 12 CUPCAKES

When taking the temperature of the caramel in steps 3 and 4, remove the pot from the heat and tilt the pan to one side. Use your thermometer to stir the caramel back and forth to equalize hot and cool spots, which will help ensure an accurate reading.

CUPCAKES

- 1¾ cups (8¾ ounces) all-purpose flour
- 1 cup (7 ounces) granulated sugar
- 1½ teaspoons baking powder
- ¾ teaspoon salt
- 12 tablespoons unsalted butter, cut into 12 pieces and softened
- 3 large eggs
- ¾ cup milk
- 1½ teaspoons vanilla extract

SALTED CARAMEL SAUCE

- ⅔ cup (4⅔ ounces) granulated sugar
- 2 tablespoons light corn syrup
- 2 tablespoons water
- ½ cup heavy cream
- 4 tablespoons unsalted butter, cut into 4 pieces
- ½ teaspoon vanilla extract
- ½ teaspoon salt

FROSTING

- 20 tablespoons (2½ sticks) unsalted butter, cut into 10 pieces and softened
- 2 tablespoons heavy cream
- 2 teaspoons vanilla extract
- ⅛ teaspoon salt
- 2½ cups (10 ounces) confectioners' sugar
  Flake sea salt

1. FOR THE CUPCAKES: Adjust oven rack to middle position and heat oven to 350 degrees. Line 12-cup muffin tin with paper or foil liners. Using stand mixer fitted with paddle, mix flour, sugar, baking powder, and salt on low speed until combined. Add butter, 1 piece at a time, and mix until mixture resembles coarse sand, about 1 minute. Add eggs, one at a time, and mix until combined. Add milk and vanilla, increase speed to medium, and mix until light, fluffy, and no lumps remain, about 3 minutes.

2. Divide batter evenly among prepared muffin cups. Bake until toothpick inserted in center comes out clean, 18 to 20 minutes, rotating muffin tin halfway through baking. Let cupcakes cool in muffin tin on wire rack for 10 minutes. Remove cupcakes from muffin tin and let cool completely on rack, about 1 hour. (Cupcakes can be refrigerated for up to 2 days; bring to room temperature before continuing with recipe.)

3. FOR THE SALTED CARAMEL SAUCE: Combine sugar, corn syrup, and water in small saucepan. Bring to boil over medium-high heat and cook, without stirring, until mixture is light amber colored, 4 to 6 minutes. Reduce heat to low and continue to cook, swirling saucepan occasionally, until mixture is medium amber and registers 355 to 360 degrees, about 1 minute longer.

4. Off heat, carefully stir in cream, butter, vanilla, and salt (mixture will bubble and steam). Return saucepan to medium heat and cook, stirring frequently, until smooth and caramel reaches 240 to 245 degrees, 2 to 4 minutes. Remove from heat and allow bubbles to subside. Carefully measure ¼ cup caramel into heatproof liquid measuring cup and set aside for frosting. Transfer remaining caramel to heatproof bowl and let both cool until just warm to touch, 15 to 20 minutes.

5. While caramel is cooling, use paring knife to cut out cone-shaped wedge from top of each cupcake, about 1 inch from cupcake edge and 1-inch-deep into center of cupcake. Discard cones. Fill each cupcake with 2 teaspoons warm caramel sauce; set aside remaining caramel for frosting.

6. FOR THE FROSTING: Using stand mixer fitted with paddle, beat butter, cream, vanilla, and salt on medium-high speed until smooth, about 1 minutes. Reduce speed to medium-low, slowly add sugar, and beat until incorporated and smooth, about 4 minutes. Increase speed to medium-high and beat until frosting is light and fluffy, about 5 minutes. Stop mixer and add ¼ cup caramel to bowl. Beat on medium-high speed until fully incorporated, about 2 minutes.

7. Spread or pipe frosting evenly on cupcakes, drizzle with remaining caramel sauce (rewarming sauce as needed to keep fluid), and sprinkle with sea salt. Serve. (Cupcakes can be stored at room temperature for up to 4 hours before serving.)

APPLE BUNDT CAKE

✓ **WHY THIS RECIPE WORKS:** A Bundt pan is a practical vessel for baking a moist cake, such as our Cider-Glazed Apple Bundt Cake, because the central hole allows heat to quickly reach the center of the batter, which would remain dense and underbaked by the time the exterior was cooked through if baked in a conventional round cake pan. We also wanted more apple flavor in our cake, but simply adding extra apples made the crumb soggy and dense. We limited the apples to 1½ pounds and bolstered their flavor with a reduction of apple cider mixed into the batter, brushed onto the warm exterior of the baked cake, and stirred into an icing. Minimizing the amount of spices allowed the apple flavor to shine.

If you're making an apple cake, there are some very good reasons to bake it in a Bundt pan. For starters, the generous size and graceful, undulating ring shape of a Bundt cake looks impressive—especially considering that Bundt cakes come together fairly easily. What's more, instead of making a buttercream, ganache, or other frosting that requires cooking or mixing in a large appliance, Bundt cakes are adorned with a stir-together icing that's either drizzled or poured over the top of the cake so that it drips attractively down the sides. But the most compelling reason to make an apple cake in a Bundt pan? Enhanced energy transfer.

I know that sounds hopelessly nerdy, but bear with me. Apple flavor is relatively mellow, so if you want a cake with robust apple flavor, you have to pack in a ton of fruit. And to accommodate the moisture that all those apples will release, the batter has to be pretty thick and stiff, which can be a problem when it comes to baking: The denser the batter, the lower the moisture and the longer it takes for the oven's heat to penetrate from the outside to the middle. That's especially problematic if you bake the batter in a standard round pan, since heat transfer can take so long that the edges of the cake overcook while the middle stays wet.

Enter the Bundt. The central hole in a Bundt pan does more than just eliminate the problematic middle—it

CIDER-GLAZED APPLE BUNDT CAKE

actually allows heat to flow through the center of the cake so that it bakes simultaneously from the inside out and from the outside in, producing a more evenly baked cake. I theorized that if I used a Bundt pan, I could pack my cake with enough apples to produce plenty of flavor without harming the texture—and to some degree, I was right. But all the cakes were light on apple flavor, and in some cases that flavor was completely obscured by assertive warm spices such as cinnamon, clove, nutmeg, and allspice.

Most of the apple Bundt cake recipes I'd tried called for 1 to 2 pounds of apples, which honestly didn't sound like that much; depending on size, there are from two to four apples in a pound. But once I'd baked the cakes, it was obvious why recipes didn't call for more. The fruit-heavy cakes were so flooded with moisture that the crumb was soggy and dense. And even then, the fruit flavor was lacking. Somehow I needed to boost the apple flavor while decreasing the amount of apples, which sounded like a job for an apple concentrate of some kind.

Until now, I'd been mixing up a thick batter by combining dry ingredients (flour, salt, leaveners, and small amounts of cinnamon and allspice) in one bowl and wet (melted butter, brown sugar, eggs, milk, and vanilla) in another and then gently stirring the two together. Going forward, I could replace the milk with some form of apple concentrate—but what, exactly? Applesauce and apple butter were out—making either would be too much work, while commercial versions would have inconsistencies in water content or sweetness across brands that would make the flavor and texture of the cake unpredictable.

But what about apple cider? It takes more than 12 pounds of apples to make a single gallon of cider, so I reasoned that it can be considered a concentrated form of the fruit. Also, its simplicity—cider is just the juice of crushed apples—means it's pretty consistent. I swapped it in for the milk and also added 1½ pounds of grated Granny Smith apples, since their tartness would deliver brighter flavor than sweeter apples would. I deliberately avoided cutting the apples into chunks for two reasons: They leave pockets of gooey, underbaked batter around them, and they shrink, so that gaps form around them and make the cake look pocked. I poured the batter into a greased and floured Bundt pan, baked it for about an hour in a 350-degree oven, allowed the cake to cool briefly, and carefully unmolded

it. To further bolster the apple flavor, I whisked some cider into confectioners' sugar to make an icing, which I drizzled over the cake. The crumb was much improved, neither soggy nor gooey, but the fruit flavor was only slightly stronger, and the icing, while pretty, was not particularly appley.

Since cider lacked the required intensity, I considered enhancing my cake with boiled cider, a super-reduced, syrupy form of the juice. I placed a 12-inch skillet (the greater the surface area, the speedier the reduction) on the stovetop, poured in 4 cups of cider, and boiled it over high heat until it was reduced to 1 cup. That took a good 25 minutes, but during that time I was able to gather and measure all my other ingredients and peel and grate another 1½ pounds of apples.

My reduction wasn't as viscous as boiled cider from a bottle (which can be hard to find), but it had a similarly intense sweetness and acidity. I stirred ½ cup into the wet ingredients and proceeded with the recipe as before. While the cake baked, I whisked 2 tablespoons of the remaining reduced cider into some confectioners' sugar to make an icing that I hoped would taste brighter and fruitier. I had about 6 tablespoons of cider reduction left over, which I hated to waste, so I brushed it over the surface of the cake once I'd unmolded it. Once the liquid had sunk in, I drizzled the cake with the icing and set it aside to cool.

I took a bite of the final product, which really was packed with true, vibrant apple flavor. And since the cake itself was nothing more than a simple dump-and-stir style, it was a dessert I could casually throw together as a snack for tea or as an easy but elegant dessert for a crowd.

ANDREA GEARY, *Cook's Illustrated*

Cider-Glazed Apple Bundt Cake

SERVES 12 TO 16

For the sake of efficiency, begin boiling the cider before assembling the rest of the ingredients. Reducing the cider to exactly 1 cup is important; if you accidentally overreduce it, make up the difference with water. To ensure that the icing has the proper consistency, we recommend weighing the confectioners' sugar. We like the tartness of Granny Smith apples in this recipe, but any variety of apple will work. You can shred the apples with the shredding disk of a food processor or on the large holes of a paddle or box grater.

4 cups apple cider

3¾ cups (18¾ ounces) all-purpose flour

1½ teaspoons salt

1½ teaspoons baking powder

½ teaspoon baking soda

¾ teaspoon ground cinnamon

¼ teaspoon ground allspice

¾ cup (3 ounces) confectioners' sugar

16 tablespoons unsalted butter, melted

1½ cups packed (10½ ounces) dark brown sugar

3 large eggs

2 teaspoons vanilla extract

1½ pounds Granny Smith apples, peeled, cored, and shredded (3 cups)

1. Bring cider to boil in 12-inch skillet over high heat; cook until reduced to 1 cup, 20 to 25 minutes. While cider is reducing, adjust oven rack to middle position and heat oven to 350 degrees. Grease and flour 12-cup nonstick Bundt pan. Whisk flour, salt, baking powder, baking soda, cinnamon, and allspice in large bowl until combined. Place confectioners' sugar in small bowl.

2. Add 2 tablespoons cider reduction to confectioners' sugar and whisk to form smooth icing. Cover with plastic wrap and set aside. Set aside 6 tablespoons cider reduction.

3. Pour remaining ½ cup cider reduction into large bowl; add melted butter, brown sugar, eggs, and vanilla and whisk until smooth. Pour cider mixture over flour mixture and stir with rubber spatula until almost fully combined (some streaks of flour will remain). Stir in apples and any accumulated juice until evenly distributed. Transfer mixture to prepared pan and smooth top. Bake until skewer inserted in center of cake comes out clean, 55 minutes to 1 hour 5 minutes.

4. Transfer pan to wire rack set in rimmed baking sheet. Brush exposed surface of cake lightly with 1 tablespoon reserved cider reduction. Let cake cool for 10 minutes. Invert cake onto wire rack and remove pan. Brush top and sides of cake with remaining 5 tablespoons reserved cider reduction. Let cake cool for 20 minutes. Stir icing to loosen, then drizzle evenly over cake. Let cake cool completely, at least 2 hours, before serving. (Cooled cake can be wrapped loosely in plastic wrap and stored at room temperature for up to 3 days.)

POMEGRANATE WALNUT CAKE

✓ **WHY THIS RECIPE WORKS:** The combination of earthy walnuts and sweet-tart pomegranates is especially popular in savory dishes of the Middle East. We thought this pairing would also shine in a sweet application and set our sights on creating an elegant layer cake. We fortified a buttery yellow cake with tangy pomegranate molasses and a full cup and a half of walnuts that we finely chopped; toasting the walnuts deepened their flavor for an unmistakable presence. We tested a few frosting options, but the winner was a simple American buttercream flavored with more pomegranate molasses. We topped the cake with jewel-like fresh pomegranate seeds and stunning quick candied walnuts.

Cake is the all-occasion dessert. There are everyday cakes (snack cakes, pound cakes, rustic fruit cakes, and the like), and there are sky-high stunners (multilayered affairs with different fillings and swirls of buttercream). But then there's something in between: occasion cakes whose beauty is in their refined elegance. These are my favorite cakes to make; they're impressive but don't require complicated techniques, and they don't need to reach showy heights or hide under a heavy coat of frosting. I love a low, lush ganache-slicked torte or a flourless chocolate cake, but I had my sights set on something a little out of the ordinary.

After some consideration, my thoughts turned to a pairing commonly found in Middle Eastern cuisine: pomegranate and walnuts. Pomegranate seeds have a rich, jewel-like hue and provide bursts of tart-sweet flavor that elevate any dish, while walnuts contribute richness and a subtle toasted, nutty flavor. I pictured a modestly sized cake—two layers—filled, frosted, and topped with an attractive no-fuss garnish.

I knew that pomegranate flavor would be hard to infuse into the actual cake layers, and I didn't want to pockmark my cake with seeds. Instead I would focus on incorporating the walnuts into the cake itself and integrating the pomegranate flavor in other ways. Grinding the walnuts would make a nut "flour," but I didn't want the layers to get their structure from walnuts alone: A flourless walnut cake would be too delicate to stack and fill. Instead, I started with yellow cake layers (whose buttery flavor would be more appropriate here than white cake) and then added walnuts to the batter for flavor and texture. Baking powder provided some lift, so the cake batter wasn't too heavy and could handle the extra density and fat from the walnuts while still remaining fluffy and moist. The batter was also light enough that I could fold in the walnuts—a generous cup and a half, finely chopped—easily and disperse them evenly for a cake with great structure. Toasting the walnuts before chopping them deepened their flavor. These layers weren't too sweet and they had a rich, nutty flavor.

Filling and frosting the cake were my next tasks, and it was time to add in the pomegranate. A pomegranate buttercream sounded like a great idea: The tangy pomegranate would offset the rich sweetness inherent in buttercream. I tested a few fancy frostings, but they all were either too rich, too sweet, or simply too much work. In the end, the best was the most basic: an American buttercream, in which butter, sugar, salt, and a little cream are simply mixed until smooth. The addition of pomegranate juice incorporated too much moisture and made the frosting too loose; pomegranate molasses worked much better, contributing a concentrated hit of tartness. I whipped the frosting a little longer than is traditional to achieve an extra-fluffy texture. The pomegranate molasses gave the frosting a beautiful warm caramel color.

Although I knew one bite would reveal that this cake was something different, I wanted it to be unique in appearance as well, so I frosted only the center and top of the cake, leaving the sides exposed. This guaranteed that each bite was perfectly balanced and that the beautiful layers of cake and frosting were on display. For garnish, shiny vibrant pomegranate seeds were a given, but I also wanted to hint at the walnut flavor of the layers. Candying some walnuts gave them a sheen as brilliant as that of the pomegranate seeds. My process for candying the nuts was foolproof: I combined sugar, salt, more pomegranate molasses, and a splash of water with toasted walnut halves in a saucepan on the stovetop and mixed them over medium heat. As the mixture came to a boil and the water evaporated, the sugar began to caramelize and thicken. At this point, I turned the mixture out onto a baking sheet and let it sit until it was crunchy.

My frosted and topped pomegranate walnut cake features complex flavors and textures—crunchy topping; creamy frosting; fluffy, nutty cake layers; and a balance of sweetness, richness, and tang—that belie its relative simplicity. And it is everything I wanted—distinctive but approachable, modest but impressive, simultaneously rustic and regal. That to me is the perfect cake.

KATHRYN CALLAHAN, *America's Test Kitchen Books*

Pomegranate Walnut Cake

SERVES 10 TO 12

Pomegranate molasses is a pantry staple throughout the eastern portion of the Mediterranean that is made by reducing pomegranate juice. It can be found in the international aisle of most well-stocked supermarkets.

CAKE

- 2 cups (8 ounces) cake flour
- 2 teaspoons baking powder
- ¾ teaspoon salt
- 1½ cups walnuts, toasted
- 16 tablespoons unsalted butter, softened
- 1½ cups (10½ ounces) granulated sugar
- 4 large eggs, room temperature
- ½ cup whole milk, room temperature
- 1 tablespoon pomegranate molasses
- 2 teaspoons vanilla extract

CANDIED WALNUTS

- ⅔ cup walnuts, toasted
- 2 tablespoons granulated sugar
- 2 tablespoons water
- 2 teaspoons pomegranate molasses
- ¼ teaspoon salt

FROSTING

- 20 tablespoons (2½ sticks) unsalted butter, cut into 20 pieces and softened
- 2¼ cups (9 ounces) confectioners' sugar
- ⅛ teaspoon salt
- 2 tablespoons heavy cream
- 2 tablespoons pomegranate molasses
- 2 teaspoons vanilla extract
- 1 cup pomegranate seeds

1. FOR THE CAKE: Adjust oven rack to middle position and heat oven to 350 degrees. Grease two 9-inch round cake pans, line with parchment paper, grease parchment, and flour pans. Whisk flour, baking powder, and salt together in bowl.

2. Process walnuts in food processor until finely chopped, about 1 minute; transfer to bowl. Process butter, sugar, eggs, milk, pomegranate molasses, and vanilla in now-empty processor until mostly smooth, about 30 seconds (mixture may look slightly curdled). Add flour mixture and pulse until just incorporated, about 5 pulses. Add walnuts; pulse until just combined, about 5 pulses. Divide batter evenly between prepared pans and smooth tops with rubber spatula. Bake until toothpick inserted in center comes out clean, 24 to 28 minutes, switching and rotating pans halfway through baking. Let cakes cool in pans on wire rack for 10 minutes. Remove cakes from pans, discarding parchment, and let cool completely on rack, about 2 hours.

3. FOR THE CANDIED WALNUTS: Line rimmed baking sheet with parchment. Bring all ingredients to boil in medium saucepan over medium heat. Cook, stirring constantly, until water evaporates and sugar mixture coats nuts and looks glossy, about 5 minutes. Transfer walnuts to prepared sheet and spread into even layer. Let cool completely, about 10 minutes.

4. FOR THE FROSTING: Using stand mixer fitted with paddle, beat butter on medium-high speed until smooth, about 20 seconds. Add sugar and salt and mix on medium-low speed until most of sugar is moistened, about 45 seconds. Scrape down bowl. Add cream, pomegranate molasses, and vanilla and beat on medium-high speed until light and fluffy, about 5 minutes, scraping down bowl as needed.

5. Place 1 cake layer on platter. Spread half of frosting evenly over top, right to edge of cake. Top with second cake layer and press lightly to adhere. Spread remaining frosting evenly over top, right to edge of cake, leaving sides of cake exposed. Arrange candied walnut halves in ring around edge of cake. Spread pomegranate seeds in even layer inside ring of walnuts, covering all of exposed frosting. Serve.

BLACKBERRY-MASCARPONE LEMON CAKE

✔ **WHY THIS RECIPE WORKS:** In search of a truly show-stopping dessert, we created a cake that features layers of contrasting flavors and textures: tart lemon, sweet blackberries, and a silky rich mascarpone whipped cream. Lemon chiffon cake was the perfect base; it has a light fluffy texture but enough structure to stand four layers tall. Replacing half of the mascarpone with tangy cream cheese ensured a creamy texture for our frosting, while folding in gelatin-enhanced whipped cream provided structure. A final addition of a vibrant homemade blackberry jam made for a sophisticated frosting that was as beautiful as it was delicious. For a look as modern as the flavor profile, we scraped a thin veil of our frosting around the sides of our cake so the lovely layers peeked through.

One of my favorite recreational culinary hobbies is cake baking. I love stacking layers and decorating my creations to share with family and friends, so naturally I was thrilled when I was tasked with developing a recipe for a creative multilayer cake. And while I didn't know exactly how it would all come together, I had a basic vision in mind. I wanted my cake to be impressive in stature, standing four layers tall. And I wanted the flavors to be refreshing and unique, so rather than settle for the standard chocolate or vanilla layers, I would use a bright lemon cake as the base. Finally, I wanted a light whipped cream–style frosting. I decided to also feature blackberries, which would offer just enough sweet-tart flavor as well as a vibrant hue.

Many lemon cakes achieve the lemon flavor with a filling—often lemon curd—but I wanted the cake itself to carry the lemon flavor. I thought a chiffon-style cake, which features the airy lightness of angel food cake but the richness and moistness of pound cake, would be ideal here. However, when I followed a standard chiffon cake recipe, the initial results didn't exactly live up to my expectations: The layers were cottony and fluffy rather than moist and airy, and they lacked flavor. Decreasing the amount of flour meant a moister, more flavorful cake but also less structure, so instead I increased the

BLACKBERRY-MASCARPONE LEMON CAKE

amount of egg yolks. Also, instead of whipping all of the egg whites and later folding them into the batter, I found that mixing some of the whites into the dry ingredients along with the yolks, water, melted butter, and lemon juice provided the structure my cake needed. A modest amount of both lemon zest and juice made the layers refreshingly citrusy but not overpowering.

Even I don't own four 8-inch round cake pans, so my next task was determining the best way to bake four cake layers. I thought about dividing the batter between two pans and then carefully slicing the cakes in half horizontally, but I was hoping for a more foolproof approach. I decided the safest way didn't save time but it was certainly the easiest way: I made the batter twice, baking each batch after mixing the batter.

I had settled on a light frosting rather than a rich buttercream, but this was a special cake, so I wanted to do something more than whip cream and top the cake with blackberries. I decided to incorporate the fruit into the frosting. I was also intrigued by the possibility of adding mascarpone cheese, which would not only add a rich tanginess but also help fortify the frosting. But as I whipped batch after batch of frosting, I learned that incorporating mascarpone cheese takes some finesse—its high fat content can cause it to separate when over-agitated. Replacing half of the mascarpone with cream cheese solved this problem and made my frosting fool-proof. I whipped the two cheeses with sugar until just light and fluffy before folding in whipped cream, which I enhanced with gelatin to give it more structure; this gave me a frosting that was light but stable enough to support the cake layers.

I tried incorporating fresh pureed blackberries into my frosting, but the results were too tart and watery. To fix both problems, I made an easy homemade blackberry jam. This made for a sophisticated frosting that was as beautiful as it was delicious—the jam provided a lovely violet hue that stood out against the light-colored layers.

The combination of lemon, blackberry, and mascarpone had certainly created a unique flavor profile and I wanted to give my cake a look as modern as its taste. My thoughts immediately turned to naked cakes, which feature a sheer coating of frosting or completely bare sides. At once elegant and rustic, naked cakes showcase the juxtaposition of layer and filling to beautiful effect.

My whipped frosting was perfect for highlighting the first style of naked cake; a thin veil of this frosting revealed the yellow layers underneath for a stunning presentation. With its impressive height, bright flavors, and striking appearance, this was one cake that didn't need any fanciful decorations.

LEAH COLINS, *America's Test Kitchen Books*

Blackberry-Mascarpone Lemon Cake

SERVES 12 TO 16

Be sure to let the cake pans cool completely before repeating with more batter.

BLACKBERRY JAM

- 1 pound (3¼ cups) blackberries, plus extra for garnish
- 1 cup (7 ounces) granulated sugar

CAKE

- 2½ cups (10 ounces) cake flour
- 2 cups (14 ounces) granulated sugar
- 1 tablespoon baking powder
- ½ teaspoon salt
- 10 large eggs (4 whole, 6 separated), room temperature
- 12 tablespoons unsalted butter, melted and cooled
- ¼ cup water
- 2 teaspoons grated lemon zest plus ¼ cup juice (2 lemons)
- 4 teaspoons vanilla extract

MASCARPONE FROSTING

- 1 teaspoon unflavored gelatin
- 2 tablespoons water
- 8 ounces (1 cup) mascarpone cheese, room temperature
- 8 ounces cream cheese, softened
- ¼ cup (1 ounce) confectioners' sugar
- 1 teaspoon vanilla extract
- ⅛ teaspoon salt
- 2 cups heavy cream, chilled

1. FOR THE BLACKBERRY JAM: Process blackberries in food processor until smooth, about 1 minute; transfer to large saucepan. Stir sugar into blackberries and bring to boil over medium-high heat. Boil mixture, stirring often and adjusting heat as needed, until thickened and measures 1½ cups, 15 to 20 minutes. Transfer jam to bowl and let cool completely. (Jam can be refrigerated for up to 1 week; stir to loosen and bring to room temperature before using.)

2. FOR THE CAKE: Adjust oven rack to lower-middle position and heat oven to 325 degrees. Lightly grease two 8-inch round cake pans, line with parchment paper, grease parchment, and flour pans. Whisk 1¼ cups flour, ¾ cup sugar, 1½ teaspoons baking powder, and ¼ teaspoon salt together in large bowl. Whisk in 2 eggs and 3 yolks, 6 tablespoons butter, 2 tablespoons water, 1 teaspoon lemon zest and 2 tablespoons juice, and 2 teaspoons vanilla until smooth.

3. Using stand mixer fitted with whisk attachment, whip 3 egg whites on medium-low speed until foamy, about 1 minute. Increase speed to medium-high and whip whites to soft, billowy mounds, about 1 minute. Gradually add ¼ cup sugar and whip until glossy, soft peaks form, 1 to 2 minutes. Whisk one-third of whites into batter to lighten. Using rubber spatula, gently fold remaining whites into batter in 2 batches until no white streaks remain.

4. Divide batter evenly between prepared pans and smooth tops with rubber spatula. Bake until toothpick inserted in center comes out clean, 30 to 40 minutes, switching and rotating pans halfway through baking.

5. Let cakes cool in pans on wire rack for 10 minutes. Remove cakes from pans, discarding parchment, and let cool completely on rack, about 2 hours. Repeat steps 2 through 5 with remaining cake ingredients to make two more cake layers.

6. FOR THE MASCARPONE FROSTING: Sprinkle gelatin over water in bowl and let sit until gelatin softens, about 5 minutes. Microwave mixture in 5-second increments until gelatin is dissolved and liquefied.

7. Using clean, dry mixer bowl and whisk attachment, whip mascarpone, cream cheese, sugar, vanilla, and salt on medium speed until light and fluffy, about 30 seconds, scraping down bowl as needed; transfer to large bowl. Using clean, dry mixer bowl and whisk attachment, whip cream on medium-low speed until foamy, about 1 minute. Increase speed to high and whip until soft peaks just begin to form, about 1 minute, scraping down bowl as needed. Slowly pour in gelatin mixture, and continue to beat until stiff

peaks form, about 1 minute. Using rubber spatula, stir ⅓ of whipped cream into mascarpone mixture to lighten; gently fold remaining whipped cream into mixture in 2 additions. Stir room-temperature blackberry jam to loosen, then gently fold jam into mascarpone mixture until combined. Refrigerate frosting for at least 20 minutes or up to 24 hours before using.

8. Line edges of cake platter with 4 strips of parchment to keep platter clean and place small dab of frosting in center of platter to anchor cake. Place 1 cake layer on platter. Spread 1 cup frosting evenly over top, right to edge of cake. Repeat with 2 more cake layers, pressing lightly to adhere and spreading 1 cup frosting evenly over each layer. Top with remaining cake layer and spread 1½ cups frosting evenly over top. Spread remaining frosting evenly over sides of cake to cover with thin coat of frosting. Run edge of offset spatula around cake sides to create sheer veil of frosting. (Cake sides should still be visible.) Refrigerate cake for 20 minutes. Garnish with blackberries and carefully remove parchment strips before serving. (Cake can be refrigerated for up to 24 hours; bring to room temperature before serving.)

NOTES FROM THE TEST KITCHEN

FROSTING BLACKBERRY-MASCARPONE LEMON CAKE

1. After filling cake, spread 1½ cups frosting over top. Spread remaining frosting evenly over sides of cake to cover with thin coat of frosting.

2. Run edge of offset spatula around cake sides to create sheer veil of frosting.

HOOSIER PIE

WHY THIS RECIPE WORKS: Hoosier pie, also known as sugar cream pie, is an Indiana staple. To stay true to its humble roots, we used basic ingredients to make a creamy, sweet, custardy pie without even using eggs (which were once a precious commodity). While we loved the pie's simplicity, we encountered a few challenges wrangling the ingredients into a consistent product. To eliminate inconsistency, we opted to cook the custard and the pie crust separately and then marry the two. This gave us a crisp, crust and a creamy but sliceable custard filling every time.

Hoosier pie was born in Indiana as a "desperation dessert" in the 1800s, when fresh fruit was scarce and eggs weren't always easy to come by. In dreary winter months, innovative home cooks in need of a sweet fix turned to the basics: sugar, cream, and flour (and, whenever it was available, a tiny hit of nutmeg). They'd gently stir the handful of modest ingredients together right in the pie shell before baking it to produce a custardy, pudding-like pie.

I loved the poetic simplicity and ingenuity of the antique recipes I dug up, and as I read, I imagined how satisfying it would be to pull a perfectly thickened pie from the oven without even dirtying a mixing bowl. But the fantasy did not play out well in reality. After an hour in the oven, my first attempt at a modern-day Hoosier pie emerged soupy. Tasters happily slurped it up with spoons; they said it tasted like warm melted ice cream. But it was definitely not pie.

During subsequent tests varying timing and technique, I watched through the oven window as one erratic pie after another bubbled and sputtered, hot custard dripping onto the oven floor. A couple eventually set up, but most remained soupy. The only aspect all the pies shared was a soggy, raw bottom crust. Desperation? I was certainly feeling it now.

I decided to divide and conquer. Maybe tackling the crust and the filling separately and then marrying them would do the trick. By prebaking the pie shell, I could control the shape, color, and doneness before adding the filling. We've been down this road before, so this was an easy task. On to the filling.

I got out a saucepan and whisked cream, sugar, a touch of salt, and a couple of tablespoons of flour over medium heat until the mixture thickened. And thickened. And thickened some more, until it resembled paste. I adjusted the flour amount and cooking time until I got something that was still sliceable once chilled but not so pasty. I poured the cooked custard into a prebaked pie shell and let it set up in the refrigerator. Finally, a satisfying slice of pie with a crisp crust. Unfortunately, it tasted like raw flour.

Switching to cornstarch was another option. Since cornstarch has more thickening power than flour, I could use less of it in the mixture. Another bonus: Cornstarch doesn't have that floury flavor. And while eggs were off the table, nobody said I couldn't add butter. I threw in a little more than half a stick. The custard's flavor blossomed, and the butter helped it set.

Hoosier pie also goes by the name "sugar cream pie." We get it—it's supposed to be sweet. After experimenting with varying amounts of white sugar and even brown sugar, I found that the best balance came from 1 cup of white sugar boosted with a healthy dose of vanilla. A final dusting of ground nutmeg—but not too much!—pulled the whole pie together. I had a balanced, simple, sweet treat that delivered clear, comforting, old-timey flavor to my eager tasters.

KATIE LEAIRD, *Cook's Country*

Hoosier Pie

SERVES 8 TO 10

We opted for store-bought pie crust in this recipe for convenience (our favorite is Pillsbury Refrigerated Pie Crusts), but you can use any fully baked pie crust and proceed with the recipe from step 4.

CRUST

- 1 (9-inch) store-bought pie dough round

FILLING

- 1 cup (7 ounces) sugar
- ¼ cup cornstarch
- ¼ teaspoon salt
- 3 cups heavy cream
- 5 tablespoons unsalted butter, cut into 5 pieces
- 1 tablespoon vanilla extract
  Ground nutmeg

1. FOR THE CRUST: Adjust oven rack to lower-middle position and heat oven to 375 degrees. Roll dough into 12-inch circle on lightly floured counter. Loosely roll dough around rolling pin and gently unroll it onto

9-inch pie plate, letting excess dough hang over edge. Ease dough into plate by gently lifting edge of dough with your hand while pressing into plate bottom with your other hand.

2. Trim overhang to ½ inch beyond lip of plate. Tuck overhang under itself; folded edge should be flush with edge of plate. Crimp dough evenly around edge of plate using your fingers. Wrap dough-lined plate loosely in plastic wrap and freeze until dough is firm, about 15 minutes.

3. Line chilled pie shell with parchment paper or double layer of aluminum foil, covering edges to prevent burning, and fill with pie weights. Bake until edges are light golden brown, about 20 minutes, rotating plate halfway through baking. Remove parchment and weights and continue to bake until crust is golden brown, 7 to 11 minutes longer. Transfer plate to wire rack. (Pie shell needn't cool completely before proceeding.)

4. FOR THE FILLING: Whisk sugar, cornstarch, and salt together in large saucepan. Whisk in cream until combined. Add butter and cook over medium heat, whisking constantly, until mixture is thick and large bubbles appear at surface, 6 to 8 minutes. Continue to whisk 20 seconds longer. Off heat, whisk in vanilla. Pour custard into pie shell and smooth top with rubber spatula. Let cool completely, about 2 hours, then refrigerate until cold, about 2 hours. Garnish with nutmeg and serve.

COCONUT CREAM PIE

✓ **WHY THIS RECIPE WORKS:** We packed coconut into all three elements of this retro pie. Grinding sweetened shredded coconut together with Nilla Wafers made a crisp and flavorful cookie-crumb crust. Folding coconut into a milk custard gave us just the tamed tropical taste we wanted. And sprinkling toasted coconut over the whipped cream topping dressed the whole pie up with an inviting garnish.

I can still feel the magnetic pull of the rotating glass dessert displays that drew me into diners as a kid growing up in New Jersey. I found just about any greasy spoon's voluminous, mile-high cakes and pies mesmerizing. The coconut cream pie, with its lofty profile, billowing cream topping, and shaggy coconut garnish, especially called to me.

Fast-forward to the present day. When I started developing this recipe, I was dead set on building my pie in a traditional flaky crust because that is what I remembered about the pies from my childhood. But I loyally followed our test kitchen process, which entails testing a diverse range of recipes. Surprisingly, we all fell in love with the pie baked in one particular cookie crust. Nilla Wafers, shredded coconut, and an unconventionally hearty dash of salt added up to a clear winner. Plus, it was supereasy to work with. Prebaking the crust until it was golden brown and aromatic ensured that it was crisp and snappy—a texture that nicely contrasted with the creamy custard filling.

With my crust set, I turned my attention to the filling. Coconut is a versatile ingredient: Coconut milk gives Southern Indian curry its earthy creaminess, shredded coconut flakes make sweet macaroons and chewy confections, coconut cream is used in many tropical mixed drinks, and coconut extract finds its way into cookies and cakes. With so many products to choose from, I had to try them all to find the coconut flavor I craved.

Subtlety is not the name of the game with this pie, so I quickly dismissed coconut milk, as it delivered muted coconut flavor. And my team of tasters revolted when I snuck a few drops of coconut extract into the custard filling, reacting negatively to its artificial tinge.

Our favorite filling was fairly straightforward: a standard milk-based custard with sweetened shredded coconut stirred in once the custard had thickened. It had the light but stable texture I was after. For added richness, I used egg yolks, forgoing the egg whites, which can cause a custard to turn grainy (because whites coagulate faster than yolks when cooked).

It's customary to thicken a custard pie filling with a starch to make it sliceable, and I quickly ruled out flour because it made a stodgy filling. I ultimately chose cornstarch, which thickened the filling without announcing its presence. A thick custard also safeguarded against a soggy bottom crust.

No coconut cream pie would be complete without a heavy-handed pile of whipped cream on top. I did not shy away from tradition as I spread 3 cups of lightly sweetened, vanilla-scented whipped cream over my coconut custard. And then, to really dress it up, I sprinkled some toasted shredded coconut over the creamy white mountain. This final maneuver meant that all three components of this pie—crust, filling,

COCONUT CREAM PIE

and topping—contained forthright coconut flavor. My pie was ready for the diner dessert case—if only I could keep it away from my tasters.

KATIE LEAIRD, *Cook's Country*

Coconut Cream Pie

SERVES 8 TO 10

Let the crust cool completely before you begin making the filling—at least 30 minutes. Plan ahead: For the filling to set completely, this pie needs to be refrigerated for at least 3 hours or up to 24 hours before serving.

CRUST

- 2 cups (4½ ounces) Nilla Wafer cookies (34 cookies)
- ½ cup (1½ ounces) sweetened shredded coconut
- 2 tablespoons sugar
- 1 tablespoon all-purpose flour
- ¼ teaspoon salt
- 4 tablespoons unsalted butter, melted

FILLING

- 3 cups whole milk
- 5 large egg yolks
- 5 tablespoons cornstarch
- ¼ teaspoon salt
- ½ cup (3½ ounces) sugar
- ½ cup (1½ ounces) sweetened shredded coconut
- ½ teaspoon vanilla extract

TOPPING

- 1½ cups heavy cream, chilled
- 3 tablespoons sugar
- 1 teaspoon vanilla extract
- ¼ cup (¾ ounce) sweetened shredded coconut, toasted

1. FOR THE CRUST: Adjust oven rack to middle position and heat oven to 325 degrees. Process cookies, coconut, sugar, flour, and salt in food processor until finely ground, about 30 seconds. Add melted butter and pulse until combined, about 6 pulses. Transfer mixture to 9-inch pie plate. Using bottom of dry measuring cup, press crumbs firmly into bottom and up sides of plate. Bake until fragrant and set, 18 to 22 minutes. Transfer plate to wire rack and let crust cool completely.

2. FOR THE FILLING: Whisk ¼ cup milk, egg yolks, cornstarch, and salt together in large bowl. Bring sugar and remaining 2¾ cups milk to simmer in large saucepan over medium heat. Slowly whisk half of hot milk mixture into yolk mixture to temper.

3. Return milk-yolk mixture to remaining milk mixture in saucepan. Whisking constantly, cook over medium heat until custard is thickened and registers 180 degrees, 30 to 90 seconds. Remove from heat and stir in coconut and vanilla. Pour filling into cooled crust and spread into even layer.

4. Spray piece of parchment paper with vegetable oil spray and press flush onto surface of custard to cover completely and prevent skin from forming. Refrigerate until cold and set, at least 3 hours or up to 24 hours.

5. FOR THE TOPPING: Using stand mixer fitted with whisk attachment, whip cream, sugar, and vanilla on medium-low speed until foamy, about 1 minute. Increase speed to high and whip until stiff peaks form, 1 to 3 minutes. Spread whipped cream evenly over pie. Sprinkle coconut over top. Serve.

MODERN FRESH FRUIT TART

WHY THIS RECIPE WORKS: We traded the traditional rolled pastry and pastry cream filling of a classic fresh fruit tart for easier, faster alternatives. Stirring melted butter into the dry ingredients yielded a malleable dough that could be pressed into the pan. A mix of mascarpone cheese and melted white baking chips gave us a quick-to-make filling that was lush and creamy but also firm enough to slice cleanly. Arranging sliced peaches in lines radiating from the center of the tart to its edge created cutting guides between which we artfully arranged a mix of berries. A glaze of apricot preserves and lime juice brightened the fruit and gave the tart a polished, professional look.

A fresh fruit tart is the showpiece of a bakery pastry case—with its clean crust edge and ornate arrangement of fruit glistening with glaze, this dessert is beautiful and conveys a sense of occasion. But the pretty presentation literally falls apart when the knife meets the tart. Instead of neat wedges, you get shards of pastry oozing messy fruit and juice-stained filling. It seemed to me that the classic fresh fruit tart needed to be reconceptualized from crust to crown. I wanted the crust and filling to be sturdy and stable enough to retain their form when cut, and I wanted to streamline the preparation of these two components.

As it turned out, there were plenty of published recipes touting innovative approaches to the fresh fruit tart, starting with the crust. The most promising one traded the traditional *pâte sucrée*—in which cold butter is worked into flour and sugar, chilled, and rolled out—for a simpler pat-in-the-pan crust. This style of crust calls for nothing more than stirring melted butter into the flour mixture to create a pliable dough that is easily pressed into the pan and baked. I tried one such recipe: While the result was crisp and cookie-like rather than flaky, it still made a nice contrast to the creamy filling.

I had one tweak in mind: Since I would be melting the butter anyway, I'd try browning it to give the pastry a richer, nuttier character. But when I did this, the dough seemed dry and produced a sandy, cracked crust. I realized that by browning the butter, I had cooked off all its water. That meant there wasn't enough moisture for the proteins in the flour to form the gluten necessary to hold the crust together. Hoping the fix was as simple as putting some moisture back, I added a couple of tablespoons of water to the browned butter before mixing it with the dry ingredients. This worked perfectly: The dough was more cohesive and, after 30 minutes in a 350-degree oven, formed a crust that held together.

On to the filling. I wasn't keen on the traditional pastry cream, since you have to cook it, strain it, and let it cool before it's ready to use. Plus, I wanted a filling that wouldn't ooze from the crust when sliced. I needed something that was thick and creamy from the get-go, and mascarpone, the creamy, tangy-sweet cheese that's the star of tiramisù and many other Italian desserts, seemed like a good option. Sweetened with a little sugar and spread over the tart shell, it was a workable starting point, but it still wasn't dense enough to hold its shape when sliced. Thickeners such as gelatin, pectin, and cornstarch required either cooking or hydrating in liquid to be effective, as well as several hours to set up. A colleague had a better idea: white chocolate. I could melt it in the microwave and stir it into the mascarpone. Since white chocolate is solid at room temperature, it would firm up the filling as it cooled.

I melted white baking chips (they resulted in a firmer texture than white chocolate, which contains cocoa butter) and quickly realized that the melted mass was too thick to incorporate evenly into the mascarpone. I started again, this time adding ¼ cup of heavy cream, which loosened up the baking chips just enough for them to blend into the cheese. I smoothed the filling into the cooled crust, gently pressed in the fruit while the filling was still slightly warm (once cooled completely it would be too firm to hold the fruit neatly), brushed on a glaze, and refrigerated the tart for 30 minutes so the filling would set. I then allowed the tart to sit at room temperature for 15 minutes before slicing it.

The filling was satiny and, thanks to the baking chips, nicely firm. But I wondered if I could give it a little more oomph. In my next attempt I added bright, fruity lime juice, which—despite being a liquid—wouldn't loosen the filling. Instead, the acid would act on the cream's proteins, causing them to thicken; meanwhile, the cream's fat would prevent any graininess.

Since heating the lime juice would drive off its bright flavor, I stirred it in with the mascarpone; it paired beautifully with the rich cheese and white chocolate. For even more lime flavor, I added a teaspoon of zest, heating it with the chocolate and cream to draw out its flavor-packed oils.

Up to this point I'd been topping the tart with just berries; for even more appeal, I decided to add a couple of ripe peaches, peeled and cut into thin slices. But before I placed the fruit on the filling, I thought carefully about how to arrange it. Many tarts feature fruit organized in concentric circles. These look great when whole, but since you have to cut through the fruit when slicing, it winds up mangled, with the berries bleeding juice into the filling. Why not arrange the fruit so that the knife could slip between pieces?

First, I spaced eight berries around the outer edge of the tart. I then used these berries as guides to help me evenly arrange eight sets of three slightly overlapping peach slices so that they radiated from the center of the tart to its outer edge. The peach slices would serve as cutting guides for eight wedges. Next, I artfully arranged a mix of berries on each wedge. The final touch: I made a quick glaze using apricot preserves that I thinned with lime juice for easy dabbing.

The crisp, sturdy, rich crust; satiny yet stable filling; and bright-tasting fruit added up to a classic showpiece with modern flavor. Best of all, it was quick to make, and each slice looked just as polished and professional as the whole tart.

LAN LAM, *Cook's Illustrated*

FRESH FRUIT TART

Fresh Fruit Tart

SERVES 8

This recipe calls for extra berries to account for any bruising. Ripe, unpeeled nectarines can be substituted for the peaches, if desired. Use white baking chips here and not white chocolate bars, which contain cocoa butter and will result in a loose filling. Use a light hand when dabbing on the glaze. If the glaze begins to solidify while dabbing, microwave it for 5 to 10 seconds.

CRUST

1⅓ cups (6⅔ ounces) all-purpose flour

¼ cup (1¾ ounces) sugar

⅛ teaspoon salt

10 tablespoons unsalted butter

2 tablespoons water

TART

⅓ cup (2 ounces) white baking chips

¼ cup heavy cream

1 teaspoon grated lime zest plus 7 teaspoons juice (2 limes)

Pinch salt

6 ounces (¾ cup) mascarpone cheese, room temperature

2 ripe peaches, peeled

20 ounces (4 cups) raspberries, blackberries, and blueberries

⅓ cup apricot preserves

1. FOR THE CRUST: Adjust oven rack to middle position and heat oven to 350 degrees. Whisk flour, sugar, and salt together in bowl. Melt butter in small saucepan over medium-high heat, swirling saucepan occasionally, until foaming subsides. Cook, stirring and scraping bottom of saucepan with heatproof spatula, until milk solids are dark golden brown and butter has nutty aroma, 1 to 3 minutes. Remove saucepan from heat and add water. When bubbling subsides, transfer butter to bowl with flour mixture and stir until well combined. Transfer dough to 9-inch tart pan with removable bottom and let dough rest until just warm, about 10 minutes.

2. Use your hands to evenly press and smooth dough over bottom and up side of pan (using two-thirds of dough for bottom crust and remaining third for side). Place pan on wire rack set in rimmed baking sheet and bake until crust is golden brown, 25 to 30 minutes, rotating pan halfway through baking. Let crust cool completely, about 1 hour. (Cooled crust can be wrapped loosely in plastic wrap and stored at room temperature for up to 24 hours.)

3. FOR THE TART: Microwave baking chips, cream, lime zest, and salt in bowl, stirring every 10 seconds, until baking chips are melted, 30 to 60 seconds. Whisk in one-third of mascarpone, then whisk in 6 teaspoons lime juice and remaining mascarpone until smooth. Transfer filling to tart shell and spread into even layer.

4. Place peach, stem side down, on cutting board. Placing knife just to side of pit, cut down to remove 1 side of peach. Turn peach 180 degrees and cut off opposite side. Cut off remaining 2 sides. Place pieces cut side down and slice ¼ inch thick. Repeat with second peach. Select best 24 slices.

5. Evenly space 8 berries around outer edge of tart. Using berries as guide, arrange 8 sets of 3 peach slices in filling, slightly overlapping slices with rounded sides up, starting at center and ending on right side of each berry. Arrange remaining berries in attractive pattern between peach slices, covering as much of filling as possible and keeping fruit in even layer.

6. Microwave preserves and remaining 1 teaspoon lime juice in small bowl until fluid, 20 to 30 seconds. Strain mixture through fine-mesh strainer. Using pastry brush, gently dab mixture over fruit, avoiding crust. Refrigerate tart for 30 minutes.

7. Remove outer metal ring of tart pan. Slide thin metal spatula between tart and pan bottom to loosen tart, then carefully slide tart onto serving platter. Let tart sit at room temperature for 15 minutes. Using peaches as guide, cut tart into wedges and serve. (Tart can be refrigerated for up to 24 hours. If refrigerated for more than 1 hour, let tart sit at room temperature for 1 hour before serving.)

NOTES FROM THE TEST KITCHEN

MAKING AN EDIBLE SLICING GUIDE

Evenly arrange 8 berries around edge of tart, then arrange 8 sets of 3 overlapping peach slices from center to edge of tart on right side of each berry. Arrange remaining berries in attractive pattern between peach slices.

CARAMEL-CHOCOLATE-PECAN ICEBOX PIE

✓ **WHY THIS RECIPE WORKS:** What better way to showcase our Caramel-Chocolate-Pecan Sauce than in a decadent turtle pie? We opted for a cookie-crumb crust made with chocolate wafer cookies, which had a pleasant mild sweetness that contrasted with the sweet sauce. Many recipes save the caramel sauce for the topping only, but we preferred the sauce to be more integrated into the pie, so we decided to put a generous layer right on the baked crust. We then topped it off with a filling made with marshmallow crème, cream cheese, heavy cream, peanut butter, and butter. The cream cheese tempered the sweetness of the marshmallow crème, while the heavy cream helped to make the filling fluffy and light. Drizzling some additional sauce on top of the pie gave it an appealing finish and drove the turtle flavor home.

When I was assigned to work on the dessert chapter of our new book on sauces, I happily accepted the task. The test kitchen already has great recipes for caramel sauces, chocolate sauces, fruit-based sauces, and custardy sauces like crème anglaise, so I was looking for a new and unique concoction. It didn't take me long to decide that I wanted to create a recipe featuring a trio of ingredients—rich chocolate, buttery caramel, and crunchy pecans—based on the classic confection called a turtle.

I knew from the outset that I would use a caramel sauce as the base. Classic caramel sauces typically require a thermometer and careful timing; but since I would be adding lots of additional flavor in the form of chocolate and pecans, I wondered if the process of making a "true" caramel was really necessary.

A second type of caramel sauce is a butterscotch sauce. It uses brown sugar for deep toffee flavor and requires heating the sugar with corn syrup, butter, and water only until the sugar dissolves—no temping needed. You then stir in the cream and vanilla and the sauce is done. It's less fussy to make than traditional caramel but still boasts rich, buttery flavor. I decided to use this as the starting point for my turtle sauce.

Next I needed to figure out how to best incorporate the chocolate. I started by making a batch of butterscotch sauce and then adding a couple ounces of finely chopped semisweet bar chocolate off the heat. I left it to sit for a few minutes so the chocolate could melt, then gave it a whisk to blend everything together. To my dismay, this sauce turned out broken, greasy, and grainy. Thinking that the butterscotch may have been too hot, I tried letting it cool until it was merely warm before adding the chocolate. But the problem persisted. After a few more botched attempts with different amounts of chocolate as well as chocolate chips (which contain stabilizers that I hoped would help), I took a step back. What was happening?

After consulting with our science editor, I realized my problem: When chocolate is melted, its ingredients—mainly cocoa solids, sugar, and cocoa butter—disperse evenly, creating a fluid mass. But if moisture is introduced, the liquid and the sugar will form a syrup which cements the cocoa particles together, creating grainy clumps (a process known as "seizing"). In the case of my butterscotch sauce, the moisture was coming from the butter—which contains water—as well as the sugar itself. That water never has a chance to fully evaporate since the sauce cooks so briefly.

Counterintuitively, the best way to smooth out seized chocolate is by adding more liquid, which dissolves most of the sugar and disperses the cocoa particles in the chocolate clumps. With that in mind, I tried stirring in more cream, but by the time I had stirred in enough to smooth out the sauce, the sauce's flavor was so diluted it was barely recognizable as either caramel or chocolate.

I decided it was time to reverse course and try the real-deal caramel instead. Because this caramel is cooked to such a high temperature, most of the water in the sugar is cooked off. And although the cream that gets stirred in at the end does contain some water, much of it evaporates quickly on contact with the hot caramel; meanwhile, the fat in the cream further stabilizes the mixture.

I made a traditional caramel and then followed the same process as before of adding chopped chocolate to the caramel off the heat, allowing it to melt, and then whisking the two ingredients together. This sauce was beautifully smooth and shiny, if a bit too sweet. Switching to bittersweet chocolate easily solved this problem.

Of course, to make this a true turtle sauce, it still needed pecans. Toasting the nuts deepened their flavor and highlighted the flavor of the caramel, and chopping them allowed the pecans to easily blend in to the sauce.

I could easily just pour this sauce over ice cream, but I wanted to develop a truly special dessert that would make this sauce shine. Since the sauce itself was a riff on a classic candy, I decided to run with that theme but translate it into an impressive yet simple pie.

Rather than traditional pie crust, I opted for a cookie crust made from chocolate wafer cookies and melted butter that could simply be pressed into the pie plate. I wanted my sauce to be truly integrated into the pie, so I decided to pour a thin layer right onto the baked crust. For the filling itself, I took inspiration from another candy bar element: nougat. Wanting to keep the filling simple, I started by combining marshmallow crème with peanut butter (to highlight the nutty flavors in my sauce), along with some butter and heavy cream for a fluffy, luxurious texture.

I was getting close, but tasters felt the filling was a bit too sweet and there wasn't enough of the turtle sauce—it got lost. Adding some tangy cream cheese to the filling easily solved the sweetness issue. I also upped the amount of sauce that I was pouring onto the crust and drizzled some on top of the pie as well. When I called my tasters back, I took their contented smiles as confirmation that my turtle sauce had found its true calling.

JOSEPH GITTER, *America's Test Kitchen Books*

Caramel-Chocolate-Pecan Icebox Pie

SERVES 8 TO 10

The sauce will need to be warm so that it is pourable. We developed this recipe with Fluff brand marshmallow crème, but any brand of marshmallow crème will work; do not use products labeled marshmallow sauce or marshmallow topping. When working with the marshmallow crème, grease both the inside of your measuring cup and a spatula with vegetable oil spray to prevent sticking.

CRUST

- 25 chocolate wafer cookies (5½ ounces), broken into coarse pieces
- 4 tablespoons unsalted butter, melted

FILLING

- 1 recipe Caramel-Chocolate-Pecan Sauce (recipe follows)
- 8 ounces cream cheese, softened
- 1 cup marshmallow crème

- ½ cup heavy cream
- ½ cup creamy peanut butter
- 2 tablespoons unsalted butter, softened

1. FOR THE CRUST: Adjust oven rack to middle position and heat oven to 325 degrees. Process cookie pieces in food processor until finely ground, about 30 seconds. Add melted butter and pulse until combined, about 6 pulses. Sprinkle mixture into 9-inch pie plate. Using flat bottom of dry measuring cup, press crumbs firmly into even layer on bottom and sides of pie plate. Bake until crust is fragrant and set, about 15 minutes. Transfer to wire rack and let cool slightly.

2. FOR THE FILLING: Pour 1 cup of sauce into bottom of cooled crust and refrigerate, uncovered, until set, about 30 minutes.

3. Using stand mixer fitted with paddle, beat cream cheese, marshmallow crème, heavy cream, peanut butter, and butter on medium-high speed until light and fluffy, about 5 minutes, scraping down sides of bowl as needed. Spread filling evenly into crust. Cover pie and refrigerate until filling is chilled and set, at least 2 hours or up to 1 day. Drizzle remaining sauce attractively over top of pie and serve.

Caramel-Chocolate-Pecan Sauce

MAKES ABOUT 1½ CUPS

We prefer an instant-read thermometer for measuring the temperature of caramel. To ensure an accurate reading, swirl the caramel to even out hot spots, then tilt the pot so that the caramel pools 1 to 2 inches deep. Move the thermometer back and forth for about 5 seconds before taking a reading.

- 1 cup (7 ounces) sugar
- ⅓ cup water
- 3 tablespoons light corn syrup
- ¾ cup heavy cream
- 2 ounces bittersweet chocolate, chopped
- 1 tablespoon unsalted butter, chilled
- ½ cup pecans, toasted and chopped
- 1 teaspoon vanilla extract
- ⅛ teaspoon salt

1. Bring sugar, water, and corn syrup to boil in large saucepan over medium-high heat. Cook, without stirring, until mixture is straw-colored, 6 to 8 minutes.

CARAMEL-CHOCOLATE-PECAN ICEBOX PIE

Reduce heat to low and continue to cook, swirling saucepan occasionally, until caramel is amber-colored, 2 to 5 minutes. (Caramel will register between 360 and 370 degrees.)

2. Off heat, carefully stir in cream; mixture will bubble and steam. Stir in chocolate and butter and let sit for 3 minutes. Whisk sauce until smooth and chocolate is fully melted. Stir in pecans, vanilla, and salt. Let cool slightly. (Sauce can be refrigerated for up to 2 weeks; gently warm in microwave, stirring every 10 seconds, until pourable, before using.)

CHOCOLATE SEMIFREDDO

WHY THIS RECIPE WORKS: For a chocolate *semifreddo* that was rich and creamy but not overly complicated, we started by preparing a custard-style base of whole eggs, sugar, cream, and water directly on the stovetop (rather than over a fussy water bath). We conveniently melted the chocolate by straining the hot custard directly over it. To ensure a rich, creamy, and sliceable semifreddo that was also cold and refreshing, we had to balance fat and water: Using whole eggs instead of yolks and cutting the cream in the custard base with a bit of water were key. Garnishing the semifreddo with a sweet cherry sauce and crunchy candied nuts added contrast and made for an elegant presentation.

I love ice cream, but it isn't the most elegant way to cap off an evening. Serving a scoop (even homemade) at a dinner party always feels a little too casual. Enter *semifreddo*, a classic Italian dessert that's often described as a frozen mousse. (Though it's fully frozen, its name roughly translates as "half-frozen.") There are many styles, but like ice cream (or gelato), semifreddo typically starts with a custard base. However, instead of being churned in an ice cream maker, semifreddo is lightened with whipped cream and/or beaten egg whites. Then it's frozen in a loaf pan until solid, unmolded, and cut into neat slices. But instead of being hard and densely packed, semifreddo is soft enough that it easily caves to the pressure of a spoon. Better yet, unlike ice cream, it can sit out of the freezer for an extended period of time without melting, which makes it ideal for serving to company. An elegant frozen dessert that doesn't require an ice cream maker, doesn't melt easily,

and is make-ahead by design? That checks a lot of boxes for me, so I tried a bunch of chocolate versions (my favorite flavor) that looked appealing.

I ruled out using whipped egg whites to lighten the custard, as they tended to produce a marshmallow-like semifreddo. I wanted a version that was lush and rich, so whipped cream would be my aerator of choice.

I started with a particularly rich custard from my research: I heated ¾ cup of heavy cream in a saucepan, thoroughly whisked it into five beaten egg yolks mixed with a few tablespoons of sugar, and poured the custard back into the saucepan to cook gently until it reached 160 degrees. I poured the hot custard over 8 ounces of chopped bittersweet chocolate so that the chocolate melted, which saved me the extra step of melting it beforehand. Once the custard cooled, I gently folded in softly whipped cream. Finally, I poured the custard into a plastic wrap–lined loaf pan and froze it until solid, which took about 6 hours.

But I had gone overboard: While the semifreddo had deep chocolate flavor, it was so rich that I couldn't eat more than a few bites. Also, despite the fact that it had just come out of the freezer, it seemed to lack a certain refreshing coldness. I tried replacing the heavy cream with an equal amount of milk, but now my semifreddo was too lean. It also seemed overly cold, almost like a popsicle, and melted a lot faster.

I would obviously need to add back some fat, so for my next batch, I used heavy cream cut with ¼ cup water (this combo still had more fat than milk alone). This time I nailed it: The semifreddo was lush, sliced neatly, and—interestingly—tasted cold without feeling numbingly so. The only drawback was the fussy step of separating all those eggs, so I tried again with a combination of heavy cream, water, and three whole eggs instead of five yolks. The results were even better—the perfect balance of decadent and refreshing, thanks to the extra water in the egg whites.

After a conversation with our science editor, I learned why the dessert had seemed more or less cold, depending on how much fat was in it: When you put a spoonful of frozen dessert on your tongue and you feel its coldness, that's because heat energy is transferring from your tongue into the dessert, making your tongue colder. The extent to which that happens—and hence the amount of coldness you feel—depends not only on the temperature of the dessert but also on its ingredients, such as the amount of fat versus water.

Though some semifreddo recipes call for mixing candied fruit, nuts, or cookies into the custard, I enjoyed my version's smooth, creamy texture and was hesitant to change it. But a garnish would offer textural contrast and make the dessert look more festive.

In my research I'd seen a chocolate semifreddo with a cherry sauce spooned over each slice, so I put together my own version made with frozen sweet cherries, sugar, kirsch (cherry brandy), and a little cornstarch for body. The color and flavor were vivid, and the plump fruit nicely complemented the satiny semifreddo. For a bit of crunch, I made a batch of candied nuts.

Rich and satiny. Elegant. Deeply chocolaty. Make-ahead (you can even slice off a portion and freeze the rest for later). No ice cream maker required. Time to plan another dinner party.

ANNIE PETITO, *Cook's Illustrated*

Chocolate Semifreddo

SERVES 12

The *semifreddo* needs to be frozen for at least 6 hours before serving. We developed this recipe with Ghirardelli 60% Cacao Bittersweet Chocolate Premium Baking Bar. Do not whip the heavy cream until the chocolate mixture has cooled. If the semifreddo is difficult to release from the pan, run a thin offset spatula around the edges of the pan or carefully run the sides of the pan under hot water for 5 to 10 seconds. If frozen overnight, the semifreddo should be tempered before serving for the best texture. To temper, place slices on individual plates or a large tray, and refrigerate for 30 minutes. Serve the semifreddo as is or with our Cherry Sauce and/or Quick Candied Nuts (recipes follow).

8	ounces bittersweet chocolate, chopped fine
1	tablespoon vanilla extract
½	teaspoon instant espresso powder
3	large eggs
5	tablespoons sugar
¼	teaspoon salt
2	cups heavy cream, chilled
¼	cup water

1. Lightly spray loaf pan with vegetable oil spray and line with plastic wrap, leaving 3-inch overhang on all sides. Place chocolate in large heatproof bowl; set fine-mesh strainer over bowl and set aside. Stir vanilla and espresso powder in small bowl until espresso powder is dissolved.

2. Whisk eggs, sugar, and salt in medium bowl until combined. Heat ½ cup cream (keep remaining 1½ cups chilled) and water in medium saucepan over medium heat until simmering. Slowly whisk hot cream mixture into egg mixture until combined. Return mixture to saucepan and cook over medium-low heat, stirring constantly and scraping bottom of saucepan with rubber spatula, until mixture is very slightly thickened and registers 160 to 165 degrees, about 5 minutes. Do not let mixture simmer.

3. Immediately pour mixture through strainer set over chocolate. Let mixture stand to melt chocolate, about 5 minutes. Whisk until chocolate is melted and smooth, then whisk in vanilla-espresso mixture. Let chocolate mixture cool completely, about 15 minutes.

4. Using stand mixer fitted with whisk attachment, beat remaining 1½ cups cream on low speed until bubbles form, about 30 seconds. Increase speed to medium and beat until whisk leaves trail, about 30 seconds. Increase speed to high and continue to beat until nearly doubled in volume and whipped cream forms soft peaks, 30 to 45 seconds longer.

5. Whisk one-third of whipped cream into chocolate mixture. Using rubber spatula, gently fold remaining whipped cream into chocolate mixture until incorporated and no streaks of whipped cream remain. Transfer mixture to prepared pan and spread evenly with rubber spatula. Fold overhanging plastic over surface. Freeze until firm, at least 6 hours.

6. When ready to serve, remove plastic from surface and invert pan onto serving plate. Remove plastic and smooth surface with spatula as necessary. Dip slicing knife in very hot water and wipe dry. Slice semifreddo ¾ inch thick, transferring slices to individual plates and dipping and wiping knife after each slice. Serve immediately. (Semifreddo can be wrapped tightly in plastic wrap and frozen for up to 2 weeks.)

Cherry Sauce

MAKES ABOUT 2 CUPS

This recipe was developed with frozen cherries. Do not thaw the cherries before using. Water can be substituted for the kirsch, if desired.

CHOCOLATE SEMIFREDDO

12 ounces frozen sweet cherries

¼ cup sugar

2 tablespoons kirsch

1½ teaspoons cornstarch

1 tablespoon lemon juice

1. Combine cherries and sugar in bowl and microwave for 1½ minutes. Stir, then continue to microwave until sugar is mostly dissolved, about 1 minute longer. Combine kirsch and cornstarch in small bowl.

2. Drain cherries in fine-mesh strainer set over small saucepan. Return cherries to bowl and set aside.

3. Bring juice in saucepan to simmer over medium-high heat. Stir in kirsch mixture and bring to boil. Boil, stirring occasionally, until mixture has thickened and appears syrupy, 1 to 2 minutes. Remove saucepan from heat and stir in cherries and lemon juice. Let sauce cool completely before serving. (Sauce can be refrigerated for up to 1 week.)

Quick Candied Nuts

MAKES ½ CUP

We like this recipe with pistachios, walnut or pecan halves, roasted cashews, peanuts, and sliced almonds. If you want to make a mixed batch, cook the nuts individually and then combine once you've chopped them.

½ cup nuts

1 tablespoon sugar

1 tablespoon hot water

⅛ teaspoon salt

1. Adjust oven rack to middle position and heat oven to 350 degrees. Spread nuts in single layer on rimmed baking sheet and toast until fragrant and slightly darkened, 8 to 12 minutes, shaking sheet halfway through toasting. Transfer nuts to plate and let cool for 10 to 15 minutes. Do not wash sheet.

2. Line now-empty sheet with parchment paper. Whisk sugar, hot water, and salt in large bowl until sugar is mostly dissolved. Add nuts and stir to coat. Spread nuts on prepared sheet in single layer and bake until nuts are crisp and dry, 10 to 12 minutes.

3. Transfer sheet to wire rack and let nuts cool completely, about 20 minutes. Transfer nuts to cutting board and chop as desired. (Nuts can be stored at room temperature for up to 1 week.)

MAINE POTATO-COCONUT CANDY

WHY THIS RECIPE WORKS: Also known as potato fudge or potato candy, Needhams are an heirloom candy from Maine featuring a creamy, coconut-studded base built on mashed potatoes. To avoid boiling and then mashing only part of one potato, we instead used dried potato flakes: Just ¼ cup mixed with hot milk and melted butter made the perfect amount of unseasoned mashed potatoes for the candy base. We stirred in confectioners' sugar, sweetened shredded coconut, and vanilla and then let the mixture firm up in the refrigerator. To create the candies' snappy-textured chocolate coating, it was essential to slowly melt the chocolate so it would recrystallize around the candies. We melted 12 ounces of finely chopped bittersweet chocolate and then added another 4 ounces of finely chopped chocolate and stirred until smooth to get the chocolate to set up once the candies were coated.

Needhams (also known as potato fudge or potato candy) are an heirloom Maine candy with an unexpected twist: their creamy, coconutty base is built on mashed spuds. You can't taste the potatoes in these treats, which resemble Mounds candy bars in texture and flavor. They were popularized in the late 1800s by their namesake, the Reverend George C. Needham of Aroostook County, Maine (a big potato-growing region), who, the story goes, made them for his parishioners.

I was admittedly skeptical when I made the first batch of these sweets, but I was pleasantly surprised to discover that plain, unseasoned mashed potatoes (the flavor of which disappeared when I mixed them with milk, butter, powdered sugar, and coconut) did a great job of binding the filling together. A few versions I tried were too sweet. Also, I wasn't thrilled about having to peel, chop, boil, and mash potatoes to make them. (Some recipes simply call for leftover mashed potatoes, but they are usually seasoned with salt and pepper and wouldn't do here.)

First, I tackled the filling. Many recipes call for boiling and mashing one potato and measuring it (discarding any extra potato), but I turned to a shortcut—dried potato flakes. Adding hot milk and melted butter to just ¼ cup of potato flakes gave me the perfect amount of unseasoned mashed potatoes. After stirring in confectioners' sugar and sweetened coconut (and a little vanilla), I spooned the filling into an 8-inch baking pan and refrigerated it until firm. Once it was firm, I cut the slab into bite-size pieces and got ready to dip them in melted chocolate.

But producing a hard, snappy chocolate shell that didn't melt in your hands wasn't as easy as merely melting chocolate and dipping the candies in, as some recipes suggest. When chocolate is melted and cooled, its chemical structure changes and it becomes squishy and looks dull. To avoid this, chocolate can be tempered (carefully heated, cooled, and reheated on the stovetop). Luckily, the test kitchen has developed an easy method for tempering chocolate in the microwave that worked great here.

When tasters bit into the coated and cooled candies, the chocolate snapped to reveal a perfectly sweet—but not cloying—coconut-rich filling that only I knew was bound by a most unlikely candy-making ingredient: potato. I think I just became an honorary Mainer.

CECELIA JENKINS, *Cook's Country*

Needhams (Potato Candy)

MAKES 36 PIECES

We prefer Ghirardelli 60% Cacao Bittersweet Chocolate Premium Baking Bars here. For the coating to set properly, you must chop the chocolate fine and then melt it gently and slowly in the microwave, stirring often so it heats evenly. In step 5, the chocolate will still be lumpy; do not be tempted to microwave it until completely smooth. The residual heat from the bowl, along with continued stirring and mashing with a rubber spatula, should melt the remaining chocolate plus any leftover lumps. The chocolate is divided here, so if you don't have a scale, note that each Ghirardelli bar weighs 4 ounces. Do not use chocolate chips in this recipe.

    6 tablespoons unsalted butter
    3 tablespoons whole milk
    ¼ teaspoon salt
    ¼ cup (½ ounce) plain instant mashed potato flakes
    1 teaspoon vanilla extract
    1½ cups (6 ounces) confectioners' sugar
    1½ cups (4½ ounces) sweetened shredded coconut
    1 pound bittersweet chocolate, chopped fine

1. Make foil sling for 8-inch square baking pan by folding 1 long sheet of aluminum foil so it is 8 inches wide. Lay foil sheet in pan with extra foil hanging over edges of pan. Push foil into corners and up sides of pan, smoothing foil flush to pan. Spray foil with vegetable oil spray.

2. Microwave butter, milk, and salt in medium bowl until butter is melted and mixture is bubbling, about 2 minutes. Stir in potato flakes and vanilla until mixture resembles applesauce, about 30 seconds (mixture will look oily). Stir in sugar and coconut until no dry spots remain and mixture forms loose paste.

3. Transfer coconut mixture to prepared pan and, using rubber spatula, press firmly into thin, even layer reaching into corners of pan. Cover with plastic wrap and refrigerate until firm, at least 2 hours or up to 24 hours.

4. Flip coconut mixture onto cutting board; discard foil. Cut into 36 (1-inch) squares (5 horizontal cuts by 5 vertical cuts). Separate squares into 2 batches and keep half refrigerated while working with other half. Line rimmed baking sheet with parchment paper.

5. Microwave 12 ounces chocolate in medium bowl at 50 percent power, stirring with rubber spatula every 15 seconds, until about two-thirds melted, about 1½ minutes (chocolate should still be lumpy). Remove bowl from microwave and add remaining 4 ounces chocolate. Stir and mash until chocolate is just melted and smooth, about 3 minutes. (If lumps remain, you may return chocolate to microwave at 50 percent power for no more than 5 seconds at a time, stirring at each interval, until fully melted.)

6. Drop several coconut squares into chocolate. Using 2 forks, gently flip squares to coat on all sides. One at a time, use fork to lift squares from chocolate. Tap fork against edge of bowl and then wipe underside of fork on edge of bowl to remove excess chocolate from bottom of candy. Use second fork to slide candy onto prepared sheet.

7. Repeat with remaining coconut squares and remaining chocolate, cleaning forks as needed. (As chocolate begins to set, microwave it at 50 percent power for no more than 5 seconds at a time, stirring at each interval, until fluid. Expect to microwave chocolate at least twice during coating process.)

8. Refrigerate candy until chocolate is set, 25 to 30 minutes. Serve. (Candy can be refrigerated in airtight container for up to 1 week.)

NEEDHAMS (POTATO CANDY)

TEST KITCHEN RESOURCES

*Every product tested may not be listed in these pages. Please visit
CooksIllustrated.com and CooksCountry.com to find complete
listings and information on all products tested and reviewed.*

BEST KITCHEN QUICK TIPS

STACKING BOWLS OF SOFT FOOD

Creamy desserts, such as pudding or crème brûlée, are often portioned into small dishes and covered with plastic wrap to chill before serving, but they take up a lot of refrigerator space. Mary Veazey Clark of Greensburg, Pa., makes them stackable by covering the dishes with stiff plastic lids she saves from yogurt containers. (This also works for portioned sauces, dips, and condiments.)

FITTING BREAD TO A TOASTER

To fit oblong artisan-style breads into her pop-up toaster, Diane Delu of Pleasant Hill, Calif., cuts the bread against a homemade cardboard pattern that mirrors the dimensions of her toaster's slot.

MAKESHIFT PIE CARRIER

To safely transport her homemade pies, Jeanne Carl of Port Washington, N.Y., slips the pie inside an empty large cereal box.

TRIM LEMONS TO GET THE MOST JUICE

While juicing lemons, Barbara Belknap of Oneonta, N.Y., found that the hard, pointy end of the fruit kept her from squeezing out the maximum amount of juice. By trimming off the end and creating a flat edge, she discovered she could press out more juice.

RECYCLE SODA CANS AS GREASE RECEPTACLES

Jeff Bartlett of Hopedale, Mass., uses empty soda cans as receptacles for hot cooking fats, such as bacon grease or frying oil. He removes the top of the can completely with a can opener, making it easy to pour the fat into the wide opening.

A TIGHT FOIL COVER

When covering a roasting pan of braising meat with aluminum foil, Richard Le of Cambridge, Mass., uses metal binder clips to hold the foil in place.

STORING FRAGILE FIGS

Figs bruise and spoil quickly if kept in a bowl or dish where they are all touching each other, so Emma Brinkmeyer of San Luis Obispo, Calif., keeps them in an empty egg carton. Each fig gets its own space, and the spaces are just big enough to allow the figs to sit upright.

SUGAR SHAKER

Lorna Freed of Grand Rapids, Mich., doesn't own a dedicated sugar shaker, so when she needs to dust confectioners' sugar or cocoa powder over desserts or sprinkle flour on a counter, she fashions a shaker from cheesecloth. She cuts a small square, heaps the powder in the center, and knots the top of the cheesecloth.

PICNIC KNIFE HOLDER

When packing utensils for a picnic, Jeanne Fletcher of Telford, Pa., likes to have a paring knife on hand for cutting fruit, cheese, or sandwiches. For a make-shift knife guard, she purchased a plastic toothbrush holder, which holds the knife securely. (The holder also works well to contain knives in the utensil drawer.)

SAVE STALE CRACKERS FOR BREADING

Pamela Berube of Columbus, Ohio, collects stale plain crackers in a zipper-lock bag and stores them in the freezer.

After a couple of months of adding to the bag, she has enough crackers to blitz in the food processor and combine with herbs or spices to make a flavorful breading for baked chicken, fish, or pork chops.

PINCH-CRIMP PIE PASTRY

Claire Schaffer of Denver, Colo., crimps the edges of pie dough with a pair of tongs. Gently pressing the pincers into the pastry leaves identical impressions for a neat-looking finish.

WHISK A WHISK CLEAN

To clean a whisk after mixing pancake batter, Diane Scalisi of Aptos, Calif., puts warm soapy water in the dirty mixing bowl and beats it with the whisk. To rinse it, she repeats the process with plain warm water.

RUBBER-GLOVE RUBBER BANDS

Eleanor Hammonds of Austin, Texas, has found a way to reuse part of her old pairs of rubber gloves. She turns them into rubber bands by cutting narrow rings from the cuffs.

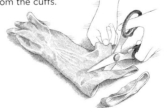

RECORDING BOWL WEIGHTS

Sometimes Cindy Hoyt of Kennard, Texas, forgets to tare her kitchen scale after putting a bowl on it and adding the first ingredient, forcing her to dump it out and start over. To remedy this, she wrote the bowls' weights on the side of each using permanent marker (masking tape comes off in the dishwasher). Now, if she forgets to tare the scale, she just subtracts the bowl weight from the weight of the first ingredient.

REHEATING WAFFLES IN A WAFFLE IRON

Rose Stewart of Burlington, Vt., was going to turn on the oven to reheat leftover homemade waffles when she realized she could just use her waffle iron. She preheated the iron to a low setting and put a waffle inside to warm up. All the nooks and crannies recrisped to a texture just like that of a freshly cooked waffle.

MINIMIZING THE MESS OF STOVETOP SPLATTER

To keep stovetop grease from splattering onto unused burners, Drew Goodwin of Maynard, Mass., puts a new 12 by 12-inch floor tile over each one. The tiles are easy to clean, and they act as added counter space.

BEST KITCHEN QUICK TIPS

KEEPING COOKBOOKS OPEN FOR COOKING

John Sauve of Toronto, Ontario, figured out a way to keep cookbooks open while he's cooking from them: He straps an elastic band to each side of the book on the page he wants open and braces the book with a wooden spoon on the cover side, spanning the spine like a cross. The book sits perfectly on the counter without bending the spine.

HOT POT FOR GRAVY

To keep gravy hot for serving, Kathleen Quinn of Wilmington, Del., stores it in a ceramic teapot instead of in a traditional gravy boat. The lidded pot keeps the gravy hotter than a gravy boat can, and the spout makes for tidy pouring.

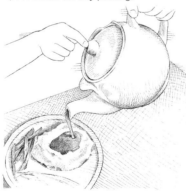

MAKESHIFT STOCK SACHET

Michele Hershey of Kihei, Hawaii, uses the netting she's saved from onions, oranges, and other produce as a sachet when making stock. She places ingredients such as shrimp shells or herbs in the netting (using two layers of netting if the holes are large) and adds the bundle to the pot; once the flavors have been extracted, she can easily retrieve and discard the bundle.

CLIP—OR STITCH—TACOS CLOSED

To prevent a soft taco from spilling open while stuffing others, Sue Wallin of Seattle, Wash., uses one of two tricks for keeping the stuffed tortillas closed: She pinches them with a bag clip, or threads a toothpick through the top of the tortilla, holding the taco together much like it would a club sandwich.

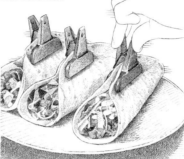

"SKIMMING" FAT WITH SUCTION

Holly Elmsley of Detroit, Mich., removes fat from the top of her pot of soup or stew with a turkey baster. The tool quickly suctions off the grease and can remove more at a time than a spoon can.

STOP CUTTING BOARDS FROM SLIDING

To prevent her cutting boards from sliding in the kitchen cabinet, Janyce Turturici of Novato, Calif., glues rubber doorstops to the floor of the cabinet. The angled doorstops are sturdy enough to keep the boards upright so that she can store several of them in the same space.

IMPROVISED LAME FOR BREAD BAKING

Ben Sobel of Cambridge, Mass., doesn't own a *lame*, a French handled blade used to slash rustic bread loaves before baking, so he devised a homemade alternative. He carefully holds a standard safety razor blade by the tabs on the short sides, bends the blade slightly, and then threads the narrow end of a chopstick through the holes on either side of the blade. The curved blade mimics the shape and function of a lame, and the chopstick is easy to grip.

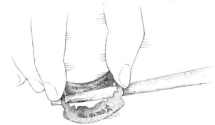

HOLLOW OUT CUPCAKES FOR FILLING

Kristin Peek of Charleston, S.C., found that the fastest, most efficient way to hollow out cupcakes for filling is with a strawberry huller.

MAKE SUPERSMOOTH GUACAMOLE WITH A RICER

To make silky guacamole without wearing out her arm, Rochelle Rougier-Maas of Mahtomedi, Minn., presses the peeled and pitted avocado halves through the fine holes of a potato ricer.

RINSING FRUIT ON THE GO

Jaime Kriss of New York City, N.Y., knows its best to wash fruits such as berries just before you eat them to prevent molding. To rinse them on the go, she packs them in a zipper-lock bag and then cuts or pokes some small holes in the bottom with scissors to make a tiny "colander." When she's ready to eat, she simply fills the bag with water and then lets it drain out.

QUICK-SOFTEN BUTTER FOR A BAKING PAN

If she's forgotten to soften butter for greasing a baking pan, Sandra Fried of Seattle, Wash., melts some in the pan while the oven preheats. Once the butter has softened or is just melted, she spreads it evenly over the pan with a pastry brush and then lets the pan cool before adding the dough or batter.

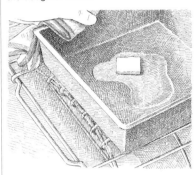

ANOTHER WAY TO FREEZE AND PREP CHIPOTLES

Rachel Delany of Charleston, S.C., finds that freezing leftover canned chipotle chiles in adobo sauce in ice cube trays makes for easy portioning. Instead of defrosting the chiles, she prefers to mince them when they're still frozen and stiff.

CUT-YOUR-OWN LEVELING TAB FOR SPICES

Karen Cofino of Bridgeville, Del., doesn't completely remove the seal on new jars of spices. She cuts half away with a paring knife and then uses the straight edge of the remaining seal to level off measuring spoons.

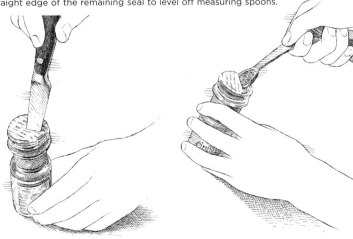

BUFFER FOR WINE BOTTLES

Bill Lewis of Mount Kisco, N.Y., found a way to safely transport multiple bottles of wine without a divided cardboard box. He packs two rolls of paper towels next to each other in a sturdy bag and slips the bottles on either side of them. The snug fit prevents the bottles from moving.

OUR GUIDE TO FRESH CORN

Corn is quite possibly summer's most anticipated produce. Here's how to make the most of the season's best crop, from shucking to storing to knowing when boiled corn is perfectly cooked.

SHOP SMART

DO AN EAR CHECK

To see if corn is at its best, you don't need to peel back the husk and silk (which makes ears less desirable for other shoppers). Instead, gently press on the kernels through the husk; they should feel tightly packed, plump, and firm. The silk should look white and clean, and the husk should be green and pliable and closely wrapped around the ear.

FOUR MYTHS, BUSTED

MYTH **Fresh corn tastes good only the day it is picked.**
FACT **These days, most varieties of fresh corn will taste good for at least several days.**

While older varieties of corn would convert about half their sugar to starch within 24 hours of being picked, that conversion occurs more slowly in the supersweet varieties sold at most markets today. Some start to lose their sweetness four days after being picked while others stay sweet for seven days.

MYTH **Adding milk, sugar, or salt to the cooking water can improve corn's flavor.**
FACT **Flavoring the cooking water doesn't make a difference.**

In taste tests, we couldn't tell the difference between corn cooked in water and corn cooked in a combination of water and milk. Likewise, corn cooked in water that had been seasoned with sugar or salt tasted no different from corn cooked in plain water. In tests, we found that the only way seasonings migrate into the kernels is by first being absorbed by the cob, and that takes far too long to be feasible. Bottom line: You're better off seasoning corn at the table.

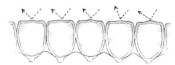

A corn kernel's skin is virtually impenetrable to seasonings such as salt, sugar, and milk.

MYTH **Kernel color indicates sweetness.**
FACT **The color of the kernels is not related to the corn's sweetness.**

The color of corn is an indication of its carotene content, not its sugar content. Furthermore, many of the corn varieties found in supermarkets today have sugar contents approaching 35 percent. That's almost three times sweeter than the varieties of corn sold decades ago, and it's true whether you buy ears that are yellow, white, or bicolor.

White Corn

Bicolor Corn

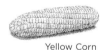
Yellow Corn

MYTH **Cold temperatures can damage corn.**
FACT **While corn plants are sensitive to chilling injury, harvested ears of corn actually benefit from cold storage.**

The colder the storage temperature, the better—as long as the corn doesn't freeze. That's because cold temperatures, along with humidity, slow the rate at which the corn's sugar turns to starch; the moist air of a refrigerator also transfers heat from the corn to the environment more efficiently than dry air does and prevents the kernels from drying out. Our preferred way to store corn is to place the unhusked ears in a wet paper bag, place the wet bag in a plastic shopping bag, and refrigerate them for up to two days.

TIPS AND TECHNIQUES

DON'T SHUCK IN ADVANCE

Some markets and farm stands allow you to shuck the corn on-site. Do this only if you plan to eat the corn that day, since the exposed kernels will be prone to drying out.

EASIEST-EVER WAY TO SHUCK

Odd as it might sound, we've found that the easiest way to shuck corn is to briefly microwave it and then shake it, which makes the husk and silk slide right off. The cob will heat up a bit, but the kernels won't be cooked.

Cut off stalk end of cob just above first row of kernels. Microwave 3 or 4 ears at a time on plate for 30 to 60 seconds. Hold each ear by uncut silk end; shake up and down until cob slips free, leaving behind husk and silk.

HOW TO MILK CORN

Corn "milk" is the term for the sweet pulp and juices that are left behind when kernels are stripped from the cob. Many recipes call for capturing this liquid to add to dishes such as soups and chowders, risotto, or polenta. But don't bother freezing it—we found that its fresh flavor faded noticeably.

Hold stripped corn cob over bowl and firmly scrape up and down all sides of cob with back of butter knife.
YIELD About 1 tablespoon corn milk per ear

HOW TO STRIP KERNELS

With a Knife

Halving the cob and standing the pieces on the cut side prevents them from sliding around the cutting surface.

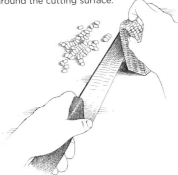

Cut cob in half crosswise, then stand each half on its flat cut end. Using chef's knife, cut kernels off cob, 1 side at a time.

With a Corn Stripper

Shaped like a computer mouse, the **OXO Good Grips Corn Stripper** ($11.99) features a sharp, toothlike blade that removes several rows of kernels at a time, which fall neatly into the attached cup. Cut kernels are poured out of the top of the cup, and the device snaps apart for easy cleaning. It's no faster or more effective than a chef's knife, but it's safer and mess-free.

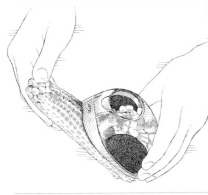

SAVE THE COBS FOR CORN STOCK

Briefly simmering stripped corn cobs can produce a surprisingly flavorful stock that can enrich polenta, cornbread, and vegetable soups. It also freezes well.

METHOD Cut 8 corn cobs into quarters. Place in large saucepan with 2 quarts water, bring to simmer, and cook for 15 minutes. Strain liquid through fine-mesh strainer.
YIELD About 7½ cups

THE BEST WAY TO FREEZE CORN

Corn, which is botanically a cereal grain, freezes better than most vegetables because it is low in water and relatively high in starch and cellulose (which strengthens the kernels' cell walls). Both starch and cellulose also make the kernels less susceptible to damage by ice crystal formation. Commercial manufacturers blanch corn before freezing it, but when we froze batches of blanched and unblanched kernels for one month, we didn't find any flavor differences between them. What did matter: drying the kernels well and freezing them in a single layer before bagging them for long-term freezer storage. This step ensured that no ice crystals formed on the surface and that the kernels didn't stick together once frozen.

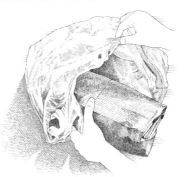

METHOD Spread kernels on dish towel-lined rimmed baking sheet and pat dry. Remove towel from sheet, spread kernels into even layer, and freeze for 1 hour. Transfer kernels to zipper-lock bag, press out air, seal bag, and return to freezer.

DISH RACK–DRAINED CORN

A clean, empty dish rack accommodates many more ears of corn than a colander. Put the ears into the dish rack as you remove them from the pot.

BOILED CORN FOR A CROWD

Our recipe for Foolproof Boiled Corn works best when cooking six ears. But what if you're cooking corn for a crowd? After discovering a method online for cooking as many as 24 ears of corn at a time in a large cooler, we tested the process and came up with our own method. Thanks to its insulation, the cooler will also keep the corn hot for hours—without continuing to cook it.

METHOD: Place up to 24 husked ears in 50-quart cooler, pour enough boiling water over corn to cover by 1 inch, and close cooler lid for 45 minutes. Serve. (Corn can be held in water for up to 2 hours.)

Foolproof Boiled Corn

SERVES 4 TO 6

Bringing the water to a boil, shutting off the heat just before adding the corn, and then covering the pot ensures that the corn's temperature will rise to between 150 and 170 degrees—the sweet spot where its starches have gelatinized but little of its pectin has broken down. The result: perfectly sweet, snappy kernels every time.

- **6 ears corn, husks and silk removed**
  Unsalted butter, softened
  Salt and pepper
- **1 recipe Chili-Lime Salt (optional) (recipe follows)**

1. Bring 4 quarts water to boil in large Dutch oven. Turn off heat, add corn to water, cover, and let stand for at least 10 minutes or up to 30 minutes.

2. Transfer corn to large platter and serve immediately, passing butter, salt (or Chili-Lime Salt, if using), and pepper separately.

Chili-Lime Salt

MAKES 3 TABLESPOONS

The mixture can be refrigerated for up to 1 week.

- **2 tablespoons kosher salt**
- **4 teaspoons chili powder**
- **¾ teaspoon grated lime zest**

Combine all ingredients in small bowl.

A COOK'S GUIDE TO RICE

The world of supermarket rice options has grown in recent years, but the same old problem remains: how to cook it perfectly. Here's what you need to know to get it right every time.

ABOUT RICE

Brown versus white: All rice starts out as brown rice, which is made up of the endosperm, germ, aleurone, bran, and hull or husk. Brown rices have simply been hulled and cleaned; since their bran layers are intact, they take longer to cook, boast nuttier flavor and more distinct chew, and cook up less sticky and/or creamy compared with equivalent white varieties. White rices are hulled and milled to remove the bran, aleurone, and germ.

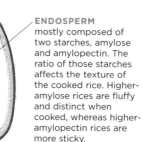

HULL the outer layer removed during the milling process

BRAN the fiber-rich interior of the rice grain beneath the hull

ALEURONE oil- and enzyme-rich cells protected by the bran

GERM responsible for reproduction in the rice grain

ENDOSPERM mostly composed of two starches, amylose and amylopectin. The ratio of those starches affects the texture of the cooked rice. Higher-amylose rices are fluffy and distinct when cooked, whereas higher-amylopectin rices are more sticky.

OUR FAVORITE RICE COOKER

Aroma 8-Cup Digital Rice Cooker and Food Steamer ($29.92)

WHY WE LIKE IT It produces perfectly tender-chewy white, brown, and sushi rice; comes with useful features such as a digital timer that lets the cook know when the rice is nearly ready, a clear audio alert, and a delayed-start function; is inexpensive and takes up only a small amount of counter space; has inner lid that pops out for easy cleanup.

KEYS TO SUCCESSFUL COOKING

Producing evenly cooked rice via the absorption method depends on the grains soaking up just enough liquid, so we use particular tools and precise methods to ensure perfect results.

1. PICK THE RIGHT PAN
Our favorite pan for making rice is a sturdy, heavy-bottomed saucepan with a tight-fitting lid. To ensure that a saucepan is big enough for the rice grains to cook evenly, dump in the raw grains; if the layer of rice is deeper than 1½ inches, switch to a larger saucepan.

2. GO LOW
After bringing the liquid to a boil and covering the saucepan, turn down the heat to a bare simmer. If more than a wisp or two of steam escapes, the heat is too high.

3. DON'T STIR
The rice will release extra starch, and grains may break.

4. KEEP A LID ON IT
To avoid releasing essential moisture, don't start checking for doneness until near the end of the recommended cooking time.

5. COVER THE PAN WITH A CLEAN DISH TOWEL AND LID
Off the heat, remove the lid, cover the saucepan with a folded clean dish towel, and replace the lid. The towel will absorb excess moisture that would make the grains mushy.

6. GIVE IT A REST
Letting the rice stand for 10 to 15 minutes off the heat (covered with a towel and lid) allows the starch granules to firm up so they won't break.

7. FLUFF IT WITH A FORK
The small tines of a fork gently separate the grains without breaking or crushing them.

SIZE

Long-, medium-, and short-grain are three loosely defined categories of brown and white rices based on the grains' length-to-width ratio. This ratio and the rice's starch composition (see illustration at left) determine whether the rice cooks up fluffy, sticky, or somewhere in between.

LONG-GRAIN

Includes conventional long-grain rice as well as aromatic basmati and jasmine rices

STARCH About 22% amylose, 78% amylopectin

TYPICAL APPLICATIONS: Steamed, pilaf, pudding, biryani, fried rice

MEDIUM-GRAIN

Includes conventional and specialty rices such as Italian Arborio, Spanish Valencia, and Bomba

STARCH About 18% amylose, 82% amylopectin

TYPICAL APPLICATIONS Risotto (Arborio), paella (Valencia and Bomba), rice bowl (conventional)

SHORT-GRAIN

Includes conventional short-grain and sushi rices

STARCH About 15% amylose, 85% amylopectin

TYPICAL APPLICATIONS Rice bowl, sushi, fried rice

YOU CAN—AND SHOULD—FREEZE RICE

Raw brown rice should be stored in a zipper-lock bag in the freezer to prevent oxidation from turning its oil-rich bran and germ rancid; be sure to use it within six months. Cooked rice can also be frozen. Simply spread the cooked rice (we tested long-grain brown and white varieties) on a rimmed baking sheet and let it cool completely. Transfer the cooled rice to a zipper-lock bag and lay it flat to freeze. There's no need to thaw it before use.

FOUR METHODS FOR COOKING LONG-GRAIN RICE

These basic methods can be dressed up by tossing the rice with butter or extra-virgin olive oil, minced herbs, and/or finely grated citrus zest.

ABSORPTION/STEAMING (FOR WHITE RICE)

Simmering rice slowly in a measured amount of liquid, covered, until tender and liquid is absorbed, is the standard way to cook it.

Combine 1 cup rinsed rice, 1½ cups liquid, and ½ teaspoon salt in saucepan. Bring to boil over medium-high heat. Reduce heat to low, cover, and simmer until tender, 18 to 20 minutes. Let stand off heat, covered with folded clean dish towel and lid, for 10 to 15 minutes. Fluff with fork and serve.
YIELD 3 cups

TO COOK 1 cup of medium- or short-grain white rice: Reduce liquid to 1¼ cups and cooking time to 16 to 20 minutes.
YIELD 2¾ cups

PILAF (FOR WHITE RICE)

Sautéing rice in butter or oil with onion before adding liquid is an effortless way to enrich rice's flavor.

1. Heat 2 teaspoons butter or oil in saucepan over medium heat. Add ½ cup finely chopped onion and cook until softened, about 3 minutes. Add 1 cup rinsed rice and cook, stirring occasionally, until chalky and opaque, about 3 minutes.

2. Add 1½ cups liquid and ½ teaspoon salt, increase heat, and bring just to boil. Reduce heat to low, cover, and simmer until liquid is absorbed and rice is tender. Let stand off heat, covered with folded clean dish towel and lid, for 10 to 15 minutes. Fluff with fork and serve.
YIELD 3¼ cups

PASTA/BOIL (FOR BROWN RICE)

Boiling rice in lots of salted water is a speedy way to cook it.

1. Bring 3 quarts water to rapid boil. Add 1 cup rice and 2½ teaspoons salt, reduce heat to low, and simmer until tender, 25 to 30 minutes.

2. Drain and serve.
YIELD 3¼ cups

TO COOK 1 cup of medium- or short-grain brown rice: Reduce cooking time to 22 to 27 minutes.
YIELD 2¾ cups

OVEN/ABSORPTION (FOR BROWN RICE)

Cooking brown rice in a measured amount of water in a covered baking dish in the oven can cook it more evenly than in a pot on the stove, especially if the pot lacks a tight-fitting lid and heavy bottom.

1. Adjust oven rack to middle position and heat oven to 375 degrees. Spread 1½ cups rice in 8-inch square baking dish.

2. Bring 2⅓ cups water and 2 teaspoons butter or vegetable oil to boil in covered saucepan. Add ½ teaspoon salt and pour over rice. Cover tightly with double layer of aluminum foil. Bake until tender, about 1 hour. Let stand for 5 minutes, uncover, fluff with fork, and serve.
YIELD 5 cups

WANT TO DOUBLE THE RICE? DON'T DOUBLE THE WATER

Despite what many recipes suggest, rice-to-water ratios can't be scaled up proportionally when multiplying a recipe for steamed or pilaf-style rice. After a series of tests, we confirmed that rice absorbs water in a 1:1 ratio, no matter the volume. For example, in our rice pilaf recipe, which calls for 1½ cups of rice and 2¼ cups of water, the rice absorbed 1½ cups of water. The remaining ¾ cup of water evaporated.

BUT HERE'S THE CATCH: The amount of water that evaporates doesn't double when the amount of rice is doubled. In fact, we found that when doubling a batch of rice using the same conditions as we'd used for a single batch, the same quantity of water evaporated. Hence, simply doubling the recipe leads to mushy rice because there is an excess of water.

THE BOTTOM LINE: When multiplying a rice recipe that uses the absorption or pilaf method, the ratio of raw rice to water should always be 1:1, plus the amount of water that will evaporate. To figure out how much will evaporate, subtract the amount of rice from the total volume of water in the original recipe and add that amount to the 1:1 volume of water.

WHEN—AND WHEN NOT—TO RINSE

Rinsing white rice removes excess surface starch that would otherwise absorb water and swell, causing the grains to stick together.

DO rinse for pilaf, steamed rice, and rice salad, where you want separate, distinct grains.

DON'T rinse for applications such as risotto or rice pudding; we found that rinsing compromises the desirably sticky, creamy consistency.

DON'T bother rinsing brown rice. With the bran layer intact, there is no exterior starch to wash away.

METHOD: Rinse rice in fine-mesh strainer under cold running water until water runs clear. (To check if water is starchy, capture some in bowl. If water is cloudy, keep rinsing and check again.)

HOW TO ROAST A GREAT CHICKEN

Whether you need dinner on the table in a hurry during the week or have time to pull out all the stops on the weekend, follow our tips and techniques to guarantee great roast chicken.

WEEKNIGHT ROAST CHICKEN

1. SWAP ROASTING PAN FOR SKILLET

Adjust oven rack to middle position, place 12-inch ovensafe skillet on rack, and heat oven to 450 degrees. Combine 1 tablespoon kosher salt and ½ teaspoon pepper. Pat 3½- to 4-pound whole chicken (giblets discarded) dry. Rub surface with 1 tablespoon olive oil. Rub salt mixture evenly over surface. Tie legs together with kitchen twine and tuck wingtips behind back.

WHY Juices pool deeply in a skillet, which prevents them from burning so that they can be used later to make a pan sauce.

2. SEAR THIGHS

Transfer chicken, breast side up, to preheated skillet in oven. Roast until breast registers 120 degrees and thighs register 135 degrees, 25 to 35 minutes.

WHY Direct contact with a preheated skillet gives the thighs a head start so that they cook in sync with the breast.

3. CUT HEAT

Turn off oven and leave chicken in until breast registers 160 degrees and thighs register 175 degrees, 25 to 35 minutes. Transfer chicken to carving board and let rest, uncovered, for 20 minutes.

WHY Cutting the heat allows the chicken to finish cooking gently.

4. SKIM FAT

While chicken rests, remove all but 1 tablespoon fat from skillet, leaving any fond and jus in skillet.

WHY Removing most of the fat prevents the sauce from being greasy.

5. USE FOND

Place skillet over medium-high heat. Add 1 minced shallot, 2 minced garlic cloves, and 2 teaspoons chopped fresh thyme and cook until softened, about 2 minutes. Stir in 1 cup chicken broth and 2 teaspoons Dijon mustard, scraping up any browned bits. Cook until reduced to ¾ cup, about 3 minutes. Off heat, whisk in 2 tablespoons unsalted butter and 2 teaspoons sherry vinegar until butter has melted. Season with pepper to taste; cover and keep warm. Carve chicken and serve with sauce.

WHY It takes minutes to transform the savory browned bits into a flavorful pan sauce with just a few extra ingredients.

BE SAVVY ABOUT THE LABEL

NOT JUST HYPE

AIR-CHILLED means the chickens weren't water-chilled in a chlorinated bath, so they didn't absorb water during processing, which dilutes flavor and makes the skin harder to crisp. Air-chilled meat is typically more tender.

USDA ORGANIC poultry must eat organic feed that doesn't contain animal byproducts, be raised without antibiotics, and have access to the outdoors (how much access isn't regulated).

BUYER BEWARE

RAISED WITHOUT ANTIBIOTICS and similar claims are important but not strictly enforced. (Poultry is randomly monitored for residues, but the only rigorous enforcement is when the claim is subject to the USDA Organic seal.)

NATURAL AND ALL NATURAL mean only that the bird was minimally processed with no added synthetic ingredients. (Chickens may be raised under unnatural circumstances and on unnatural diets.)

HORMONE-FREE is meaningless; the USDA does not allow the use of hormones or steroids in poultry production.

VEGETARIAN FED AND VEGETARIAN DIET sound healthy, but the terms aren't regulated.

HOW TO CARVE A WHOLE CHICKEN

1. EXPOSE LEG JOINT Using chef's knife, make cut through skin to expose where thigh meets breast.

2. SEPARATE JOINT TO REMOVE LEG QUARTER Pull leg quarter away from carcass, gently pull leg out to side, and push up on joint. Cut through joint to remove leg quarter from carcass.

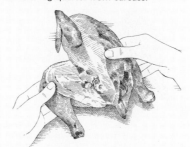

3. SEPARATE DRUMSTICK AND THIGH Cut through joint that connects drumstick to thigh. Repeat steps 1 through 3 on chicken's other side.

FOUR ROAST CHICKEN RULES

1. PORTION SEASONINGS

To avoid constantly washing and rewashing your hands—and to reduce the risks of cross-contamination—portion and set aside any seasonings, such as salt and pepper, before you start handling the meat.

2. DON'T RINSE RAW POULTRY

The United States Department of Agriculture (USDA) advises against rinsing raw poultry. Doing so will not remove much bacteria, and the splashing of water can spread the bacteria found on the surface of the raw chicken.

3. LET MEAT REST TO MAXIMIZE JUICINESS

When meat cooks, its proteins contract and squeeze out moisture. Carving meat without letting it rest causes it to lose this moisture. Resting before carving allows the contracted proteins to relax and reabsorb some of the expelled moisture.

4. TEMP PROPERLY

Inserting the thermometer incorrectly can give you an inaccurate reading. Here's our method:

White Meat Insert probe low into thickest part of breast, just above bone. Withdraw probe slowly, checking for lowest registered temperature.

Dark Meat Insert probe down into space between tip of breast and thigh. Slightly angle probe outward so that it pierces meat in lower part of thigh.

OUR FAVORITE WHOLE CHICKENS

MARY'S Free Range Air Chilled Chicken
(also sold as Pitman's)
Price: $1.99 per lb

WHY WE LIKE IT
Air chilling plus a higher percentage of fat (compared with the more diluted water-chilled chicken)

added up to a bird that tasters raved was "clean," "buttery," "savory," and "juicy," with "richly flavored" dark meat that was "so moist" and "tender."

BELL & EVANS Air Chilled Premium Fresh Chicken
Price: $3.29 per lb

WHY WE LIKE IT
Thanks to almost three hours of air chilling, this bird's white meat was "perfectly moist," and "chicken-y," and its dark meat "silky-tender" yet "firm." Several tasters remarked that it seemed "clean-tasting." Also helpful to flavor: It had the highest fat percentage of any bird in the tasting.

4. REMOVE BREAST MEAT Cut down along side of breastbone, pulling breast meat away from breastbone as you cut.

5. SLICE BREAST MEAT Remove wing from breast by cutting through wing joint. Slice breast crosswise into slices. Repeat with other side.

CRISP ROAST CHICKEN

1. CUT CHANNELS, LOOSEN SKIN, POKE HOLES

Place 3½- to 4-pound whole chicken (giblets discarded), breast side down, on cutting board. Using tip of paring knife, make four 1-inch incisions along back. Using your fingers, gently loosen skin covering breast and thighs. Using metal skewer, poke 15 to 20 holes in fat deposits on top of breast and thighs. Tuck wings behind back.

WHY These cuts create escape routes for fat and juices, which helps the skin crisp.

2. RUB AND CHILL

Combine 1 tablespoon kosher salt, 1 teaspoon baking powder, and ½ teaspoon pepper in bowl. Pat chicken dry with paper towels and sprinkle evenly with salt mixture. Rub in mixture with your hands, evenly coating entire surface. Set chicken, breast side up, in V-rack set on rimmed baking sheet and refrigerate, uncovered, for at least 12 hours or up to 24 hours.

WHY Salt and baking powder, plus air drying, dehydrate the skin so that it will crisp and brown.

3. ROAST HIGH AND FLIP

Adjust oven rack to lowest position and heat oven to 450 degrees. Using paring knife, poke 20 holes about 1½ inches apart in 16 by 12-inch piece of aluminum foil. Place foil loosely in roasting pan. Flip chicken so breast side faces down and set V-rack in prepared pan on top of foil. Roast chicken for 25 minutes. Remove pan from oven. Using 2 large wads of paper towels, flip chicken breast side up. Continue to roast until breast registers 135 degrees, 15 to 25 minutes longer.

WHY A hot oven browns the skin quickly so that the meat doesn't have time to dry out; a foil liner prevents rendered fat from burning and smoking. Flipping the chicken helps it cook evenly.

4. BLAST IT

Increase oven temperature to 500 degrees. Continue to roast chicken until skin is golden brown and crispy, breast registers 160 degrees, and thighs register 175 degrees, 10 to 20 minutes longer. Transfer chicken to carving board and let rest for 20 minutes. Carve chicken and serve immediately.

WHY A final high-heat blast deeply browns and crisps the skin.

QUICK PASTA SAUCES, PERFECTED

We retooled a week's worth of classic sauces so you can keep them in your back pocket for busy nights.

Quick Tomato Sauce
COOKING TIME 15 MINUTES

What Can Go Wrong With little time to simmer and meld flavors, quick tomato sauces can taste dull or, worse, like you simply dumped a can of tomatoes on the pasta.

How We Fixed It Minimally processed crushed tomatoes offer bright, fresh flavor and preclude the need to puree whole canned tomatoes ourselves. Grating the onion releases a lot of its flavor quickly. Sautéing the onion in butter, versus oil, contributes rich meatiness from the browned milk solids. Garlic, oregano, a touch of sugar, basil, and olive oil further ramp up the flavor.

- 2 **tablespoons unsalted butter**
- ¼ **cup grated onion**
- 1 **teaspoon minced fresh oregano or ¼ teaspoon dried**
   Salt and pepper
- 2 **garlic cloves, minced**
- 1 **(28-ounce) can crushed tomatoes**
- ¼ **teaspoon sugar**
- 2 **tablespoons chopped fresh basil**
- 1 **tablespoon extra-virgin olive oil**

Melt butter in medium saucepan over medium heat. Add onion, oregano, and ½ teaspoon salt and cook, stirring occasionally, until onion is softened and lightly browned, 5 to 7 minutes. Stir in garlic and cook until fragrant, about 30 seconds. Stir in tomatoes and sugar, bring to simmer, and cook until slightly thickened, about 10 minutes. Off heat, stir in basil and oil and season with salt and pepper to taste. Add sauce to pasta and toss well to coat, adjusting consistency with pasta cooking water as needed.

GRATE ONION
Efficiently creates more of the compounds that give cooked onion complex flavor.

Puttanesca
COOKING TIME 15 MINUTES

What Can Go Wrong Assertive flavors like anchovies, garlic, olives, and pepper flakes can overwhelm a sauce.

How We Fixed It Gently sautéing the garlic, anchovies, and pepper flakes in oil mellows and blends their flavors. We use diced tomatoes, since they retain their shape better than whole or crushed products; the bright, sweet-tasting tomato pieces balance the other flavors and yield a sauce with a chunky texture. Drizzling olive oil over each portion adds richness.

- 2 **tablespoons extra-virgin olive oil, plus extra for drizzling**
- 8 **anchovy fillets, rinsed, patted dry, and minced**
- 4 **garlic cloves, minced**
- 1 **teaspoon red pepper flakes**
- 1 **(28-ounce) can diced tomatoes, drained**
- ½ **cup pitted kalamata olives, chopped coarse**
- ¼ **cup minced fresh parsley**
- 3 **tablespoons capers, rinsed**
   Salt

1. Heat oil, anchovies, garlic, and pepper flakes in 12-inch skillet over medium heat. Cook, stirring often, until garlic turns golden but not brown, about 3 minutes. Stir in tomatoes and cook until slightly thickened, about 8 minutes.

2. Stir olives, parsley, and capers into sauce. Add sauce to pasta and toss well to coat, adjusting consistency with cooking water as needed. Season with salt to taste. Drizzle additional olive oil over individual portions and serve immediately.

SAUTÉ AROMATICS
Mellows and melds assertive anchovy and garlic flavors.

Classic Basil Pesto
PREP TIME 10 MINUTES

What Can Go Wrong Sharp raw garlic can overpower delicate, aromatic basil. The basil can also turn a drab, unappealing dark green.

How We Fixed It To mellow the garlic, we toast unpeeled cloves in a dry skillet before processing. Adding parsley (which doesn't discolor as easily as basil) helps keep the pesto green. Pounding the herbs before pureeing them releases their flavorful oils.

- 3 **garlic cloves, unpeeled**
- 2 **cups fresh basil leaves**
- 2 **tablespoons fresh parsley leaves**
- 7 **tablespoons extra-virgin olive oil**
- ¼ **cup pine nuts, toasted**
   Salt and pepper
- ¼ **cup grated Parmesan cheese, plus extra for serving**

1. Toast garlic in small, heavy skillet over medium heat, shaking skillet occasionally, until fragrant and color of cloves deepens slightly, about 7 minutes. Let garlic cool slightly, then peel and chop.

2. Place basil and parsley in heavy-duty 1-gallon zipper-lock bag. Pound bag with flat side of meat pounder or rolling pin until all leaves are bruised.

3. Process oil, pine nuts, ½ teaspoon salt, garlic, and basil-parsley mixture in food processor until smooth, about 1 minute, scraping down sides of bowl as needed. Stir in Parmesan and season with salt and pepper to taste. Add sauce to pasta and toss well to coat, adjusting consistency with pasta cooking water as needed. Serve, passing extra Parmesan separately.

TO MAKE AHEAD Pesto can be covered with thin layer of oil (1 to 2 tablespoons) and refrigerated for up to 4 days or frozen for up to 1 month.

TOAST UNPEELED GARLIC CLOVES
Softens and sweetens harsh bite.

Garlic and Oil Sauce (Aglio e Olio)

COOKING TIME 15 MINUTES

What Can Go Wrong The garlic tastes harsh, and the oil-based sauce doesn't cling to the pasta.

How We Fixed It Treating the minced garlic two different ways—gently sautéing some of it until pale golden brown and then stirring in the rest raw—yields garlic flavor that is nutty, mellow, and sweet, with a pleasantly sharp finish. We use the pasta cooking water as the sauce's base, not just to adjust its consistency. The starchy liquid helps the sauce cling to the noodles and helps evenly distribute the garlicky oil.

- 6 tablespoons extra-virgin olive oil
- 12 garlic cloves, minced
  Salt
- 3 tablespoons chopped fresh parsley
- 2 teaspoons lemon juice
- ¾ teaspoon red pepper flakes
  Grated Parmesan cheese

1. Heat 3 tablespoons oil, two-thirds of garlic, and ½ teaspoon salt in 10-inch nonstick skillet over low heat. Cook, stirring constantly, until garlic foams and is sticky and straw-colored, about 10 minutes. Off heat, add parsley, lemon juice, pepper flakes, remaining garlic, and 2 tablespoons reserved pasta cooking water.

2. Add garlic mixture and remaining 3 tablespoons oil to pasta and toss well to coat, adjusting consistency with pasta cooking water as needed. Season with salt to taste, and serve immediately, passing Parmesan separately.

**BUILD SAUCE WITH
PASTA COOKING WATER**
Helps sauce cling to pasta; evenly
distributes garlic flavor.

Simple Italian-Style Meat Sauce

COOKING TIME 30 MINUTES

What Can Go Wrong The ground meat dries out. The meaty flavor is only superficial.

How We Fixed It We brown mushrooms, onion, and tomato paste to develop meaty flavor without browning (and drying out) the beef. Blending bread and milk into the meat keeps it tender. Crushed and diced tomatoes add body and bright flavor.

- 4 ounces white mushrooms, trimmed
- 1 slice hearty white sandwich bread, torn into quarters
- 2 tablespoons whole milk
  Salt and pepper
- 1 pound 85 percent lean ground beef
- 1 tablespoon olive oil
- 1 large onion, chopped fine
- 6 garlic cloves, minced
- 1 tablespoon tomato paste
- ¼ teaspoon red pepper flakes
- 1 (14.5-ounce) can diced tomatoes, drained with ¼ cup juice reserved
- 1 teaspoon dried oregano
- 1 (28-ounce) can crushed tomatoes
- ¼ cup grated Parmesan cheese, plus extra for serving

1. Process mushrooms in food processor until finely chopped, about 8 pulses, scraping down sides of bowl as needed; transfer mushrooms to bowl. Process bread, milk, ½ teaspoon salt, and ½ teaspoon pepper in now-empty processor until paste forms, about 8 pulses. Add beef and pulse until mixture is well combined, about 6 pulses.

2. Heat oil in large saucepan over medium-high heat until just smoking. Add onion and mushrooms and cook, stirring frequently, until vegetables are browned and dark bits form on saucepan bottom, 6 to 12 minutes. Stir in garlic, tomato paste, and pepper flakes; cook until fragrant, about 1 minute. Add reserved tomato juice and oregano, scraping up any browned bits. Add beef mixture and cook, breaking meat into small pieces, until beef is no longer pink, 2 to 4 minutes.

3. Stir in crushed tomatoes and diced tomatoes and bring to simmer. Reduce heat to low and gently simmer until sauce has thickened and flavors have blended, about 30 minutes. Stir in Parmesan and season with salt and pepper to taste. Add sauce to pasta and toss well to coat, adjusting consistency with pasta cooking water as needed. Serve, passing extra Parmesan separately.

**BROWN VEGETABLES,
NOT MEAT**
Develops meaty flavor
without drying out meat.

PASTA SAUCE PANTRY STAPLES

High-quality ingredients make a big difference in any sauce. Here are our favorites.

MUIR GLEN Organic Whole Peeled Tomatoes

HUNT'S Diced Tomatoes

SMT Crushed Tomatoes

GOYA Tomato Paste

CALIFORNIA OLIVE RANCH Extra Virgin Olive Oil

KING OSCAR Anchovies—Flat Fillets in Olive Oil

BOAR'S HEAD Parmigiano-Reggiano

BOAR'S HEAD Pecorino Romano

CHOOSE YOUR NOODLE

Each recipe will sauce 1 pound of pasta, serving 4 to 6, and the sauces pairs well with any pasta shape.

DON'T DUMP THE WATER!

Each sauce relies on the addition of pasta cooking water, so be sure to reserve at least ½ cup before draining. Set a measuring cup in the colander to remind yourself.

MAKE THE MOST OF YOUR MICROWAVE

Your microwave oven can do so much more than simply reheat last night's leftovers. It can also be a big timesaver and prevent messes, all without heating up your kitchen.

HOW MICROWAVE OVENS WORK

Microwave ovens use electric current and spinning magnets to generate electromagnetic waves (the same sort of phenomenon as radio waves and light waves) called "microwaves," which create a field with a positive and a negative charge. These charges reverse direction an astounding 4.9 billion times per second.

HOW DO MICROWAVES HEAT FOOD?

Microwaves interact with water molecules and, to a lesser extent, oil. When water molecules, which have positive and negative charges, are exposed to the oscillating positive and negative charges of microwaves, they move at the same incredibly fast rate, bumping into one another (and into nearby molecules, such as fats and proteins) and increasing their temperature.

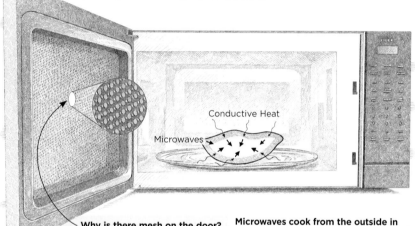

Why is there mesh on the door?

The holes allow users to see into the oven, and the metal reflects some microwaves back toward the food. The holes are small enough that microwaves can't fit through.

Why is the interior metal?

Microwaves bounce off the metal surfaces, back toward the center of the oven.

Why do microwaves have turntables?

By rotating the food, the turntable helps microwaves reach—and heat—more of a food's surface.

Microwaves cook from the outside in

Microwaves strike the exterior of food and in most cases penetrate about an inch into the interior, causing water molecules to heat up. That heat energy then transfers to adjacent molecules, heating the rest of the food via conduction.

How does the power level work?

The power level indicates the ratio of time that the power is on to total cooking time. So, 50 percent power means the microwave is emitting electromagnetic waves for 30 seconds out of a 1-minute cooking time by rapidly pulsing on and off.

EASY MICROWAVE CLEANUP: JUST ADD WATER

Microwave 2 cups water at full power until steaming but not boiling, about 2 minutes. Let sit for 5 minutes. Steam will loosen dried, stuck-on food. Wipe clean.

TIPS FOR HEATING FOOD EFFICIENTLY IN THE MICROWAVE

After many years of working with the microwave, we've come up with a few best practices. Below are a few of our tips to ensure you get the best results, whether you're reheating leftovers or jump-starting cooking.

STIR OR FLIP OFTEN: Movement allows the microwaves to hit new parts of the food and promotes heat transfer via conduction.

COVER FOOD: Using a plate or an inverted bowl to cover the food traps steam, which provides more cooking via conduction.

LET FOOD REST: Letting food rest for a few minutes after cooking it allows hot and cool spots to even out through conduction.

9 UNEXPECTED WAYS TO USE THE MICROWAVE OVEN

1. TOAST NUTS, COCONUT, WHOLE SPICES, OR BREAD CRUMBS

Precise Control = No Burning

Place ingredient in shallow bowl or glass pie plate in thin, even layer. Microwave, stirring and checking color every minute. When ingredient starts to color, microwave in 30-second increments until golden brown.

2. MELT OR TEMPER CHOCOLATE

Faster and less fussy than double boiler

TO MELT 4 OUNCES CHOCOLATE

Microwave finely chopped chocolate in bowl at 50 percent power, stirring occasionally, until melted, 2 to 4 minutes.

MELTING CHOCOLATE

5 MINUTES
Microwave

15 MINUTES
Double Boiler

TO TEMPER CHOCOLATE

Place three-quarters of chocolate, chopped fine, in bowl. Heat at 50 percent power, stirring every 15 seconds, until melted but not much warmer than body temperature, about 93 degrees. Add remaining one-quarter of chocolate, grated, and stir until smooth, microwaving for no more than 5 seconds at a time, if necessary, to finish melting.

3. MELLOW RAW GARLIC

Easy way to ease garlic's edge

Place unpeeled garlic cloves in small bowl. Microwave at full power for 15 seconds or until cloves are warm to the touch but not cooked. Warming garlic prevents formation of allicin (molecule that gives raw garlic its edge). Mince or otherwise prep garlic as called for in cooked applications such as pesto, hummus, and dressings.

Bonus The quick spin in the microwave makes the cloves a cinch to peel.

RAW AT 70°
Loads of allicin; sharp bite

HEATED TO 140°
Not much allicin; mellow flavor

4. DRY FRESH HERBS

Ready in minutes versus weeks

Place hardy herbs (sage, rosemary, thyme, oregano, mint, or marjoram) in single layer between 2 paper towels on microwave turntable. Heat at full power for 1 to 3 minutes, until leaves turn brittle and fall easily from stems—sure signs of dryness.

Not all inks used on printed paper towels are food-safe. We recommend plain paper towels without any printing for use in the microwave.

5. DEHYDRATE CITRUS ZEST

Speedy way to always have this versatile flavoring on hand

Use vegetable peeler to remove strips of citrus zest, avoiding bitter pith. Place strips on paper towel–lined plate. Heat at full power for 2 to 3 minutes, let cool, then store in airtight container. Steep in tea, pan sauces, custards, or cooking water for grains to add subtle citrus flavor.

6. MAKE AN EMERGENCY ROUX

No whisking or saucepan required

Mix 2 tablespoons flour with 2 tablespoons oil. Microwave at full power for 1½ minutes. Stir, then microwave for 45 seconds. Stir, microwave for another 45 seconds, and stir again. For darker roux, continue microwaving and stirring in 15-second increments. Stir roux, 1 tablespoon at a time, into hot stew or gravy base until desired consistency is reached.

7. CARAMELIZE SUGAR

Quick and foolproof method for making caramel

Stir 1 cup sugar, 2 tablespoons corn syrup (prevents crystallization), 2 tablespoons water, and ⅛ teaspoon lemon juice together in 2-cup liquid measuring cup. Microwave at full power until mixture is just starting to brown, 5 to 8 minutes. Remove from microwave and let measuring cup sit on dry surface until caramel darkens to rich honey brown, about 5 minutes.

TO MAKE CARAMEL SAUCE

Stir ½ cup hot heavy cream into caramel few tablespoons at a time, followed by 1 tablespoon unsalted butter and pinch salt.

Fresh from the microwave

After 5 minutes on the counter

8. FRY SHALLOTS

No splatter and less stirring than on stovetop

Place 3 shallots, peeled and sliced thin, in medium bowl with ½ cup vegetable oil. Microwave at full power for 5 minutes. Stir, then microwave for 2 minutes. Repeat stirring and microwaving in 2-minute increments until shallots begin to brown (4 to 6 minutes), then stir and microwave in 30-second increments until shallots are deep golden (30 seconds to 2 minutes). Using slotted spoon, transfer shallots to paper towel–lined plate; season with salt. Let drain and turn crisp, about 5 minutes, before serving. Sprinkle on salads and sandwiches; use cooked oil in dressing.

9. DRY EGGPLANT FOR FRYING OR SAUTÉING

Speedier and more effective than salting alone

Toss cubed eggplant with salt in bowl. Line large plate with double layer of paper towels and lightly spray with vegetable oil spray. Spread eggplant in even layer on paper towels. Microwave until dry and shriveled to about one-third of original size, 8 to 15 minutes (it should not brown). Transfer immediately to paper towel–lined plate. This technique eliminates much of eggplant's air and moisture, allowing it to easily brown and absorb less oil during cooking.

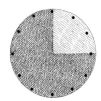

HOT SAUCE

While hot sauces haven't caught up to mayonnaise or ketchup, the top-selling condiments in America, their sales have seen an increase of more than 30 percent since 2012. In a previous tasting, we declared Huy Fong Sriracha Hot Chili Sauce our favorite, but since then, more Sriracha sauces have hit supermarket shelves and we've come to think of them as a separate category. So we decided it was time to find a new winner among traditional hot sauces. We sampled seven brands plain, drizzled over cheesy grits, and on chicken wings. The sauces showed a range of textures, from watery to viscous to gritty, but tasters didn't have a clear preference there. What did matter was complexity. Our favorite sauces were tangy and sweet, with discernible heat. By contrast, our lowest-ranked sauce was deemed hot but flavorless—or, as one taster put it, "all pain, no gain." Our top two sauces got their complexity from aged peppers and a decent dose of sodium. After sending the sauces to a lab to measure their Scoville Heat Unit (SHU) ratings, which quantify how hot a food is, we learned that our winner was on the milder end at a pleasant, "spicy but not too spicy" 690 SHUs. While a potent 3,000-SHU sauce also ranked high, we came away from this tasting appreciating those sauces that boasted complexity rather than just eye-watering burn. Hot sauces are listed in order of preference.

RECOMMENDED

FRANK'S Original RedHot Cayenne Pepper Sauce
PRICE: $3.49 for 12 oz ($0.29 per oz)
PEPPER TYPE: Aged cayenne peppers
SHU: 690
SODIUM: 190 mg
COMMENTS: Our favorite hot sauce had a thick texture and "vibrant" flavor that was "tangy" and "not too hot." When used in Buffalo wing sauce, it created a "good coating" on chicken wings. Tasters even liked it plain, praising its "assertive" flavor.

LOUISIANA BRAND Hot Sauce The Original
PRICE: $1.29 for 6 oz ($0.22 per oz)
PEPPER TYPE: "A special blend of aged peppers"
SHU: 1,700
SODIUM: 200 mg
COMMENTS: This "thin" sauce's "hard-hitting heat" was "bold" but balanced by a "fruity," flavor. There was a "good amount of burn," but we liked its "layers of flavor." Tasters also thought it clung nicely to chicken wings.

TAPATÍO Hot Sauce
PRICE: $2.19 for 10 oz ($0.22 per oz)
PEPPER TYPE: Not disclosed
SHU: 3,000
SODIUM: 110 mg
COMMENTS: With the highest SHU rating in the lineup, this sauce had "lots of heat," which "builds and lingers." Some tasters noted it was "sweet at first, then spicy." It had "a lot of complexity"; its "thick," "gritty" texture was noteworthy but inoffensive.

TEXAS PETE Original Hot Sauce
PRICE: $2.19 for 12 oz ($0.18 per oz)
PEPPER TYPE: Proprietary blend of cayenne peppers
SHU: 710
SODIUM: 90 mg
COMMENTS: We especially liked this sauce plain, with its "good balance of heat and vinegar." It tasted a bit "sweet" on grits, and we liked its "mild heat" on chicken wings: It "builds slowly" toward a "good spice finish."

RECOMMENDED (continued)

CHOLULA Hot Sauce
PRICE: $3.99 for 5 oz ($0.80 per oz)
PEPPER TYPE: Arbol and piquin peppers
SHU: 450
SODIUM: 110 mg
COMMENTS: Tasters noted that this "citrusy," "tart" sauce had "very mild heat," which made sense given that it had the lowest Scoville Heat Unit rating in the lineup. This sauce had an "acidic kick" and a "subtle," "balanced," "smoky" flavor that was also "a bit sweet" on grits and chicken wings. Its "thin" texture still coated wings well.

RECOMMENDED WITH RESERVATIONS

VALENTINA Salsa Picante
PRICE: $1.29 for 12.5 oz ($0.10 per oz)
PEPPER TYPE: Serrano, puya, and paprika peppers
SHU: 490
SODIUM: 64 mg
COMMENTS: This "grainy" hot sauce was "thick and ketchup-like," with a "mild" spice level. It tasted "dull" and "flat" on chicken wings, with "not enough heat." It "doesn't seem like your classic hot sauce," said one taster, though others enjoyed its "fruity," "rich" flavor, especially on grits.

NOT RECOMMENDED

TABASCO BRAND Pepper Sauce
PRICE: $4.59 for 5 oz ($0.92 per oz)
PEPPER TYPE: Tabasco peppers
SHU: 2,800
SODIUM: 35 mg
COMMENTS: As one taster said, the "spice punches you in your face, and you can't taste anything but heat." This hot sauce tasted "like a shot of vinegar," with "overpowering heat." It thin consistency "barely coated" the chicken wings.

WHITE WINE VINEGAR

White wine vinegar is a utility player: It isn't as distinct as other vinegars, which means it can deliver a jolt of clean acidity and balanced fruity sweetness to just about any dish. We rounded up eight vinegars, priced from $0.16 to $0.58 per ounce, and tasted them, first in a simple vinaigrette served with mild salad greens and then simmered with sugar, salt, and herbs to make a flavorful brine for pickled vegetables. Most of the vinegars were a well-balanced combination of punchy acidity and sweetness, but our winner stood out for its complex vibrancy. That's because it's made with Trebbiano grapes, a variety known for being crisp and fruity. Its high acidity gave it a robust flavor, and with no added sugar, we knew its sweetness came from the wine itself. Vinegars are listed in order of preference.

RECOMMENDED

NAPA VALLEY NATURALS Organic White Wine Vinegar
PRICE: $4.19 for 12.7 oz ($0.33 per oz)
INGREDIENTS: Organic white wine vinegar
TITRATABLE ACIDITY: 6.21
ACIDITY: 6%
TYPE OF WINE: White wine made from Trebbiano grapes
SOURCE: Produced in Italy, packaged in California
COMMENTS: This vinegar boasted high levels of acidity and sweetness, which accounted for the "vibrant" vinaigrette it produced. Its sweetness brought out "aromatic" flavors in the pickled vegetables.

STAR White Wine Vinegar
PRICE: $2.99 for 12 oz ($0.25 per oz)
INGREDIENTS: White wine vinegar, water, potassium metabisulfite (as a preservative)
TITRATABLE ACIDITY: 5.31
ACIDITY: 5%
TYPE OF WINE: White wine made from Chardonnay, Xarel-lo, Macabeo, and Parellada grapes
SOURCE: Spain
COMMENTS: The particular wine grapes in this vinegar might have accounted for the "fruity" flavor tasters noted in the vinaigrette. But its low acid content had tasters wishing that the pickled vegetables tasted sharper.

COLAVITA Aged White Wine Vinegar
PRICE: $3.49 for 17 oz ($0.21 per oz)
INGREDIENTS: Aged white wine vinegar
TITRATABLE ACIDITY: 6.08
ACIDITY: 6%
TYPE OF WINE: Unspecified white wines
SOURCE: Italy
COMMENTS: The acidity of this vinegar was "punchy" and "assertive." It also had a sweetness that brought out similarly "fruity," "floral" notes in the pickled vegetables.

POMPEIAN White Wine Vinegar
PRICE: $2.49 for 16 oz ($0.16 per oz)
INGREDIENTS: White wine vinegar reduced with water to 5% acidity
TITRATABLE ACIDITY: 5.09
ACIDITY: 5%
TYPE OF WINE: Blend of unspecified varieties
SOURCE: California
COMMENTS: Low acid and moderate sweetness produced a "mellow" vinegar. The vinaigrette and pickles lacked "punch," but they were "clean" and "balanced."

RECOMMENDED (continued)

SPECTRUM ORGANIC White Wine Vinegar
PRICE: $6.99 for 12 oz ($0.58 per oz)
INGREDIENTS: Organically grown and processed white wine vinegar
TITRATABLE ACIDITY: 6.34
ACIDITY: 6%
TYPE OF WINE: Unspecified white wines
SOURCE: Italy
COMMENTS: The strong acid in this product was "potent," with "very citrusy" flavor. In the pickles, those flavors mellowed to a "balanced" brine that all tasters liked.

REGINA White Wine Vinegar
PRICE: $2.79 for 12 oz ($0.23 per oz)
INGREDIENTS: White wine vinegar, potassium metabisulfite (as a preservative)
TITRATABLE ACIDITY: 5.16
ACIDITY: 5%
TYPE OF WINE: Champagne wine stock
SOURCE: Predominantly USA
COMMENTS: Relatively low in acid and sweetness, this vinegar didn't "wow" anyone, but it also didn't offend. Fans of mellower flavors might consider this product if what you want is a simple, "clean" source of acid.

HOLLAND HOUSE White Wine Vinegar
PRICE: $2.99 for 12 oz ($0.25 per oz)
INGREDIENTS: White wine vinegar, water, potassium metabisulfite (as a preservative)
TITRATABLE ACIDITY: 5.08
ACIDITY: 5%
TYPE OF WINE: Unspecified white wine
SOURCE: California
COMMENTS: "Rather soft vinegar presence" is a good way to describe this low-acid product. Tasters could better taste the oil in the vinaigrette and the carrots in the pickle mix while the vinegar "played second fiddle."

MONARI FEDERZONI White Wine Vinegar
PRICE: $3.99 for 16.9 oz ($0.24 per oz)
INGREDIENTS: White wine vinegar
TITRATABLE ACIDITY: 6.91
ACIDITY: 7%
TYPE OF WINE: Unspecified
SOURCE: Italy
COMMENTS: The most acidic vinegar we tasted also contained less sugar, so it packed a little too much punch for some. But tasters who preferred a vinaigrette with "bold" acidity liked the intensity of this "lively" vinegar.

DARK CHOCOLATE CHIPS

Today's dark chocolate chips are full of premium products touting their cacao percentages and artisan origins, but we wanted to look past labels to find the best product available. While our tasters were pleased with all 14 products we sampled, there were clear preferences. The chips ranged from 40 to 70 percent cacao; the lower-cacao chips seemed overly sweet, while those with high cacao percentages yielded deep, rich chocolaty flavor with mild sweetness. High-fat chips had a creamier, richer texture, and chips in the traditional dewdrop shape or in chunks with curved edges distributed more evenly in cookie dough than did their more angular counterparts. Chocolate chips are listed in order of preference.

HIGHLY RECOMMENDED

GHIRARDELLI
60% Premium Baking Chips
PRICE: $4.39 for 10 oz ($0.44 per oz)
INGREDIENTS: Bittersweet chocolate (unsweetened chocolate, sugar, cocoa butter, milk fat, soy lecithin—an emulsifier, vanilla)
TOTAL CACAO: 60%
COMMENTS: "Creamy, raisiny, intense," and "cocoa-y" when tasted plain, in cookies these slightly oversize chips were "very rich" but "balanced." "This is the perfect chocolate chip cookie," said one taster.

GUITTARD
Extra Dark Chocolate Chips 63%
PRICE: $4.49 for 11.5 oz ($0.39 per oz)
INGREDIENTS: Cacao beans, sugar, sunflower lecithin, and real vanilla
TOTAL CACAO: 63%
COMMENTS: This product nearly tied with the top-ranked chips. Its high percentage of cocoa solids made "a more bitter chocolate chip, which I enjoyed." It was "creamy and full-flavored. Not overly sweet but intensely chocolaty" with "coffee/espresso" notes.

RECOMMENDED

HERSHEY'S KITCHENS Special Dark Mildly Sweet Chocolate Chips
PRICE: $3.29 for 12 oz ($0.27 per oz)
INGREDIENTS: Sugar, chocolate, cocoa butter, cocoa processed with alkali, milk fat. Contains 2% or less of lecithin (soy), natural flavor, milk
ESTIMATED TOTAL CACAO: 46.7%
COMMENTS: Since these chips had a lower cacao percentage, we thought they might not be as chocolaty, but their additional cocoa made them "rich" but "not bitter." Their high ratio of fat to cocoa solids made them "smooth" and "gooey." Some found them "a touch too sweet." But most agreed that "this tastes like the quintessential chip."

NESTLÉ Toll House Bittersweet Chocolate Morsels 62%
PRICE: $2.99 for 10 oz ($0.30 per oz)
INGREDIENTS: Chocolate, sugar, cocoa butter, milk fat, nonfat milk, natural flavor
TOTAL CACAO: 62%
COMMENTS: These chips "toe the line between 'about right sweet' and 'too sweet.'" In cookies, the chips had "a nicely dense, chewy, almost fudgy quality." And they taste dark, "like good-quality bar chocolate." Some tasters felt that these chips held their shape "a little too well" when baked.

RECOMMENDED *(continued)*

GUITTARD Super Cookie Chips Semisweet Chocolate Chips 48%
PRICE: $4.49 for 10 oz ($0.45 per oz)
INGREDIENTS: Sugar, cacao beans, cocoa butter, sunflower lecithin, and vanilla
TOTAL CACAO: 48%
COMMENTS: These "big disks of chocolate," —by far the largest chips in our lineup—left "naked cookie bits" due to "poor coverage." The chocolate was "milky," "very creamy and rich," and offered "complexity," though the chips were "maybe a hair too sweet." Tasters enjoyed their "dense," "chewy" texture.

BARRY CALLEBAUT
Semisweet Chocolate Chips
PRICE: $9.95 for 16 oz ($0.62 per oz)
INGREDIENTS: Cocoa mass, sugar, anhydrous dextrose, soy lecithin (emulsifier), vanilla extract
TOTAL CACAO: 49.9%
COMMENTS: Tasters described these chips as having "sweet, simple," and "classic" chocolate flavor. They contained the lowest fat level in the lineup but had added anhydrous dextrose, a glucose compound that helps make chocolate smoother. However, we still found them slightly "hard" and "grainy."

HERSHEY'S KITCHENS
Semi-Sweet Chocolate Chips
PRICE: $3.29 for 12 oz ($0.27 per oz)
INGREDIENTS: Semisweet chocolate (sugar, chocolate, cocoa butter, milk fat, lecithin (soy), natural flavor, milk)
ESTIMATED TOTAL CACAO: 40%
COMMENTS: With the lowest cacao percentage in the lineup and an ingredient list that starts with sugar rather than chocolate, these petite chips tasted "almost like milk chocolate" and, to some, a little "too sweet." They held their shape well in cookies.

GHIRARDELLI Semisweet Premium Baking Chips 44%
PRICE: $4.39 for 12 oz ($0.37 per oz)
INGREDIENTS: Sugar, unsweetened chocolate, cocoa butter, whole milk powder, soy lecithin—an emulsifier, vanilla
TOTAL CACAO: 44%
COMMENTS: "Sweet with some roasty notes" and with a "caramelly" quality, these chips were "less creamy" than others in the lineup. A few tasters complained that the chocolate flavor lacked "depth." In cookies, the chips kept their shape and seemed "well balanced" in flavor and texture. One taster wrote, "What I'd expect in a chocolate chip!"

COCOA POWDER

Cocoa powder has a higher proportion of flavorful cocoa solids than any other form of chocolate, so ounce for ounce, it tastes more intensely chocolaty. While natural cocoa is made from ground cocoa solids, Dutched cocoa is treated with an alkalizing agent to neutralize its acidity, mellowing the cocoa's astringent notes. To find out once and for all if there was a difference, we gathered four natural cocoa powders and four Dutched and used them in cakes and cookies. The natural powders produced some of the tallest, airiest, and crumbliest cookies and cakes while most of the Dutched powders produced baked goods that hadn't risen quite as tall. This makes sense: Baking soda (which was in all the recipes we tested) releases carbon dioxide bubbles when it reacts with acid and moisture; this is one of the reasons that doughs and batters rise in the oven. The cakes and cookies made with natural cocoa were perceived as drier; our tasters preferred the fudgier, moist desserts made with Dutched powders. In fact, a Dutch-processed cocoa won every tasting, so we're confident in recommending out winner for all applications—it produces moist, tender, intensely chocolaty baked goods every time. Cocoa powders are listed in order of preference.

RECOMMENDED

DROSTE Cacao
PRICE: $9.99 for 8.8-oz package ($1.14 per oz)
STYLE: Dutched
PH: 7.90
FAT: 20.14%
COMMENTS: Our longtime favorite Dutched supermarket cocoa powder was the clear winner. With a high fat content and less starch, cookies were "perfectly chewy and moist." Cakes were very "moist," "rich," and "fudgy." We also loved its dark color and "earthy," "woodsy" chocolate flavor.

GUITTARD Cocoa Rouge Cocoa Powder
PRICE: $7.99 for 8-oz package ($1.00 per oz)
STYLE: Dutched
PH: 7.22
FAT: 22.09%
COMMENTS: With the most fat and least starch in our lineup, this cooca made for baked goods that were decadent and "fudgy." With less starch and no acidity to react with baking soda, it produced wide, flat cookies. Cookies and cakes had "deeper chocolate flavor" reminiscent of "espresso."

VALRHONA Cocoa Powder
PRICE: $14.99 for 8.82-oz package ($1.70 per oz)
STYLE: Dutched
PH: 6.91
FAT: 20.73%
COMMENTS: The priciest cocoa in our lineup delivered "intense," "rich chocolate flavor." Some tasters even detected slightly "smoky," "bitter" notes, which added complexity. Cookies were tender and chewy, and cakes had a "brownie-like" and "velvety crumb."

HERSHEY'S Natural Unsweetened Cocoa
PRICE: $3.99 for 8-oz package ($0.50 per oz)
STYLE: Natural
PH: 5.36
FAT: 10.97%
COMMENTS: By far our favorite natural cocoa, this product had "mild" yet pleasant chocolate flavor that "tasted familiar." Cookies rose higher than with Dutched powders due to the fairly high acidity and levels of starch. Cakes were deemed "light and almost airy," though perhaps "a little dry."

RECOMMENDED *(continued)*

SCHARFFEN BERGER Unsweetened Natural Cocoa Powder
PRICE: $7.99 for 6-oz package ($1.33 per oz)
STYLE: Natural
PH: 5.51
FAT: 21.54%
COMMENTS: Although high in fat, this natural cocoa powder couldn't compete with Dutched cocoas. Its flavor was "bright" and "fruity," and some tasters wanted "a bit more bitterness." Desserts were "fluffy" and "light" and tended toward dryness.

NESTLÉ Toll House Baking Cocoa
PRICE: $2.69 for 8-oz package ($0.34 per oz)
STYLE: Natural
PH: 5.73
FAT: 11.46%
COMMENTS: Alongside other samples, this inexpensive, low-fat cocoa tasted "like milk chocolate." It produced "tall," light-colored desserts that were a little "crumbly."

GHIRARDELLI 100% Unsweetened Cocoa
PRICE: $4.99 for 8-oz package ($0.62 per oz)
STYLE: Natural
PH: 5.57
FAT: 20.51%
COMMENTS: Baked goods made with this natural cocoa tasted "sweet" and "bright" but weren't as intensely chocolaty as those made with other products. The textures of the cakes and cookies were "perfectly OK," but we preferred products that combined big chocolate flavor and fudgy consistency.

EQUAL EXCHANGE Organic Baking Cocoa
PRICE: $7.99 for 8-oz package ($1.00 per oz)
STYLE: Dutched
PH: 6.88
FAT: 11.95%
COMMENTS: This was the only low-fat Dutch-processed cocoa in our lineup, and we missed the extra fat. Its "dark," "deep," almost "bitter" flavor earned mixed scores. While cookies made with it had "nice height" one cake was a little too dry.

SHREDDED MOZZARELLA

It's hard to top fresh-grated mozzarella. While convenient preshredded cheeses usually contain anticaking agents that make the cheese stiff and dry, the real thing melts evenly and tastes great out of hand or atop a salad. To see if any bagged options were worth buying, we sampled seven shredded mozzarellas plain and on pizza. None was great when eaten raw—texture was a problem—but when melted on pizza a handful emerged from the oven perfectly stretchy and chewy. Fat helps cheese retain a tender, milky texture when melted, so the higher-fat products (such as our winner, the only one made with whole milk) were more tender and boasted a buttery, rich flavor. Moderate salt amounts were also important to flavor, adding just the savory complexity we craved. While thin shreds clumped for uneven melting, larger, chunkier strands were easy to sprinkle on and melted uniformly. While we still prefer fresh mozzarella on our pizzas, we have no qualms about turning to our winner for a reliably rich, cheesy topping. Cheeses are listed in order of preference.

RECOMMENDED

POLLY-O Low Moisture Whole Milk Shredded Mozzarella
PRICE: $2.98 for 8 oz ($0.37 per oz)
MILK: Whole
FAT IN SOLIDS: 45%
SODIUM: 210 mg
AVERAGE THICKNESS: 2.8 mm
COMMENTS: These "chunky" strands were easy to spread over pizza dough and were "stringy," "evenly browned," and "chewy" when melted. Tasters praised their "classic," "creamy" milkiness and "tang," which added a "rich" sharpness to pizza.

SARGENTO Off the Block Shredded Low Moisture Part-Skim Mozzarella Cheese
PRICE: $4.29 for 8 oz ($0.54 per oz)
MILK: Part-skim
FAT IN SOLIDS: 38%
SODIUM: 229 mg
AVERAGE THICKNESS: 1.8 mm
COMMENTS: This cheese's "big, fat shreds" were "soft" and "pliable," melting into an "even," "golden-brown" sheet atop pizza. Its flavor was "rich" and mildly "funky," with a "vegetal" tanginess. Though a few tasters found its melted strands "a bit tough," most agreed this was an all-around "good support cheese."

KRAFT Shredded Low-Moisture Part-Skim Mozzarella Cheese
PRICE: $3.99 for 8 oz ($0.50 per oz)
MILK: Part-skim
FAT IN SOLIDS: 41%
SODIUM: 207 mg
AVERAGE THICKNESS: 1.1 mm
COMMENTS: These moderately thick shreds were "mild," with a "familiar" "string cheese" flavor. Though fairly "starchy" when sampled plain, this cheese was perfectly "stretchy" and "chewy" when melted on pizza. A few picked up on a slightly "dusty" aftertaste, but most agreed that this "simple" cheese was a "safe bet."

RECOMMENDED WITH RESERVATIONS

KRAFT With a Touch of Philadelphia Mozzarella Shredded Cheese
PRICE: $3.99 for 8 oz ($0.50 per oz)
MILK: Part-skim
FAT IN SOLIDS: 40%
SODIUM: 253 mg
AVERAGE THICKNESS: 1.4 mm
COMMENTS: Tasters deemed this cheese "nutty," and "sharp" (if a "tad salty"). However, some couldn't get past the anticaking agents' "powdery" coating. Though texture improved with melting, some still found the cheese "rubbery" and "grainy" on pizza.

HORIZON ORGANIC Shredded Mozzarella Cheese
PRICE: $4.49 for 6 oz ($0.75 per oz)
MILK: Part-skim
FAT IN SOLIDS: 39%
SODIUM: 231 mg
AVERAGE THICKNESS: 1.5 mm
COMMENTS: This cheese made the "greasiest" pizza of the bunch, which was surprising considering its moderate fat level. Tasters that weren't put off by the "oil slick" enjoyed its "tangy" creaminess and "gooey" texture.

POLLY-O Low Moisture Part Skim Shredded Mozzarella
PRICE: $2.98 for 8 oz ($0.37 per oz)
MILK: Part-skim
FAT IN SOLIDS: 36%
SODIUM: 175 mg
AVERAGE THICKNESS: 2.8 mm
COMMENTS: Many tasters thought this cheese was "too lean" and "could use more salt," but some liked its "lightly nutty" flavor. "Springy" and easy to spread on pizza, it was a bit "rubbery" and "dry" when melted.

NOT RECOMMENDED

ORGANIC VALLEY Shredded Low Moisture Mozzarella Cheese, Part Skim
PRICE: $4.99 for 6 oz ($0.83 per oz)
MILK: Part-skim
FAT IN SOLIDS: 36%
SODIUM: 121 mg
AVERAGE THICKNESS: 0.9 mm
COMMENTS: "Was that cheese?" asked one taster after sampling these "plasticky," "bland" shreds. On pizza, the melted cheese was "rubbery," "tough," and "flavorless."

SUPERMARKET EXTRA-SHARP CHEDDAR

Supermarket shelves are bursting with American cheddar options, which makes choosing one a daunting task. Typically, the older the cheese, the stronger it tastes, which is why we choose extra-sharp cheddar when we want bold flavor. To find out which block deserved top billing, we tasted seven top-selling brands plain, in grilled cheese, and in stovetop macaroni and cheese. The cheeses aged closer to 24 months did not melt well; those products aged for 12 months or less melted beautifully but ranged in flavor from bold to bland. It turns out that meltability and flavor came down to moisture, fat content, and terroir. Relatively high fat and moisture contents made for optimum melting. Contaminant cultures picked up from the air where the cheese is made have a particularly large impact on extra-sharp cheddar's flavor. (For this reason, because the two Cracker Barrel cheeses tasted markedly different, we suspect they're made in different locations.) While we were able to recommend most of the cheeses we tried, only our winner had it all: richness, complexity, and a creamy, even texture when melted. Cheeses are listed in order of preference.

RECOMMENDED

CRACKER BARREL Extra Sharp White Cheddar Cheese
PRICE: $3.99 for 8 oz ($0.50 per oz)
COLOR: White
AGE: Proprietary
FAT: 35%
MOISTURE: 36%
MADE IN: Proprietary
COMMENTS: Described by one taster as "sharp to please all palates," this white cheddar was "rich" with the "perfect balance of tang." Its moderate amounts of fat and moisture ensured it was "crumbly" when sampled plain but still "creamy" when cooked.

CABOT Vermont Extra Sharp Cheddar Cheese
PRICE: $3.59 for 8 oz ($0.45 per oz)
COLOR: White
AGE: 12 months
FAT: 33%
MOISTURE: 37%
MADE IN: Vermont
COMMENTS: This white cheddar had an "assertive" sharpness that tasters loved. It melted with a "creamy" smoothness, though a few tasters noted some "graininess." This "firmer" cheese was great on crackers.

KERRYGOLD Reserve Cheddar
PRICE: $7.99 for 7 oz ($1.14 per oz)
COLOR: White
AGE: 24 months
FAT: 32%
MOISTURE: 36%
MADE IN: Ireland
COMMENTS: This Irish import softened into a "creamy" layer in grilled cheese and coated pasta nicely. Its "fragrant," "grassy" flavor reminded some tasters more of "Parmesan" or "Swiss" than of cheddar.

CABOT Private Stock Cheddar Cheese
PRICE: $5.00 for 8 oz ($0.63 per oz)
COLOR: White
AGE: 18 to 24 months
FAT: 34%
MOISTURE: 37%
MADE IN: Vermont
COMMENTS: When melted, this aged cheddar was "gritty." Said one taster: "I would eat the heck out of that cheese on a cracker, but it's way too sharp for a sandwich."

RECOMMENDED (continued)

CRACKER BARREL Extra Sharp Cheddar Cheese
PRICE: $3.99 for 8 oz ($0.50 per oz)
COLOR: Orange
AGE: Proprietary
FAT: 34%
MOISTURE: 37%
MADE IN: Proprietary
COMMENTS: This orange cheese was "mild," with a "soft," almost "plasticky" texture. When melted, tasters deemed it "familiar" and "creamy." However, many thought it lacked the sharpness for snacking plain.

RECOMMENDED WITH RESERVATIONS

GRAFTON VILLAGE CHEESE 2 Year Aged Vermont Raw Milk Cheddar Cheese
PRICE: $5.50 for 8 oz ($0.69 per oz)
COLOR: White
AGE: 24 months
FAT: 36%
MOISTURE: 33%
MADE IN: Vermont
COMMENTS: This "pungent" cheddar was the sharpest of the bunch. Sampled plain, most thought its boldness was "out of place" in grilled cheese and mac and cheese. Its low moisture also meant it wasn't a great melter.

KRAFT NATURALS Extra Sharp Cheddar Cheese
PRICE: $3.14 for 8 oz ($0.39 per oz)
COLOR: Orange
AGE: Proprietary
FAT: 36%
MOISTURE: 37%
MADE IN: Proprietary
COMMENTS: While this cheddar tasted "familiar," many thought it was too "plain" and "dull." However, we liked it melted into mac and cheese, where it was "sweet" and "buttery" like "classic blue box mac and cheese." In grilled cheese, it was "creamy," though some found it a tad "greasy."

FETA

Although feta remained a specialty item in the United States for most of the last century, it is now as as common in American refrigerators as cheddar. This rise in popularity has meant more options to choose from—and those options can vary wildly depending on where they're made. We sampled eight cheeses plain, crumbled into couscous salad, and baked in Greek spinach and feta pie. In the European Union, only cheeses made in Greece using at least 70 percent sheep's milk may bear the Protected Designation of Origin (PDO) seal and be labeled "feta." Of the samples we tasted, three were authentic PDO fetas, one was French, and the rest were domestic, and we quickly determined you can't beat the real deal. While the domestic cheeses were too salty and lean, the Greek fetas were complexly flavored with a moist, lush texture owing to their higher fat contents. The difference came down to salting. While the Greeks salt-age their fetas for a day or two before submerging the cheese in brine, domestic cheesemakers skip this step, going straight for the brine. While a few domestic fetas showed merit, it's hard to top our winner's indulgent texture and complex taste. Cheeses are listed in order of preference.

RECOMMENDED

REAL GREEK FETA Feta Cheese
PRICE: $13.99 per lb ($0.87 per oz)
ORIGIN: Greece
SODIUM: 260 mg
MILK: Sheep
FAT: 7 g
COMMENTS: This superb sheep's-milk feta was complex yet balanced. It was "buttery" and "savory" with "clean dairy flavor" but also "tart" and "lemony," with a "perfect" salt level. Texture-wise, it was "silky" and "tender" but "firm" enough to maintain its presence when stirred into salads or baked.

DODONI Feta Cheese
PRICE: $9.49 per lb ($0.59 per oz)
ORIGIN: Greece
SODIUM: 310 mg
MILK: Sheep and goat
FAT: 6 g
COMMENTS: This Greek feta was "bracingly tangy." Tasters called it "grassy" and "gamy." A few found it too strong, but most raved, especially when it was baked into pastry, which muted its flavor a bit. It was "moist" and "dense," with tender crumbles.

BOAR'S HEAD Feta Cheese
PRICE: $4.99 for 8 oz ($0.62 per oz)
ORIGIN: USA
SODIUM: 370 mg
MILK: Cow
FAT: 4 g
COMMENTS: This American-made feta was "quite salty," with a "subtle milky" flavor and a "vinegary tang." if you're looking for a simple feta, this "fairly mild" one might be fo you. Its texture was drier and a few tasters found it "pebbly," but most didn't mind.

NIKOS Feta Cheese
PRICE: $8.99 per lb ($0.56 per oz)
ORIGIN: USA
SODIUM: 320 mg
MILK: Cow
FAT: 6 g
COMMENTS: "Inoffensive but undistinguished" is how one taster described this feta. When sampled plain, it had a "rubbery" texture, but mixed into couscous or baked in phyllo, most tasters found it acceptable.

RECOMMENDED WITH RESERVATIONS

EUPHRATES Feta Cheese
PRICE: $6.49 per lb ($0.41 per oz)
ORIGIN: USA
SODIUM: 360 mg
MILK: Cow
FAT: 4 g
COMMENTS: When eaten plain and in couscous salad, this American feta was too salty for most tasters. But it was good baked in phyllo. Its texture was pleasing throughout: "discrete without being dry" and "creamy."

VALBRESO Feta Cheese
PRICE: $12.99 per lb ($0.81 per oz)
ORIGIN: France
SODIUM: 270 mg
MILK: Sheep
FAT: 6 g
COMMENTS: Made from excess milk from Roquefort cheese production, this feta was "almost spreadable." It "melted" into salad and disappeared in spanakopita. It was "creamy" and "rich," with a mild funk. We liked it, but it's not what we want in a feta.

MT. VIKOS Feta Cheese
PRICE: $9.50 for 8 oz ($1.19 per oz)
ORIGIN: Greece
SODIUM: 350 mg
MILK: Sheep and goat
FAT: 7 g
COMMENTS: Our old winner couldn't compete with bolder new products. It was "fine, nice even," with a "pleasant sheepy-goaty" flavor, but it wasn't as strong or rich-tasting as we wanted. It was dense but crumbled well.

NOT RECOMMENDED

ORGANIC VALLEY Feta Cheese
PRICE: $7.99 for 8 oz ($1.00 per oz)
ORIGIN: USA
SODIUM: 430 mg
MILK: Cow
FAT: 4 g
COMMENTS: Tasters described this feta as having a "sour" tang. Its high sodium content didn't cover up its funk in a salad where it was described as "bitter." Baked into spanakopita, it was "bland." Texture-wise, it was "firm" and "on the drier side."

PECORINO ROMANO CHEESE

Pecorino Romano cheese is one of the world's oldest cheeses; it has a firm, slightly oily, crystalline texture and salty, funky flavor. We use it in salads, vegetable dishes, soups, and frittatas, not to mention classic Italian pasta dishes such as cacio e pepe, pasta all'amatriciana, and lasagna. We sampled imported Pecorino Romanos, made with sheep's milk, and domestic Romanos, made with cow's milk. The different milks had obvious flavor implications: Sheep's milk develops complex flavors as it ages, and while some domestic producers try to create intensity by adding the enzyme lipase to cow's milk, the reaction results in cheese that tastes more like aged provolone. Because American sheep breeds produce less milk than European breeds and aging ties up inventory for long stretches of time, domestic producers simply cannot match European cheese makers. As such, the results of our blind tastings were of little surprise: Both plain and in pasta, tasters preferred the imported cheeses for their sharper, funkier flavor and crumbly, crystalline texture. (When we took a closer look, we noticed that the imports were aged for over eight months while the domestics were aged for as few as five.) The imports also had higher sodium, giving them a deeper, more savory taste. Cheeses are listed in order of preference.

RECOMMENDED

BOAR'S HEAD Pecorino Romano
PRICE: $6.99 for 7 oz ($1.00 per oz)
SOURCE: Sardinia, Italy (non-DOP)
MILK: Sheep
AGED: More than 8 months
INGREDIENTS: Pasteurized sheep's milk, cultures, rennet, salt
PH: 5.3
FAT: 8.4 g
SODIUM: 672 mg
COMMENTS: "Delicious! Rich, complex, deeply savory," and "crystalline" crunch, "dense, nicely dry, salty in a fruity, fatty kind of way," this sheep's-milk Pecorino Romano was our tasters' overall favorite. It also had the highest sodium level by far in our lineup, adding to its savory appeal.

ZERTO Pecorino Romano `BEST BUY`
PRICE: $4.99 for 7.5 oz ($0.67 per oz)
SOURCE: Sardinia, Italy (DOP)
MILK: Sheep
AGED: 9 months
INGREDIENTS: 100% sheep's milk, rennet, salt
PH: 5.4
FAT: 8 g
SODIUM: 550 mg
COMMENTS: With "lots of crystals," this "salty, rich, funky" cheese was "pleasingly pungent" when nibbled plain, "without being overbearing." Its "coarse texture" was "perfect for grating." In cacio e pepe, the flavor was "a little mild," but it achieved a "good balance of salt + cheese + pepper."

LOCATELLI Pecorino Romano
PRICE: $9.99 for 7.5 oz ($1.33 per oz)
SOURCE: Sardinia, Italy (DOP)
MILK: Sheep
AGED: Minimum 9 months
INGREDIENTS: 100% pure pasteurized sheep's milk, cultures, rennet, salt
PH: 5.3
FAT: 9 g
SODIUM: 550 mg
COMMENTS: "Full-flavored, crystalline, crumbly, and salty," this imported sheep's-milk Pecorino Romano had a "lovely sheepy, briny flavor." In cacio e pepe, it was "velvety," "creamy and buttery."

RECOMMENDED (continued)

GENUINE FULVI Pecorino Romano
PRICE: $7.99 for 7.5 oz ($1.07 per oz)
SOURCE: Nepi, Lazio, Italy (DOP)
MILK: Sheep
AGED: 10 months to 1 year
INGREDIENTS: Pasteurized sheep's milk, rennet, salt
PH: 5.6
FAT: 11.2 g
SODIUM: 560 mg
COMMENTS: With "a little kick!" and "some funk on the finish," this Pecorino won fans. "Firm and crumbly yet also creamy. It's grassy and fruity with some crunch." On spaghetti, it made for a "velvety," "nutty" sauce.

RECOMMENDED WITH RESERVATIONS

SARTORI Cheese Romano
PRICE: $4.19 for 5 oz ($0.84 per oz)
SOURCE: Wisconsin, USA
MILK: Cow
AGED: 8 months
INGREDIENTS: Pasteurized milk, cheese cultures, salt, enzymes
PH: 5.3
FAT: 7 g
SODIUM: 280 mg
COMMENTS: With "mild," "nutty" flavor, this Romano was "very soft" and "not as pungent as it should be." "It's mild, creamy, and toothsome with good milkiness," but others noted it "could stand to be saltier." In pasta, it had "nice sauciness" but "the cheese is really overwhelmed by the pepper."

BEL GIOIOSO Romano
PRICE: $6.99 for 8 oz ($0.87 per oz)
SOURCE: Wisconsin, USA
MILK: Raw cow's milk, rBST-free
AGED: 5 months
INGREDIENTS: Cultured milk, enzymes, salt
PH: 5.1
FAT: 7 g
SODIUM: 330 mg
COMMENTS: "Mildly salty" and slightly creamy," with a "pebbly" texture, this domestic cow's-milk Romano "eats like cheddar," "provolone," or "Swiss." "This is missing that gritty saltiness I crave," one taster noted.

JARRED PASTA SAUCE

Opting for jarred pasta sauce is an easy way to get a head start on dinner, but the array of supermarket sauces is dizzying. We focused on simple sauces from the 10 best-selling national brands, simmering and sampling them plain and tossed with spaghetti. Sauces that contained added sugar or corn syrup tasted sickly sweet. Use of whole tomatoes made for a fresh tomato taste we loved, and plenty of olive oil made for rich sauce that clung nicely to spaghetti. Our lower-ranking sauces were plagued with old, cooked flavors from their tomato paste bases and heavy use of dried herbs. After giving the sauces a try in lasagna, we discovered that our winner still reigned supreme. Containing the least amount of liquid, this sauce kept the lasagna layers distinct without sogging the noodles. Our top sauces aren't cheap, but we think they're worth the money. Pasta sauces are listed in order of preference.

RECOMMENDED

RAO'S Homemade Marinara Sauce
PRICE: $9.39 per 24-oz jar ($0.39 per oz)
INGREDIENTS: Italian tomatoes, olive oil, fresh onions, salt, fresh garlic, fresh basil, black pepper, oregano
SUGAR: 3 g
FAT: 7 g
LIQUIDS: 18%
SOLIDS: 82%
COMMENTS: This sauce offered "vibrant tomato flavor" and "bright" acidity. A dose of olive oil lent a "creamy" richness to pasta.

VICTORIA FINE FOODS Premium Marinara Sauce
PRICE: $6.99 per 24-oz jar ($0.29 per oz)
INGREDIENTS: Whole tomatoes, onions, olive oil, salt, garlic, basil, spices
SUGAR: 4 g
FAT: 4 g
LIQUIDS: 35%
SOLIDS: 65%
COMMENTS: This sauce was "zippy," with "roasted" notes. Added olive oil made for a sauce that "coated pasta nicely."

RECOMMENDED WITH RESERVATIONS

BARILLA Marinara Sauce
PRICE: $3.99 per 24-oz jar ($0.17 per oz)
INGREDIENTS: Tomato puree (water, tomato paste), diced tomatoes (tomatoes, citric acid), sugar, dried onions, dehydrated garlic, salt, basil, extra-virgin olive oil, oregano, citric acid, natural flavor
SUGAR: 9 g
FAT: 1 g
LIQUIDS: 34%
SOLIDS: 66%
COMMENTS: This product had "deep tomato flavor," but some tasters were distracted by its "sweet" and "herby" notes. Still, many liked the simplicity of this "mild" sauce.

FRANCESCO RINALDI Marinara Sauce
PRICE: $1.79 per 24-oz jar ($0.07 per oz)
INGREDIENTS: Tomato puree (water, tomato paste, citric acid), diced tomatoes in tomato juice, sugar, salt, extra-virgin olive oil, dried onions, spices, dried garlic
SUGAR: 7 g
FAT: 1 g
LIQUIDS: 38%
SOLIDS: 62%
COMMENTS: This sauce tasted of "tomato paste." Its "thick" texture "coated pasta well," but most agreed it was "middle of the road."

RECOMMENDED WITH RESERVATIONS *(continued)*

PREGO Traditional Italian Sauce
PRICE: $3.49 per 24-oz jar ($0.15 per oz)
INGREDIENTS: Tomato puree (water, tomato paste), diced tomatoes in tomato juice, sugar, contains less than 1% of: canola oil, salt, dehydrated onions, spice, dehydrated garlic, citric acid, onion extract, garlic extract
SUGAR: 10 g
FAT: 1.5 g
LIQUIDS: 36%
SOLIDS: 64%
COMMENTS: This sauce was "complex" but its "thick" texture and sweetness drew comparisons to "ketchup." This "familiar" brand evoked nostalgia for some, but most agreed this sauce lacked fresh tomato flavor.

NOT RECOMMENDED

RAGÚ Marinara Sauce
PRICE: $2.99 per 23.9-oz jar ($0.13 per oz)
INGREDIENTS: Tomato puree (water, tomato paste), crushed tomatoes in puree (crushed tomatoes, tomato puree, calcium chloride [firming aid], citric acid), soybean oil, extra-virgin olive oil, salt, sugar, dehydrated onions, spices, natural flavor
SUGAR: 7 g
FAT: 2.5 g
LIQUIDS: 41%
SOLIDS: 59%
COMMENTS: "Is this ketchup?" asked one taster about this "suspiciously smooth" sauce. It reminded tasters of "cafeteria spaghetti." Most deemed it "boring" and "bland."

CLASSICO Tomato & Basil Sauce
PRICE: $3.59 per 24-oz jar ($0.15 per oz)
INGREDIENTS: Tomato puree (water, tomato paste), diced tomatoes in juice (tomatoes, tomato juice, citric acid, calcium chloride), contains 2% or less of: olive oil, onions, salt, basil, garlic, spices, natural flavors
SUGAR: 5 g
FAT: 2 g
LIQUIDS: 22%
SOLIDS: 78%
COMMENTS: A lack of added sugars actually worked against this product, which was "blindingly acidic." It fell short on fresh tomato flavor and was "overpowered" by "dusty" notes of dried oregano and basil.

SMOOTH PEANUT BUTTER

Smooth peanut butter can be found in three forms: the familiar products made with hydrogenated vegetable oil and sugar, "natural" options that use palm oil, and "natural" peanut butters made with just peanuts and salt. We gathered top-selling jars in each category and tasted them in PB&Js, peanut butter cookies, and plain. The peanuts-and-salt products sank right to the bottom; they tended to be thin, runny, and gritty. Because they contain only peanut oil and therefore had the least amount of saturated fat, cookies made with these peanut butters didn't spread in the oven and baked up cakey. The peanut butters made with palm oil made cookies that spread significantly into thin, crumbly disks. The best cookies were made with peanut butters that used hydrogenated oils: They tasted rich; had a thick, chewy texture; and just the right amount of bend. These peanut butters also had a touch more salt, which helped balance them against sweet jams in sandwiches. Peanut butters are listed in order of preference.

RECOMMENDED

SKIPPY Creamy Peanut Butter
PRICE: $2.69 per 16.3-oz jar ($0.17 per oz)
STYLE: Hydrogenated oil
ADDED SUGAR: Yes
SATURATED FAT: 3 g
SUGAR: 3 g
SODIUM: 150 mg
COOKIE THICKNESS: 0.4 in
COMMENTS: This favorite was praised for its "balance of sweet and salty." We loved its "classic smoothness" in sandwiches. It made cookies that were perfectly chewy.

JIF Creamy Peanut Butter
PRICE: $3.29 per 16-oz jar ($0.21 per oz)
STYLE: Hydrogenated oil
ADDED SUGAR: Yes
SATURATED FAT: 2.5 g
SUGAR: 3 g
SODIUM: 135 mg
COOKIE THICKNESS: 0.4 in
COMMENTS: This "familiar" peanut butter was "smooth" and produced "well-balanced" sandwiches. Cookies were "chewy" and "moist" but a bit lacking in peanut flavor.

PETER PAN Natural Creamy Peanut Butter
PRICE: $4.93 per 28-oz jar ($0.18 per oz)
STYLE: Palm oil
ADDED SUGAR: Yes
SATURATED FAT: 3.5 g
SUGAR: 3 g
SODIUM: 130 mg
COOKIE THICKNESS: 0.3 in
COMMENTS: Tasters thought this offering was "spreadable," with a "rich," "roasty" flavor in sandwiches. Cookies were a bit too "flat" and, to some, a tad "greasy."

SKIPPY Natural Peanut Butter Spread
PRICE: $2.69 per 15-oz jar ($0.18 per oz)
STYLE: Palm oil
ADDED SUGAR: Yes
SATURATED FAT: 3.5 g
SUGAR: 3 g
SODIUM: 150 mg
COOKIE THICKNESS: 0.3 in
COMMENTS: Like other palm oil products, this peanut butter made cookies that were "a touch too flat." But tasters loved it on sandwiches, where it was "creamy," with "a hint of sweetness" and a "pleasant nutty aftertaste."

RECOMMENDED (continued)

JIF Natural Creamy Peanut Butter Spread
PRICE: $3.29 per 16-oz jar ($0.21 per oz)
STYLE: Palm oil
ADDED SUGAR: Yes
SATURATED FAT: 3 g
SUGAR: 3 g
SODIUM: 80 mg
COOKIE THICKNESS: 0.3 in
COMMENTS: This peanut butter had a "roasty" flavor and "thick" texture that made a sturdy sandwich. Cookies spread but most liked this peanut butter's "fluffy" lightness.

ADAMS Natural Creamy Peanut Butter
PRICE: $6.01 per 26-oz jar ($0.23 per oz)
STYLE: Just peanuts and salt
ADDED SUGAR: No
SATURATED FAT: 2.5 g
SUGAR: 1 g
SODIUM: 105 mg
COOKIE THICKNESS: 0.5 in
COMMENTS: This product was "drippy" in sandwiches and made "cakey" cookies, but most enjoyed its "pure peanut" flavor.

RECOMMENDED WITH RESERVATIONS

SMUCKER'S Natural Creamy Peanut Butter
PRICE: $4.29 per 16-oz jar ($0.27 per oz)
STYLE: Just peanuts and salt
ADDED SUGAR: No
SATURATED FAT: 2.5 g
SUGAR: 1 g
SODIUM: 105 mg
COOKIE THICKNESS: 0.5 in
COMMENTS: This peanut butter was "runny." Tasters liked its "roasted" notes. Cookies were "moist," but "cakey."

PETER PAN Creamy Original Peanut Butter
PRICE: $3.59 per 16.3-oz jar ($0.22 per oz)
STYLE: Hydrogenated oil
ADDED SUGAR: Yes
SATURATED FAT: 3 g
SUGAR: 3 g
SODIUM: 140 mg
COOKIE THICKNESS: 0.4 in
COMMENTS: This product had sweetness, "toasty" notes, and a "spreadable" texture, but many noted a "stale" aftertaste.

READY-MADE PIE CRUSTS

There's no doubt that good homemade pie crust has better flavor and texture than store-bought versions. But when time is of the essence, it's nice to have a ready-made crust you can count on, so we put store-bought pastry crusts and graham cracker crusts through their paces. For the former, we prefer the convenience of rolled pastry crusts, so we tested three nationally available products only to find that two needed extra rolling in order to fit into a standard 9-inch pie plate. The same two crusts began burning halfway through baking while our winner emerged tender, flaky, and evenly browned. A look at the nutritional labels explained this: The two burned crusts contained sugar, speeding their browning, while the winner contained no sugar at all. Another important factor was fat content. While our winner's use of lard made for pockets of slow-melting fat for tender, flaky layers, the two lesser products used palm oil, a less stable fat that melts more readily, creating a heavy, dense crust.

When we tested graham cracker crusts plain and in lemon icebox pie, we vastly preferred products with a mix of white and whole-wheat flours, which produced the nutty flavor and tender texture we were looking for. Fat content was also key: Products with more fat were tender and moist and could be cut into neat slices. Our winner aced each test, offering the right balance of sweet, nutty flavor and crisp texture. Crusts are listed in order of preference.

PASTRY CRUST: RECOMMENDED

PILLSBURY Refrigerated Pie Crusts
PRICE: $3.99 for 2 crusts ($2.00 per crust)
FAT: Lard and modified lard
SUGAR: 0 g per 25-g serving
COMMENTS: "Flaky," "buttery," and "user-friendly," this product met all our requirements for an ideal supermarket crust. It fit perfectly in our pie plate right out of the package, with "plenty of overhang" that allowed us to make "picture-perfect" crimped edges. Tasters loved its "light," "crispy" texture and "clean," "toasty" flavor that "allowed the filling to shine."

RECOMMENDED WITH RESERVATIONS

WHOLLY WHOLESOME Bake At Home Organic Pie Dough
PRICE: $6.99 for 2 crusts ($3.50 per crust)
FAT: Palm oil
SUGAR: <1 g per 25-g serving
COMMENTS: Though most testers liked the "savory" nuttiness of this "thick," "short-bread"-like crust, some thought the texture was a bit "dense" and "dry." It was also difficult to use: The dough cracked when we tried to unroll it, had to be rolled further to fit in our pie plate, and browned too quickly. While it required more work than we prefer in a supermarket crust, this product makes a decent pie if you prefer a vegetarian crust.

NOT RECOMMENDED

IMMACULATE BAKING CO. Ready to Bake Pie Crusts
PRICE: $3.99 for 2 crusts ($2.00 per crust)
FAT: Palm fruit oil and canola oil
SUGAR: <1 g per 25-g serving
COMMENTS: There was little to like about this crust: It tasted "fishy," and "sour" even though it was well within its sell-by date, and its texture was "tough" and "dense," like "cardboard." Though it unrolled easily, we had to stretch it paper-thin for it to fit in our pie plate, so the bottom crust baked up "soggy." Added sugar caused the crust to burn halfway through a 1½-hour bake.

GRAHAM CRACKER CRUST: RECOMMENDED

KEEBLER Ready Crust Graham Pie Crust
PRICE: $2.59 per 6-oz crust ($0.43 per oz)
FAT: 5 g
SUGAR: 6 g
COMMENTS: This crust nailed the balance of "sugary" and "wheaty" and had a flourishing "touch of saltiness" and "hint of vanilla" that reminded tasters of "homemade." The texture was "crisp" yet "tender," and the crust cut neatly for picture-perfect slices.

HONEY MAID Graham Cracker Crust
PRICE: $2.49 per 6-oz crust ($0.42 per oz)
FAT: 5 g
SUGAR: 6 g
COMMENTS: "Exactly like graham crackers I ate as a kid," said one taster about this "familiar" product's "buttery flavor" and "honey sweetness." Most also appreciated its "light," "tender" texture that was still "sturdy" enough to hold its shape when sliced.

NOT RECOMMENDED

ARROWHEAD MILLS Graham Cracker Pie Crust
PRICE: $3.79 per 6-oz crust ($0.63 per oz)
FAT: 4 g
SUGAR: 7 g
COMMENTS: This lower-fat crust "crumbled like a dry sand castle" when we sliced into it and had a "dusty" texture that coated tasters' mouths. Its flavor was "too sweet," and a few noted a "raw flour" aftertaste.

MI-DEL Gluten-Free, Allergen Safe Graham Style Pie Crust
PRICE: $3.99 per 7.1-oz crust ($0.56 per oz)
FAT: 5 g
SUGAR: 7 g
COMMENTS: From its "overpowering" after-taste of "raisin" and "banana" to its "cloying" sweetness, tasters found little to like about the flavor of this gluten-free crust. They were equally perplexed by its texture, which was somehow both "soggy" and "gritty," like "eating a mouthful of wet sand."

SUPERMARKET TURKEY

A well-tested recipe and the right equipment go a long way toward a better bird, but the turkey itself matters just as much. To find the best supermarket bird, we purchased eight best-selling turkeys from both national and regional brands. All birds were in the 12- to 14-pound range, which we like for its 10- to 12-serving yield and easy maneuverability. After salting and roasting the turkeys the differences became immediately clear. Half of the birds tasted weak and washed out, with musty, gummy textures. On the flip side, our top turkeys were deeply flavorful, juicy, and tender. Why this broad range? It all came down to diet and treatment. Though it was hard to get details on what each producer feeds its birds, we noticed that turkeys labeled "vegetarian-fed" and "antibiotic-free" tended to taste better. And although injections of salt-based solutions are intended to enhance flavor and moisture, all the treated birds we tasted were rife with texture issues. The untreated birds also had far fattier, more flavorful meat. In the end, we were convinced that untreated, vegetarian-fed turkeys were the best holiday table candidates because they offer clean turkey flavor and allow you to control the seasoning. Turkeys are listed in order of preference.

RECOMMENDED

MARY'S Free-Range Non-GMO Verified Turkey
PRICE: $2.69 per lb
INGREDIENT: Turkey
AGE: 10 to 12 weeks
PERCENT OF RETAINED LIQUID: Up to 6%
ANTIBIOTIC-FREE: Yes
VEGETARIAN-FED: Yes
FAT IN DARK MEAT: 2.61%
FAT IN WHITE MEAT: 0.48%
COMMENTS: "Tastes like what I think turkey should taste like," wrote one happy taster. Our winner has relatively high fat levels and is fed a vegetarian diet. As a result, it had "clean," "robust" turkey flavor. It had "great texture" and was "very tender and juicy."

PLAINVILLE FARMS
Young Turkey `BEST BUY`
PRICE: $1.19 per lb
INGREDIENT: Turkey
AGE: 13 weeks
PERCENT OF RETAINED LIQUID:
Less than 6%
ANTIBIOTIC-FREE: Yes
VEGETARIAN-FED: Yes
FAT IN DARK MEAT: 4.11%
FAT IN WHITE MEAT: 0.46%
COMMENTS: Our Best Buy was "amazingly flavorful." Tasters liked the "rich" flavor of the dark meat, which was so good that there was "no need for gravy." Its dark meat had the highest fat level in our lineup and was deemed "firm, juicy, tender."

DIESTEL TURKEY RANCH
Non-GMO Verified Turkey
PRICE: $3.49 per lb
INGREDIENT: Turkey
AGE: About 24 weeks
PERCENT OF RETAINED LIQUID: Up to 3%
ANTIBIOTIC-FREE: Yes
VEGETARIAN-FED: Yes
FAT IN DARK MEAT: 3.58%
FAT IN WHITE MEAT: 0.78%
COMMENTS: Raised for six months, this turkey had dark meat with a purplish hue, "savory" flavor, and "subtle minerality" that reminded us of duck and expensive heritage turkeys. As for texture, panelists commented that even the white meat was "perfect."

RECOMMENDED (continued)

BELL & EVANS Turkey Raised Without Antibiotics
PRICE: $2.99 per lb
INGREDIENT: Turkey
AGE: 10 to 12 weeks
PERCENT OF RETAINED LIQUID:
Less than 4%
ANTIBIOTIC-FREE: Yes
VEGETARIAN-FED: Yes
FAT IN DARK MEAT: 3.61%
FAT IN WHITE MEAT: 1.51%
COMMENTS: Tasters loved the "flavorful" and "tender and moist" meat. The white meat had the highest fat level of the bunch, and its dark meat was almost purple—a sign of older or relatively well-exercised birds.

RECOMMENDED WITH RESERVATIONS

JENNIE-O Frozen Whole Turkey
PRICE: $0.69 per lb
INGREDIENTS: Young turkey containing approximately 9.5% of a solution of turkey broth, salt, sodium phosphate, sugar, flavoring
AGE: About 12 weeks
PERCENT OF RETAINED LIQUID:
Approximately 9.5%
ANTIBIOTIC-FREE: No
VEGETARIAN-FED: No
FAT IN DARK MEAT: 1.50%
FAT IN WHITE MEAT: 0.16%
COMMENTS: Tasters found the white meat "very bland" and wished the dark meat were "a little richer." Some praised its texture, but others found it "almost mushy."

HONEYSUCKLE WHITE
Frozen Young Turkey
PRICE: $1.16 per lb
INGREDIENTS: Turkey, broth, salt, sugar, natural flavoring
AGE: 10 to 13 weeks
PERCENT OF RETAINED LIQUID: 9.5%
ANTIBIOTIC-FREE: No
VEGETARIAN-FED: No
FAT IN DARK MEAT: 2.71%
FAT IN WHITE MEAT: 0.49%
COMMENTS: "Weak" and "generic" were apt descriptions of this bird's flavor. This turkey contains 9.5 percent absorbed moisture, prompting remarks such as "leaning toward mushy" and "a little waterlogged."

SANTOKU KNIVES

With their petite build and curved tips, santoku knives have been giving Western-style chef's knives a run for their money. To find out if they offer something unique, we tested 10 santoku knives and also compared their feel and performance to that of our favorite chef's knife. We used them to dice onions, break down whole raw chickens into parts, and quarter unpeeled butternut squashes. To assess precision, we cut carrots into matchsticks. Handles with big bumps, curves, and strongly tapered shapes lost points, as they forced our hands into uncomfortable positions, and handles made from all metal or smooth plastic slipped if our hands were wet or greasy. The angle of the bevel—the slim strip on either side of the blade that narrows to form the cutting edge—is what determines the sharpness of the blade. Nearly all were 15 degrees, a standard angle for an Asian-style knife, but a couple were even narrower—just 10 degrees. Most of the models we tested featured gently curved bottom edges that allow for a subtle rocking motion, which we found effective for mincing herbs. In the end, we decided that if you prefer a smaller tool, one of our top-ranked santokus might suit you just fine. However, if you're comfortable with the extra length and heft of a chef's knife and would miss the pointed tip (as opposed to the santoku's turned-down tip), you might want to consider a santoku only as an addition to your arsenal, not as a replacement. Products are listed in order of preference.

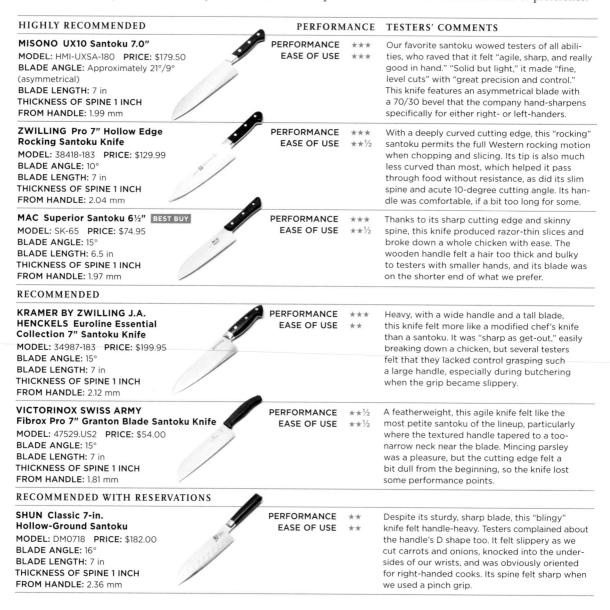

HIGHLY RECOMMENDED

	PERFORMANCE		TESTERS' COMMENTS

MISONO UX10 Santoku 7.0"
MODEL: HMI-UXSA-180   PRICE: $179.50
BLADE ANGLE: Approximately 21°/9° (asymmetrical)
BLADE LENGTH: 7 in
THICKNESS OF SPINE 1 INCH FROM HANDLE: 1.99 mm

PERFORMANCE ★★★
EASE OF USE ★★★

Our favorite santoku wowed testers of all abilities, who raved that it felt "agile, sharp, and really good in hand." "Solid but light," it made "fine, level cuts" with "great precision and control." This knife features an asymmetrical blade with a 70/30 bevel that the company hand-sharpens specifically for either right- or left-handers.

ZWILLING Pro 7" Hollow Edge Rocking Santoku Knife
MODEL: 38418-183   PRICE: $129.99
BLADE ANGLE: 10°
BLADE LENGTH: 7 in
THICKNESS OF SPINE 1 INCH FROM HANDLE: 2.04 mm

PERFORMANCE ★★★
EASE OF USE ★★½

With a deeply curved cutting edge, this "rocking" santoku permits the full Western rocking motion when chopping and slicing. Its tip is also much less curved than most, which helped it pass through food without resistance, as did its slim spine and acute 10-degree cutting angle. Its handle was comfortable, if a bit too long for some.

MAC Superior Santoku 6½" **BEST BUY**
MODEL: SK-65   PRICE: $74.95
BLADE ANGLE: 15°
BLADE LENGTH: 6.5 in
THICKNESS OF SPINE 1 INCH FROM HANDLE: 1.97 mm

PERFORMANCE ★★★
EASE OF USE ★★½

Thanks to its sharp cutting edge and skinny spine, this knife produced razor-thin slices and broke down a whole chicken with ease. The wooden handle felt a hair too thick and bulky to testers with smaller hands, and its blade was on the shorter end of what we prefer.

RECOMMENDED

KRAMER BY ZWILLING J.A. HENCKELS Euroline Essential Collection 7" Santoku Knife
MODEL: 34987-183   PRICE: $199.95
BLADE ANGLE: 15°
BLADE LENGTH: 7 in
THICKNESS OF SPINE 1 INCH FROM HANDLE: 2.12 mm

PERFORMANCE ★★★
EASE OF USE ★★

Heavy, with a wide handle and a tall blade, this knife felt more like a modified chef's knife than a santoku. It was "sharp as get-out," easily breaking down a chicken, but several testers felt that they lacked control grasping such a large handle, especially during butchering when the grip became slippery.

VICTORINOX SWISS ARMY Fibrox Pro 7" Granton Blade Santoku Knife
MODEL: 47529.US2   PRICE: $54.00
BLADE ANGLE: 15°
BLADE LENGTH: 7 in
THICKNESS OF SPINE 1 INCH FROM HANDLE: 1.81 mm

PERFORMANCE ★★½
EASE OF USE ★★½

A featherweight, this agile knife felt like the most petite santoku of the lineup, particularly where the textured handle tapered to a too-narrow neck near the blade. Mincing parsley was a pleasure, but the cutting edge felt a bit dull from the beginning, so the knife lost some performance points.

RECOMMENDED WITH RESERVATIONS

SHUN Classic 7-in. Hollow-Ground Santoku
MODEL: DM0718   PRICE: $182.00
BLADE ANGLE: 16°
BLADE LENGTH: 7 in
THICKNESS OF SPINE 1 INCH FROM HANDLE: 2.36 mm

PERFORMANCE ★★
EASE OF USE ★★

Despite its sturdy, sharp blade, this "blingy" knife felt handle-heavy. Testers complained about the handle's D shape too. It felt slippery as we cut carrots and onions, knocked into the undersides of our wrists, and was obviously oriented for right-handed cooks. Its spine felt sharp when we used a pinch grip.

HIGH-END BLENDERS

In terms of a luxury blender that can pulverize anything and will likely outlast its seven-year warranty, the Vitamix 5200 has been our top choice for years. It is admittedly a stripped-down machine, with three features on its control panel. But recently, Vitamix and other manufacturers have released new models with more power and extra bells and whistles. We tested some newcomers to see if more money gets you a superior blender. The answer was, mostly, no. The LCD touch screen on one wasn't responsive enough to be a practical upgrade. A cavitation warning was unnecessary as well (you don't need the machine to tell you when an air pocket has formed; you can hear it). Presets weren't especially helpful and can add as much as $200.00 to a blender's price. And more power wasn't necessarily better: The most powerful model wasn't able to make mayonnaise because its lowest speed was too fast. While we can ultimately recommend three of the four new high-end models, the Vitamix 5200 is still the best high-end blender for the money; while some blenders produced more finely textured results, it's hard to beat the velvety, creamy blends produced in the tall, narrow jar of the Vitamix 5200. Products are listed in order of preference.

HIGHLY RECOMMENDED	PERFORMANCE		TESTERS' COMMENTS
VITAMIX 5200  MODEL: 5200 PRICE: $449.00 JAR DIAMETER: 4 in DECIBELS ON HIGH: 96.1 WATTS: 1,380 WARRANTY: 7-year full	SMOOTHIE HUMMUS CRUSHED ICE MAYONNAISE ALMOND BUTTER HOT SOUP JUICE MANEUVERABILITY EASE OF USE	★★★ ★★★ ★★★ ★★★ ★★★ ★★ ★½ ★★★ ★½	This quiet, high-powered blender has intuitive controls. Its blending capability was top notch, producing fine-textured foods without incorporating excess air. The tamper accessory was helpful when blending thicker foods, and the seven-year warranty insured our investment. It's tall, so it can't be stored on a counter beneath a standard cabinet, and its narrow jar made scraping out its contents a minor challenge.
VITAMIX Professional Series 750  MODEL: 750 PRICE: $574.99 JAR DIAMETER: 4.5 in DECIBELS ON HIGH: 104 WATTS: 1,440 WARRANTY: 7-year full	SMOOTHIE HUMMUS CRUSHED ICE MAYONNAISE ALMOND BUTTER HOT SOUP JUICE MANEUVERABILITY EASE OF USE	★★½ ★★★ ★★★ ★★★ ★★★ ★★ ★½ ★★★ ★★½	This model is the higher-end version of our winner, with presets for tasks such as making smoothies and cleaning. With its slightly more powerful motor, the Vitamix 750 blended food more finely than the Vitamix 5200, but its wider jar allowed more air to be incorporated into the food and it was louder. It's shorter, so it can be stored beneath a standard cabinet, and its wider jar was slightly easier to scrape food out of.

RECOMMENDED			
KITCHENAID Pro Line Series Blender with Thermal Control Jar  MODEL: KSB8270CA PRICE: $524.95 JAR DIAMETER: 4.5 in DECIBELS ON HIGH: 105.7 WATTS: 1,800 WARRANTY: 10 years	SMOOTHIE HUMMUS CRUSHED ICE MAYONNAISE ALMOND BUTTER HOT SOUP JUICE MANEUVERABILITY EASE OF USE	★★½ ★★★ ★★★ ★★★ ★★★ ★★ ★½ ★½ ★★½	This blender made creamy almond butter and mayonnaise; smoothies and soups were very smooth albeit slightly aerated. Its motor was loud, and the blender rocked at higher speeds. The thermal control jar didn't keep contents any hotter than regular jars. At a whopping 20 pounds, this model is cumbersome to move and will probably need a fixed spot on your counter.

RECOMMENDED WITH RESERVATIONS			
BREVILLE The Boss  MODEL: BBL910XL PRICE: $399.95 JAR DIAMETER: 4.5 in DECIBELS ON HIGH: 99.1 WATTS: 1,500 WARRANTY: 7 years	SMOOTHIE HUMMUS CRUSHED ICE MAYONNAISE ALMOND BUTTER HOT SOUP JUICE MANEUVERABILITY EASE OF USE	★★½ ★★★ ★★★ ★★★ ★½ ★ ★½ ★★½ ★★★	This blender had a bright screen and a handy built-in timer. Smoothies and soups were smooth, though slightly aerated. We made almond butter twice in it; the first time it overheated. The second time it smelled like it was burning but it powered through. Breville also makes our winning midpriced blender, The Hemisphere Control, which makes slightly less smooth food but costs $200.00 less.

NOT RECOMMENDED			
BLENDTEC Designer 725  MODEL: CTB3 PRICE: $679.95 JAR DIAMETER: 5.75 in DECIBELS ON HIGH: 103.2 WATTS: About 2,800 WARRANTY: 8 years	SMOOTHIE HUMMUS CRUSHED ICE MAYONNAISE ALMOND BUTTER HOT SOUP JUICE MANEUVERABILITY EASE OF USE	★★½ ★★½ ★★ ○ ★★ ★★½ ★½ ★★½ ★	This powerful blender had a propeller-like blade. It was too vigorous to emulsify mayonnaise, and despite all that power, bits of food also got stuck in the corners of the squared-off jar. The "cavitation warning," which signals the formation of air bubbles, was unnecessary; a tamper (which this model lacks) is better for preventing air pockets. The touch screen wasn't very responsive; it also constantly scrolled messages.

MIDPRICED BLENDERS

Our favorite midpriced blender from five years ago, The Hemisphere Control from Breville ($199.95), has held up incredibly well. That said, it's our job to periodically scour the marketplace to make sure nothing new has come along that might topple the current champ. We found six contenders to pit against the Breville (capping the price at $300.00) and put them through a range of tests. We found stark differences among the models in the new lineup. Four utterly failed at emulsifying mayonnaise, and only one was successful in turning almonds into a smooth butter. Some smoothies had green flecks of kale speckled throughout or were overly aerated. We thought the difference might be due to the shape of the blades or power, but what really mattered was the design of the jar. Jars with rounded interiors and smooth, seamless bottoms didn't trap food and created the best vortices. Wider jars were easier to scrape out, but ingredients spattered, they required lots of scrape-downs, and they incorporated too much air. Narrower jars kept the food contained and required less scraping down. When we tallied the scores, our old favorite once again won out. It wasn't as high-powered as some of the other models but it features a rounded, narrow jar; a powerful-enough motor; and a good range of speed. It produced nicely blended smoothies, perfect mayo, and snowy crushed ice, and it even did well in our almond butter abuse test. Products are listed in order of preference.

HIGHLY RECOMMENDED

BREVILLE
The Hemisphere Control
MODEL: BBL605XL   PRICE: $199.95
JAR WIDTH: 4.8 in
DECIBELS: 87.3 (low), 91.4 (high)
WATTS: 750
WARRANTY: 1 year
LOWEST RPM: 3,812

PERFORMANCE	
SMOOTHIE	★★½
CRUSHED ICE	★★★
MAYONNAISE	★★★
ALMOND BUTTER	★★½
EASE OF USE	★★½
NOISE	★★★

TESTERS' COMMENTS

Our previous winner once again beat out the competition, reliably passing every test. Its jar was comparatively narrow, so it required relatively few scrape-downs and combined foods efficiently. Its built-in timer stopped the blender every minute, so we had to restart it during longer projects, but it's durable and has stood the test of time in the test kitchen.

RECOMMENDED

KITCHENAID 5-Speed
Diamond Blender
MODEL: KSB1575ER   PRICE: $159.99
JAR WIDTH: 4.5 in
DECIBELS: 83.1 (low), 97.3 (high)
WATTS: 550
WARRANTY: 5-year limited
LOWEST RPM: 11,008

PERFORMANCE	
SMOOTHIE	★★
CRUSHED ICE	★★★
MAYONNAISE	★★★
ALMOND BUTTER	★★½
EASE OF USE	★★
NOISE	★★★

The least expensive model in our lineup, this blender had a narrow jar that combined food well, but it was relatively low-powered, so its smoothies had large flecks of kale scattered throughout. While this blender had a smaller footprint and was easy to move and store, its jar was sometimes hard to twist off, and its partially downturned blade was hard to clean.

RECOMMENDED WITH RESERVATIONS

OSTER Versa Pro
Performance Blender with
Tamper 1400 Watts
MODEL: BLSTVB-RV0   PRICE: $199.99
JAR WIDTH: 5.8 in
DECIBELS: 87.4 (low), 94.8 (high)
WATTS: 1,400
WARRANTY: 7-year limited
LOWEST RPM: 10,210

PERFORMANCE	
SMOOTHIE	★★½
CRUSHED ICE	★★
MAYONNAISE	○
ALMOND BUTTER	★★½
EASE OF USE	★★½
NOISE	★★★

This blender made smoothies that were slightly aerated but impressively fine-textured, and we liked its intuitive controls. The downside: It had a wide jar and a very fast low speed, so it produced a lot of splatter, couldn't make mayonnaise, and required many midblend scrape-downs.

BRAUN PureMix
MODEL: JB7172BK   PRICE: $179.95
JAR WIDTH: 4.75 in
DECIBELS: 85.6 (low), 89.4 (high)
WATTS: 670
WARRANTY: 2 years
LOWEST RPM: 1,980

PERFORMANCE	
SMOOTHIE	★★
CRUSHED ICE	★★★
MAYONNAISE	★
ALMOND BUTTER	★★
EASE OF USE	★½
NOISE	★★★

This smaller, low-powered blender made OK smoothies, but it couldn't dependably make mayonnaise. Its buttons were hard to press, and its heavy jar was taxing to pour from. The blade can be detached for cleaning, but we found this more frustrating than helpful since food got stuck in the seam where the blade attached.

NOT RECOMMENDED

NUTRI NINJA
Ninja BlendMAX DUO
MODEL: BL2013   PRICE: $199.99
JAR WIDTH: 6.8 in
DECIBELS: 92.2 (low), 96 (high)
WATTS: 1,600
WARRANTY: 5-year VIP limited
and lifetime limited
LOWEST RPM: 2,264

PERFORMANCE	
SMOOTHIE	★★
CRUSHED ICE	★★★
MAYONNAISE	○
ALMOND BUTTER	★★★
EASE OF USE	★
NOISE	★★★

This blender created a raucous vortex, so its smoothies were extremely aerated albeit smooth. Its lid opens via a spout on the side, so when we drizzled in oil to make mayonnaise, it ran down the side of the jar, resulting in a mayo that didn't emulsify. Its lid and jar had chambers that collected water and food particles. We had to be very careful when removing its six-pronged blade for cleaning.

INEXPENSIVE BLENDERS

Could we find a good blender for less than $100.00? To find out, we selected seven top sellers priced from $60.68 to $99.99 and conducted a taxing series of tests. Overall, we preferred blenders with narrower jars; they kept their contents more contained so that their blends were dense and smooth, and they required fewer scrape-downs. Mayonnaise is especially tricky because it's a small-volume recipe that has to be combined slowly to emulsify properly. Two of the blenders' blades were set too high, so they couldn't reach the ingredients underneath to combine them. And three blenders had low speeds that were simply too fast, preventing the mixture from emulsifying. We preferred easy-to-press, clearly labeled buttons; lighter plastic jars to heavier glass ones; and jars that were easy to attach, detach, and pour from. Our top-rated model was simple to operate and blended exceptionally well. It couldn't make almond butter—the toughest task—but its overheat protection system stopped its motor so it wouldn't burn out while trying to. For those who just want a darn margarita, a smoothie, or some soup, our winner, from Black + Decker, is an excellent choice. Products are listed in order of preference.

RECOMMENDED	PERFORMANCE	TESTERS' COMMENTS
BLACK + DECKER Performance FusionBlade Blender MODEL: BL6010 PRICE: $80.26 JAR WIDTH: 4.25 in DECIBELS: 84.5 (low), 95.3 (high) LOWEST RPM: 8,558	BLENDING/CRUSHING ★★★ MAYONNAISE ★★★ ALMOND BUTTER ○ CLEANING/HANDLING ★★ CONTROLS/OPERATION ★★★ NOISE LEVEL ★★★	Our top-rated blender made impressively silky smoothies, frozen margaritas, mayonnaise, and pureed soups that were on par with those produced by blenders costing five times as much. It was notably quiet. It overheated during the almond butter test but recovered thanks to its overheat protection system. Its tall, narrow jar was easy to attach, detach, and pour from.

RECOMMENDED WITH RESERVATIONS		
BRAUN PureMix MODEL: JB7000BKS PRICE: $75.92 JAR WIDTH: 4.5 in DECIBELS: 89.4 (low), 95 (high) LOWEST RPM: 10,928	BLENDING/CRUSHING ★★ MAYONNAISE ○ ALMOND BUTTER ★★ CLEANING/HANDLING ★★½ CONTROLS/OPERATION ★★ NOISE LEVEL ★★★	This blender made well-blended soup and margaritas, but tougher textures such as kale took longer to get good results. It took a long time to make almond butter (and it was a bit stodgy). Chunks occasionally remained when crushing ice. Sometimes it took us two tries to engage the buttons. Its lowest speed splattered ingredients too chaotically to emulsify mayonnaise.
NINJA Professional Blender MODEL: BL610 PRICE: $64.89 JAR WIDTH: 6 in DECIBELS: 93.6 (low), 97.3 (high) LOWEST RPM: 3,440	BLENDING/CRUSHING ★★ MAYONNAISE ○ ALMOND BUTTER ★★½ CLEANING/HANDLING ★★ CONTROLS/OPERATION ★★★ NOISE LEVEL ★★	This blender crushed ice and pureed soup well, and it made acceptably smooth smoothies, but margaritas had small chunks. It had intuitive controls. Although its almond butter was quite good, it couldn't make mayonnaise because its blades were too high to reach the egg mixture at the bottom. Its removable blade was hard to clean.
CUISINART Velocity Ultra 7.5 1 HP Blender MODEL: SPB-650 PRICE: $99.99 JAR WIDTH: 5.4 in DECIBELS: 92.2 (low), 96.7 (high) LOWEST RPM: 3,411	BLENDING/CRUSHING ★★ MAYONNAISE ○ ALMOND BUTTER ★★ CLEANING/HANDLING ★★½ CONTROLS/OPERATION ★★ NOISE LEVEL ★★	This blender had intuitive controls. It splattered a lot due to its wide jar. It was too chaotic to emulsify mayonnaise; soups and smoothies were mostly well blended but a little frothy. It made slightly chunky almond butter, though we had to scrape down the jar 12 times. It was fairly loud, and it was slightly hard to clean under its blade.

NOT RECOMMENDED		
OSTER PRO 1200 PLUS Blend-n-Go Smoothie Cup & Food Processor Attachment MODEL: BLSTMB-CBF-000 PRICE: $88.28 JAR WIDTH: 4.5 in DECIBELS: 79.2 (low), 95 (high) LOWEST RPM: 4,590	BLENDING/CRUSHING ★½ MAYONNAISE ○ ALMOND BUTTER ★★½ CLEANING/HANDLING ★½ CONTROLS/OPERATION ★½ NOISE LEVEL ★★★	This blender had a blade that reversed directions while running. This helped make smooth almond butter, but it still left traces of almonds uncombined, and smoothies and soups had chunks. The blades were set too high to make mayonnaise and the buttons were hard to read. At the end of testing, the blade had some dings and a part on the underside of the jar showed some rust.
HAMILTON BEACH Multiblend Blender with Built-in Travel Jar MODEL: 53517 PRICE: $60.68 JAR WIDTH: 4.75 in DECIBELS: 91.6 (low), 95.3 (high) LOWEST RPM: 15,460	BLENDING/CRUSHING ★½ MAYONNAISE ○ ALMOND BUTTER ○ CLEANING/HANDLING ★★★ CONTROLS/OPERATION ★ NOISE LEVEL ★★	The cheapest and lightest model in our lineup had buttons that were hard to read and confusing. This blender made slightly chunky smoothies, margaritas, and crushed ice, and it died for good while trying to make almond butter. Its extremely fast lowest speed couldn't properly emulsify mayonnaise. Part of the rubber grip on its handle started to peel off after a few uses.

LARGE SAUCEPANS

A saucepan may be simple—it's basically a bowl with a handle and a lid—but it's a kitchen essential. To zero in on a reliable, hard-wearing saucepan, we tested 10 large (3- to 4-quart) saucepans with lids in a variety of styles and materials. We put each saucepan through its paces, stirring, scraping, and pouring custard; making rice pilaf; and browning butter. We timed how long it took for water to come to a boil and noted how easy (or not) each model was to pour from. We even abused them by heating them and plunging them into ice water and whacking them on a concrete step. Pans with straight sides and light interiors allowed us to easily monitor the color and texture of food—particularly important when browning butter—while those with bulging or dark interiors made this difficult. The thinner, lightweight frames of nonstick and anodized aluminum pans caused them to run hot and forced us to constantly adjust the heat to avoid burning the onions. Only a few saucepans came away from our abuse tests with just a few minor dings. Ultimately, our longtime favorite still proved to be the best of the bunch: Its fully clad construction provided uniform and steady heat, and its light-colored interior and relatively broad cooking surface offered good visibility. It also survived abuse testing with almost negligible dents, and since we've used it in the test kitchen for almost a decade, we know that was not just a flash in the pan. Products are listed in order of preference.

HIGHLY RECOMMENDED

	PERFORMANCE	TESTERS' COMMENTS
ALL-CLAD Stainless 4-Qt Sauce Pan MODEL: 4204 PRICE: $179.13 FULLY CLAD: Yes FEATURES: Helper handle, dishwasher-, oven-, and broiler-safe to 600 degrees (without lid) WEIGHT WITH LID: 4 lb, 2⅜ oz COOKING SURFACE DIAMETER: 7½ in	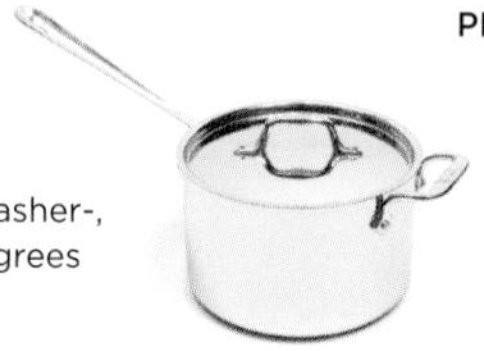 PERFORMANCE ★★★ EASE OF USE ★★★ CLEANUP ★★★ DURABILITY ★★★	Our longtime winner excelled, with uniform, steady heating and good visibility to monitor browning. Its cup-shaped stay-cool handle was easy to grip, and a helper handle provided another grabbing point when the pan was full. Even after whacking on concrete, this model emerged with only minor dents and it still sat flat on the counter.

RECOMMENDED

	PERFORMANCE	TESTERS' COMMENTS
ZWILLING J.A. HENCKELS Aurora 5-ply 4-qt Stainless Steel Saucepan MODEL: 66085-220 PRICE: $214.99 FULLY CLAD: Yes FEATURES: Oven- and broiler-safe to 500 degrees, dishwasher-safe WEIGHT WITH LID: 5 lb, 5⅝ oz COOKING SURFACE DIAMETER: 8¼ in	 PERFORMANCE ★★★ EASE OF USE ★★½ CLEANUP ★★★ DURABILITY ★★½	Onions cooked evenly and rice came out fluffy and separate in this wide, sturdy saucepan. The round handle stayed completely cool but sometimes slipped in our hands when we were scooping and scraping out food because the saucepan is heavy. It cleaned up well and emerged from abuse testing with only small dents.
TRAMONTINA Gourmet Tri-Ply Clad 4 Qt. Covered Sauce Pan MODEL: 80116/024DS PRICE: $89.95 FULLY CLAD: Yes FEATURE: Helper handle WEIGHT WITH LID: 3 lb, 14⅞ oz COOKING SURFACE DIAMETER: 7 in	 PERFORMANCE ★★½ EASE OF USE ★★½ CLEANUP ★★½ DURABILITY ★★	This saucepan ran a little fast and hot, so onions browned slightly around the perimeter of the pan. The cooking surface is relatively narrow. The frame was easy to lift and scrape food from, but its handle gets hot. Its shiny interior dulled after cleaning, and it suffered more in our abuse testing than higher-ranked models.
CUISINART MultiClad Unlimited 4 Quart Saucepan with Cover `BEST BUY` MODEL: MCU194-20N PRICE: $65.12 FULLY CLAD: Yes FEATURES: Oven- and broiler-safe, dishwasher-safe WEIGHT WITH LID: 3 lb, 5 oz COOKING SURFACE DIAMETER: 7½ in	 PERFORMANCE ★★★ EASE OF USE ★★½ CLEANUP ★★ DURABILITY ★★	This lightweight pan had a few drawbacks: It cooked fast, leading to minor browning when we softened onions; the pan got hot, so a pot-holder was needed; and it lacked a helper handle. In abuse tests, it warped slightly and suffered minor dents and surface cracks at the points of impact. But given its bargain price, its performance was impressive.

RECOMMENDED WITH RESERVATIONS

	PERFORMANCE	TESTERS' COMMENTS
OXO Stainless Steel Pro 3.5 qt. Sauce Pan + Cover MODEL: CW000975-003 PRICE: $79.99 FULLY CLAD: Yes FEATURE: Helper handle WEIGHT WITH LID: 4 lb, 6 oz COOKING SURFACE DIAMETER: 7½ in	 PERFORMANCE ★★½ EASE OF USE ★★ CLEANUP ★★ DURABILITY ★★½	While this low, wide, rounded saucepan made it easy to see inside and cooked pilaf and browned butter well, its flared shape was problematic for custard. It was also too small, holding far less than its advertised capacity. The handle became very hot, and the rivets easily trapped food. The glass lid steamed up.

PARCHMENT PAPER

Recently, parchment has become available in sheets, a precut version of the rolls that we have long used. Curious how these products would compare with traditional rolls, we purchased 10 parchment paper products: seven rolls and three packages of precut sheets. All the papers produced cakes, cookies, and pizzas that were evenly baked and released cleanly. None tore easily or caught fire in a hot oven. None stuck, tore, or crumpled when used to roll out cookie dough. But in terms of how easy they were to use, scores were anything but even and two things mattered: size and cutting mechanism. Most rolls were too wide to fit in a standard rimmed baking sheet, forcing us to trim them and resulting in wasted paper. Rolls that came in sturdy boxes and relied on tension were easy to tear into sheets with straight, clean edges. The precut sheets all fit in a standard baking sheet and were big enough to use for other tasks. But just as with the parchment rolls, packaging mattered: Our favorite sheets were stored flat in a large zipper-lock bag, so they never got wrinkled, curled, or creased. Sized just right and perfectly smooth, they practically floated into baking sheets. Products are listed in order of preference.

HIGHLY RECOMMENDED		PERFORMANCE		TESTERS' COMMENTS
KING ARTHUR FLOUR **Baking Parchment Paper** **100 Half-Sheets** PRICE: $19.95 per package ($0.20 per sheet), plus shipping STYLE: Precut sheets DIMENSIONS: 16½ x 12¼ in SHEETS PER PACKAGE: 100		PERFORMANCE SIZE HANDLING PACKAGING	★★★ ★★½ ★★★ ★★★	These precut parchment sheets are the only ones in our lineup that are stored completely flat. They're sized just right for a standard rimmed baking sheet. Their superior convenience made them the runaway favorite. Don't let the price distract you: The per-sheet cost falls squarely in the middle of our lineup.

RECOMMENDED

		PERFORMANCE		
PAPERCHEF **Parchment Rolls** PRICE: $12.95 per package (approximately $0.18 per sheet) STYLE: Roll DIMENSIONS: 15 in x 98.4 ft SHEETS PER PACKAGE: Approximately 73		PERFORMANCE SIZE HANDLING PACKAGING	★★★ ★★ ★★½ ★★★	Our favorite rolled parchment paper had clever packaging: The lid fits inside the front of the box, which holds the roll in place and provides tension for neat, even tears. Our biggest criticism was that we had to trim about 3 inches from the paper to fit it in a rimmed baking sheet.
REYNOLDS **Parchment Paper** PRICE: $5.33 per package (approximately $0.20 per sheet) STYLE: Roll DIMENSIONS: 15 in x 36 ft SHEETS PER PACKAGE: Approximately 27		PERFORMANCE SIZE HANDLING PACKAGING	★★★ ★★ ★★ ★★★	We liked working with this parchment. When the lid was tucked inside the box, it was easy to tear off sheets with clean edges. However, sheets had to be trimmed significantly to fit in rimmed baking sheets. The edges tended to curl, especially when the paper was near the end of the roll.

RECOMMENDED WITH RESERVATIONS

		PERFORMANCE		
GOOD COOK **Parchment Roll** PRICE: $5.27 per package (approximately $0.35 per sheet) STYLE: Roll DIMENSIONS: 12 in x 20 ft SHEETS PER PACKAGE: Approximately 15		PERFORMANCE SIZE HANDLING PACKAGING	★★★ ★★½ ★★½ ★½	This roll was the only one in our lineup whose width matched that of a standard rimmed baking sheet, but the packaging was poorly designed. The boxes were beat up by the end of testing, and one side came unglued. Per sheet, it was the most expensive product in our lineup.
NORPRO Unbleached **Baking Paper** PRICE: $7.04 per package (approximately $0.16 per sheet) STYLE: Roll DIMENSIONS: 15 in x 59 ft SHEETS PER PACKAGE: Approximately 44		PERFORMANCE SIZE HANDLING PACKAGING	★★★ ★★ ★★ ★★	We have no complaints about the performance of this paper, but we had to trim about 3 inches from its width to fit it in a standard rimmed baking sheet. We thought the sharp serrations on the box would guarantee a clean tear, but sheets often had uneven or jagged edges. The box lacked a closure and always stayed slightly ajar.
WILTON **Parchment Paper** PRICE: $12.98 per 2-box package (approximately $0.27 per sheet) STYLE: Roll DIMENSIONS: 14.9 in x 32.8 ft SHEETS PER PACKAGE: Approximately 48 (24 per box)		PERFORMANCE SIZE HANDLING PACKAGING	★★★ ★★ ★★ ★★	This parchment performed well, but we had to trim off about 3 inches to make it fit. Even with the box's plastic serrated teeth, the paper routinely tore with a jagged chunk of extra paper at one end. The paper remained fairly flat even when we got to the end of the roll.

PLASTIC FOOD STORAGE CONTAINERS

Whether you're storing leftovers or taking lunch to work, food storage containers are essential. In our last testing, we chose the Snapware Airtight 8 Cup Rectangular Container as our favorite plastic model, but we've heard complaints about the performance of recently purchased copies; plus, new competitors have emerged. We purchased six plastic containers, including our former winner, to find out which functioned best. After container boot camp—filling them with water to test for leaking; adding moisture-detecting crystals to the containers to determine if they were truly airtight; using them to store and reheat chili to monitor staining; and filling them with pungent oil-packed tuna and anchovies to determine how easy they were to keep clean and odor-free—we had a winner. The Rubbermaid Brilliance Food Storage Container, Large, 9.6 Cup is roomy, with a flat shape that was easy to stack and helped food heat more evenly. We liked its pair of lid clips that doubled down on its already-tight seal. Best of all, it didn't leak, and it emerged from extensive testing still looking good as new. Products are listed in order of preference.

HIGHLY RECOMMENDED	PERFORMANCE	TESTERS' COMMENTS
RUBBERMAID Brilliance Food Storage Container, Large, 9.6 Cup MODEL: 1991158 PRICE: $12.99 MATERIAL: Tritan CAPACITY: 9.6 cups 	MICROWAVE HEATING ★★★ STORAGE ★★★ LEAKS ★★★ ODORS ★★½ DESIGN ★★★ DURABILITY ★★★	The lightweight Tritan plastic stayed as stain-free as glass, and its seal didn't leak. Foods chilled and heated evenly. Lid vents left the container fully sealed while keeping splatters contained and extended rims stayed cool. The attached gasket is nice, but you need to clean carefully under its open side. It's also sold in sets, in varying sizes.

RECOMMENDED		
KINETIC Fresh Series 54-Ounce Rectangular Food Storage Container with Lid MODEL: 49014 PRICE: $10.99 MATERIAL: Polypropylene CAPACITY: 6.75 cups 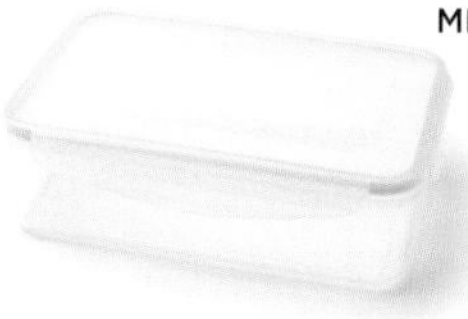	MICROWAVE HEATING ★★½ STORAGE ★★½ LEAKS ★★★ ODORS ★★ DESIGN ★★ DURABILITY ★★½	This container was leakproof and airtight. It acquired a slightly orange, cloudy look from the microwaved chili, but didn't warp or spill. Its 6.5-cup capacity did seem a bit cramped. Its teensy silicone gasket is nearly impossible to remove for cleaning and retained slight odors. The lid can't be used in the microwave, so we put paper towels over the food to prevent splatter.
LOCK & LOCK Easy Match, 10.1 Cup MODEL: HPL341EM PRICE: $25.97 MATERIAL: Polypropylene CAPACITY: 10.1 cups 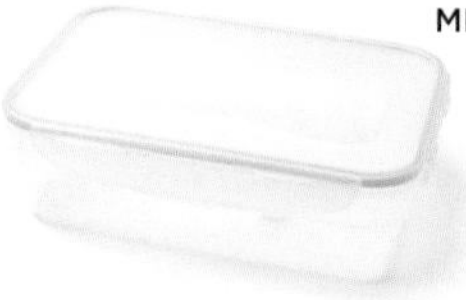	MICROWAVE HEATING ★★½ STORAGE ★★½ LEAKS ★★ ODORS ★★ DESIGN ★★ DURABILITY ★★★	This container had solid construction and flaps that seal firmly, but it leaked and admitted a bit of moisture when submerged. It also retained a mild odor and an orange tint from chili. The gasket is hard to budge from its channel for cleaning, but we liked the feature where a colored dot on the base matches the trim of the lid.

RECOMMENDED WITH RESERVATIONS		
OXO Good Grips 9.6 Cup Smart Seal Container MODEL: 11174900 PRICE: $12.99 MATERIAL: Polypropylene CAPACITY: 9.6 cups 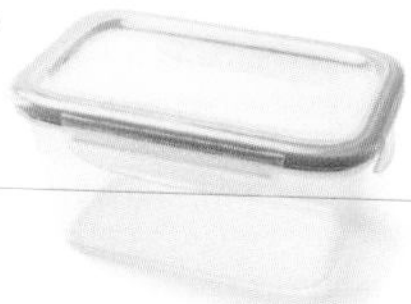	MICROWAVE HEATING ★★ STORAGE ★★ LEAKS ★★★ ODORS ★½ DESIGN ★★½ DURABILITY ★½	This container sealed well and didn't leak. The gasket required careful washing and drying or it would trap odors and moisture. The container's tall, narrow shape meant foods took longer to heat or chill. The plastic stained in our chili test, and when we filled the container with water and pushed it onto the floor, all four flaps flew open.

NOT RECOMMENDED		
SNAPWARE Airtight Food Storage 8 Cup Rectangular Container MODEL: 1098434 PRICE: $7.99 MATERIAL: Polypropylene CAPACITY: 8 cups 	MICROWAVE HEATING ★★½ STORAGE ★★½ LEAKS ★ ODORS ★½ DESIGN ★★ DURABILITY ★	Our former winner stained and retained odors, and the gasket split in our first round of testing and continued to degrade. When we dropped the container off the counter full of water, its flaps opened. While we still like its snappy seal, stackable lid, and low profile, the failure of the gasket means we can no longer recommend it.
JOSEPH JOSEPH Nest Storage Plastic Food Storage Containers Set MODEL: 81009 PRICE: $35 for set of six graduated sizes (we tested the 3-liter model) MATERIAL: Polypropylene CAPACITY: 12.6 cups 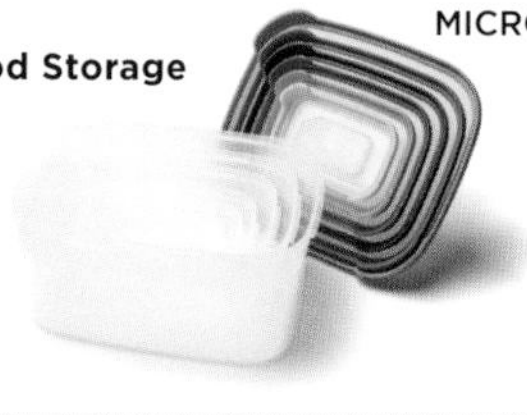	MICROWAVE HEATING ★★ STORAGE ★★ LEAKS ★ ODORS ★½ DESIGN ★½ DURABILITY ★★	The lid leaked when the container was shaken, and the container quickly filled with water when submerged. When dropped, the lid flew off. The container retained odors, and its depth meant food chilled and heated unevenly. While we liked its generous size, nesting storage, and the system of matching a colored dot on the bottom to the lid trim, this container isn't the best choice.

PAPER TOWELS

We use paper towels for everything from cleaning up messes and patting meat dry to oiling grill grates and simply drying our hands. For our testing we included five full-sheet and seven variable-sheet rolls priced from $0.87 to $2.49 per roll. After putting these paper towels through their paces, we determined there was no difference in performance between full- and variable-sheet towels. However, most towels completely bombed our tests, and in the end, we found only two we liked. In terms of price, we did some sleuthing and discovered something sneaky: Budget paper towels have about 17 percent fewer sheets than premium products. While they might be cheaper if you're looking solely at the price per roll, a deeper truth becomes evident when you calculate the price per square foot. Our favorite product was also the national top seller: Bounty Paper Towels. The two-ply sheets were thick, ultrastrong, and highly absorbent. Products are listed in order of preference.

HIGHLY RECOMMENDED	PERFORMANCE		TESTERS' COMMENTS
BOUNTY Paper Towels **AVAILABLE IN:** Full sheet and Select-A-Size **PRICE:** $2.49 for 1 roll (full sheet, regular and Select-A-Size, regular) **PRICE PER SQUARE FOOT:** $0.07 (full sheet and Select-A-Size) **NUMBER OF SHEETS:** 48 (full sheet), 84 (Select-A-Size) **WATER ABSORBENCY:** 0.4 g per sq in **PLY:** 2 **THICKNESS:** 0.4 mm	ABSORBENCY STRENGTH LINTING EASE OF USE	★★★ ★★★ ★★★ ★★★	Every tester who tried these towels gave a positive review. The sheets were thick, soft, and sturdy, and a single full-size towel could hold nearly ¼ cup of water—about twice as much as lower-ranked towels. Thanks to their double-ply thickness, the sheets were unscathed after 300 passes across a semiabrasive cutting board—and we detected nary a hair of lint, even on glass.

RECOMMENDED

| **BRAWNY Paper Towels**
AVAILABLE IN: Full sheet and Pick-A-Size
PRICE: $1.99 for 1 roll (full sheet, regular), $3.16 for 2 (Pick-A-Size, big)
PRICE PER SQUARE FOOT: $0.05 (full sheet), $0.03 (Pick-A-Size)
NUMBER OF SHEETS: 48 (full sheet), 117 (Pick-A-Size)
WATER ABSORBENCY: 0.4 g per sq in
PLY: 2 **THICKNESS:** 0.4 mm | ABSORBENCY
STRENGTH
LINTING
EASE OF USE | ★★★
★★★
★★½
★★½ | These two-ply paper towels were durable and strong, easily holding more than 1 pound of weight and muscling through all our scrubbing tests without fraying or tearing. Said one tester: "They felt like I could have rinsed one, wrung it out, and used it again, like they do in paper towel commercials." A few testers lamented that these towels were a bit linty and not as soft as our winner. |

RECOMMENDED WITH RESERVATIONS

| **VIVA Towels**
AVAILABLE IN: Full sheet and Choose-A-Sheet
PRICE: $3.83 for 2 rolls (full sheet, regular), $2.29 for 1 (Choose-A-Sheet, regular)
PRICE PER SQUARE FOOT: $0.04 (full sheet) and $0.05 (Choose-A-Sheet)
NUMBER OF SHEETS: 68 (full sheet), 102 (Choose-A-Sheet)
WATER ABSORBENCY: 0.4 g per sq in
PLY: 1 **THICKNESS:** 0.5 mm | ABSORBENCY
STRENGTH
LINTING
EASE OF USE | ★★★
★½
★
★★ | These ultrasoft, cloth-like towels sure felt luxurious, but testers were split on their performance. While their thick, plush weave easily soaked up messes and kept our hands thoroughly dry when we scrubbed, their strength waned when wet, and they tore under less than ½ pound of weight. They were also ultralinty: Paper scraps lingered on every surface we scrubbed, and multiple testers noted a cloud of lint whenever they tore off a sheet. |
| **VIVA Vantage Towels**
AVAILABLE IN: Choose-A-Sheet
PRICE: $2.19 for 1 roll
PRICE PER SQUARE FOOT: $0.05
NUMBER OF SHEETS: 88
WATER ABSORBENCY: 0.3 g per sq in
PLY: 1 **THICKNESS:** 0.4 mm | ABSORBENCY
STRENGTH
LINTING
EASE OF USE | ★★
★★
★★
★½ | The "budget" offering by Viva, these towels were just as expensive once we calculated the price per square foot, and they weren't as plush or absorbent. However, these one-ply towels managed to muscle through our scrubbing tests. They also didn't lint as much as their premium counterpart, though testers detected some residue when we used them to dry wineglasses. |

NOT RECOMMENDED

| **SCOTT Towels**
AVAILABLE IN: Choose-A-Sheet
PRICE: $2.29 for 1 roll
PRICE PER SQUARE FOOT: $0.05
NUMBER OF SHEETS: 102
WATER ABSORBENCY: 0.2 g per sq in
PLY: 1 **THICKNESS:** 0.3 mm | ABSORBENCY
STRENGTH
LINTING
EASE OF USE | ★
★
★½
★ | This product initially fooled us with its plush texture, but not for long. Steaks were linty, meat juices soaked onto our hands, gaping holes formed in the towels after fewer than 100 passes across a cutting board, and grease seeped through three layers. |

PIE PLATES

Pie plates come in a variety of styles, and the differences aren't just aesthetic—material, thickness, and color all affect the final product. Since the Pyrex Basics 9" Pie Plate won our last testing, new pie plates have become available. It was time to retest, so we selected seven widely available pie plates priced from $7.59 to $39.95: two metal, two ceramic, and three glass models, including our former winner. All were close to the standard 9 inches in diameter. We baked three pies per plate, each with a different type of crust. While all the pie plates produced nicely cooked fillings, the quality of the crusts varied wildly. All three glass pie plates struggled with the graham cracker crust, which stuck to the glass, while none of the metal or ceramic plates had release issues. While the metal and ceramic plates produced picture-perfect bottom crusts, the glass plates disappointed, as their bottom crusts were soft and pale. Metal is generally a better conductor of heat than ceramic or glass; also, metal plates can be made thinner, which helps them heat faster. In the end, the Williams-Sonoma Goldtouch Nonstick Pie Dish ($18.95) outshone the rest. It made evenly baked pies with beautifully browned crusts on both top and bottom, and its slices were easy to cut and remove. Products are listed in order of preference.

HIGHLY RECOMMENDED	PERFORMANCE	TESTERS' COMMENTS

WILLIAMS-SONOMA Goldtouch Nonstick Pie Dish
MODEL: 5-1978204 PRICE: $18.95
MATERIAL: Commercial-grade aluminized steel with Goldtouch ceramic nonstick coating
COLOR: Gold
DIAMETER: 9 in
THICKNESS: 0.8 mm

BROWNING ★★★
RELEASE ★★★
DURABILITY ★★
VERSATILITY ★★★

This golden-hued metal plate baked crusts beautifully without overbrowning; even bottom crusts emerged crisp and flaky. Additionally, we liked this plate's nonfluted lip, which allowed for maximum crust-crimping flexibility. One minor drawback: The metal surface is susceptible to scratches and nicks, but we found that this didn't affect its performance.

RECOMMENDED

ROSE LEVY BERANBAUM'S Perfect Pie Plate, Bayberry
MODEL: RL3BB PRICE: $22.54
MATERIAL: High-fired ceramic with scratch-free glaze
COLOR: Blue
DIAMETER: 8.8 in
THICKNESS: 5.2 mm

BROWNING ★★★
RELEASE ★★★
DURABILITY ★★★
VERSATILITY ★½

Our runner-up produced impressive pies with golden exteriors and lightly tanned bottom crusts. Pie slices were easy to cut and remove. While the fluted lip gave us pretty pies and made this plate easy to maneuver, we found that it hindered versatility. Its built-in crust guide may be helpful for some, but we preferred nonfluted lips, which allow for more crimping options.

EMILE HENRY Pie Dish, Oak
MODEL: 966131 PRICE: $39.95
MATERIAL: Burgundy clay
COLOR: Tan
DIAMETER: 9.25 in
THICKNESS: 7.4 mm

BROWNING ★★★
RELEASE ★★★
DURABILITY ★★★
VERSATILITY ★½

This ceramic plate delivered delightfully crisp crusts on top and bottom. Slices were easy to cut and remove, with no crust sticking whatsoever. However, the fluted lip wasn't as versatile as we'd have liked; we preferred a straight edge to give us more flexibility in forming pie crusts.

NORPRO Stainless Steel Pie Pan, 9"
MODEL: 3811 PRICE: $8.83
MATERIAL: Stainless steel
COLOR: Silver (mirrored finish)
DIAMETER: 9.125 in
THICKNESS: 0.4 mm

BROWNING ★★½
RELEASE ★★★
DURABILITY ★★
VERSATILITY ★★★

Despite its lack of nonstick coating, this mirrored stainless-steel plate easily released crusts and produced nicely colored crusts that were slightly less browned than those produced by our winner. It was prone to light scratches, but they did not hinder performance. This model isn't dishwasher-safe, but is easy to wash by hand.

PYREX BASICS 9" Pie Plate
MODEL: 6001003 PRICE: $7.59
MATERIAL: Pyrex glass
COLOR: Clear
DIAMETER: 8.875 in
THICKNESS: 4.3 mm

BROWNING ★★
RELEASE ★★
DURABILITY ★★★
VERSATILITY ★★★

We encountered crust-release issues for two of the three pies baked in this plate. Moreover, we found that bottom crusts were less browned and less crisp than was ideal. In general, this glass plate produced satisfactory pies; they were simply paler in color and harder to remove.

RECOMMENDED WITH RESERVATIONS

OXO Good Grips Glass 9" Pie Plate
MODEL: 11175900 PRICE: $8.99
MATERIAL: Borosilicate glass
COLOR: Clear
DIAMETER: 9.25 in
THICKNESS: 6.2 mm

BROWNING ★★
RELEASE ★★
DURABILITY ★★★
VERSATILITY ★★½

This glass plate was the deepest in the lineup, with sides that sloped further outward—which made it a little awkward to work with. The graham cracker crust was difficult to release from after baking. Bottom crusts generally skewed paler, and this pie plate also felt slippery and difficult to securely grip.

KITCHEN TONGS

When we previously tested tongs, the OXO Good Grips 12-Inch Tongs were our favorite. But with new models on the market, we decided to retest, selecting eight models priced from $12.88 to $19.99. We used them to fry delicate tortillas, move a roast, and stir and portion pasta. While we didn't have a strong preference regarding tong length (as long as they measured between 10 to 12 inches long), other issues definitely influenced performance. We noticed big differences in tension; some were so stiff that they were painful to use. But those that were comfortable still had to do their job: securely hold food without tearing or shredding it. Pincers with scalloped edges were more precise and secure than tongs with oar-like blades; those coated with silicone or plastic were thicker and less precise than stainless-steel ones, which offered better control. All the tongs had locking mechanisms designed to keep them closed for easy storage. We preferred tongs that required us to push the mechanism to unlock because we could do it with one hand. All told, the OXO Good Grips kept the top spot; they gripped foods well and were comfortable to hold. Products are listed in order of preference.

		PERFORMANCE		TESTERS' COMMENTS
HIGHLY RECOMMENDED				
OXO Good Grips 12-Inch Tongs MODEL: 28581 PRICE: $12.95 LENGTH: 12 in TENSION: 0.55 lb		PRECISION COMFORT PINCER DESIGN	★★★ ★★★ ★★★	The scalloped, uncoated pincers on our longtime favorite felt very precise. The silicone-padded handle made them comfortable and the tension didn't strain our hands. They didn't securely grip ramekins, but they excelled at every other task and felt like a natural extension of our hands.
RECOMMENDED				
OXO Good Grips 12-Inch Tongs with Silicone Heads MODEL: 110198 PRICE: $14.95 LENGTH: 12 in TENSION: 0.44 lb		PRECISION COMFORT PINCER DESIGN	★★½ ★★★ ★★★	This model is similar to our winner, but has coated pincers. Even with a silicone coating these tongs still offered a precise grip most of the time, but we struggled when transferring the beef roast. The coated pincers didn't grip as well as the uncoated version, though they were advantageous when moving ramekins.
EDLUND (4412 HDL) 12 inch Heavy Duty Tong with Lock MODEL: 4412 HDL PRICE: $12.88 LENGTH: 11.75 in TENSION: 0.57 lb		PRECISION COMFORT PINCER DESIGN	★★★ ★★★ ★★½	These pared-down metal tongs—with uncoated pincers and no silicone grip—were light and precise. Though they didn't securely hold ramekins, their slightly more concave scalloped pincers held food with precision. Tension was comfortable, so holding them closed when frying taco shells was no problem at all.
NOT RECOMMENDED				
ERGO CHEF Pro Series 12" DUO Tongs MODEL: 2112 PRICE: $19.99 LENGTH: 12 in TENSION: 0.79 lb		PRECISION COMFORT PINCER DESIGN	★★ ★ ★★½	These tongs had the second-highest tension in the lineup and took more strength to hold closed. The half-coated, half-uncoated pincers confused users, and while they had shallow scallops along one side and something resembling rounded teeth on the other, they didn't grip well.
JOSEPH JOSEPH Elevate Steel Tongs MODEL: 10120 PRICE: $16.99 LENGTH: 10.625 in TENSION: 0.42 lb		PRECISION COMFORT PINCER DESIGN	★½ ★★ ★	Batter got stuck in the holes on the silicone-coated heads. Ramekins were hard to transport and meat slid around, as there was virtually no grip. An "integrated tool rest" is meant to keep tong heads off the counter, but liquid dripped down. They locked when we didn't want them to.
MASTRAD Quick Tongs MODEL: A17610 PRICE: $14.99 LENGTH: 11 in TENSION: 0.84 lb		PRECISION COMFORT PINCER DESIGN	★ ★ ★½	With the highest tension in the lineup, these tongs were tiring. The bulky locking mechanism cut down on handle grip space. They stand on end to prevent a dirty counter, but dripping oil gave us a greasy handle instead. The pincers' wavy edges were ineffective and dropped pasta.
KITCHENAID Silicone Tipped Tongs MODEL: KC094OHOBA PRICE: $13.87 LENGTH: 10.25 in TENSION: 0.51 lb		PRECISION COMFORT PINCER DESIGN	★ ★ ★	These tongs were the shortest and heaviest in the lineup, making them tiring to use. The thicker, silicone-coated rectangular pincers weren't very precise and failed to pick up a single strand of pasta. These tongs never got a good grip on the roast. The metal handle got noticeably warm.

MULTICOOKERS

While multicookers promise to replace a pressure cooker, slow cooker, rice cooker, and more, we have found that they don't stack up against said equipment and require recipe rejiggering to get good results. Still, the appeal of their versatility is undeniable. Armed with recipes designed for these appliances, we tested five multicookers with a large 8-quart capacity. All but one made great pressure-cooked food, and almost all the machines made acceptable rice. As for slow cooking, we found two problems. First, multicookers heat up fast, so we often had to reduce the cooking time to make slow-cooker recipes work. Second was that all the machines cooked unevenly. Whether on low or high, the Instant Pot was significantly cooler—and thus slower—than other models. While these machines aren't as good as the individual products they promise to replace, we liked them much more than before. Our winner, the Fagor LUX LCD Multicooker ($199.95), cooks well on all modes and is intuitive and easy to use. Products are listed in order of preference.

RECOMMENDED	PERFORMANCE	TESTERS' COMMENTS
FAGOR LUX LCD Multicooker MODEL: 935010063 PRICE: $199.95 AVERAGE LOW PRESSURE: 233.8°, 7.6 psi AVERAGE HIGH PRESSURE: 238.0°, 9.4 psi SLOW COOKER MAX, LOW: 203.8° SLOW COOKER MAX, HIGH: 213.1°	PRESSURE COOKING ★★★ SLOW COOKING ★★ RICE COOKING ★★★ SEARING/SAUTÉING ★★★ EASE OF USE ★★★ MANEUVERABILITY ★★★	This new model from the maker of our old winner has a couple of upgrades. Pressure-cooked food was good, and the slow-cook function worked with some recipe tweaking. It has a clearly labeled lid, which helped us latch it quickly and accurately, and its LCD interface was easy to use and read. It also has a sensor that alerts you when the lid isn't properly sealed. Lastly, we likead that you can lock the control panel.

FAGOR LUX Multicooker MODEL: 670041960 PRICE: $169.95 AVERAGE LOW PRESSURE: 235.9°, 8.5 psi AVERAGE HIGH PRESSURE: 240.6°, 10.5 psi SLOW COOKER MAX, LOW: 200.1° SLOW COOKER MAX, HIGH: 213.9°	PRESSURE COOKING ★★★ SLOW COOKING ★★ RICE COOKING ★★★ SEARING/SAUTÉING ★★★ EASE OF USE ★★½ MANEUVERABILITY ★★★	Our old winner still made great pressure-cooked food. Like other models, it tended to cook less efficiently than a traditional slow cooker because of its shape, but we were able to tweak our recipes to get good results. It had a simple interface and we liked the clear "locked" and "unlocked" symbols, which made it easier to attach the lid. Its interface isn't quite as streamlined as that of our new winner, but it's still a good option.

GOWISE USA 8-Quart 10-in-1 Electric Pressure Cooker/Slow Cooker `BEST BUY` MODEL: GW22623 PRICE: $89.95 AVERAGE LOW PRESSURE: 235.2°, 8.3 psi AVERAGE HIGH PRESSURE: 240.4°, 10.5 psi SLOW COOKER MAX, LOW: 198.0° SLOW COOKER MAX, HIGH: 214.1°	PRESSURE COOKING ★★★ SLOW COOKING ★★ RICE COOKING ★★★ SEARING/SAUTÉING ★★★ EASE OF USE ★★ MANEUVERABILITY ★★★	This multicooker had a ripping-hot sauté function that browned meat nicely. It also worked great as a pressure cooker. It ran a bit hotter than a traditional slow cooker, so you'd have to adjust some recipes. Its interface was a little confusing, and like most models it has a busy control panel with a ton of vague, superfluous buttons such as "poultry" and "meat/stew." Testers also found the "hours" label next to the timer confusing because it was often counting down minutes, which gave us pause.

RECOMMENDED WITH RESERVATIONS

INSTANT POT Duo 7-in-1 Multi-Use Programmable Pressure Cooker MODEL: DUO80 PRICE: $129.95 AVERAGE LOW PRESSURE: 234.4°, 7.9 psi AVERAGE HIGH PRESSURE: 246.5°, 13.4 psi SLOW COOKER MAX, LOW: 186.7° SLOW COOKER MAX, HIGH: 206.2°	PRESSURE COOKING ★★★ SLOW COOKING ★ RICE COOKING ★★★ SEARING/SAUTÉING ★★★ EASE OF USE ★★½ MANEUVERABILITY ★★	This machine did a good job at pressure-cooking, making rice, and searing, but its slow-cooking function took way too long (even on high). Thick, large-volume recipes take an excessive amount of time. Cooking was unevenly concentrated in the bottom of the pot. This model runs a little hotter under pressure, but this was easy to fix by adjusting the cooking time. Its instructions were confusing and the metal on its lid got really hot.

PLASTIC WRAP

We rely on plastic wrap to help store and freeze food and to perform certain kitchen tasks, such as pounding cutlets and making logs of cookie dough. We rounded up the seven top-selling plastic wraps, as well as a bulk food-service wrap that is available online, ranging in price from $1.33 to $4.19 per 100 square feet. All the wraps clung well to metal, glass, and ceramic, but two products refused to adhere to a plastic bowl. When resealing, some wraps tore at the edges while thinner wraps bent out of shape or ripped right down the middle. Serrated blades felt less safe and made it tricky to get a clean-edged piece of plastic. Slide cutters felt safer and were easier to use, resulting in clean, straight cuts. Our winner, Freeze-Tite Clear High Cling Freezer Wrap, consists of thick plastic that is superclingy, remarkably durable, and an ideal width. Products are listed in order of preference.

HIGHLY RECOMMENDED	PERFORMANCE		TESTERS' COMMENTS
FREEZE-TITE Clear High Cling Freezer Wrap PRICE: $13.21 for 315 sq ft ($4.19 per 100 sq ft) WIDTH: 15 in THICKNESS: 0.68 mm CUTTING MECHANISM: Slider and serrated blade 	CLING WRAP DURABILITY EASE OF USE DISPENSER DURABILITY	★★★ ★★★ ★★★ ★★★	This ultraclingy wrap was the thickest in the lineup, making it nearly impossible to rip. At an unusual 15 inches wide, it could cover our large cutting board with a single sheet, though it was great for smaller jobs as well. Its dispenser came with both a serrated blade and slide cutter. While the blade worked fine, the slide cutter was a revelation: It makes it a breeze to produce smooth, perfectly sized sheets.

RECOMMENDED			
STRETCH-TITE Premium Plastic Food Wrap `BEST BUY` PRICE: $5.99 for 250 square feet ($2.40 per 100 sq ft) WIDTH: 12 in THICKNESS: 0.44 mm CUTTING MECHANISM: Slider or serrated blade 	CLING WRAP DURABILITY EASE OF USE DISPENSER DURABILITY	★★★ ★★ ★★★ ★★★	This wrap was just as clingy as our winner, sticking to containers of every type. It comes in a more standard 12-inch width, which was fine for most jobs. It's thinner, so it isn't quite as durable as our winner. It's sold with either a serrated blade or slide cutter. We tested both and preferred the latter, which makes the product slightly easier to use.

RECOMMENDED WITH RESERVATIONS			
REYNOLDS Food Service Film PRICE: $39.90 for 3000 sq ft ($1.33 per 100 sq ft) WIDTH: 18 in THICKNESS: 0.36 mm CUTTING MECHANISM: Slider	CLING WRAP DURABILITY EASE OF USE DISPENSER DURABILITY	★★★ ★ ★★ ★★½	This commercial plastic wrap was very clingy; it was also wide, so it excelled at larger tasks. Testers loved its slide cutter, which cleanly severed sheets. But its top flap didn't always stay put inside the box. It's one of the thinnest wraps, so it stretched and tore fairly easily. Finally, buying 3,000 square feet of wrap is a commitment.
GLAD FreezerWrap PRICE: $10.04 for 150 sq ft ($6.69 per 100 sq ft) WIDTH: 12 in THICKNESS: 0.55 mm CUTTING MECHANISM: Serrated blade	CLING WRAP DURABILITY EASE OF USE DISPENSER DURABILITY	★★ ★★½ ★ ★★	This wrap clung to containers of every type, and its thickness made it durable; its average width meant we needed an extra pass to wrap baking sheets and cutting boards. Its serrated blade was located on a flimsy interior flap, making it hard to get a clean sheet. The wrap's blue shade makes it difficult to monitor the color of food.
GLAD Cling Wrap PRICE: $3.19 for 200 sq ft ($1.60 per 100 sq ft) WIDTH: 11.6 in THICKNESS: 0.3 mm CUTTING MECHANISM: Serrated blade	CLING WRAP DURABILITY EASE OF USE DISPENSER DURABILITY	★★★ ★ ★½ ★★	Reformulated since we last tested, our former winner was very clingy, but had little else going for it. The thinnest wrap in our lineup, it tore easily. It had a flap-mounted serrated blade that made it hard to dispense the wrap neatly. At 11.6 inches, it was the narrowest wrap we tested.

NOT RECOMMENDED			
GLAD Press'n Seal PRICE: $4.19 for 140 sq ft ($2.99 per 100 sq ft) WIDTH: 11.8 in THICKNESS: n/a (textured wrap could not be analyzed properly) CUTTING MECHANISM: Serrated blade	CLING WRAP DURABILITY EASE OF USE DISPENSER DURABILITY	★★★ ★★★ ½ ½	This wrap seemed thick and durable, and its one sticky side clung to containers of all types. But it left a gluey residue on some surfaces, and testers disliked its translucent, textured finish, which made it impossible to see the food underneath. Its dispenser was the hardest to use. Mounted on a weak flap, its plastic serrated blade mangled the wrap instead of cutting it cleanly.

CONVERSIONS & EQUIVALENTS

Some say cooking is a science and an art. We would say that geography has a hand in it, too. Flour milled in the United Kingdom and elsewhere will feel and taste different from flour milled in the United States. So, while we cannot promise that the loaf of bread you bake in Canada or England will taste the same as a loaf baked in the States, we can offer guidelines for converting weights and measures. We also recommend that you rely on your instincts when making our recipes. Refer to the visual cues provided. If the bread dough hasn't "come together in a ball," as described, you may need to add more flour—even if the recipe doesn't tell you so. You be the judge.

The recipes in this book were developed using standard U.S. measures following U.S. government guidelines. The charts below offer equivalents for U.S., metric, and imperial (U.K.) measures. All conversions are approximate and have been rounded up or down to the nearest whole number. For example:

1 teaspoon = 4.929 milliliters, rounded up to 5 milliliters
1 ounce = 28.349 grams, rounded down to 28 grams

VOLUME CONVERSIONS

U.S.	METRIC
1 teaspoon	5 milliliters
2 teaspoons	10 milliliters
1 tablespoon	15 milliliters
2 tablespoons	30 milliliters
¼ cup	59 milliliters
⅓ cup	79 milliliters
½ cup	118 milliliters
¾ cup	177 milliliters
1 cup	237 milliliters
1¼ cups	296 milliliters
1½ cups	355 milliliters
2 cups	473 milliliters
2½ cups	591 milliliters
3 cups	710 milliliters
4 cups (1 quart)	0.946 liter
1.06 quarts	1 liter
4 quarts (1 gallon)	3.8 liters

WEIGHT CONVERSIONS

OUNCES	GRAMS
½	14
¾	21
1	28
1½	43
2	57
2½	71
3	85
3½	99
4	113
4½	128
5	142
6	170
7	198
8	227
9	255
10	283
12	340
16 (1 pound)	454

CONVERSIONS FOR INGREDIENTS COMMONLY USED IN BAKING

Baking is an exacting science. Because measuring by weight is far more accurate than measuring by volume, and thus more likely to achieve reliable results, in our recipes we provide ounce measures in addition to cup measures for many ingredients. Refer to the chart below to convert these measures into grams.

INGREDIENT	OUNCES	GRAMS
Flour		
1 cup all-purpose flour*	5	142
1 cup cake flour	4	113
1 cup whole-wheat flour	5½	156
Sugar		
1 cup granulated (white) sugar	7	198
1 cup packed brown sugar (light or dark)	7	198
1 cup confectioners' sugar	4	113
Cocoa Powder		
1 cup cocoa powder	3	85
Butter†		
4 tablespoons (½ stick, or ¼ cup)	2	57
8 tablespoons (1 stick, or ½ cup)	4	113
16 tablespoons (2 sticks, or 1 cup)	8	227

* U.S. all-purpose flour, the most frequently used flour in this book, does not contain leaveners, as some European flours do. These leavened flours are called self-rising or self-raising. If you are using self-rising flour, take this into consideration before adding leavening to a recipe.

† In the United States, butter is sold both salted and unsalted. We generally recommend unsalted butter. If you are using salted butter, take this into consideration before adding salt to a recipe.

OVEN TEMPERATURES

FAHRENHEIT	CELSIUS	GAS MARK (imperial)
225	105	¼
250	120	½
275	135	1
300	150	2
325	165	3
350	180	4
375	190	5
400	200	6
425	220	7
450	230	8
475	245	9

CONVERTING TEMPERATURES FROM AN INSTANT-READ THERMOMETER

We include doneness temperatures in many of our recipes, such as those for poultry, meat, and bread. We recommend an instant-read thermometer for the job. Refer to the table above to convert Fahrenheit degrees to Celsius. Or, for temperatures not represented in the chart, use this simple formula:

Subtract 32 degrees from the Fahrenheit reading, then divide the result by 1.8 to find the Celsius reading.

EXAMPLE:

"Roast chicken until thighs register 175 degrees." To convert:

175° F − 32 = 143°
143° ÷ 1.8 = 79.44°C, rounded down to 79°C

INDEX

Note: Page references in *italics* indicate photographs.

Bubble and Squeak, 69–71, *70*

Buffalo Chicken Wings, Multicooker, 7–10, *8*

Buns, Hot Cross, 199–201, *200*

Butter, quick-softening, for baking pans, 265

Buttery Spring Vegetables, *46,* 48–49

C

Cabbage

Bubble and Squeak, 69–71, *70*

Chicken Shawarma, 100–102, *101*

Chinese Pork Dumplings, 10–14, *11*

preparing, 71

Red Wine Risotto with Beans (Paniscia), 86–88, *87*

savoy, about, 71

Cakes

Blackberry-Mascarpone Lemon, 240–43, *241*

Cider-Glazed Apple Bundt, 235–38, *236*

Coffee, with Pecan-Cinnamon Streusel, 201–3

Pomegranate Walnut, 238–40

Candied Nuts, Quick, *256, 257*

Candy, Potato (Needhams), 257–58, *259*

Caper(s)

Almond, and Raisin Relish, 56

Puttanesca, 272

Capicola

Prosciutto Bread, 213–14, *215*

Prosciutto Bread with Provolone, 214

Caramel

-Chocolate-Pecan Icebox Pie, 251–54, *253*

-Chocolate-Pecan Sauce, 252–54, *253*

Salted, Cupcakes, *216,* 233–35

Caramelized Onion Dip, 2–4, *3*

Caramelized Onions, 4

Carrot(s)

Harissa-Rubbed Roast Boneless Leg of Lamb with Warm Cauliflower Salad, 148–49

Multicooker Chipotle Pork and Hominy Stew (Posole), 35–38, *36*

Pot Roast with Rosemary–Red Wine Simmering Sauce, 121–24, *122*

Carrot(s) *(cont.)*

Salad, Chopped, with Celery and Raisins, *20,* 22

Salad, Chopped, with Fennel, Orange, and Hazelnuts, 22

Salad, Chopped, with Mint, Pistachios, and Pomegranate Seeds, 21–22

Salad, Chopped, with Radishes and Sesame Seeds, 22

Cast-Iron Baked Chicken, 163–64

Cast-iron skillets, test kitchen favorite, 163

Cauliflower

Grilled, 55–56, *57*

Salad, Warm, Harissa-Rubbed Roast Boneless Leg of Lamb with, 148–49

Celery and Raisins, Chopped Carrot Salad with, *20,* 22

Cheddar, supermarket extra-sharp, test kitchen favorites, 281

Cheese

American, test kitchen favorite, 96

Blackberry-Mascarpone Lemon Cake, 240–43, *241*

Blintzes with Raspberry Sauce, 195–98, *197*

Blue, Dressing, Creamy, *8, 9*

Blue, Pear, and Parsley, Radicchio Salad with, *17, 18*

Boogaloo Wonderland Sandwiches, 94–97, *95*

Bread-Crumb Topping, 75

cheddar, supermarket extra-sharp, test kitchen favorites, 281

Creamy Parmesan Polenta, *76,* 79

Detroit-style Pizza, *92,* 93–94

feta, test kitchen favorites, 282

Fresh Fruit Tart, 247–50, *249*

Gougères, 207–9

Gougères with Aged Gouda and Smoked Paprika, 209

Gougères with Manchego and Black Pepper, 209

Grilled Sweet Potato Salad, 23

Macaroni and, Slow-Cooker Grown-Up, with Comté and Porcini, 74–75

Make-Ahead Baked Ziti with Sausage and Broccoli Rabe, 80–83, *81*

Make-Ahead Chicken Parmesan, 155–58, *156*

Migas, 192, *193*

One-Hour Pizza, 88–93, *91*

Parsley-Cucumber Salad with Feta, Pomegranate, and Walnuts, *98,* 100